Janet Teissier du Cros

A Scotswoman in Occupied France

Divided Loyalties

Edited by Janet Adam Smith
Foreword by Richard Cobb

**CANONGATE
CLASSICS
43**

First published in Great Britain in 1962 by
Hamish Hamilton Ltd. This edition first pub-
lished as a Canongate Classic by Canongate
Press Plc, 14 Frederick Street, Edinburgh EH2
2HB. Copyright © Estate of Janet Teissier du
Cros 1962. Note and Afterword © Janet Adam
Smith 1992. Foreword © Richard Cobb 1992.
   The publishers gratefully acknowledge gen-
eral subsidy from the Scottish Arts Council
towards the Canongate Classics series and a spe-
cific grant towards the publication of this title.
Set in 10pt Plantin by Falcon Typographic
Art Ltd, Fife, Scotland. Printed and bound
in Great Britain by BPCC Hazells Ltd.

Canongate Classics
Series Editor: Roderick Watson
Editorial Board: Tom Crawford, J. B. Pick

British Library Cataloguing in Publication Data
A catalogue record for this book is available
from the British Library.

ISBN 0 86241 375 3

Contents

Note on New Edition

Divided Loyalties is a unique account by a Scotswoman of her experiences in the Cevennes region of France during the Second World War. After the German victory in France in 1940, Janet Teissier du Cros was torn between the loyalty she felt as a Scot and a Briton, and the loyalty she felt for the country she loved and into which she had married. She was also sensitive to the division of loyalties – to Vichy, or to the Free French abroad and the Resistance at home – between which the French themselves were torn.

For me – a Scot, a contemporary and friend of the author, who also had spent the war in the countryside with children, though in far easier circumstances than hers – the book has always had a special appeal.

During Janet Teissier du Cros's funeral service in October 1990, it suddenly struck me that of all the crowded congregation in the church at La Gardiole, I had known her the longest. We met in Aberdeen in 1910 when she was five, and I nearly five. Her father, Herbert Grierson, who held the chair of English at the University of Aberdeen, was a friend of my father George Adam Smith, newly appointed Principal of the University. The Griersons offered to take in the younger Adam Smiths while my parents and their older children moved into their new house in Old Aberdeen. So for a month my sister Kathleen and I were part of the Grierson family of five daughters. Janet was the youngest of them as I then was of my family.

A few years later the Griersons moved to Edinburgh and Janet and I met only occasionally. 'Our friendship,' she wrote me in 1988, 'has consisted of – as far as I am concerned – enchanted islands. I suppose when a friendship is two generations long, and has even planted some seeds in the third generation, it has a unique quality.' By that time her sons had stayed with my family in London and Scotland, my daughter and sons had stayed with hers in the Cevennes and Paris, and in the 1980s I had often visited Janet and François at Mandiargues. The 'enchanted islands' were close together.

Re-reading *Divided Loyalties* after seeing the places where so much of it had been lived, I hated to think a book which had won such high praise on its first appearance should now be out of print. I asked Janet's permission to try and find a publisher in this country for a new edition, and she readily agreed. The search's happy ending came too late for Janet to know of it. I had much help along the way, and I warmly thank Peter Janson-Smith, who cleared up copyright matters; Hugo Brunner, who encouraged me to keep trying, and helped at every stage; and Tristram Powell, who introduced *Divided Loyalties* to the Canongate Press, whose response was heartwarmingly positive.

This reissue would not have been possible without the help and encouragement of Janet's family: her husband François Teissier du Cros, her sons Henri, André and Nicolas Teissier du Cros, and her daughter Marie Dalbard. François searched out photographs and supplied much of the information in the Afterword, which tells what happened to the main characters of Janet's story after the war. I owe them a great deal.

My thanks go also to Professor Richard Cobb, for writing the new Foreword, which replaces the Preface contributed by D.W. Brogan to the original edition of 1962. Professor Brogan could count on most of the book's readers remembering the Second World War. Thirty years later Professor Cobb sets the events of the book in their historical context for a new generation of readers for whom that war is history rather than memory or lived experience. Thanks also to others who have supplied information, photographs and help generally: Janet's niece Jane Garnett, Renée Fedden, Rosie Peto, Sally Morphet, Caroline Taylor, Germaine Dieterlen, and members of my family.

In this edition, the Foreword, the Afterword, the photographs and the map are new, and there have been minor additions to the Chronology. Otherwise, apart from corrections of a very few printer's errors, the text of the book is exactly as published in the original edition in 1962.

Janet Adam Smith
London, January 1992

Foreword

Divided Loyalties was first published thirty years ago in 1962, that is at a time when the chronicle of dramatic public events in wartime France, which form the background to this very personal story, was much more familiar to the average reader than it would be now. It would perhaps be useful to recall the principal dates of what was happening in the outside world beyond the isolated and to some extent protected territory of the Cevennes.

Most of the narrative contained in the author's marvellously vivid, understanding and gently humorous book falls between September 1938 and August 1944. September 1938 marks the date of the Munich Agreement. In March 1939 the Germans entered Prague. In September of that same year Hitler's armies invaded Poland, and Britain and France entered the war. The period from September 1939 to May 1940, apart from the collapse of Poland and the invasion of eastern Poland by the Soviet forces, was one of almost complete military inactivity in the West. This is the period known as the 'Phoney War' (in French *'la drôle de guerre'*).

In May 1940 the German armies invaded Belgium, Holland and France, and a month later, with the French armies in disarray, the French government, which had taken refuge in Bordeaux, sued for an armistice. Italy meanwhile had entered the war against Britain and France. As a result of the military terms of the armistice in June 1940, France was divided between the areas of direct German and Italian military occupation, which together formed what became known as Occupied France, and most of central and south-central France (including *le pays cévenol*) which remained unoccupied till November 1942. In July 1940 the two chambers of the French Parliament, meeting in the spa town of Vichy, entrusted Marshal Pétain with unlimited powers; and unoccupied France was administered direct from Vichy.

In July 1940 the British Mediterranean Fleet under the command of Admiral Cunningham bombarded a section of the French Fleet at anchor in the North African port of Mers-el-Kébir. In June 1941 the Germans invaded the Soviet Union, and in December of the same year the Japanese attacked the US fleet at Pearl Harbour. In November 1942 the Americans and the British landed in French North Africa, and the Germans moved into what had been the unoccupied zone of France. In 1943 and in the first half of 1944 France entered a bitter period of near-civil war, and the pressure of compulsory labour service in Germany (STO – *Service du Travail Obligatoire*) fell more and more heavily on young Frenchmen, inducing many of them to go into hiding or to join a Resistance group. *Le pays cévenol*, thanks to its isolation and poor communications, offered particularly favourable conditions both to clandestinity and to local Resistance activities. It was also an area that, owing to its predominantly Protestant population, could look back on a long tradition of resistance to central authority from the last years of the seventeenth-century. Both Paris and *le pays cévenol* were finally liberated in late August 1944, which is the concluding date of the book.

Divided Loyalties has two supreme virtues: first, it is a reminder that nothing is quite as simple as it might at first seem, and that there are more areas of grey than those of black and white. Some Protestants, including the author's own in-laws, retained their loyalty to Marshal Pétain. Some Protestant parishioners seem to have shown sympathy to local Communists. The close friend of the Teissier du Cros family, Monsieur Passemard, was shot after the Liberation of Nîmes, as head of the local *milice*. The other virtue is the author's admirable ability to relate an account of dramatic public events to the banality of everyday existence: the terrible cold, the endless February rain, the health of her ill-nourished children, and the increasingly difficult situation with regard to the most primitive necessities of life – food, heat and clothing. The reader must take over from here . . .

Richard Cobb
Oxford, January 1992

Chronology

Spanish Civil War, July 18, 1936–March 31, 1939.
Munich Agreement handing over NW Czechoslovakia to Germany, made between France, Britain, Germany, and Italy, Sept. 30, 1938.

1939
Hitler occupied all Czechoslovakia, March 15.
Italy invaded Albania, April 28.
Germany denounced Anglo-German Naval Agreement of 1934, April 28.
Non-Aggression Pact signed by Germany and the USSR, Aug. 23.
Britain and Poland signed Pact of Mutual Assistance, Aug. 24.
Germany invaded Poland and annexed Danzig, Sept. 1.
France and Britain declare war on Germany, Sept. 3.
Russians invaded eastern Poland, Sept. 17.
Warsaw surrendered to the Germans, Sept. 27; partition of Poland between Germany and Russia.

1940
Germany invaded Denmark and Norway, April 9; the Netherlands, Belgium, Luxemburg, May 10.
Winston Churchill formed coalition government, May 11.
Germany invaded France, May 14; Netherlands army surrendered same day.
Evacuation of British and French troops from Dunkirk, May 26–June 4.
Belgian army surrendered, May 28.
Italy declared war on France and Britain, June 10.
Occupation of Paris by German Army, June 14.
Following meetings in Bordeaux in unoccupied France, 84-year-old Marshal Pétain became Prime Minister of France, June 16.
France signed armistice with Germany, June 22; with Italy, June 24.
Pétain and his ministers moved to the spa town of Vichy in the unoccupied zone of France as their temporary capital, July 1.
British attack on French ships in Oran and Mers el-Kébir, July 3.
French National Assembly, meeting at Vichy, authorised the assumption of full powers by the Prime Minister, Marshal Pétain, July 10. (Later the same day he declared himself 'Head of the French State'.)
Battle of Britain (decisive period), Aug. 8–Sept. 15.

1941

German siege of Tobruk, N. Africa, began April 11; raised Nov. 26.
Yugoslavia capitulated to the Germans, April 17.
Germans captured Athens, April 27; conquered Crete, June 1.
Germans invaded Russia, June 22.
Churchill and President Roosevelt drew up Atlantic Charter, Aug. 14.
Leningrad beleaguered by Germans by end of September.
Germans captured Kiev, Sept. 21; Briansk, Oct. 12; Odessa, Oct. 16.
Japanese attacked Pearl Harbor, Dec. 7, and brought the USA into
the war; landed in Philippines, Dec. 10; captured Hong Kong,
Dec. 25.

1942

Japanese conquered Singapore, Feb. 15; took Bataan, Philippines,
April 8.
British evacuated Burma, May 15.
Germans captured Tobruk, June 21.
Russians evacuated Sevastopol, July 3; Rostov, July 27.
US forces landed on Guadalcanal, in the Solomons, Aug. 7.
British reconnaissance at Dieppe, Aug. 19.
Fighting reached outskirts of Stalingrad, Sept. 16.
Battle of Alamein, Oct. 23.
Allied landings in French North Africa, Nov. 8.
German forces invaded the unoccupied zone of France, Nov. 11.

1943

Siege of Leningrad raised, Jan. 18.
Seige of Stalingrad raised, Jan. 27; last Germans at Stalingrad
surrendered Feb. 2.
Americans cleared Guadalcanal, Feb. 10.
German and Italian forces in Tunisia capitulated, May 12.
Allied conquest of Sicily, July 10–Aug. 17.
Unconditional surrender of Italy to the Allies, Sept. 3.
Russians recaptured Briansk, Sept. 17; Smolensk, Sept. 25,
Dniepropetrovsk, Oct. 25.
Allies occupied Naples, Oct. 1.

1944

German blockade of Leningrad cleared, Jan. 27.
Russians liberated Odessa, April 10; Savastopol, May 9.
Allies occupied Rome, June 4.
Allies landed in Normandy, June 6.
Allies occupied Florence, Aug. 11.
Allies landed in southern France, Aug. 15.
Paris liberated, Aug. 25.

Introduction

In a diary I kept off and on during the last war I find the
following lines, dated February 11th, 1940:

We sat and rested from our walk in the mouth of a
cave, Papa, Maman, the Passemards, and I. They spoke
of dolmens, of granite and schist and fossils, they spoke of
war aims. I lay back and listened with half my attention on
Henri, who was playing by himself farther down the hill.
Then suddenly a breath of cool air shivered over my bare arms
and legs, and at its touch I was back in Istria. It was Easter
in the year 1924 and I was eighteen again. My sister Alice,
another friend and myself had been spending the winter in
Vienna, and we had come to Istria for our Easter holidays.
We left Vienna one cold evening at the end of March, its
pavements banked high along the edge with filthy snow.
We woke the next morning to the sight of almond-blossom
against the blue sky of Trieste. We sailed along the coast of
the Adriatic to Strugnano in an orange-sailed fishing-smack,
and there we spent three weeks in a *pension* by the sea. Every
morning we used to wander round the bay till we reached the
villa that once was Tartini's. There in Tartini's garden we
would lie and bask in the sun on the low wall over the sea,
and listen to the dry rustle of the lizards on the one side, and
on the other to the ripple and rush of the pebbles, washed to
and fro by the deep-breathing sea. Every now and then just
such a light cool wind would play on my bare arms and legs
and my heart give an unreasoning leap of joy at the thought
of all life spread before me. But now, looking back from my
hillside in the Cevennes, it occurred to me that even then my
feet had been set in a passage between high narrowing walls
that led me ineluctably to where I lay in the mouth of a cave
in France at war. The vast and various world I dreamed of
was in fact contained in the thin shell of my skull.

When I came on those lines a few years ago they set me

feeling my way back along the passage in an attempt to distinguish at what point I first put foot in it. I found it led me beyond the bounds of memory to where in a nursery in Aberdeen I spoke my first words of French; and I realised that though I had always thought my marrying a Frenchman a matter of blind chance, in fact France had been like a hound on my trail from the moment I left the cradle.

I was born into a family where some knowledge of French was counted as essential to one's happiness. My mother might have been content if we had picked up enough to allow us to discuss private matters in front of the maids, but my father, who read poetry aloud to us before we were of an age to grasp more than its music, wanted to make us free of French as well as of English literature. Swiss-French governesses succeeded one another in our nursery, and it is not surprising that I, as the youngest of five, learned French before English, though I have only my mother's word for this. Certainly one of my earliest memories is of our governess of the moment standing by the fire in our night-nursery in Aberdeen, waiting to turn the light out till we had finished our conversation. We children, the three of us who slept in that room, were in bed and chattering French to each other. Our father came upstairs to say goodnight, and he stopped at the door to listen. 'You'll all grow up and marry foreigners!' he said in disgusted tones, and in chorus we all replied: 'Oh no we won't!' But my father was right. The three of us who were chattering French that evening in bed did in fact all marry foreigners.

In spite of such an auspicious beginning, until it actually occurred nothing on the face of it could have seemed more unlikely than that I should marry a Frenchman and come to live in France. It is not merely that it is a far cry from Aberdeen to Paris. Quite early my life took a turn in a very different direction, and by the time I lay dreaming in Tartini's garden I was the most romantic of Germanophiles. It was as though the hound had lost my trail. On looking back I realise that it often plucked at the hem of my garment.

In 1916 we moved from Aberdeen to Edinburgh. My father had been appointed from the chair of English Literature of King's College, Aberdeen, to that of Edinburgh University. We left the comfort of a world where it was the right thing to be Scotch and glorious to be connected with the University, for a city where no one is considered as quite respectable who has not an English accent, or what passes for such, and where the Law Courts take precedence of the University. Our last Swiss governess left us early in the First War. By the time it ended I had almost forgotten I could speak French, and with a child's contrariness I emerged from the war years with a romantic enthusiasm for everything German. Not but what I had very clear memories of the atrocity stories I had heard recounted in the second-rate hotel where a school-friend of my sister Letty lived with her mother, and where we sometimes went to visit her. It was an intensely depressing hotel that smelled of bad cooking. I gradually came to associate the atrocity stories with the smell, and with the elderly women who used to gather in the 'lounge' for tea and horror-talk. I doubt whether we ever told our mother of our visits to that hotel. She would strongly have disapproved of the conversations we listened to. We kept our visits to ourselves, and I quickly came to discount all I heard. I thrust it from me with the memory of that dreary hotel.

No doubt it was my growing love of music that made me so interested in Germany. Very early my dream was to become a concert pianist, and as I had settled in my mind that it was in Vienna I would study, I began to learn German in my last year at school. At the same time I fell under the spell of (Sir) Donald Tovey (1875–1940). I went to as many of his lecture-recitals as I could, and I hung on his lips at an evening class in musical interpretation which he took under the auspices of the WEA. Better still, he often dined at our house. To say that he unwittingly bewitched me with his playing, as Othello bewitched Desdemona with his story-telling, would be an understatement. It was something even beyond that. I believe that no one who heard Tovey play when he was at the height of his powers will ever forget the experience, or cease to feel there was something there which no other pianist possessed. Not only had he the great executant's powers; he understood the whole genesis of what he was playing, it spoke to him in the language he best understood and initiated him into the composer's inmost thoughts, those he could never express in words. Both his understanding — not the cerebral appreciation of the musicologist, but the re-creation of a fellow-artist — and his emotion were things he succeeded in transmitting more directly than any other player I ever heard. For as long as he played he made you a person far superior to what in fact you were, and the language became intelligible to you, too, which before had simply been intoxicating sound. Every now and then at a crucial moment, it might be some unexpected modulation that cut the ground from under your feet and plunged you reeling and giddy into the fourth dimension, or a blazing forth in the major mode of some tragic minor theme, its message of hope no sooner uttered than you were cast down again by a return to the minor key; whatever it was, you were always warned to the tiptoe of attention by a fleeting glance of blue fire from Tovey's wide-apart eyes, and for a brief moment you were absorbed into him and understood not with your own heart and mind but with his. It was such an unforgettable experience that when he died and the gates of that paradise closed, which I never visited in my own right, I was left an outcast.

For years Tovey was to be the strongest influence in my life, and it was an influence that did more than any other to sever me from my French roots. The most English of Englishmen, the most Balliol of Balliol men, he had been fated to receive his early musical education at the hands of a redoubtable German woman who kept a school in England for the daughters of the English upper class. She was in many ways a fascinating woman even in her old age, which was all I knew of her, but in a sense she was Tovey's undoing. Because it was she who discovered his great musical gifts when he was still a child of five, she considered him as her property. She bound him to her by ties of gratitude, and she guarded him jealously against any influence not chosen by herself, right up to the time of his death. By that time she was a rabid Nazi and her influence was null; but her power to make him suffer was still considerable. Of the influence she had on his youth I know only what Mr R C Trevelyan (1872–1951) told me. He once spoke to me with great bitterness of her having taken upon herself to smooth the path of a youth whose genius was so great that he could have fought, and should have had to fight, his own battles; and of how she isolated him from his contemporaries and by arranging for him to make his first public appearances with the great violinist of his time, Joachim, then an old man hampered by rheumatism and only the shadow of the player he had been, first made him the object of the jealous criticism that was to dog him all his life. She steeped his native genius in a foreign culture — and incidentally infected him with the perennial German suspicion of the French. Small wonder that, having sat at his feet in mute adoration for a couple of very impressionable years, by the time I left for Vienna I was as ready as a sponge to soak up Germanic culture, Germanic prejudice, Germanic everything. And if I escaped a Germanic marriage it was because I had scarcely reached Vienna when the hound was on my trail.

It happened at a ball I was taken to about ten days after I arrived. I was dancing with a Hungarian, and he soon discovered that my school German was insufficient for conversation. He knew no English; he asked me whether I spoke French. Before I had time to reflect I answered, 'No'; then suddenly it came upon me with a rush that of course I spoke French! I was humiliated to discover that I had now a British accent with an occasional Swiss inflection, and that my vocabulary was that of a child. But from then on I spoke far more French than English or German. I spoke it with Hungarians and Bulgarians, with Russians, Rumanians, and Greeks, but never with anyone French, for I met none. It grew more fluent as my vocabulary increased, but was unwittingly starred with expressions unfamiliar to French ears, translations from more exotic tongues.

No doubt it was because French was the only foreign language in which I was fluent enough to keep pace with my need for communication that, in spite of my love for all things Germanic, I chose my intimate friends from among those elements of Vienna student life that were not Germanic. But I do not think it was the only reason; a great many Austrians spoke French. I think that the compass we carry hidden in the last and inmost box of our complex natures was pointing the way I had to go. All my Central European friends were steeped in French culture and loved everything France stands for. Through their influence I began to read French authors and take an interest in French music.

Actually there was another way in which, paradoxically, I was being prepared to receive the full impact of the French way of life. Our existence in Vienna in the 20s was, I suppose, an extraordinary one. Normal standards of value were upside-down, to some extent at least. The old upper classes were ruined; money was no longer a criterion of respectability as it tends to be elsewhere. Generally speaking, it was taken for granted that you would be poor, and life was planned accordingly. We lodged in the flats of ruined aristocrats; we could buy our cigarettes one at a time; we could spend half the day in the warmth of a comfortable café on the strength of a single cup of coffee; we could dress as we liked, for no extreme either of elegance or of bare-legged simplicity shocked; we moved in no closed circle, but switched indifferently from the drawing-room of an impoverished aristocrat to the bare bed-sitting-room of a struggling composer, and on through the café where we forgathered with our student friends to a dinner-dance in one of the Central European embassies. Life was so uncertain that it was always a shock to learn that one of our friends was taking it seriously enough to get married, and we came to rejoice when another was appointed to the security of a post in the United States.

That was the general picture, but in my own case a stable element was provided by an introduction Tovey gave me when on a flying visit to Vienna. It was to old Clara Wittgenstein, and it was round her that my real cultural life revolved during all the time I eventually stayed in Vienna. She was of an old, very distinguished Jewish family, and even after the ruin of Austria she was rich. She spent both her time and her money in giving intelligent help to struggling Austrian musicians and artists, not necessarily Jewish. Before the first war her drawing-room was one of the chief musical centres of Vienna, and when I met her music was still her real world. She was nothing of a Bohemian; she lived the most ordered and harmonious life it was ever my good fortune to witness. Her time was divided between an immense flat she owned in Vienna, and a 'palace' built in Laxenburg by Maria Theresa for one of her ambassadors. To this day I am homesick for the cool shadow of silence that fell on you like a cloak when you penetrated, hot and dusty from the hour's train journey from Vienna, to the hall of the 'palace' and climbed the broad white staircase that led to her front door; homesick for the tall white doors with their gilt edging, the huge white and gold porcelain stoves that could have served as a background for *Rosenkavalier*, the bedrooms big as ballrooms where we could rest after our coffee, the rose-scented garden we were offered as an alternative ('Shall we now separate to collect our thoughts,' was the formula she used), and especially for the white and gold music-room reserved for great occasions, where long ago both Haydn and Mozart had played, and, in Clara Wittgenstein's own times, Brahms. In short, though the topsy-turvy life we led in Vienna in the 20s was in its way an excellent preparation for life under enemy occupation, it was an echo of Clara Wittgenstein's way of life with its high standards of behaviour and customs of ceremonious simplicity that I found when I first made contact with the great French bourgeoisie, and that not only appealed to me by analogy, but struck me as wildly romantic.

But at the end of the first year in Vienna my parents wrote and told me to come home. They softened the blow by adding that Tovey had offered to take me as a private pupil. And so it came about that the following autumn I went round one misty Edinburgh afternoon to George Square for my first lesson. It was a little, as my father remarked, like going to Saint Paul for Sunday school, for I went to Tovey with for sole baggage my cocky ambition to play in public and the feeling for Mozartian style that had been fostered in me in Vienna. But he successfully bridged the gulf and did far more for me than teach me to play.

But Tovey left Edinburgh every year as soon as the musical academic year was over. In Edinburgh it lasts only two terms, which meant that from March onward I was without a teacher. I soon persuaded both Tovey and my parents that it would be a good thing for me to go back to Vienna for the six or seven months that he was absent, and right up to the time of my marriage I spent from March to October in Austria.

It happened almost accidentally during those years that I went three times to France. Looking back, I see those visits as so many breakwaters set up at irregular intervals to stem the rising tide of my German romanticism. The first was when I stopped in Paris for a week on my way home from my first year in Vienna. The Hungarian of that first ball was now Paris correspondent of a Budapest newspaper, and I had promised him that I would break my journey in Paris. But I could scarcely tear myself away from Vienna, and I kept sending him telegrams postponing my arrival. When at last, on July 14th, I landed at the Gare de l'Est, the only room he had been able to find for me at such short notice was in a rather disreputable hotel in the Rue St André des Arts. I had no idea that I was making things especially difficult for him by arriving on that day of all days; the Fourteenth of July was a date that meant nothing to me. I had, of course, heard of the storming of the Bastille, but I had no idea it could be an occasion for public rejoicing. What little I know of the French Revolution I had learned from *The Scarlet Pimpernel* and *A Tale of Two Cities*. On the other hand, I had often heard my German acquaintances speak slightingly of *französische Frivolität*, so it seemed to me a right and proper thing that the French should be dancing in their streets. I dined with my Hungarian friend on the Place St Michel, and danced for a part of the night.

My next visit occurred a year later. I came back to the same hotel, for I knew no other, with Margaret Ludwig, now the wife of Herbert Read, and the life we led was like some enchanting dream. We had only to lean out of the window to enjoy sights and sounds so foreign as to be an adventure in themselves. But there was more to it than that. A student who occupied the room above us sent us each a madonna lily; a young architect who worked over the way from our hotel watched us assiduously with opera-glasses, and once stood boldly at his window holding a large sheet of paper on which he had printed: *Dans la cours*. We shook our heads vigorously; we were much too young and much too interested to pay no attention to him. He returned with resignation to his opera-glasses. To crown it all, we saw Chaliapin at the Opera in *Boris Godunov*, with Koussevitzky conducting. We were so excited we nearly fell out of our box, and at the end we threw Chaliapin a red rose and got a bow all to ourselves.

My third visit to France occurred some three months later. My parents took two of my sisters and myself to Brittany. Of this visit only a few photographic images remain. I remember walking round the ramparts of St Malo by night and looking over the parapet to watch the hungry sea beating against the city walls, where only that morning had been a vast expanse of smooth sandy beach. I remember visiting Mont St Michel, and how the feeling of fathomless gloom I associate with afternoons spent at Portobello, Edinburgh's most accessible and most depressing beach, caught up on me as we climbed the winding lane that leads to the abbey. It was caused by the booths full of shell-ornamented wares that stand on either side, like traps for tourists. But at the top I remember how the gloom vanished and the ghost of Tristan emerged, inescapable, from the grey legendary stones of the abbey and the grey line of legendary sea beyond the wet stretches of sand.

I remember, too, that day in day out I was a prey to the wild nostalgia of adolescence. Wherever I went, it went with me; whether we were watching the fishing-boats dancing into the harbour of Concarneau, or were sitting perched on rocks that rose sheer from the sea, while the spray from the foaming breakers played about us. I think it is because my memories of that nostalgia are so vivid, and because it marred so much of what should in the ordinary course of things have been happy, that I have so little regret for my lost youth. '*À quoi rêvent les jeunes filles?*' '*À ne plus l'être*', my father-in-law would answer. At the time it did not seem nearly so simple as that.

And so at last what I took for a series of incidents having no real bearing on the trend of my life, led to my marrying a Frenchman and coming, willy-nilly, to know the French. I soon came to love first the everyday people with whom I made daily contact, the butcher, the baker, and the candlestick-maker; and at last everything that France stands for.

The native of one country who falls in love with another can be as tiresome to those who have never had to change their skin as the wearer of Solomon's Ring must have been to those who knew nothing of the language of birds and beasts. I think this is because we are apt to take for a change of heart what is really an extension of it. Because you come to see world history from a new angle and lose your early belief in the infallibility of your country of origin, your loyalty to it is not affected; nor, because you come to see that the English way of doing things may be right for the English but is not necessarily a norm, do you cease to believe it is right for the English.

It took me years really to come to know the French, and there is a great deal I got to understand only through bringing up French children. The surface difference between the French and the English is so great that it blinds us and them to certain fundamental resemblances. The French do not make things easy. They carry their faults on their sleeve and keep their immense qualities for the privacy of family life. Those who touch only on the periphery of their lives come up against their irritability — the reverse side of their great rapidity of thought and reflex action; their suspicion of foreigners — the reverse side of their strong family feeling; their lack of civic sense and rooted dislike of all authority — the reverse side of the independence of judgement that is fostered in them at school; their cruel wit that has its roots in no hardness of heart, but in a love of laughter so great that they can resist no occasion for it. They are misleading, too, because they are full of contradictions — at once anti-clerical and, on the whole, profoundly Catholic; anti-militarist, but loving military display; pleasure-loving, but hard-working; caring deeply for quality in all things, but pastmasters in the art of making something out of nothing; taking what they do seriously, but feeling themselves in honour bound not to take themselves seriously; little given to cherishing illusions about human nature, but easily fired to expect great things of it. France is the country where no one trusts the government, but where everyone strives for state employment; the land of public scandals and of such monuments of disinterested integrity as the Michelin guide book.

Certainly there are many ways in which the French differ from ourselves. They are much more given to abstract reasoning, and suspicious of our empirical methods. But it would be wrong to take too seriously this love of abstraction. A French biologist once told me how distressed the German delegates are when in an international conference the French delegates ask for a diagram of whatever is being discussed. The Germans point out that you cannot isolate anything from its context. 'We would never dream', said my French friend, 'of isolating anything from its context. But we do love a diagram!'

The French differ from us in their attitude to the spoken word. Like Pericles, they consider that until thought has found verbal expression it is scarcely worthy of the name of thought. I think we feel that by dragging thought up to the level of utterance we may in some sort disturb its processes. We believe in intuitive reasoning which, to quote my own father, 'works on more subtle and complex data than the thinker can hope to define clearly'. It is not, I think, for his swashbuckling 'panache' that Cyrano de Bergerac lies so near the heart of the great French public; it is because he triumphs over physical deformity through qualities of the mind, and because in him real greatness of heart finds witty expression.

Perhaps the English are more aware than the French of the dangerous power of words; and the French more alive than the English to the danger of muddled thinking. There is something to be said for both points of view.

The French and the English differ in their attitude towards nature. The English love nature for herself and they like everyone and everything to be natural, by which they mean unstudied. Like one great Englishman, Dr Johnson, the French like to see the trace of man's hand in nature, and have a cult for the moral quality of effort. The difference is evident if you compare a French with an English garden. An English garden is man's idea of what nature would do if she were right-minded; a French garden is decorative art carried out in live materials.

There are qualities which both the French and the English possess, but which find different expression in each. I shall give only one example or I shall never have done. Both are idealists, but on the whole with the English it is especially on the individual, with the French on the public, level that idealism finds expression.

Before I mention briefly what both peoples have in common, I would like to draw attention to one curious thing, and that is the matter of what is taboo in each country as a subject of conversation. In England it used to be love. It no longer is, but the fact that it is now called 'sex' shows that although the taboo has been cast aside, its ghost has not been laid. With the French the only real taboo is money. Money may not be mentioned. Perhaps love for the English and money for the French are the pieces of the puzzle that have never found their rightful place in the metaphysical scheme of things generally accepted by the community. They are always knocking at the door to be allowed in. In England and America we blame our Puritan ancestors for our shortcomings in the realm of love. Is it because France is a Catholic country that money remains a misfit? I think that Protestants more readily than Catholics embrace the Old Testament notion of material prosperity coming as a reward for moral virtue. No doubt it seemed in the old days a fitting thing that our missionaries, by teaching the 'heathen savage' to hide his nakedness, incidentally opened up markets for the cotton wares of Manchester. I am not suggesting any connection was made in the minds of the missionaries. I merely doubt whether, if the connection had occurred to them, it would have shocked them. The Catholic ideal is an ideal of poverty. That must be difficult to fit into one's scheme of things in the country of all countries where money can do most for you, not in the material sense, but because it buys beauty in so many forms. How tempting to thrust deep down into the unconscious the problem of how to reconcile a love of money with a sincere desire to shake off the fetters of materialism.

As regards the fundamental resemblance between the French and the English, I think they may be summed up in the fact that both are at the same stage of civilization, and that their civilizations have common roots. To use an image of Kipling's, they were formed in the same womb. But Kipling speaks only of Rome (as including Greece) as the common ancestor. It is true that Greece is the ancestor that probably had most influence in forging the French mind, and it is certain that she left her mark also on the English. But what of the other spiritual ancestor, common to both, but which left the stronger mark on the English? The English, as Protestants, were nourished for generations on the Bible, whereas Catholic France, alarmed at the explosive effects of the Bible on people's minds at the time of the Reformation, inclined until quite recently to treat it almost as a museum piece, and take her nourishment especially from Greece. Today it is as though each held in his hand one half of the apple of Christendom.

Small wonder I feel that, born British and French by adoption, I have the best of all worlds. And this brings me to the last thing the two peoples have in common. It is so much a second nature with both to believe that there is no one like them that the notion scarcely even reaches the level of conscious thought, but is manifest in the atmosphere of exclusiveness in which both take refuge as naturally as does an octopus in a cloud of ink. It is probably one of the reasons they often find each other so oddly irritating.

Janet Teissier du Cros

Part One
'Things fall apart...'

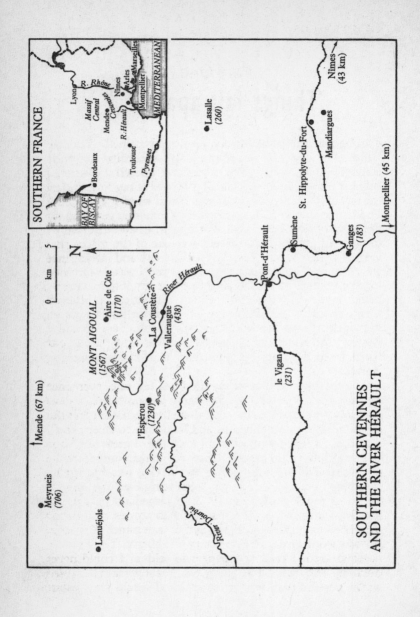

SOUTHERN FRANCE

R. Rhône
Lyon
Massif
Central
Mende
Cévennes
R. Hérault
Toulouse
Pyrenees
Bordeaux
BAY OF BISCAY
Arles
Marseilles
Montpellier
MEDITERRANEAN

Mende (67 km)

Meyrueis
(706)

Lanuéjols

MONT AIGOUAL
(1567)

l'Espérou
(1230)

Aire de Côte
(1170)

La Coustète

Valleraugue
(438)

River Hérault

River Dourbie

le Vigan
(231)

N

0   km   5

Lasalle
(260)

Nîmes
(43 km)

Mandiargues

St. Hippolyte-du-Fort

Sumène

Pont-d'Hérault

Ganges
(183)

Montpellier (45 km)

SOUTHERN CEVENNES
AND THE RIVER HÉRAULT

Throughout the whole of my youth I lived in the childish belief that one can order one's life according to one's convictions and plan one's future for oneself. I believed that I was Captain of my Soul and Master of my Fate and all the rest of the nonsense that was in the air when I was a child. I had no feeling of patriotism except a romantic yearning for the countryside of Scotland. Patriotism, I had been told by those a little older than myself, was one of the myths that led our fathers astray. Maturity, objectivity and intelligence were the three gods of my generation, and I was determined to take maturity by storm and to prove my intelligence by being objective. I took no account of frontiers, I believed I had no racial prejudice nor any class-feeling. I was an individualist and the world was my oyster. So I thought. But in truth when the Second World War broke about our heads I was the shornest lamb that ever was loosed among wolves.

The trouble was that all my life I had felt safe, ever since my mother persuaded me that there are no bears, cobras nor wolves in England, and that there has been no successful invasion since 1066. The sea had lulled me to sleep, and I remained in that condition until long after I grew up. Mine was a glorious world in which there was danger only from the other sex. The possibility of an Act of God was admittedly suspended over all our heads, but it troubled me only as a part of my fear of death. Politics played no part in my life. I associated the word vaguely with stories read in my childhood about Czarist Russia and the salt mines of Siberia. It was a word shrouded in mystery and horror. The mystery never cleared. I read newspapers so seldom I could never catch up with what was going on. If conversation turned on the possibility of war or revolution, I would grow aware of a creeping feeling in my scalp and a cold feeling down my spine. But I played the ostrich till the very end, that is to say till the Munich crisis.

'Munich' burst upon us like a mountain thunderstorm one glorious day in the Cevennes, out of the purest of blue skies. It so cleft my life in two that all that came before seems to have taken place in some phantom world of innocence. The person I had been died in some sort a sudden death. The one I was to become emerged only after months and years of painful but unheroic gestation. And now when I look back on my old self it is as though I saw in a looking-glass my own reflection gazing out at me with the eyes of a stranger. For the thoughts and beliefs that lend it expression are so utterly different from what are now my thoughts and beliefs.

In the summer of 1938 we were spending the holidays at L'Espérou, a mountain village in the southern part of the Cevennes. We never saw a newspaper and we had no wireless. It was from Parisian cousins who came up from the valley of Valleraugue to see us that we learned of Hitler's ultimatum to Czechoslovakia. They imparted the news with the truly Parisian blend of agitation and cool-headedness which I always find so shattering. The look in their eyes as they spoke filled me with awful foreboding. It seemed to fix some distant horizon visible only to themselves, as though French history was so much a part of them that it could shed light not only on the future but also on the means whereby they could arm themselves to face it. What knowledge I had of French history was academic, not atavistic. The sense of imminent catastrophe I had, catastrophe beyond anything I had ever dreamed of; but I felt completely disarmed before it. It seemed to me that I was being treacherously measured for circumstances that would prove too big for me.

The immediate outcome of our cousins' visit was that my husband and I felt we could no longer bear to remain isolated in those indifferent enduring heights. The very human need to herd together for our greater mutual agitation and our occasional mutual comfort drove us down into the valley with our cousins, Pierre and Germaine Dieterlen, and their friend, Solange de Ganay.

We went from L'Espérou to Valleraugue on foot by the

longer and more beautiful route. First it took us higher
still, to Mount Aigoual, by the *draille*, the broad track that
leads through beech forests and over bare hilltops, the track
along which sheep have been driven, spring and autumn,
since prehistoric times. From Mount Aigoual we descended
slowly along the shoulders of the hills, at one point along
a fragment of Roman road. I doubt whether the scene we
saw about us was so very different from what the Roman
legionaries must have seen when they went that way. It
is wild, back-of-beyond country. Steep rugged mountains
tower over narrow valleys. You can tell roughly the height
you are at from the vegetation that surrounds you. The
terraced lower slopes are planted with vine and mulberry.
Above, to a level of about two thousand five hundred feet,
are chestnut groves. Then come beech forests broken by
wild stony stretches where only gorse and juniper bushes
grow. When you look across the valley to the opposite
heights the impression you have is not of wooded hills,
but of the giant limbs of some hirsute monster. Only the
chestnut-trees seem really to clothe the hills because of the
way the light catches their glossy leaves. Few landscapes can
look wilder, yet the mountains raised their heads that day
against the serenest of blue skies and the grass at our feet was
bejewelled with the wild version of some of our homeliest
garden flowers—carnation, pansy and snapdragon.

At last we saw the green ribbon of the valley of Valleraugue
far below us, and directly and precariously we descended into
it by the rough path called the Four Thousand Steps which
leads straight into the village of Valleraugue.

At this point I must make a digression and explain
our connection with the Cevennes, for they are the background against which much of the drama that followed was
played.

I first saw the valley of Valleraugue in the year 1929. I
had been staying in Montpellier with my future parents-in-
law, and their eldest son, François, to whom I was then
engaged, drove me and his younger brother, Jacques,
to Valleraugue to visit the house their great-grandfather
made by throwing together two much older dwellings.
Our way took us through the fantastic country that lies

north of Montpellier, dry, dusty, beautiful, its bone-white
rocks forever breaking through their thin covering of poor
earth. It took us through the vine-grown plains among the
first foothills of the Cevennes where another old family
house stands: Mandiargues, now the permanent home of
my parents-in-law but then a house the family occupied
only during the vine harvest in September. From that point
onward the road leads deeper and deeper into the wild
mountainous country I have come to love so well. It was
spring, the season when innumerable tumultuous streams
come gushing down from the heights on either side to join
the Hérault. A light wind was blowing and it stirred the
olive-trees to silver so that for a moment I imagined they
had blossomed.

And so at length, after twisting and turning and crossing
the river and crossing back again, we drove into the village
of Valleraugue.

Valleraugue was once one of the chief centres of the
silk industry to which the Cevennes owed a period of
considerable prosperity and on which the fortunes of my
husband's family were originally founded. By the time
I came to know the village it had fallen with the silk
industry (and the family fortunes) on evil days. Gone was
the time when eighty gentlemen's families found it worth
their while to settle in the village and neighbouring valley,
and every inhabitant hastened to build on an extra storey to
lodge the great silkworm nurseries, giving an impression of
disproportionate height to the houses. By the time I came
there all the part of the village which was built on rising
ground, and through which we descended that day in the
middle of the Munich crisis, was falling to ruin. And along
the Quai, what were once the houses of the gentry now
shelter the post-office, the baker's and draper's shops, the
workshops of plumber, mechanic and locksmith. All that
remains of former glory are the finely vaulted ceilings, the
wrought-iron arabesques of balcony and balustrade.

A few of the once prosperous houses have remained in the
hands of the original families though their descendants now
earn their living elsewhere. They stand empty all winter and
blossom to life only at the first sign of summer when their

owners are due to arrive for the holidays. It was to one of
these that François took me on that April day in 1929, and
it was in the same house, the house of Germaine's father,
our Oncle Ernest, that we took refuge at the time of the
Munich crisis.

I remember how puzzled I was at first by the approach
to the house. I was accustomed to the clear-cut position
of the 'big hoose' in a Scotch community. It is generally
approached by a long avenue of Scotch pines. It stands
aloof. The house where François took me that day in 1929
was something very different. He stopped the motor in an
open square in the village where grew a purple-flowering tree
that was new to me. We left the square and picked our way
up a steep, narrow, cobbled lane between tall houses built
of the lovely dark schist that is characteristic of the region.
The stonework stood out in all its harsh beauty, unmasked
by the coating of white or rose-coloured roughcast that gives
a gay tone to the houses of the more prosperous villagers.
But against that sombre background how jewel-like shone
the geraniums, the fuchsias, the petunias, the begonias
and the China asters, set out in pots and old tins on the
windowsills and along the outer edges of the stone steps.
I once read somewhere that the gardens sung by the poets
of Persia were probably poor enough compared with our
English gardens, that they owed the miraculous impression
they produced on people's minds to their desert setting. I
understood that statement fully that day for the first time
when I found myself catching my breath at the sight of a
few pots of radiant flowers, and saw the thin crystalline jet
of water from a fountain play in the sun with more effect,
in a region where water that flows the whole year round
is a luxury, than all the watery wonders of the Versailles
gardens.

To this fountain the village women came with their prosaic
water-cans to fetch water for their households, and at the
sight I fell to wondering what the local plumbing was like.
But I cared little. The sun was hot, the sky was blue, there
was a gaiety in the air to which I was peculiarly sensitive, for
the mists of Scotland still hung about my mind and gave me
a gloomy tendency. What mattered the plumbing? Besides,

François and Jacques had stopped in front of a great double green door with an immense and highly polished knocker which stood a little back from the cobbled lane, in the wall of a house that seemed no different from the others. A smaller door was, as it were, carved out of one of the great doors, much as you sometimes see a door for the cat at the foot of an ordinary-sized door. This door François opened and through it, cat-like, I went. It led, I discovered, not into the house but under a part of it, by a short vaulted tunnel, and into the courtyard round which the colossal house is built. There on the doorstep stood, not the master of the house—he was in Paris at that time of year—but the littlest of old women, her face alight with joy at the sight of us. That was the first time I met old Lucinde who had been with the family since she was fourteen.

It was not till the following summer that I was taken to the family's other house, at L'Espérou. In summer the heat in the valley is intense although the nights are cool, and François's grandfather built one house and bought two more at L'Espérou to lodge the various branches of the family in July and August. In those times, and even when François was still a child, L'Espérou was a primitive mountain village, a small cluster of granite houses with slate roofs, each with an impressive dunghill before its door, sign of the peasants' wealth, for their fortune is in their cows and sheep and in the slow-moving oxen whose yokes the owners carve out themselves from wood cut in the neighbouring forests. It is the only visible sign of wealth; it would be difficult to imagine a more primitive way of life than theirs, even at the present time.

The country round the village is of exceptional beauty and the air at that altitude, about four thousand feet, is incomparable. My husband's family was not the only one that sought refuge there from the heat of the valley. Two other families share with his the honour of being the oldest non-indigenous inhabitants of L'Espérou, though all three are of Cevenol origin. The de Lapierres bought what had once been the schoolhouse and adapted it to their needs. The Nicks bought what had been the curé's house, and their grandfather, Monsieur Lecque, built on a large annexe. These three families form the nucleus of what has since become a summer resort. In their heart of hearts to this day they consider themselves as the lords of L'Espérou and a mystic bond binds them to the hills, to the peasants and to each other. It is something more mysterious and fundamental than a bond of friendship, and to be honest their relationship is sometimes stormy. To the peasants they still rank to some extent as outsiders, though they are accorded pride of place over the 'summer visitors'. The peasants belong to a far older civilization and to them our legal rights to this or that piece of land are artificial. The land is theirs, as naturally as it belongs to the wild boar, the foxes and hares they hunt in the winter. As soon as we leave they take over. Our backs are scarcely turned when their cows are cropping the grass in our gardens, and when the following summer we open the doors of the outhouse where we shelter our motor-car (when we have one) we find it mysteriously filled with sheep's dung.

For me there is an added bond between our family and the Nicks; it was through one of the Nick daughters, Madeleine, that I first met François. Madeleine Nick spent a year in Edinburgh giving French conversation lessons *au pair* in a girls' school, and she soon became an intimate friend first of my sister Letty and then of myself. In fact she became almost a part of our household, and when François after her return to France wrote that he was passing through Scotland on his way home from Sweden and Norway, she sent him a letter he has kept to this day. In it she gave him our address and the advice to 'turn up as though by chance at tea-time because of the cherry cake'.

Little by little I came to know all Madeleine's family except her brother André, the flower of the family, who died before ever I met her. In fact, it was his death that drove Madeleine to Scotland because home was emptied of his presence. They were (today only two of them remain) an extraordinarily beautiful family and they are of an heroic race. The father, Pasteur Nick, was probably the finest French Protestant clergyman of his time, both by reason of his courage in the First World War and because of his influence among the working population of Lille. He was a tremendous personality but he never weighed upon his children. He left them free scope to develop and he always encouraged their sense of adventure. He had six children in all. The eldest was Jeanne. She had been married but when I knew her she was living with her father and working as a biologist in a laboratory in Lille. The eldest son, Paul, died some time before the war and I knew him only slightly. The second son, Pierre, was a country doctor in the region of Lille. I learned after the war of 1939–45 that although he had a wife and five children he had worked all through it both for the Resistance and for the British Intelligence Service and had even had a transmitting-set in his cellar. The second daughter, Helena, married a White Russian shortly after I came to live in France, an architect whose real name is Scobeltzine but who calls himself Scob for convenience' sake. When the war broke out they had two children; and Scob's mother, the widow of General Scobeltzine of the Russian Imperial Army, spent the war years with them. Madeleine, the youngest, was now married to François Dieterlen, a distant cousin of Germaine's husband, and they had two little girls.

All the Nicks were very tall and, as I said earlier, very beautiful. All were lighted up from within by the republican spirit of a Jaurès. It was like a torch by whose light they always clearly saw the way they had to go. They had never, like myself, to prop their failing courage on the first illusion to hand. My only merit was that I knew in my bones that, even if they failed as they sometimes did to convince me by argument, in whatever they did or thought they were pretty sure to be right.

The house at L'Espérou, the Maison Noire, had fallen to Papa's share of his father's inheritance, and that is where we were when the Munich crisis fell upon us like a thunderbolt. It was to Oncle Ernest's house at Valleraugue that we went with Germaine and Pierre for shelter, I with a secret hope that old Lucinde would reassure me as my mother used to do when she was alive. It never even occurred to us to go to our own little house farther up the valley. I shall tell of it later. At this time it still had for us something of the unreality of a toy house built in one's parents' garden—a place to play in when the sun is shining and there is nothing to fear, but not quite a safe shelter when the shadows of night begin to fall and the storm is rising.

We found Lucinde busy in her kitchen among the copper pans. She was calm enough, but her reassurance was rather too long-term to be helpful. She told me the Germans were like melons; you must wait to eat them till they are ripe. That time had not yet come but would certainly come some day. I found this cold comfort. In the meantime Germaine and Pierre were opening telegrams which had arrived in their absence and which decided them to leave for Paris at once. They now spoke of war as inevitable.

I date from that day the knowledge that came to me suddenly and has never left me—that our private lives were at an end and we were now at the mercy of forces over which we had no control. They might occasionally be restored to us like a toy, to play with, but we must not expect such a delightful state of things to last. This was the more bitter that private life had never seemed more precious than it did that summer. François had come to a turning point in his life and our hopes for the future were high. Briefly, he hoped to give up engineering for scientific research. For some time past he had felt a growing desire to do so, but with a wife and two children to support he had hesitated. As an engineer he was employed by the French state and his future was assured. Research is an uncertain and often a badly paid adventure. But suddenly a door had sprung open. My father had been suffering badly from loneliness since my mother died in 1937, and it occurred to me that both his problem and ours would be solved if we were to reconsider a suggestion my mother made a year or so before she died. The great German physicist, Max Born, had just been appointed to the chair of physics at Edinburgh left vacant by Sir Charles Darwin's departure for Cambridge, and her suggestion had been that we come home for a year and that François join Professor Born's seminar. At the time we had hesitated; François was still a little uncertain in his mind. But now he was more sure of himself, and I wrote to my father suggesting we come home the following

year. He at once agreed. All that remained was to obtain a
year's leave from the French authorities, and this proved
easier than we expected. François would be able to leave
for Edinburgh without burning his boats and we planned
to go in October 1938. Now this happy prospect seemed to
be receding beyond the bounds of possibility.

Our gathering in Valleraugue broke up rapidly. Though
the holidays were not yet over, the holiday spirit had fled.
Germaine and Pierre and Solange de Ganay left for Paris
by road. My husband took the train for Marseilles, and I
collected the children and my English nurse from L'Espérou
and joined him shortly afterwards.

I remember those last weeks in Marseilles as among the
unhappiest I have ever known. To make matters worse, I
had bad news of my father. He had come home from the
United States on the verge of a nervous breakdown and I
decided I would leave for Edinburgh with the children as
soon as our belongings were packed, and let François join
us when he could. If he were prevented by the outbreak of
war, as seemed likely, then we would return to Marseilles.

There are two incidents belonging to this period which
I am never likely to forget. One was an evening when,
on our way home from the cinema, we stopped before
the Havas Agency on the Canebière to see what news
was posted up outside. Among other things we read that
Japan had confirmed her intention of standing by Germany
in the event of war. I was shattered. François thought I
took too serious a view of the role Japan could play. He
was accustomed to thinking in terms of the continent of
Europe. I, for all my ignorance of politics, was haunted by
Empire communications. The other incident occurred when
we were packing our belongings to prepare for the removal of
our furniture. We were wrapping books in newspapers full of
sinister headlines, and we fell to wondering what our feelings
would be when we unpacked them, presumably a year later
on our return to France. Little did we guess it would be
three years before we would unpack them, or that we would
do so in Paris, in the shadow of Notre Dame, to the sound
through the window of heavy boots beating the pavement
as German soldiers dutifully went their sightseeing round of

the conquered capital. And the feeling of catastrophe that weighed upon us as we packed them emerged as intact as the books and mingled with the bleak drabness that was then our life.

And so we left Marseilles. François saw us on our way as far as Paris. Of the few days we spent with him in the capital I remember only a visit to the Jardin d'Acclimatation. We took our two little sons to see the elephants, and we fed them so successfully with bread that one of them trumpeted after us when we left. It used to haunt me during the Occupation to think we had given bread to an animal, and white bread at that.

We parted, François and I, at the Gare du Nord. When catastrophe is still only a possibility and hope not dead, we dare allow free rein to our imagination and indulge in what one can describe only as the luxury of unutterable suffering. That separation was more of a tearing asunder than when we were to part in the station of Nîmes in May 1940 at a far worse moment. When disaster is really upon us we have no choice, but a minimum of courage. I had no courage in 1938. I was desperate when the ferry-boat train drew out of the station and my husband vanished from my sight. But presently my English nurse came and poked her head through the door of my sleeper, her kindly blue eyes misty behind thick spectacles. She wiped a drop of sympathy from the tip of her nose and said, 'I've a feeling in my bones there won't be a war this time!' At once I felt immensely better.

We reached Edinburgh in time to receive Chamberlain's announcement that he brought us 'peace with honour', and I was one of the fools who believed him and rejoiced. Not for long, but long enough to send me, in my muddled way, to church (where I seldom went) on a wave of joy and gratitude. I went before breakfast and I came home bursting with happiness and a certain feeling of virtue at having given credit where credit, I felt, was due. In my ignorance and the general confusion of my mind where politics are concerned, I thought that good had triumphed over evil in the international field. My father effectually pricked that balloon. He was sitting at breakfast looking very gloomy, a crumpled newspaper beside him. He looked at my happy face with a sardonic eye and said, 'Well! We have sacrificed the whole prestige of the British Empire to postpone war some six or eight months!'

I felt a wave of fury surge in my bosom. Why, I asked myself, must prophets always prophesy disaster? Or rather, why must I be born in a period of history when prophets are of necessity pessimists? There must have been times when young women's fathers looked up from the breakfast table to prophesy the rising of shares and the conquest of new colonies. Why was not I born at such a time? As far back as I could remember, my father had had his prophetic moments. They were not cheerful memories. He was to have one more before the tide of events swept us asunder for five long years.

During the weeks that followed I caught up on world politics. I devoured every book and every review that could help to dispel my ignorance. The result was an ever-growing sense of despair and a pessimism so black that my friends began to avoid me.

In the meantime, circumstances independent of the political situation had led to my father's leaving once more for the United States on what promised to be a long visit. François had at last wound up his affairs in Marseilles and had joined us in Edinburgh. He took up the work in mathematical and physical research that for years he had longed to do, and I settled into something resembling what had once been my way of life, with the difference that in spite of the presence of my English nurse (who had ceased to have reassuring feelings in her bones) the fact of my having two children and a big house to run left but limited room for practising the pianoforte as I had hoped to do.

I remember that year in Edinburgh as feverish. François's happiness in his work made us dread more than ever the ruthless forces that were going to destroy for years his hope of its becoming his life's work. As for myself, it was not merely my duties as a mother that prevented me from working regularly at my music. Though Sir Donald Tovey had lent me one of his instruments (my own had followed me to France at the time of my marriage) and was prepared to take up once more the regular rhythm of our lessons, in the atmosphere of crisis from which we never emerged I found it impossible to work as I used to do in the old peaceful days. Besides, and as will become apparent later, when death or disaster looms I invariably develop a strong sense of duty. I hoped then that if I threw my personal life overboard I would perhaps be allowed to retain my private life as a wife and mother. I went further: in the hope of salvaging something by my good conduct I became involved in the work of helping refugees to escape out of Germany by means of affidavits; to some of them we gave temporary hospitality on their arrival in Edinburgh. I found these contacts singularly depressing. It struck me that most of these refugees, but for the accident of their being Jewish, would themselves have been Nazis. In the admiration they displayed for force and efficiency, they were far more German than Jewish. One of them in particular used to pore over our newspapers at breakfast with every now and then a short contemptuous laugh at some example of what seemed to him the weakness of the democracies. This finally so frayed my nerves that when one day I left for an excursion with François I hid a book I had been reading, *They Betrayed Czechoslovakia*, written by President Benes's secretary, I forget his name. I thought it would be safe behind a row of books, and that we would be spared our refugee's contemptuous commentaries. Alas! When we came home we found him plunged in a familiar-looking volume. He looked up from its pages and with the German accent I had so come to loathe he said, 'I have found a most interesting book, *They Betrayed Czechoslovakia*'. I sought refuge precipitately in my room.

What troubled us greatly in all this was the fear that these refugees would create anti-Semitism by an attitude of mind which, as I say, was not Jewish but German. For how were those of us to distinguish what were Jewish traits and what German who had no knowledge of either? No doubt generalizations about the Jewish race are as foolish as most generalizations, but I think no one could accuse the Jews of an exaggerated respect for force, and certainly nothing could be more foreign to their intellectual integrity than the irrational and emotional and wholly unscientific train of thought that led to Nazism.

In the meantime, we were progressing from crisis to crisis. The Italian invasion of Albania found us in Yorkshire where we were spending the Easter holidays. We had driven over to York to visit the Minster and we were having tea in a nearby tea-room when we saw the news in the headlines of our neighbour's newspaper. It is extraordinarily unpleasant to read bad news in someone else's headlines. It was to happen to us again on an even more dramatic occasion. It is as nerve-racking as to hear fragments of bad news on someone else's wireless through an open window, an experience I often had during France's collapse but which never failed to reduce me to a state of dithering nerves. I remember that on this occasion the sight of the houses opposite, harmonious and civilized as the Jane Austen novels they call to mind, heightened by contrast the sense of nightmare.

The Prague crisis is another memory whose drama for me was concentrated into the space of a few seconds and which stands out as clearly as by spot-lighting, with the same unreal, permanent quality as though lifted out of time and space. I was lying in my bath one evening before changing for dinner after a tiring day. In the far distance—very far, for the terrace where we lived is isolated on either side by gardens—I heard the raucous cry of an excited newspaper-boy. It was impossible at that distance to distinguish a word, but the sound had an urgent quality. Before I had any clear notion of what I was doing I had leaped out of my bath, flung a bath-towel round me and opened the door into the bedroom. François was there, lying resting on the bed; he too had had a tiring day. I said, 'The Germans have entered Prague!' He said, 'Nonsense!' But he got up and went out to buy a newspaper. It told us that the Germans had indeed entered Prague. The sword of Damocles had dropped a couple of inches nearer.

During the whole of that year my imagination continued to cause me torment, as no doubt happened to most women. I was haunted by the thought of the people in Prague and especially of the women who like myself had a husband and

children. Vicariously I lived through the anguish of knowing
them in danger. I did not know then what I said a few pages
back, that the imagination is a luxury indulged in only by
those who still feel safe. The Germans had scarcely swept
through France but my own closed down, and it remained
deaf and dumb and blind for four long years. Life then was
so simple it was bounded by the coming night; beyond that
the world was a new world which did not yet concern us.
No material object had value except in as far as it served
to keep breath in our bodies and warmth in our veins. Life
itself was worth only so high a price; there was a spiritual
level below which it was worth nothing, though that level
varied from one person to another. This left a wide margin,
the unheroic margin in which the shorn lambs took refuge,
fighting the daily battle for the material means to keep alive,
acting according to their lights when occasion arose, and
trusting some other self, the self that would arise tomorrow
in a new world, a new self, to take the consequences. In fact,
so speedily and so utterly do we adapt ourselves to disaster
that I used often to feel it was probably my sister Letty in
New York who was having the hardest time, because in her
anxiety for all of us she could afford to give free rein to
her imagination and had no experience to tell her how the
obscure and the mediocre survive disaster. She did not, in
fact, know the truth of what a young Frenchman once said
to me, '*On se fait à tout, même à l'Apocalypse!*'

As far as François's work went, the year in Edinburgh was a
complete success and our hopes for the future were crowned
one June evening at a party at the house of Principal Sir
Thomas Holland. The party was in honour of those who
had just been awarded *Honoris Causae* doctorates by the
University of Edinburgh. Of these Dr Boegner, the head
of the French Protestant Church, a friend of my husband's
family, was one. I was to meet him again in less happy
circumstances. On this occasion we had all been invited,
but my father, who was back once more in Edinburgh, and
my husband were both tired and disinclined to go. They
delegated my sister Letty (home for a holiday from New
York) and myself to represent them. Neither Letty nor I was

ever too tired to go to a party. We dressed for the occasion in the slow, leisurely way that had been customary to us when as girls we prepared for a dance. When we were ready we were just going to telephone for a taxi when an old friend turned up and offered to drive us to Sir Thomas Holland's house. This friend was Arthur Cardell Ryan. During all those feverish months his lightning visits had provided an element of comedy that relieved the emotional strain. His friendship with our family dated back to the First World War when we were still schoolchildren and he was a 'snotty' on board the *Warspite*. Every time the *Warspite* anchored in the Firth of Forth he would turn up at our house with a band of fellow midshipmen and glorious times would follow. He disappeared out of our lives after the First War, though an occasional postcard would reach us from Kenya or the Dead Sea or some such unlikely spot. He turned up again as suddenly as ever during our year in Edinburgh, as though war were his natural element—as indeed I think it is—and the moment he scented its approach he emerged from some secret Valhalla where he had taken refuge during the years of peace.

It was from Glasgow that Arthur appeared on the evening of Sir Thomas Holland's party. The last we saw of him he was sprinting across the garden in full pursuit of his dog which had escaped in Letty's and my wake. He was still running when the front door swallowed us up.

The party was a great success. We shook hands with the *Honoris Causae* doctors, and Dr Boegner murmured a few polite words about François's family. Then, having accomplished our duty, Letty turned her attention to Mr R. A. Butler while I retired into a small room off the main drawing-room with Professor Born, who wanted to discuss François's future with me since he was not there himself. I emerged from our conversation in a state bordering on bliss. Professor Born had spoken so highly of François's capacities and with such confidence of his future, he had expressed so clearly his wish to keep him on in Edinburgh, that I could scarcely wait to get home and repeat it all to my husband.

As soon as we reached home I ran upstairs and woke him to repeat to him every detail of my conversation with

Professor Born. For the rest of the night we lay sleepless with excitement. From our beds we could see the pale June night grow paler as dawn broke. It broke behind the trees of the terrace gardens whose every branch I knew. I used as a child to steal out of my bedroom window when I was supposed to be asleep, creeping barefoot over the roof of my father's study to go and play tennis or climb those trees with my friends in the long evenings that herald in our northern summer nights. It was through those same gardens, in the pitchy darkness of cold foggy winter evenings, that Sir Donald Tovey used to see me home after my lessons, so absorbed in his flow of talk that he scarcely noticed we had almost to grope our way. Now it was the same familiar skyline that I watched as it grew every moment more clear, and we lay sleepless from happiness that owed its acuity to the grinding fear that our hopes would all come to nothing.

It was from that height that we fell in September 1939. There can be no point in going back over the days of rising tension that culminated in the bombardment of Warsaw; we are none of us likely to forget them. We did have one last laugh before our world collapsed. One night very near the end, when we had just gone to bed—it must have been round about midnight— the door-bell rang. I threw on a dressing-gown and ran down to see what it could be. There was no one there, but a sheet of paper had been shoved into the letter-box. It was from Arthur Cardell Ryan and all that was written on it was, 'I'm off on a secret mission to raise troops at Aden. I'll look you up after the war'.

Arthur's world had gone back to normal.

There was no actual need for us to go back to France until war was declared; François's mobilization orders were that he join his regiment at Avignon eight days after declaration of war. But when on September 1st we were walking down Princes Street and saw the bombardment of Warsaw announced on the news bulletins, we were in such a fever to be gone that we went straight to Cook's to arrange our journey home, regardless of the fact that we had now no real home in France.

Like everyone else, Cook's employees expected bombing to start even before war was declared, and they were dubious of our getting farther than London. Obviously we could count on the French Consul-General to ship us home when the time came, but we felt we could not wait. Now that we knew Professor Born wanted François to stay on in Edinburgh we had been afraid our eldest son Henri might forget his French, and we had sent him to his French grandparents for the summer. We felt we could not bear to be separated from him at such a time but must hasten home. We set out that same evening. Just before we left my father had his other prophetic moment. He suggested we send for Henri and that I stay on in Edinburgh with the children. He said, 'France will be unprepared and America will take a couple of years to make up her mind. You'll be safer in Scotland.' It never even occurred to me to take this suggestion seriously. Instinctively I knew that our place was in France. Besides, I could never have borne to see François leave all alone, nor did I believe I could fetch Henri back in time of war.

When he saw my mind was made up, my father added a last if a gloomy word of comfort. He said, 'Remember that whatever may happen, America simply cannot afford to let us be beaten.' I often hugged those words to me in the years to come.

We left the house in one of the familiar taxis that used to take my sisters and me to dances. The blackout was total and we could go only at a foot pace. The Waverley Station gave me a foretaste of hell as I imagine it. It was packed with people and the faint, rather sinister blue lighting only intensified the impression of darkness. Trainloads of drunken conscripts were singing songs from the First World War. They roused memories deliberately buried of the grim bleak shadow that had darkened our childhood. We trailed up and down the London train hunting by matchlight for our sleeper. The match travelled up and down the numbers on the doors and then flickered out and we were back in the dark and the crowd. At last we found our carriage and we had just boarded it when three friends, Alison Cairns, Dr Misra and Dr Kellermann broke through the barrier (non-travellers were not allowed on the platform) and came running to say goodbye. Alison was a friend from our childhood days in Aberdeen; Dr Misra and Dr Kellermann were a Hindu and a German physicist who had been working with François in Professor Born's research group. As the train drew away from the platform Dr Kellermann pressed into my hand the sixpence he had once bet me that Hitler would not fight when it came to the point. I shouted a last recommendation to Dr Misra, who had been six years in prison under British rule as a Gandhian, not to rouse India against us now that we were in trouble, and he shouted after us, 'Never, ours are family quarrels!' And so our life in Edinburgh ended.

The porters at King's Cross Station were more sanguine than Cook's employees in Edinburgh. They thought we would get back to France all right. War was not yet declared. At Victoria Station they told us there was a train for Folkestone in an hour, but they were uncertain of there being a boat to Boulogne. We decided to risk it; anything rather than be held up in London if bombing started. The mere idea of bombardment terrified me and I was certain I could never persuade André, the baby, into his gas-mask. At Folkestone we got a boat at once though as we left the train to go on board loudspeakers warned us that the French authorities no longer guaranteed the connection between Boulogne and Paris. The crossing was dead calm and our destroyer escort gave us a feeling of security, but I never saw the cliffs of England disappear with a heavier heart.

As we approached Boulogne we formed into a crowd with the other travellers, impatient to be on shore and learn the worst. André was weary of the whole business of travelling and kept shouting, 'Off the boat!' We were not a large crowd; no doubt, most people had broken off their holiday and gone home at an earlier date. As I examined our fellow-travellers I remember having the odd impression that the France I was coming back to was not the one I had come to know and love, but that other France that used to meet me when I came there long ago as a tourist. The people round me looked hard and impenetrable, especially the women. The men simply looked foreign. In front of me a well-dressed woman of a certain age was harassing her husband about the luggage. I thought to myself, 'So they are like that after all, hard, irritable and elegant as in so many second-rate English novels!' At that very moment François smiled at me and whispered, '*Des Suisses!*' And looking round me, glancing at labels on pig-skin suitcases, I realized that hardly any of these people were French. Nor were any of them at all characteristic of their country of origin. They were simply some of the international rich whose nerves were on edge at finding themselves up against one of the few things for which money is no cure.

When we landed we were relieved to find that there was, after all, a train for Paris. By this time we were feeling pretty tired, but to our surprise we found our spirits rising. The fact was that here in France no one seemed to believe there would be a war at all, and as we heard one person after another about us voice with cheerful contempt their conviction that the crisis would blow over, a cowardly hope began to grow in my heart that we would yet escape our fate.

I often wonder what the outcome would have been if we had fought instead of giving in over the Czechoslovakian crisis. I think the temper of France would have been very

different. After the first moment of relief, Munich left
people in France with a cynical taste in their mouths.
There was a feeling later that if 'they' had wriggled out
of going to war once, then 'they' were quite capable of
doing so again—'they' being, as always with the French,
the government. Something had been lost at Munich that
could never be recovered, the certainty of having acted
in accordance with traditions of which the French are
immensely proud. There was no honour left in public life;
all one could now do was cling to what was left of private
life. The door was open for the 'realists' who were to do so
much harm.

At the Gare du Nord there was not a porter to be found and
we were told there were very few taxis. The full meaning of
a *mobilisation générale* began to dawn on me. It was the first
time I had seen a country deprived of all men of military
age and the confusion that results.

We collected our registered luggage ourselves, piled everything on to a trolley and wheeled it out of the station. I sat
down on a suitcase to wait with André, now furious with
exhaustion, on my knee, and François went off to scour the
streets for a taxi. It was nearly an hour before he found one,
and André was quite desperate by the time we got away.

Just as we had determined not to stop in London, so now
we determined not to spend so much as a night in Paris. We
went straight across to the Gare d'Austerlitz; we had to go
south by the Massif Central because all the main lines were
requisitioned for the transport of troops and only secondary
lines and slow trains were available for travel. When we
reached Austerlitz we realized that our troubles were only
beginning; our journey so far had been easy compared with
what lay ahead of us. We now found ourselves drawn into
the mass of women and children who were being evacuated
from Paris, most of them from the slum quarters. The
station was thronged and every movement that followed
took hours, every inquiry meant long standing in a queue.
André by now was so exhausted he was nearly crazy. Our
porter was kind, everyone was kind, but we were nearing
the end of our tether. André would allow me neither to set

him down nor to sit down myself for a moment; and while François went from queue to queue I stood, holding the enormous two-year-old baby in arms that ached from wrist to shoulder. I think he felt that any concession would be tantamount to accepting his fate, and he was determined to travel no more.

At last it became clear that our prospects of leaving Paris that night were hopeless. There were only refugee trains, and they were so crowded we felt it would be cruel to André to take him on farther in such conditions that night. We followed our porter's advice, registered our luggage, and left in another taxi for the Hotel Madison of happy memories. We used to stay there in the old light-hearted days when we came to Paris on a holiday. We knew we would feel safe within its walls.

By the time we reached the hotel André was fast asleep, but he was so filthy we had no choice but to wake him and give him a bath. Then when he was safe in bed and once more sound asleep, we sallied forth in search of a restaurant.

Paris was dark, but it was Paris. The very air had a galvanizing effect upon us, and when we found ourselves in the Brasserie Lipp in front of a real French dinner, once more our spirits soared. The red wine relaxed us and the thought that we were back in France and still together was enough for us in the meantime. Besides, the people round us looked more excited than depressed. There were uniforms to remind us that war was imminent, but the faces above them were cheerful.

While we were finishing dinner François caught sight of an acquaintance in officer's uniform at another table and we joined him for coffee. He spoke not as the people in the train had done, but as people had been speaking in England, saying that another Munich was out of the question and that he would be ashamed to be French if we let Poland down. I remembered my sister Letty, weeping in the Caledonian Station in Edinburgh when she left us to return to New York in the early stages of the final crisis. She had said, 'If France and Britain don't fight, however shall I face the Americans?' I quashed my cowardly hopes and told him how people felt at home; that was one of the first things he, like everyone else, asked. He had rung up a sister-in-law to tell her he was in Paris and she soon came and joined us. They both gave us a feeling of calm and confidence, and we went back to our hotel feeling more hopeful, not of our chances of escaping war but of winning it when it came. We set our alarm for 5 a.m. and fell into a deep well of sleep.

The next day was exhausting, but it was an exciting experience. We travelled all through the day, a couple of hours at a time with long stops between in crowded dark and dirty station buffets where there was only wine, beer or black coffee to drink and dry bread to eat, and where self-service was the rule now that all the waiters were mobilized. While André and I sat guarding whatever table we found free, François, bearing the dirty cups or glasses left on the table, had to fight his way through the crowd round the counter to exchange them for clean cups of black coffee.

On the platforms of the stations we passed through, officers over military age had mobilized the local Boy Scouts to help the refugees with their luggage. Members of the Red Cross doled out milk and dry bread to the children. Everywhere there was goodwill and good humour. Even at that stage, I think that if fighting had come at once instead of after the long, demoralizing months of the cock-eyed war, then things might have been different.

The first train we boarded was an electric suburban train. Like all the other trains in which we were to travel, it was packed. Peasants and officers and children and their mothers, all were piled together pell-mell with a picturesque assortment of luggage. We sat opposite a gregarious peasant who told us he owned a market garden near Paris. He gave us a glowing description of the vegetables he grew, his hands unconsciously making the gesture appropriate to picking them so eloquently that when he spoke of his string beans you could see them fall in a green shower into an invisible basket. He had been through the First War and was now called up again, but he had still a few days before he had to join his regiment and he was going to visit his wife and daughter whom he had sent for safety to a property he owned in the centre of France. He was quite confident we would win the war—all those who had fought in the First War were equally confident—but like so many of his kind he doubted it would come to war. He spoke of the Germans without hatred and showed great respect for their courage. He said he would rather be sent to the Italian front than the German because the Italians are *pas méchants*. The Germans, he said, are a warlike race, always have been and always will be; it is unfortunate but there it is.

And so we went from train to train and met the oddest people in the brief intimacy born of our common trouble. On one occasion, after travelling for two days in crowded, dirty third-class carriages, we had the good fortune to find room in an almost empty second-class carriage. But scarcely were we installed and congratulating ourselves than we discovered the train was going in the wrong direction. We had only just time to project ourselves and our belongings out on to the platform and force our way into another crowded refugee train before it left. I remember there was an old woman with a wooden leg in our compartment. It stuck out straight in front of her as she sat. She was very jovial and insisted on regaling us all with swigs from a bottle of the inevitable red wine which her finer feelings incited her to wipe, before handing it on to the next person, with a very dubious pocket-handkerchief.

Out of the medley of memories three incidents stand out more clearly than the rest. One was when, to André's huge delight, we had to do part of our journey in an open cattle-truck. By that stage we were all looking pretty bedraggled, and André was so filthy that I doubt whether I would have had the courage to touch him if he had been someone else's child. We had therefore little to lose when we settled ourselves as comfortably as we could on the floor of our cattle-truck. We were joined there by a lady from St Germain-en-Laye. She was like a breath from Paris. Though she sat on the floor with us she never lost her air of neat elegance, and the sight of her struck guilt to my soul, for it reminded me that I had been taking advantage of circumstances to let my standards down, an unpardonable thing in France. This lady was dressed in a beautiful black tailor-made suit, a white lingerie blouse that was still really white, and a small black hat which could have come only from Paris. Her one concession to the occasion was a pair of rather old brown court shoes, but I felt certain, as certain as though I had peeped inside, that in the little dressing-case she carried with her there was another pair of shoes, black and well-polished, and that she would change into them the moment she was near her destination. She had undertaken the journey to pay a visit to her husband who was mobilized somewhere in the south. She told me she was a little anxious at having to leave her eighteen-year-old daughter alone in their house in St Germain-en-Laye. She had visions of soldiers being billeted on them in her absence . . . Her mind boggled at the thought and mine boggled in sympathy. We had a confidential chat about Hitler. In low tones so that the others should not hear she told me she had it on the best authority (what, I wondered, could that authority be!) that he was impotent, and together we shook our heads to think that the fate of nations should hang on such a sorry thread.

Then I clearly remember crossing the Lozère, some of the wildest and most glorious country of all the Massif Central, in a train full of women and children from the Paris slums. We shared our carriage with two women and their innumerable offspring, some with heads as red as any Glasgow child, but a darker red. The children were very lively but the mothers sat gazing out of the windows with gloomy faces as the lovely September landscape slipped by: the rushing torrents, the glossy chestnut groves, the high rocky mountains against the purest of blue skies served but to feed their bitter nostalgia for Paris. Every now and then they would lean their heads together and moan in concert at the thought of the awful prospect before them—country life! I tried to comfort the one who sat next me; I suggested it would be fun for the children and good for their health to live in the open and breathe the mountain air. I said, 'Look what lovely country it is!' She looked. She gazed out of the window with desperate eyes and answered, 'Oh, you know, when you're used to Paris . . .' Her voice died away and I remained silent, afraid to break in on the nostalgic dream that engulfed her. She was far away, on the steep lively streets of Montmartre or in the network of narrow alleys that run between the Boulevard St Michel and the Rue Dante and have kept the same character and reputation from Villon's time to our own. Who knows where she was?

The other incident that still haunts me occurred in a little lost mountain station, I have no recollection where. To this day I have no clear notion by what route we reached the south. We zig-zagged to and fro by whatever train took us more or less in the right direction and the whole journey took us three days. Our train had been standing in the station I refer to for some time and was on the point at last of getting underway, when suddenly the most terrible wailing rose in the air, the howling of some woman whose son or husband was leaving to join his regiment. It was a sound of sheer animal pain and quite terrifying to hear. In our carriage two young women were sitting with a soldier. They said something contemptuous when they heard the sound; I thought them hard-hearted and was caught up on a wave of that most suspect of emotions, moral indignation. Just then the train began to draw out of the station. The soldier rose hurriedly to his feet. Speechless with emotion, he kissed both the young women and jumped off the train without looking back. They sat on, in bleak, silent despair, and the tears ran slowly down their cheeks.

It was a strange journey altogether. Our physical fatigue was extreme, but I discovered to my amazement that I felt it very little. After the brief moment of euphory in Paris I was in too great mental torment to care. I say 'to my amazement', because I had never really believed that mental torment could ever make one forget physical pain or even exhaustion; I heartily agreed with Papa who used often to quote whoever it was who said, *'Dieu, épargnez-moi la douleur physique; la douleur morale j'en fais mon affaire'*. I discovered for the first time during that journey how our standards shift to suit circumstances. I found I could get as great relief out of merely being able to sit instead of stand, even with a heavy sleeping child in my arms, as normally from lying on a comfortable bed.

Food for André was an insoluble problem; I think he lived through the journey like the camel, mainly on his reserves, which were considerable. All we had to give him at first was dry bread, to which as we neared the south we managed to add grapes and raw tomatoes, none of which was very suitable for his age. But after Paris he took things as they came and everything delighted him. He grumbled no more however often we changed trains, however little sleep he got, and by evening he was always so tired he would drop off wherever we set him down.

The first night of our journey we spent at Montluçon, François's birthplace. There we learned that war had been declared. We had settled André to sleep in our own bed to make him feel safe, and we had gone down to the hotel restaurant for dinner. There we were told that '*ça y est!*' There was excitement in the air but here, too, no one looked depressed. Everyone behaved as though they had known everyone else all their life and this created a pleasant atmosphere, as though we were all of one family. It set me wishing such a relationship could be possible in times other than apocalyptic. The *patronne* gave us an especially good dinner because of my being *anglaise*: I remember we got trout where the other guests were given some less distinguished fish. We drank a bottle of Beaujolais all to ourselves. It inspired me to write an illegible but optimistic letter to my father before going to bed. When we did at last go up to our room we found that André had fallen out of bed. He had not reached the floor but was caught between the wardrobe and the bedstead. There he hung suspended, peacefully sleeping.

The next night we spent at Neussargues. We arrived there by the light of a bright full moon and left again before it had set. It gave the town an unreal Gothic character which it has kept in my memory ever since. On looking back I see my husband, little André and myself walking hand in hand not through the streets of an ordinary town but through a Dürer engraving.

And so we boarded our last train. 'It's nice in the train!' said André hopefully. It took us to Tournemire where we piled into a taxi, for no train connected Tournemire with St Hippolyte-du-Fort, the station nearest to where Papa has his vineyards. And so at last, dirty, hungry and travel-weary, we alighted in front of the familiar old house of Mandiargues and found ourselves in the beloved landscape where everything breathed peace.

The village of Mandiargues is little more than a hamlet. It stands at the point where the plain that stretches east to the Rhône and south to the Mediterranean, breaks to the north-west against the first foothills of the Cevennes. Whatever the season, whatever the circumstances, the very air there is saturated with a feeling of deep peace. On every side the vineyards flow tranquilly to the hills, one of which, the Colline des Heures, is so like the convex side of a giant scallop-shell that I have always taken for granted its far side must be hollow and pale rose-coloured. Here and there a classic-looking house seems to have grown out of the arid earth as slowly and naturally as the cypress tree that gives it point. But I think the feeling of peace has its roots in something more occult than the mere fact of its being a landscape that rests the eye. There is some quality inherent in the plains and lower slopes of the Cevennes, some fundamental deep-lying charm that stirs people's memories and calls up out of the shadowy pools of the unconscious the lost landscapes of childhood. Just what it is it took me some time to discover. I knew it was no mere physical resemblance to Scotland, for there is none, though they have this in common, that both are poor countries and poor countries get at you in a way more prosperous ones do not. But the truth is that long before, when I was still a child in an Aberdeen nursery, I had seen those landscapes with my mind's eye. I cannot claim to have been brought up on the Bible in the sense that was once the rule in Scotland, but I was brought up by women who belonged to that tradition. Our old Aberdeenshire nanny taught us from the start (and thank God unsuccessfully) that all flesh is dust, and our mother used to read us stories from the Old Testament, just as she read us Grimm and Andersen. Though probably the

plains at the foot of the Cevennes are no more like Palestine
than they are like Scotland—I have never been in Palestine
so I cannot tell—I know they are like what I saw with my
mind's eye when my mother read of Jacob meeting Rachel
by the well, and that the whole glorious cycle of growing
and making wine is fraught with Biblical symbolism, from
the cutting off of the dead shoots in the late autumn to the
grape harvest in early September when the stones of the
courtyard run blood-red with grape juice from the press.
So is the name of the purple-flowering tree that blossoms in
the spring with such shattering effect against the dust-grey
aromatic herbs of the *garrigue*—the southern equivalent of
our moors: the Judas-tree. And I am certain that, though I
had no clear notion when I first came there why it already
seemed a part of me, I could not have felt more at home if
I had found myself among the rolling fields of the Marquis
of Carabas or in the underground orchards of Dame Holl.

Papa's house, where we came in September 1939 as to a
womb for shelter, just as a year earlier we had come to the
old house of Valleraugue, is as peaceful as the landscape
round it. We had scarcely stepped out of the blinding
sunlight into the cool twilight of the hall than our jangling
nerves began to relax. It is a house so old that its rhythm is
the slow rhythm of another age. You cannot hurry on the
broad shallow steps of the staircase, nor in the half-light
that in summer pervades everything, save where a vibrant
shaft of light splits its way through the shutters, kept closed
to ward off heat and flies. In the very bathroom you must
take your time, for in those days you had first to light the
stove with bundles of vine-shoots specially prepared for the
purpose; you had to keep it alive with small logs of evergreen
oak and stay beside it lest the fire burn out and the water
run cold, or the water boil and the boiler explode. An old
Scotch friend of ours once remarked with some justice to
.Papa, 'Yours, Sir, is a delightful house. Your dining-room
has a twelfth-century vaulted ceiling, your staircase is Louis
XIII, your drawing-room Empire. You have, in fact, all the
luxuries. What you lack are the necessities.'
When Papa settled permanently at Mandiargues the

necessities were to a modest extent supplied, but it is a house so old it seems to combat even the mildest forms of modern convenience with the tremendous force of inertia. Electricity has taken the place of the old oil-lamps, but if you attempt to use a vacuum-cleaner while someone else is ironing all you achieve is a short-circuit; and though central-heating has been installed in the greater part of the house, when the cold winter winds that smell of snow sweep down from the northern mountains they whistle round the old badly-fitting doors of the three main entrances and swirl about the stone-flagged hall and the bare stone staircase. Actually, before even an embryonic bathroom and limited central-heating could be achieved a major problem had to be solved, that of water. Long, long ago there must have been some water at Mandiargues for in the courtyard behind the house, in the fragrant shadow of two fig-trees, there stands an ancient well, now dry. Papa had to look elsewhere for his water-supply. In recent years water has been brought to Mandiargues by the municipality of St Hippolyte-du-Fort, but in those early days he had to mobilize the overflow from the village fountain and have it pumped up to the house by means of an electric pump. Every time a tap was turned on this pump gave voice, and it sounded as though the house were heaving sigh after sigh at the exigencies of an incomprehensible generation. Sometimes there was no overflow and the old house sighed in vain. Small wonder Papa, no friend at the best of times to modern convenience, once ironically remarked, 'Another bath! How the years fly!'

Another essential, always there in modest primitive form, had been brought, if not up to date, then at least to a level that would have been considered satisfactory in England twenty years ago. As far back as Papa can remember the lavatory at Mandiargues has been papered with an old-fashioned English wallpaper showing episodes out of the life of Robinson Crusoe, with captions in English under each episode. This wallpaper has earned for the room the name of *les Robinson*, pronounced as though it were French. When *les Robinson* was brought up to date the walls were repainted, but on either side of the door a panel of the original paper was preserved to justify the well-established name; and because Papa is a man of sentiment who hates all things new as lacking associations. To one born and bred in the British Isles this wallpaper is curiously evocative. When in splendid isolation we sit gazing at Crusoe on his raft, Crusoe gun in hand catching his first sight of the savages, Crusoe clad in goatskins with naked Friday kneeling at his feet, a vision of England rises up. The walls expand and retreat and become a background for faded chintzes and old-fashioned furniture in some bedroom where we slept, surely, long ago. Through the window, metamorphosed from a french to a sash-window and open a little at the top to let in a chillier air, there comes not the high shrill chirring of cicada but the cawing of rooks in ancient elms. Those narrow walls enclose the rural England that Cecilia in *Middlemarch* conjures up when she says to her sister, newly married and going to live in London, 'How will you bear to live in a street!' Its memory in the years to follow would rise to haunt me every time I crossed the threshold of *les Robinson*. It was as though my frail defences crumbled at the mere sight of Crusoe's goatskins, like the walls of Jericho to the piercing trumpet sound.

But that was much later. When we reached Mandiargues in those early days of the war I was in no mood to dream in Papa's lavatory.

François went and joined his centre of mobilization on the specified eighth day after the declaration of war. According to my diary, on September 18th my parents-in-law and I travelled to Avignon to see him before he left for the *Zone des Armées*. Avignon, thronged with uniforms, was no longer its sleepy, peaceful self. But it was glorious blue September weather, and once more a good French meal eaten with François in a good French restaurant relaxed our nerves and raised our spirits. We spent the afternoon wandering about the outskirts of the town on the banks of the Rhône. Towards evening we went to slake our thirst in a café before taking our train home. It was in this café that we had the same shattering experience we had already had in the York tearoom. We saw in the headlines of our neighbour's evening paper that Russia had invaded Poland. We rushed to buy a newspaper for ourselves.

I think it was then that for the first time I learned in my own flesh and blood as distinct from mere hearsay that fear is a sensation felt simultaneously in the scalp and the pit of the belly. It was later to become such a familiar sensation that I came to realize it should be possible to treat it as a purely physical phenomenon and train oneself to some degree of detachment. I never got very far along that path, only far enough to know that the thing should be possible. But that was much later. When I said goodbye to François and our train gathered speed, I had about as much courage as would serve to arm a sparrow.

There followed a period that was black indeed. I would go rooting round in my mind, like a wild animal in a cage, for some way out of my torment. I tried the New Testament, but with no success at all. The only prospect it seemed to me to offer, and indeed to recommend, was martyrdom. Besides, I still at that time conceived religion as a mixture of fairy tale and moral code, not as a change of heart, an initiation to a totally different attitude towards life. Even if I had known, I doubt whether it would have helped me then. It was one thing to understand and another to achieve, and even now I have scarcely got beyond standing on the mountaintop gazing inward at the promised land. I find in my diary:

'I try to find comfort in the Bible but . . . the whole thing frightens me, for nothing is ever prophesied but disaster and I definitely feel that I am not the stuff martyrs should be made of. I can find nothing to justify the comforting proverbs we are taught in our childhood, that "the Lord tempers the blast to the shorn lamb" and so on. Were there no shorn lambs in Poland and Czechoslovakia? Did they escape?'

I also find: 'I wish I weren't so ignorant. I wish I had some clear idea what it would really mean if . . .' There I broke off. I could in no wise face the thought of disaster.

Our anguish of mind was heightened by the tension that is always in the air before the vine harvest, tension lest it rain or do not rain as the case may be; and in that particular year lest the horses be requisitioned for the army before the work were done. But while the harvest lasted, it kept our minds busy and that was all to the good. I would often go wandering through the vineyards with the children, watching the harvesters at work. There were fifteen of them, men and women alike all sheltered from the sun under broad-brimmed straw hats. The vine branches were weighed down under their load of purple fruit and some of the leaves were already deep crimson or chrysanthemum-yellow. The harvesters stripped the grapes into pails with the slash of a tiny sickle and at once the branch stripped would spring erect. When the pails were full the grapes were emptied into wooden tubs and pressed down with great wooden pestles to make room for more. The tubs were then loaded on to horse-carts (today replaced by long low motor-lorries, and it is astonishing how rural and picturesque these lorries look) and trundled through the vineyards to the press in the courtyard. Everyone that year was working against time, for with the harvest falling so late there was a danger of its coinciding with the equinoctial rains, due any moment now. Besides, we were short-handed because of the mobilization, and to make matters worse—in a sense—it was the best harvest we had had for years.

If we were short-handed in the fields, in the kitchen it was quite the other way. Circumstances had so combined to produce there a state of things whose like I had known only in my childhood and in the home of François's banker grandfather in Switzerland. Instead of the *bonne à tout faire* who is the general rule in France except in rich families, three maids, Jeanne, Odette and Amy, provided the figured base on which the harmony of a house depends.

When we reached Mandiargues after our epic journey there was only one maid in the kitchen. Who she was I cannot remember, nor why a change was made, an unusual thing in my parents-in-law's house where maids stay longer than anywhere else I know. But a change there must have been because I clearly remember the arrival of Jeanne. She looked furious from the day she entered the house till the day she left it, some fifteen years later, to take up her abode in the sunny home for old people run by the nuns of St Hippolyte-du-Fort. But her heart was a heart of gold. She was like the cow that lets you milk her dry and then sends you away with a kick. Born in Alsace when Alsace was still under German rule, she arrived with all her nerves on edge. The state of war between France and Germany and the suspicion aroused wherever she went by her accent were almost more than she could bear. She melted towards me when she found I could speak German and had no objections to doing so. But even when she first came to Mandiargues Jeanne was an elderly woman. The work was obviously going to be too much for her. I suggested I engage another maid on my own account to second her and give a hand with the children. At that time I still considered housework as a thing to be avoided at all costs. It proved almost as difficult to find help in the French countryside as in the English. But after extensive inquiries among our tradesmen, we were told of a girl, Amy, who might be persuaded to come as housemaid. She called for an interview, accompanied by her sister Odette. The Cevennes produce two human types, the dark, long-headed serious type, usually very distinguished, and the fair-haired, blue-eyed, round-headed convivial type. Amy was the first of these, Odette the second. Amy explained to us that she was willing to come on one condition, that we engage also Odette. Odette would work *au pair*, but they could not separate. This might have given us pause but that it makes little difference at Mandiargues, where we produce most of what we consume, how many people live in the house. So we agreed to the arrangement, and soon Amy and Odette could be heard about the house, singing hymns as they worked.

In the meantime the harvest had been gathered in, the wine had been made and was safely housed in the great vats, and we had settled down to what was to be the normal routine of our lives. From then onward it is difficult to give any real chronological order to my memories, but the essence of all that period is contained to this day in the smell of wood-smoke, preserved intact in the taste of walnuts eaten with honey. The rhythm of our lives was governed by the work in the vineyards, and its cycle was the thread on which our days were strung. In that peaceful countryside time has a character of its own. It flows like a tranquil river with scarcely a landmark to distinguish one day from the next. Even the seasons seem to melt into one another, though each brings new beauty and is marked by the sight of the peasants at some new task in the fields. When the vine-harvest is over, the glorious season to which tends the whole cycle of the year, vines and trees catch fire and burn all through October in crimson and gold, while on the dust-grey bushes on the *garrigue* the red-gold pomegranates burst open. Gradually the torrid heat abates and there come mild days, blue with azure skies and wood-smoke, that linger on as often as not far into December. Then imperceptibly at the touch of winter the landscape pales to a uniform grey against which the sun picks out rare touches of colour so subtle they elude the unaccustomed eye: an occasional deep crimson copper-beech, the almost-black green of the little ilex-trees, the chrome-yellow of a water-willow down by the stream, the dark violet of the trees that have shed their leaves. The naked vines stand like an army of stunted dwarfs, their every limb lopped off, in rows of geometrical precision whose pattern changes shape as you change place but never loses its rigid severity.

Little by little the sun renews its strength and spring comes with rare tenderness. Against a background of white rock and thorny bush its isolated manifestations have each the little perfection of a lyric, as though here and there the arid earth had burst into song. It may be a wild pear-tree blossoming in immaculate white, or the guilt-red flowering of a Judas-tree. At last the moss-roses on the garden wall swell in the warm spring night and burst open at the first touch of the sun. So torrid summer comes, parching the earth and bleaching hills and *garrigue* to palest green, lavender, grey. From constant spraying with copper-sulphate the vines turn lapis-lazuli. Not a bird sings.

By the middle of October our nervous tension had relaxed. We had settled down in the respite afforded by the general inaction and had almost come to look upon our peaceful lives as immutable. Autumn had come almost overnight. I remember one morning when I opened the front-door and saw a carpet of russet leaves which a wild north wind had blown there in the night. A little orange-coloured kitten was playing among them, and for one irrational moment the thought struck me that this was one of the innumerable black kittens that haunt the village and that it had suffered in the night the same change as the leaves. Overhead was the first real autumn sky, an intenser blue than in the summer.

It was at this point that I became aware of two things. One was that it was disconcerting to have no definite framework to give shape to my personal life. There seemed to be no real function for me to fill. Maman ran the house and the work was done by Jeanne, Odette and Amy. The children took up comparatively little of my time; they were happy playing about the farm. Children in the country are never at a loss for employment. There was no pianoforte on which I might have practised. Besides, I am naturally of a lazy temperament and have never been able to get round my laziness by forming habits, except to spur myself to action by the negative habit of smoking; I am helped rather than hindered by the need to do a thing by a given date and be at a place by a certain hour. In Mandiargues there was no great need to do a thing in the morning rather than in the afternoon, today rather than tomorrow.

The other feeling that came over me was an immense sense of adventure. It came upon me quite suddenly one mild October evening when shadowy dusk was just beginning to fall. I was walking home from the village and I noticed for the first time that high piles of wood were being stacked in front of the houses for the winter fires. The smell of fermented grapes from the recent harvest mingled with the acrid breath of wood-smoke and went a little to my head, and the sense of adventure I referred to came over me in a wave. I saw the long winter ahead of me like an uncharted sea, and I felt at once excited and a little lost. Hitherto I had, like most town-dwellers, skimmed the cream off my country life, basking in the sun in the long golden days but fleeing back to city life at the first breath of autumn; I had still to learn that its real essence, the tang and soul of it, is in its bitter dregs. And though at the moment what excited me was the prospect of unlimited time at my disposal, time in which to 'stand and stare', I had also a distinct feeling of misgiving. I knew that now, with this unlimited time before me, I was going to have to put to the test and draw upon my capital of intellectual and spiritual resources. So that in a sense these two impressions were simply different aspects of the same discovery—that I had hitherto lived plugged into a wall but now must generate my own energy. Looking fearfully down a well in which I had confidently hoped to see the glitter of some hidden treasure, I was met instead by the distraught image of my own face, and the suspicion dawned on me that my intellectual and spiritual resources were perhaps more meagre than I had thought.

And so it was that I began to look about me for some object to which to harness my too great liberty. Papa, seeing me at a loose end, began persuading me that I should write about France. He pointed out that few foreigners had my opportunity of seeing France from the inside. I let myself be tempted and had in fact two articles published that winter in the *Spectator*. But at the back of my mind was always a gnawing superstitious fear that this could not be enough. No such enjoyable occupation could be all that was required of me. Some sacrifice, surely, must be made to the gods (since none was being required of us by the government) if we were to come through the war unscathed.

I am almost ashamed to confess what the task was that seemed to me unpleasant enough to carry with it some chance of allowing us to escape scot-free out of the Apocalypse. I offered my services to the wife of the local clergyman who had asked for volunteers to help her with the village children. I imagine she sized me up pretty promptly, for all she asked of me was that I take charge of a group of these children on Thursday afternoons (Thursday and not Saturday being the weekly holiday for French children), and even for that she supplied me with a helper. The idea was to keep the children out of homes where they might hear too much war-talk.

No one could have been less well-adapted than I for such a task. I never had an atom of authority and I have a demagogic tendency to play for popularity, especially with children. Besides, though I went through such a maternal stage between the ages of seven and seventeen that I have often wondered whether we were wise to combat child-marriages in India, it all petered out before I was twenty. Emotionally the birth of my first child took me so unawares that fear was the feeling uppermost when, at the sound of his first furious, impotent wail, maternal love entered my heart with the violence of a knife-thrust; I knew then that a sleeping tigress had awoken in me and that I would stick at absolutely nothing in my child's defence. It was a frightening thought.

But maternal love is one thing, child-love is another. I cannot escape a tendency to see, or think I see, just what a child is going to turn into, and I like the child only if I like what I see. I doubt whether I would have made anything of those Thursday outings if I had not had the help of a young girl from a neighbouring village who possessed the qualities I lacked. She had enthusiasm and authority—they often go together—and she knew all sorts of games for the children to play. Suzanne was her name, and events that were shortly to occur make me think she was probably a communist, though I have no real ground for saying so. Certainly she was of the very fine stuff of which French communists are often made. She burned with longing to do great things and to escape from her narrow environment; but she loved the Cevennes and she knew every path of the hills about St Hippolyte-du-Fort, and though unfortunately for me she left before the winter was over to become a nurse in a military hospital and I never saw her again, for so long as she remained I found in her a real friend, in spite of the difference in our ages. We soon began to see each other on days other than Thursdays and we went long walks together.

Our trysting-place with the children was the Protestant church, and from there we would sally forth, some fifteen to twenty of us, to the countryside beyond the village bounds. I attempted at first to kill two birds with one stone by taking Henri, then aged eight, along with me. The attempt was a failure. After one outing he refused to come again. The village children terrified him, mainly as I afterwards realized because most of them were girls. The day he came with us there was only one other boy, and I remember that he and my son stuck together like thieves and would have nothing to do with the little girls. Even on later occasions when the small boys were more numerous, I noticed that it was almost impossible to organize mixed games, which made things as complicated as possible. When we thought everything was going nicely we would suddenly discover that the boys had disappeared and as likely as not we would find them busy lighting a fire behind a hayrick.

Altogether I got a good deal of entertainment out of watching how boys and girls react to one another at an age when sex plays no conscious part as such. I noticed that the boys affected to despise such arts as skipping because the girls were better at them than they; they would slip away to the river to skip stones instead, sure there of their ground. And when a game of 'catch' was started, what the children called *trappette*, the little boys had to be prevented from chasing each other exclusively. The girls were more sociable—or more precocious. Another thing that struck me about their social behaviour was their reaction to the Spanish refugee children. There were then, there still are, a number of refugees in the region from the Spanish Civil War. Today they are, if not completely assimilated (their apparent and surprising inability to master the French tongue would make that difficult), at least accepted by the local people. But at the beginning of the war they were still frankly refugees. A number of the children of these refugees used to gather on the outskirts of whatever place we chose for our games. They would play together barefoot almost within reach of us, wrestling and rolling in the grass, as free and as ragged as gypsies. There was no mistaking them for French children; their long dark heads were as different as possible even from the dark type of Cevenol child. They knew, they must have known, what envy they roused in the respectable village children. They flaunted their freedom, source of this envy, to compensate themselves for their ragged condition. And the respectable village children reacted as respectable people will react all the world over: they feigned to despise, as something not quite respectable, the freedom they envied. The Spanish children came one day so close that I suspected they were longing to join in our game. I spoke to one of the little boys, hoping to draw him into our group. A little village girl said to me in scandalized tones, 'But, Madame, they're Spaniards!' The little Spanish boy rolled away down the hill, his bare feet beating the air. I was left to reflect on the nature of man. Seeing a shadow on my face the little girl put her hand in mine and said in earnest tones, 'I much prefer the poor Poles!'

How right she was! The Poles were far away, the Spaniards at her door.

We joined Suzanne who was organizing a new game. It turned out to be a sort of blindman's-buff that went by the name of Romeo and Juliet. Two children instead of one were blind-folded, a boy for Romeo, a girl for Juliet. The game consisted in trying to prevent their coming together. They had to call each other by name and to guide their steps by the sound of one another's voice. But the other children had also the right to call their names and they ran about shouting, to confuse the minds of poor Romeo and Juliet. Evening fell. No nightingale sang though the pomegranate bush was at hand. It was not the lark either, but children's voices that strained 'harsh discords and unpleasing sharps'. With strong southern accent they cried the tragic lovers' names 'Rômeo! Julietteuh!', while the sky changed from blue to pale gold, from pale gold to dove's wing, and with sharp needle the first star pierced its silken surface. 'How silver-sweet,' I told myself, 'sound lovers' tongues by night!'

I have so far given no description of my parents-in-law, only of the house they live in.

Papa came of a family where it was a tradition that the sons go straight from the Lycée to the famous engineering school founded during the Revolution, the École Polytechnique. The original purpose of this school was to form military engineers, and I am told Napoleon used to refer to it as the Goose that lays the Golden Eggs. Though it is still a military school and still forms military engineers, its Golden Eggs today are especially the covey of young civil engineers it looses every year upon French administrative life who form one of the most remarkable *élites* of the country. They represent the first 150 or so of the graduates, or what is known as *La Botte*. But on the military side too the tradition is high. Some of the most outstanding of the First World War generals were Polytechnicians. In the last war, proportionately as many Polytechnicians of both kinds died in the Resistance as members of the communist community.

Papa and Oncle Ernest were both sent to this school and both succeeded in passing the competitive entrance examination. But whereas Oncle Ernest emerged in the *Botte* and swam like a fish both during the years he served in the administration and when afterwards he retired (as many Polytechnicians do) into business, Papa was made from a different and more complex clay. He played the violin, painted, had great feeling for literature and a passion for geology. Only in a family like my husband's, where the maternal grandmother would inspect each new baby at birth and after a rapid calculation in her head would pronounce the words, 'Promotion such and such a year', according to what by her high standards should be the year of the baby's graduation into Polytechnique, only in such a family would anyone have dreamed of sending Papa to be metamorphosed into a Golden Egg, for no better reason than that he was as gifted for mathematics as for most other things.

Papa in 1939 was still a fine upstanding figure of a man. He used to boast that on a journey he made to India before the war he was taken on board ship for an English colonel. Illogically enough, for he is so Latin in his sympathies that he draws a line round the world at the level of Calais and refers to everything north of it as *les brumes du Nord,* he was proud of having been thus mistaken. Knowing with what ease he can spin cloth of gold from a handful of nettles, I never quite believed this story. Nothing could be less military in mind or appearance than Papa. He will wear only clothes that are both old (the older the better) and loose-fitting. He is so little dependent on the myth of paternal infallibility to preserve his ascendancy that he always frankly tells his children and grandchildren, 'Don't do what I do; do what I say!' His eyes are so expressive and his shoulders so eloquent that he scarcely needs to gesture with his hands to give speech the colour it lacks. He has no sense of discipline as such, and I never heard him moralize; but not even my own father had a greater gift for opening the minds of the young to vast unknown horizons. And with all this he is so intuitive that he can guess your troubles when they are still at the inarticulate stage, and by merely holding out his hand to you can flood your heart with a flow of self-pity.

Maman is of Swiss-French origin, the fifth of the seven children of a man who was a banker by profession but literary in his tastes and who was known in the family as Grandpapa-de-Genève. He lived with his family in a lovely manor in a huge park on the outskirts of Geneva, at Petit Saconnex. The moment you crossed the threshold of that house you were back in the pre-1914 world. Maman herself is a lively, intelligent and witty woman, perhaps the wittiest I ever met. She adapted herself with great ease to life in Paris and would willingly have spent her whole life there. But Papa, who had not graduated in the *Botte* but had gone on from Polytechnique to the École des Mines and then into business, struck a bad period after the First War as a result of a dishonest deal of which he was the victim. The outcome of it all was that he retired with Maman and his younger children to Montpellier while François was still at the Polytechnique and the second brother, Roger, was at the École Navale. It was a great blow to Maman, the more so that Papa's feeling of frustration made him unsociable and unwilling to meet strangers. She adapted herself with remarkable courage, losing neither humour nor gaiety nor, in spite of their now straitened circumstances, her exceptional generosity. She filled the little leisure left her by her family, and provided herself with an outside interest, by plunging into good works. Papa to this day has a horror of good works, and when Maman joined an association whose purpose was prison reform and whose members paid regular visits to the inmates of the local prison, he christened them *les Amis du Crime*. But she quietly went her way, the way of a very practical Christian, while Papa plunged deeper and deeper into geology and metaphysics—though ultraphysics would be an apter term. And the maddening thing is that today it is more especially he who has won his way through to serenity. He has cut the cable that bound him fast to a world of frustration and war, and now he bobs about like a balloon between the Noosphere of Teilhard de Chardin and the Neolithic Age. There not even the threat of mildew or the atomic bomb can shake him. On the political level too he has escaped, into the past and into the future. His Golden Age is lighted up by the Roi Soleil; he still calculates in terms of the *louis* and the *sou*; and pending the final and certainly hierarchical unity in which he firmly believes, the unity of the Parousia, he has no use whatever for Democracy.

Maman is the heart of Mandiargues; Papa is its soul. It was from him that I derived in the months that followed the energy I proved incapable of generating for myself. He set me writing. He introduced into my unscientific mind my first notions of geology. He took up where my Viennese friends left off my French literary education. He even sent for oil paints and was going to teach me to paint when the collapse of Belgium brought us back to earth.

My happiest memories of the months we spent in Mandiargues are the evenings when we sat round a roaring

fire in the vaulted dining-room. It is a room shaped rather
like a fat rectangular wasp. After dining in the half nearest
to the kitchen you pass through the wasp's waist to the other
half where there is a chimney-piece so vast you can put chairs
inside it, one on either side of the fire. I used to settle in one
of those chairs with my knitting (normally I never knit; my
doing so now was all of a piece with my work among the
village children, a foolish attempt to ward off disaster by
sacrifice and good works), and I sat listening while Papa
read aloud. Sometimes he would read Stendhal, sometimes
we would rock with laughter over *Docteur Knock*, or the plays
of Courteline. Occasionally he would read us poetry, and
my heart would melt with longing for peacetime Paris and
private life when his faintly ironical voice waxed tender over
Maurice Donnay's *Quatorze Juillet*. I hear still the crackle of
the fire, the regular dropping of her scissors by Maman as she
sewed or mended, the voices when the kitchen door opened,
shrill Odette, gentle Amy, scolding Jeanne. And when at last
silence fell, when the fierce blaze had died down in the great
fireplace and mulberry-log and vine-root had settled back to
smoulder on a bed of glowing embers, when the last shout
had been quieted in the nursery and Amy had brought us in
the sober French nightcap of lime-flower tea, Papa would
lay his book aside and our conversation would invariably
turn to the ever-present problem of war aims.

I remember one evening in particular when Maman was on
a visit to her parents in Geneva, and Papa and I were alone.
I remember he said to me, 'Your husband and his brothers
represent the fifth generation, since one of our forebears was
killed at Iéna, that has had to tear up its roots and go to war,
the third to fight against Germany. All of them have been
soldiers not by profession but by necessity. I am sure they
would all agree that the only thing that matters is that war
should cease. The problem at present seems to be that of
fitting a warlike Germany into a peace-loving Europe. But
for all we know the situation may be totally different by the
time this war is over. I had a thought last night. I saw the
war ending without either vanquished or vanquisher. I saw
Europe divided into two self-sufficing blocks, on the one
side Russia, Germany and the Balkan states, on the other the

French and British Empires with grouped about them the Oslo states and probably Italy. Each block would be forced by the other to live in a state of economic totalitarianism and our equal strength would keep us from going to war.'

He smoked his pipe in silence for a while, gazing into the fire. The grandfather clock struck the half-hour twice over, as is its habit. The house heaved a prodigious sigh as Amy drew water for the hot bottles. He looked up and added, 'Of course, in that case the United States would have lost the war without even being in it.'

It is curious that, like François, he took no account of Japan. On the other hand, always supposing that France and Britain retained their Empires, he would have been right about the United States. And therein lies matter for reflection.

On another evening he told me how, in his own armchair and before that very fireplace, an ancestress sat night after night during and after the Revolution, waiting for her husband and son to return from America where they had gone for safety and whence they never returned, nor were they heard of again. He told me too how his peasant forebears, many hundreds of years before, had as they grew rich, with sly peasant humour, bought up little by little the land round about the estate of their neighbour, Baron Pieyre de Mandiargues, thus gradually hemming him in. Since those days the two families have intermarried and the feud is a thing of the past.

I found in the old house of Mandiargues the same sense of security as in that of Valleraugue, and gradually it came to seem to me less irrational. There is something in the atmosphere of a family house that may be found nowhere else. You are borne up in troubled times by a feeling of continuity, the assurance that others before you have lived through and survived similar catastrophes. The knowledge comes to you that you are no mere isolated unit but a link in a chain, and that when danger comes you will not have to count on yourself alone. Even if you are not a child of the old house, you too have in your blood some latent quality inherited from your forebears which may be counted upon to take over when the time comes. So, at any rate, you hope. The spirit of the Valleraugue house was crystallized in the form of old Lucinde, and its feeling of security found expression in her words, 'Providence will do nothing to you that you cannot bear'. I was less certain of this than Lucinde, but I began to believe—or I thought I did—that I would not have to face alone whatever there would be to face.

Not only the house at Mandiargues but everything that lies about it contributes to this feeling of security. Papa would often take me walking on the *garrigue*. He would show me where, in some cave where men once lived, he had dug up broken pieces of pottery made from the very clay he was digging. Once, farther afield, he had found a bronze bracelet of the same period. He showed me dolmens too, and walking one day in the dry season along the then waterless bed of the Vidourle, in the shadow of the ruins of a medieval castle, he suddenly bent down and picked up a piece of Roman tile where it lay beside a wild vegetable-marrow. We then turned aside from the river and he led me to a spot where you could trace the very scanty remains of a Roman villa. When Nîmes was a Roman city, its citizens then as now must have had their country villas on that gentle plain. The very people of that region still bear the stamp of Roman times. I have seen Nero in dungarees spin past on a *petrolette* and Cicero pensive behind a plough. Everything in that district speaks of continuity and a life unbroken by cataclysm. You come to believe that there nothing evil can happen to you.

It was on one of our expeditions that the incident occurred to which I referred in my introduction, when we sat in the mouth of a cave and suddenly I felt the world and life and time shrink to the narrow dimensions of my skull. On that occasion I was not alone with Papa; Maman was with us and a couple whom we had lately come to know and who, in view of what later occurred, are of particular if tragic interest. I forget how Papa came to know the Passemards. Husband and wife were both palaeontologists and Papa soon struck up a lively friendship with them. They were a strange couple, but I may as well say honestly that I liked them. It would be sheer hypocrisy if, with an eye to later events, I were to pretend otherwise. Monsieur Passemard was a vastly entertaining but frankly ill-natured man. Wherever he went his neighbours were his enemies. I think we were rather flattered at being exceptions to this rule. His wife was most unattractive-looking and yet proved oddly likeable. She was one of those very feminine-shaped women who affect a masculine style of dress and who seem to be wholly devoid of coquetry, a type rather rare in France. Both were exceptionally intelligent and they had just that blend of ill-nature and wit that tends, when you are not the butt, to make people such good company. Monsieur Passemard and his wife were at once violently anti-communist and frankly anti-British, though Passemard ended by admitting that he was really only anti-Intelligence Service. He had lived and worked in Syria before the war and was familiar with a world I knew nothing of. He accused the Intelligence Service of quietly and systematically carrying on a policy of its own, without reference to its government. Its policy in the Near East—or so he said—had been to stir up trouble among the indigenous populations under French mandate. He had been working as a palaeontologist in Syria at the time of the Druse rising and he held the Intelligence Service responsible in great part for that rising. I knew nothing about the Druse rising nor about the Near East; I merely repeat what he said. At least I am certain of one thing, that he believed what he said and that having himself at one point worked in Syria for the French Intelligence Service, he was not entirely ignorant in these matters. His views were shared by many French people who had lived in those parts before the war, and this accounts in no small measure for the hostile attitude shown in many French overseas possessions to the Gaullist troops and the English, identifying as they did the former with the latter. Unfortunately I have forgotten the details of what he told me; I had no idea at the time how interested I would one day be in him and all he stood for.

I made three friends on my own account during that winter at Mandiargues, besides Suzanne. One was a girl of the same background and much the same age as Suzanne, Mademoiselle Rouveyrol, the daughter of one of the local postmen. She taught in the village school. My son Henri attended this school later on, but to begin with he needed coaching in French grammar and spelling because at his Edinburgh school he had learned to read and write in English only. I asked Mademoiselle Rouveyrol if she would agree to coach him in her free time. She took him twice a week for a couple of hours at a stretch and by Christmas she had brought him up to his normal level and he was able to attend the village school. He did so most unwillingly for he still found the village children terrifying. He told me that it was not the lessons he objected to but the 'revolution', by which he meant the recreation. The word was aptly chosen. The boys had asked him to speak English on the very first day and he had innocently complied. He had been greeted with roars of laughter and had been considered as a standing joke ever since. Besides, I have often myself heard the roar of a French village school bursting forth from the schoolhouse for its recreation. My heart bled for Henri.

My other two friends were of a background similar to my own. One, Madame Dupouy, was the wife of a colleague of my husband's and she too had her roots in the Cevennes. The other, Madame Luigi, was of Swiss origin but married to a Frenchman whose mother was then living in a house she owned in St Hippolyte-du-Fort. Both their husbands were mobilized and they had, like myself, returned with their children to the family womb. I found their company a great support, the more so that they both possessed the fortitude I so sadly lacked.

Apart from these friends we saw very few people. Life in the French countryside is not at all like life in the English countryside. Though so many French people seem to have their roots in the country, they are essentially town-dwellers; when they own a country house they go there only for their holidays. There is not the English tradition of middle-class country life. The French countryside has kept its ancient forms; a village is a group of rural dwellings centred about the church and the curé's house, and this house has not the status of a rectory or a manse but is simply one more rural dwelling, probably with a walled garden. Nearby there may be a castle, but it will be at some distance and is unlikely to be inhabited all the year round. But for the accident of war which drove so many people to take refuge in houses they normally occupied only in the summer, we would have led isolated lives.

Our circle did, however, include one family of cousins. As they lived at some distance the petrol rationing limited our contacts to an occasional visit, for we had not yet taken to bicycling such long distances. It was in the late autumn that Papa motored me over for the first time to visit the de Billy family, most of whom I already knew, and who were temporarily settled in their house, Le Campet, near Lasalle. In France it is the usual thing for a family house to be inherited collectively by all the direct descendants of the family. It is not customary nor even legal to leave property to one chosen member unless the remaining heirs are otherwise compensated. As a result many of the people I know have a share in some huge house where their ancestors once lived, as often as not as peasant owners. Papa and Oncle Ernest were the only surviving children of a man who owned more houses than he knew what to do with, and had been able to divide things between them. The de Billys, like our other cousins, the Angliviels de la Beaumelle who have a house in the valley of Valleraugue, had to share one house among several branches of the family. During the war this had certain advantages; while the men were mobilized their wives joined forces in the old house, keeping each other's courage up and sharing expenses. But in normal times the system has obvious disadvantages. Certainly it means that the land is not divided up, nor are daughters and younger sons at a disadvantage; but the house itself soon comes to have an anonymous look. No one of the women who spend their holidays there dares mark it with the stamp of her personality. Cut off from its time dimension, it remains petrified in an unending past, like the house of some man whose ephemeral greatness is forgotten save by the sleepy provincial town that preserves its framework as a museum. On the other hand, it has struck me again and again that only a highly civilized people can make such a system work at all. And from the human point of view as distinct from that of the house, it works surprisingly well. You find not only several branches of the same family but as many as four generations of them living together with every appearance of perfect harmony.

When we went to call on the de Billys we found a household of women and children. The older generation of men in the family all died young or were killed in accidents. The young generation was of course mobilized. In spite of this sad lack of men, the atmosphere was very agreeable. All the members of the de Billy family have what my mother used to call 'sterling qualities', and in our heartless youth her preference for such people was a standing joke. I began to understand her better as I drew new strength from those very qualities.

We were received in a small sitting-room, the inevitable *petit salon* of all self-respecting French families of a certain period. We sat round the fire sipping a glass of Frontignan till one of the daughters offered to show me round the house. I accepted with pleasure and left Papa with Tante Antoinette de Billy. We went from room to room of a house that had not the charm of age. It was built in the nineteenth century and its only real advantage is its park. The anonymous quality I referred to, the breath from a provincial museum, was like a blight on everything and it seemed strange to see children's toys in the heavily furnished bedrooms and beauty products on the massive, businesslike toilet-tables.

We wandered out into the park and climbed a slope where Spanish chestnut-trees grew. With memories of England still fresh in my mind's eye, it troubled me that there should be no grass underfoot. At the top of the hill we found a miniature fort built of red brick. Papa, who had joined us, told me that he and Oncle Ernest and their de Billy cousins, now dead, had built it in their childhood and that their children had played at soldiers there during the 1914–18 war. Now it would be the turn of our children's generation, in the Second World War. We could see them below us as we stood at the top of the hill, sylph-like little girls with intelligent faces and dark glossy hair playing Provençal bowls with slender adolescent boys who might have stepped out of a French reading-book.

When we left the sky was darkening and there was a magnificent rainbow; a few drops of rain were falling.

But as we drove through the park the sky cleared and the rays shone almost horizontal from the setting sun, lighting up the trees from beneath and leaving their tops in shadow. The atmosphere had freshened. Here too everything breathed peace.

Three outstanding events mark my memories of our life in Mandiargues. The first was a journey. François had left Avignon and was stationed in the region of Grenoble, and some time in the middle of November he sent me a telegram asking me to meet him in that town for the coming weekend.

Civilians could travel in the *Zone des Armées* only if they had a *laisser-passer*. These were said to be difficult to obtain. The moment the telegram arrived Papa motored me over to the *Gendarmerie* of St Hippolyte-du-Fort to make inquiries. It was late afternoon on a mild November day when we drove through the great iron gates into a courtyard full of trees where a *gendarme* with a broom was sweeping the dead leaves into heaps for some small boys to set alight. In the early twilight the fires glowed red and the smoke rose in acrid-smelling clouds. It was a glorious picture of autumn, homely with the gay shouting of children. The anguish that oppresses my bosom in the presence of any police force turned over and fell asleep.

We had drawn up our plan of action on the way. We knew that we must find some pretext for my journey other than that of joining my husband; it was forbidden for wives to visit their husbands in the *Zone des Armées*. But my own father had, I knew, a colleague in Grenoble, Monsieur Lafourcade, professor of English Literature at the University. It occurred to me that though he would scarcely remember the schoolgirl I had been when he visited us in Edinburgh, he would probably forgive me for my father's sake if I made use of his name—and if, which was unlikely, it ever came to his ears that I had done so. The only difficulty was that I did not know his address. When we reached the door of the *Gendarmerie* Papa suddenly said to me, 'Oh, by the way, Professor Lafourcade's address is 12 Place Grenette'. I had not even time to ask him how he had come by this information, for the *Gendarme-Chef* had already risen to his feet to greet us. It was a delicate moment. Some little time before Papa had accosted him in the village and asked him how I could obtain a *laisser passer* to go and visit my husband should occasion arise. 'Monsieur!' he answered reproachfully, 'It isn't her husband she'll want to visit. It's some other member of her family!' Not a tremor of his features showed that he remembered this occasion. We solemnly discussed ways and means of obtaining within twenty-four hours a permit allowing me to visit in Grenoble an old friend of my father's. The *Gendarme-Chef* promised to telephone through to headquarters at Le Vigan for the permit and to complete the formalities himself as speedily as possible. We shook hands all round with perfect gravity, and Papa and I stepped out into the twilit courtyard where the fires still crackled and smoked, sending showers of sparks to join the first stars in the darkling sky.

As we drove off I murmured, '*Vive la France!*' Papa replied, 'Do you know whose address 12 Place Grenette is?' 'Professor Lafourcade's, you said. How did you know?' 'Not Professor Lafourcade's. Stendhal's!'

When I reached Grenoble it was pouring with rain, accompanied by what I took for thunder. The mountains were stifled in clammy white mist and as the train drew near the town we passed sodden-looking vines trained along wooden frames that were dark and slippery with rain. I went straight from the station to the *Ponts et Chaussées* headquarters where I was to find or leave a message from or for François. I left the name of the hotel I was going to as there was no message for me, and as the typist wrote it down I overheard through an open door a heated discussion on the subject of anti-aircraft guns, whether or not one needed to see in order to aim, and what the chances were of seeing anything at all when the sky was pressing down on the mountaintops like a dirty feather-bed. I was surprised that people here should be troubling about anti-aircraft guns. When I left Mandiargues I had been faced with the problem of packing as much as possible into a suitcase I could carry myself because of the lack of porters. I had weighed the respective claims of my gas-mask and a pot of jelly made from our own apples. The gas-mask had not really stood a chance. Grenoble seemed to me an unlikely place for an enemy air-raid, whereas the jelly would, I knew, be of almost holy significance to François.

As I left the building I passed a group of men gathered in the doorway and several voices besought me not to go out. I felt it was my own business whether or not I got wet, so I silenced them with the sort of look I had found useful when we lived in Marseilles. As I walked off I heard a flabber-gasted, '*Eh bien! Si c'est comme ça!*' I had not far to go to the hotel and I was just settling into my room when the thunder broke out again loud and near, and it came over me in a flash that it was no thunder but anti-aircraft guns. My knees went suddenly weak. It was my first experience of the sort. The train had arrived after the sirens had sounded their warning.

As soon as the all-clear sounded I went off to the hairdresser. I was lucky enough to get the head man and as he massaged my scalp he gave ecstatic descriptions from his memories of the last war of aircraft darting through the sky amid bursting shells. He was bitterly disappointed at having been prevented that morning by the clouds from seeing what was going on.

In the meantime a message had come through from François to say he was arriving that evening. Before he came, in the late afternoon, the sirens sounded for the second time. The *patronne* of the hotel invited me to go with her and her children to the nearest air-raid shelter. We ran all the way. In front of the shelter a couple of jovial soldiers welcomed us with open arms and guided us down into the bowels of the earth. There they lit lanterns, improvised benches for the handful of us who had sought shelter, and set about entertaining us with unending jokes. They incidentally pointed out that there was nothing to be afraid of but our own anti-aircraft guns; the German planes were throwing down only anti-British tracts.

When we got back to the hotel I found that François had arrived and was sitting doing mathematics by candlelight.

The next event that broke the even flow of our lives occurred in the middle of the winter. The Mandiargues estate was run at that time by a peasant called Brunel. He is of a local family and most of his relatives live in the region. It came as a great shock to him and to all of us when the news reached us that his nephew, the orphan son of a brother who had died, had been arrested for printing and distributing communist tracts. This arrest was a result of Daladier's new laws against communism. It was the first grim foretaste of what lay ahead of us and our first experience of the corrupting influence of fear.

It was from Suzanne that I heard most of the details. She had been a great friend of young Brunel's and it is no doubt this fact that has left me with the impression that Suzanne may have been, if not a communist, then at least a fellow-traveller. She told me Brunel was an exceptionally intelligent boy who had done very well at school, and that it had been a great blow to him to have to go back to the life of a peasant when his father died instead of going on with his studies. He had been left with a bitter feeling of frustration. She said he had a small hand-printing press in his house and that he had been working for the Communist Party for some time.

We were still uncontaminated by war mentality and we all of us saw quite clearly that Daladier's methods were more likely to foster communism than to uproot it. We decided to get in touch with an advocate François and I had known in Marseilles. He had been a Marseilles member of the *Amis du Crime* and had been particularly active before the war in furthering prison reform. Papa wrote to him and he at once offered to take charge of young Brunel's defence. Unfortunately there had been so many arrests of the sort that the wretched boy languished in the prison of Nîmes for several months before he came up for trial. When he did eventually appear in court it was at the worst possible moment, for his trial coincided with the Germans' western offensive. Our friend did his best, but with little help from the prisoner himself who was determined to be a martyr in the communist cause. He was condemned to two years' imprisonment. The country was in the grip of fear at the time and the communists provided a convenient and even a likely scapegoat. As a result of Russia's foreign policy, they had come to be identified in people's minds with Germany's Fifth Column.

Though at the time of his arrest none of us dreamed of any but a happy ending to young Brunel's misfortunes, this episode cast an additional gloom over the whole of that winter.

The third outstanding event fell in the early days of April and was once more a journey to spend a few days with François, this time in Paris to whose neighbourhood his company had now been shifted. Oncle Ernest's younger daughter Lucienne, who is a painter and who occupied at the time an immense studio off her parents' flat in the Boulevard de Montparnasse, offered us the use of the flat. It was standing empty, for Oncle Ernest was running an arms factory at Châtellerault for the duration of the war. She suggested we occupy it for as long as we cared to stay.

I arrived some days before François. I found it glorious to have hot baths without having to light a fire, glorious going to parties and having Lucienne give parties for me in her studio, and above all glorious meeting artists and writers instead of minding village children. I was amused to find that whereas in peaceful Mandiargues we had done our best to respect the blackout, Lucienne in the heart of the capital had recoiled from the difficulty of masking a window that occupies one whole wall of a split-level studio. As it looked out not on the Boulevard de Montparnasse but on an interior garden, she hoped it would escape the not very vigilant eye of the Paris police. But a few days after I arrived a couple of policemen did ring our bell to complain about this window. They were obviously inclined to regard the whole thing as something of a joke, but they said they really could not close their eyes to so large a window. We explained that its size was our whole difficulty, and they saw our point. They admitted that they had no suggestions to make and as neither had we, nothing was done. In spite of the joking threats our policemen made as they took their leave, they did not return while I was in Paris.

It was during that visit that for the first time I began to hear sinister rumours about our being unprepared for war. In spite of the limpid air—and the sun that month of April shone so gaily, the air was so sparkling, such fleecy clouds chased each other across the sky that I look back on those ten days as the very pattern of what Paris in the spring should be—my spirits were badly sunk by what a friend of Lucienne told us who had come home to Paris recently from Rumania. She came in early one evening for a drink, and she enlarged on the stupidity of our pre-war policy and the hopelessness of our present situation. She told us that none of the Central European countries had faith in the Western Democracies. They were convinced that we could never stand up to Hitler and that they must look to Germany for protection against Russia.

I revenged myself on our guest for knocking the bottom out of my universe by saying in deliberately smug tones, 'We British never anticipate defeat!' I knew just how offensive I was being, but I suspected her of *le snobisme anglais* so often to be found among upper-class French Protestants, and I was pretty certain the thrust would tell. I had no notion how truly I spoke, except for myself alone.

Apart from that incident—and my time was so fully occupied that I had no leisure to brood over it—our stay in Paris was completely happy. For the few days we were together, François and I were more free than we had been since children had been born to us. He had a beautiful new uniform made by an excellent tailor. He looked very elegant and we were absurdly gay. I remember none of the places where we went, but I know we were reckless about stepping in and out of taxis—those were still the halcyon days when taxis in Paris 'cost nothing'.

After François left, Lucienne gave a last party for me, and at it I met a young man who had just written a novel about Finland where he had lived for some time, both in Helsinki and in the tundras of the north. Finland was of course very much in all our thoughts at the time because of her heroic resistance to Russia. I read the young man's typescript and was fired with a sudden desire to translate his novel. He took me to pay my respects to Grasset, his publisher, who agreed *en principe* to my undertaking the translation. All that remained was to get in touch with Routledge through Herbert Read, and submit them a sample of my work.

With the delightful prospect of this work to make me feel rich and important—it takes little more than a distant mirage to make me feel rich—I set out once more for Mandiargues in a state of high glee. The train was scarcely out of the Gare de Lyon before I had begun to discount the disquieting talk I had heard in Lucienne's studio. I put everything down to the Parisians' lack of fighting spirit and felt very superior. In a sense I was right, except in feeling superior. One of the disadvantages of being very intelligent (and I know no more intelligent people than the Parisians unless it be the Athenians) and too well-informed is that you take lucid stock of your situation and draw logical conclusions. The better your rational defences against the irrational subconscious, the more difficult it is for words or ideas to touch off the fuse that will run its burning course till it blows the impeding mountain sky-high. The generation that fell between the two wars had exceptionally good defences. They were sick to death of their fathers' heroism about which they had heard so much, sick to death of the word 'patriotism' with which their fathers had, they felt, been duped. André Malraux speaks for them all when he says:

'There is no ideal to which we can sacrifice ourselves for we are aware of the falsity of them all, we who have no knowledge of truth. The earthy shadow cast by the marble gods is enough to turn us from them. How close is the embrace that binds man to himself! Homeland, justice, grandeur, truth, which of these statues is not so defiled by human hands as to rouse in us the same rueful irony as faces grown old but once beloved . . .'

What finally touched off the fuse was no dream either of glory or liberty or even justice, first favourite with the French. It was the bare fact of defeat and the presence on French soil of the enemy occupying force. In the spring of 1940 the climate was still one of scepticism.

And so I returned once more to Mandiargues where everyone still believed that France was the same as in 1914. Change comes slowly to the French provinces. They draw their strength today as they did of old from permanent sources, or what they still hold to be permanent. Paris generates her own peculiar energy, an energy that is intellectual, spiritual, nervous, artistic. I came away as always with my batteries recharged, but with my complacency shattered and a feeling of latent anguish in my heart. It soon dissolved in the warm glow and slow peace of our evenings round the fire. While we ate our dessert of walnuts and honey, and of grapes that have hung from wires in the attics till they are slightly shrivelled and very, very sweet, we spoke judgingly of Paris and the Parisians as all provincial people do, and life went peacefully on.

It went so peacefully that before a week was out I began to make plans for leaving Papa's sheltering wing and settling with Odette and Amy and the children in our own little house in the valley of Valleraugue. We had bought it in the early years of our marriage. The moment I saw the Cevennes I knew that there I could grow roots; but to grow roots you must have a house. It seemed at the time a reckless ambition for a young couple with a small income, but the value of land was very low then in the Cevennes and houses worth only the land they stood on. There was no reason in those days to inflate prices; even today the austere beauty of those mountains is no magnet for the ordinary tourist. And so it was not long before Lucinde found us a peasant house which was going for 9,000 francs, then the equivalent of about seventy pounds. This house, La Coustète, stands against a little hill whose terraces, planted with vine and mulberry, rise from the trout-brown waters of the Hérault. Because it is built against three of these terraces it is a house that changes aspect according as you face it from the front, the side or the back. From the side it is a three-storey house rising from rocks that slope abruptly to a stream which flows to join the Hérault from a spring behind the house. From the front it is a two-storey house with a semi-basement and on the first floor a small terrace whose stone pillars give it a faintly Grecian look. From the back you see only one raised story to which you gain access up a flight of rough stone steps. There is a front door on each level and on the lowest of all a vine-trellised enclosure serves as an open-air dining-room. But perhaps the house's chiefest charm is the rocky grotto from which wells the spring I mentioned earlier. A twisting path at the back of the house leads down to it, and there we go for our bathes and to fetch our drinking water, though during the rainy season we are cut off from the spring by a foaming waterfall that pours from an overhanging rock into the pool we bathe in.

The prospect of having two maids at La Coustète made me acutely aware of all it lacked in the way of convenience from their point of view. The kitchen was then still only an alcove off one of the two first-floor rooms. The ground-floor consisted of stables as yet unconverted. The *magnanerie*, or silkworm nursery, on the top floor we had arranged as an immense and very charming living-room. Would Amy and Odette find these arrangements sufficient? I decided I must at least have electricity installed before I bring my maids, though I would have to keep my installation to the merest essentials. It was fortunate that I made so wise a decision. Not a year or even six months later it was to become impossible to procure either candles or paraffin or liquid gas, and electricity could be installed for neither love nor money.

I left Mandiargues for Valleraugue with the electrician of St Hippolyte-du-Fort in his lorry. On our way we discussed the latest blow, the German invasion of Norway. We had heard the news just as we were setting out, and I am surprised that in face of this calamity I should yet have persisted in my plans for a life of independence. Perhaps I felt it was too late to turn back; certainly the glorious weather must have had a sustaining effect and allowed me an illusion of fortitude. And when we reached La Coustète we found the lilac-bush by the house-door in flower and a swarm of bees making honey between one of the living-room windows and its shutters. Once more the feeling came that this was a magical country beyond the reach of evil, and that here at least we must be safe.

Three rooms are not many for five people. I made up a bed for myself in the living-room so as to leave the bedrooms for the maids and the children. When that was done I left the electrician to his job and went down to Valleraugue to pay a visit to Lucinde. I found her not at all dismayed by the new turn the war had taken. She thought the melons might now just possibly be ripe. On my way home I looked in at Chanel the tobacconist. Chanel was a brother of the famous Coco Chanel, the dressmaker, though this we were not supposed to know. Rumour had it that she had bought him his business on condition she hear no more about him, but this may have been pure invention. All I know is that there was a tacit understanding that the subject of his relationship to the great Chanel must never be mentioned. Undoubtedly he looked strangely like her and so did one of his daughters. Neither had her beauty, but both had the fine bone structure that is characteristic of her face. Chanel spent his time between his shop and the Café du Jardin where he consumed innumerable Pernods while playing cards with his cronies; but he was a good friend to me and generous with his cigarettes when tobacco rationing came.

I asked him too what he thought of the latest German move. He said that in his opinion any move must be a move in the right direction and an opportunity for calling what he took for Hitler's bluff. I quieted my qualms and adopted his easy optimism. Towards evening I returned to Mandiargues and the next day I brought my family back and we settled at La Coustète. Soon we were installed in the last period of peace, brief as a dream, that we were to know. It was superficial peace with anguish at its roots, but I still had the unbelievable capacity of youth for happiness, the wonderful feeling that I had still all time at my disposal to be happy in, even if thwarted in the present.

Yes; brief as it was that period was wonderful. When they had recovered from the shock of being cut off from the world by the bridge that leads to La Coustète, a bridge half of whose planks were then missing, which had no handrail, and which hangs suspended some fifteen feet above the river; when they had crossed it under my firm guidance with shrieks and loud cries of '*Boodioo!*'—*Bon Dieu* in the local patois—Amy and Odette soon fell in love with the sheer beauty and peace of the place. While I sat translating in the *magnanerie* I could hear them singing their hymns as they mended our sheets on the terrace, with one eye on the children fishing for minnows in the little irrigation canal, the *béal*.

For moral support I had Lucinde whom I visited every time I went shopping in the village, which was often, for Odette and Amy refused to venture on to the bridge again once they were over it. Lucinde was one of the most extraordinary women I ever knew. She was well over seventy when I first met her, and she had been with François's family since she was fourteen. She had come to help in the house at the time of the great-grandfather's last illness. Except for the few years of her marriage, cut short by her husband's death, she had been with them ever since. Our children were the fifth generation of the family that she had known, the third to whom she had sung cradle-songs in the local form of the Languedoc *patois*. In the course of her long association with the old house, she had gradually gathered its reins into her hands and for as long as she lived she ruled it and us with humour and spirit and an affection that embraced even those new members who chanced to be foreigners—but with a firm hand. Never a tall woman, she had been reduced by age to minute proportions; but she had the organizing powers of a general and one of the liveliest wits I ever met. We were as wax in her hands. Shorts and backless dresses she would tolerate in the house and even the garden, but they must never pass the threshold of the great green door that leads to the village streets. We were not allowed to carry our own suitcases to the village bus because she considered it would be unsuited to our walk in life. We were forbidden to enter the village cafés however hot the weather, however great our thirst, however tempting their vine-trellised terraces . . . 'Drink what you will,' said Lucinde, 'but let it be at home!'

Years afterwards I came to realize that she had spared us a good deal of the contempt that country people feel for 'summer visitors'. She taught us the difficult art of making a permanent place for ourselves in a region where we normally lived for only a couple of months in the year. She was the link between us and them, in other words between the urban and archaic civilizations we represented, that live side by side all the world over but have so few points of contact.

However democratic our principles, however reduced our circumstances compared to those of the older generation, the moment we entered the valley of Valleraugue we were expected by Lucinde to uphold the phantom of family prestige, and for very love of her we complied.

We were all proud of Lucinde, proud above all of her affection for us, but proud too of her wit and her wisdom and her divine ignorance. For Lucinde believed, or so she said, that the world is round 'not like an apple but like a plate'. We could never resist showing her off to our friends. After she had cooked us one of her inimitable meals, it was almost a ritual for her to come into the dining-room and, standing demurely by the table, to entertain the company. None of us would, I think, have dared suggest she sit down at table with us. In her own domain, the kitchen, she often enough sat while we stood; if she had considered it a fitting thing that she sit with us in the dining-room she would have needed no telling. It would have seemed to us sheer impertinence to presume to know better than Lucinde with all her years. No; we confined ourselves to drawing her out and showing her off. At least that is what we thought we were doing. But Lucinde was more subtle by far than any of us. I suspect she had the laugh of us. I suspect she took the stage like a great actress, and that when at last she went back to the kitchen, walking as always with her hands a little in front of her because of her failing sight, she was fully aware of having given a masterly performance—of having, in fact, allowed the children we ever remained in her eyes to play for a moment with a unique and glorious toy.

It was during that brief period of peace that I came really to know Lucinde. We used often to sit together in Oncle Ernest's terrace-garden and she would tell me how as a child she had worked her twelve hours a day along with her mother in François's great-grandfather's silk factory. That was even before she came to work in the house. She looked back on that time without any apparent sense of hardship and her accounts of rising by starlight to prepare the day's food in advance, and of setting out with her mother in the dark with a can of black coffee to be heated and drunk at the factory, had more in them of adventure than of servitude.

For Lucinde believed in work not as a curse but as a blessing. She believed that, equal in essence but unequal in gifts and fortune, each man is cast for a different part and that the casting is not the result of blind hazard; that man may achieve in any station his essential function of spiritual development; and that the pursuit of such development need not prevent him from enjoying what good things of life come his way, for she was no puritan. As a result of this outlook, she was against compulsory education and thought people should be taught according to their needs. 'Madame François', she would say to me, for in that valley we are known by our husbands' first names to distinguish us from each other, 'look at me! All the geography I know is that the Clarou [a local stream] joins the Hérault in front of the Hôtel Bourbon! Am I the worse for it?'

I never attempted to argue with Lucinde. The term 'social justice' would have meant nothing to her. Besides, she had in most directions such wisdom that she made me feel callow. I sat and listened and drew her out about the members of François's family I had come too late to know. She loved especially to speak of his great-grandmother. Little by little she brought back to haunt the old house the ghost of a woman who had risen every morning in time to be at the gates of her husband's factory at four o'clock to welcome the factory-hands; who had lived to see her husband and all her children but one die, but who had never failed in her duty nor ever spoken a bitter or an unkind word to any living being.

She brought back another and livelier ghost, too, that of the friend who lived with the great-grandmother and who was known by everyone as 'Miss' because she loved the English language and its literature. Now when I meet *Childe Harold* between Montaigne and Voltaire, or *Little Lord Fauntleroy* and half a dozen bound volumes of *Punch* (her tastes were catholic) between Rabelais and Eugène Sue on the shelves of Oncle Ernest's library, I know who brought them there, and I feel that if only I can turn round fast enough I shall catch a glimpse of the dynamic little lady whose dramatic gift for story-telling is remembered to this day by all those who as children fell under her spell; the

'Miss' who washed according to a system of her own, her 'sacred' half one day, her 'profane' half the next; and who by her love of all things English in a sense paved the way for me.

Yes, like a dream indeed the last days of April slipped away and it was May. The weather continued glorious. The gorse glowed yellow on the flanks of the hills, the rocks were submerged under wave upon wave of purple phlox, the apple-trees flowered and then shed their blossom on the long grass starred with wild flowers. It is the time of year when the whole valley glistens with moisture and sunlight and every flower stands out clear in the translucent air so that the landscape has the look of a Persian enamel. Night after night a nightingale sang its heart out in the trees outside the house and the fat toad that shares our bathing pool with us pierced the night air with its high pure love-call. Little by little the shorn lamb (to mix my metaphors) began to put out her horns. I ordered a very up-to-date beehive to house the swarm in the living-room window, and a rabbit-hutch for a couple of rabbits Henri had been given. I bade our neighbour's farmer, Laune, who worked for us, to extend the vegetable garden which I tended every day. And as I drank my afternoon coffee lying on a deck-chair in the sun, I dreamed of a closed economy.

But the storm was gathering. Before it broke I had a visit, a unique event in Valleraugue at that time of year. Madame Dupouy and Madame Luigi motored over to call on me. It was a delightful surprise. I had missed their company, and my spirits were beginning to flag as the news from Norway grew worse. But as we sat chattering in the living-room a more immediate shadow on my mind was that I had nothing to offer them for tea. I was wondering what to do about it when little André came panting upstairs and handed me a scrap of paper. On it was written in Amy's hand, '*Que Madame ne s'inquiète pas, nous faisons des gauffres*'. And sure enough, a little later she and Odette appeared with beaming faces, bearing in triumph a tray laden with a tea-pot and an enormous dish of hot sugared waffles.

That was the last happy day, though as the news from Norway grew steadily worse one small oasis was accorded me. It occurred the day I read in the newspaper that the *Warspite* had been the first ship to sail into Narvik harbour. I identified myself in some sort with the *Warspite* because of Arthur Cardell Ryan. On one occasion he had loosed my sisters and myself on board her for a whole afternoon. As we ran about the ship in his wake, hour after hour, an urgent need overtook me which I and my sisters were far too shy to mention to any young man. At last, when we were down in the bowels of the ship and heading for the engine-room, I pretended to feel faint and bolted in the direction of the deck, for I had no idea where I would find a lavatory. When I reached the top I found that outside darkness had fallen, which was a good thing. But I also found that between me and the deck, one on either side of the door, stood two stalwart marines with rifles over their shoulders. Seeing me come at them they made a move to stop me, but I was so desperate I dived between them and made for the darkest spot. There, as surely as though I were breaking a champagne bottle over her prow (or wherever it is that they break the champagne bottle), I baptized the *Warspite*. Now, some twenty years later, I felt some modest pride and participation in her achievement.

From then onward the wheel turned faster and faster. On May 8th I went down to Valleraugue on my bicycle to do my shopping and I came back in the late afternoon. I crossed the high rickety bridge and as I put foot on our own ground I was met as ever by the green smell of wild mint. Esther Laune, the wife of the farmer who tends our vines, was sitting under one of our apple-trees, minding her goats. She hailed me the moment she saw me and told me there must be news for me because a telegram had gone up to the house. I ran the rest of the way, weak-kneed and with a beating heart, afraid that something had happened to François. But what the telegram told me in a few brief affectionate words was that he was coming to join me the following day for a fortnight's leave.

No words can describe my state of happiness for the next twelve or fourteen hours. I filled the house with wild flowers and spent the evening arranging it to look its festive best. Late at night when everything was ready I went to bed but could not sleep. At first I was too happy. I lay listening to the nightingales singing outside and I planned how I would make that fortnight something unique in our lives. I had decided to meet François at Nîmes, and Henri had persuaded me to take him with me. The Pont d'Hérault bus left at six in the morning so I had set my alarm for five. Not only happiness but the thought that I had so few hours before me and ought to be making the most of them drove sleep from me. When at last the birds fell silent I began to be haunted by the sound of the river. Whenever I was dropping off its low rumbling would seem to my confused senses to be the distant roar of guns. Several times I leaped out of bed and hung out of the window in the warm spring air, straining my ears to catch and sift the many sounds of which a southern night is woven.

It was pitch-dark when we left the next morning and picked our way on foot down to Valleraugue. Without knowing it I had set my alarm for 4.15 a.m., for it turned out to be three-quarters of an hour fast. We had a long dark wait till the bus was ready to leave, but the first real summer day dawned as we drove along the Vallée de l'Hérault. At Pont-d'Hérault we changed buses for Nîmes. Our spirits rose with the sun and it was from mere habit that I bought a newspaper when we halted at St Hippolyte-du-Fort. '*Détente en Hollande*', I read. The cock-eyed war was going to last long enough to allow François to enjoy his leave. Nothing else mattered. Soon we were passing through Mandiargues in front of the familiar house, but at that early hour we saw no sign of the family. On we sped, between Papa's vineyards and his fields of sainfoin splashed with scarlet poppies, the eternal symbol of France at war.

A little beyond Mandiargues some soldiers stopped the bus and came on board. They told us that their leave had been cancelled because at that very moment the Nazi troops were pouring into Holland. A buzz of dismay went through the bus. I sat frozen. Something in my mind was rushing desperately hither and thither, hunting for a way out. There was none. My sister Alice was married to a Dutchman and lived in The Hague. What would become of their children and of themselves? What about François? It was the end, the terrible end I had sensed from the beginning, for all I had said about the British never anticipating defeat. Only the old habit of self-control kept me calm in appearance amid the cries of dismay that were bandied about me. And it was only a habit; it corresponded to no inner reality of fortitude. For the first time I was a prey to the feeling I was to have again and again in the weeks that followed, the feeling that my brain was on the point of boiling over and that I must hang on for all I was worth or I would go mad. Just that. Nothing constructive. Merely hang on. For the thought of my sister and the thought of my husband trod on each other's heels till my mind whirled like a relentless wheel.

I remember nothing more of our journey. At Nîmes we went to the Hôtel du Cheval Blanc. We took a room with a bathroom, a great luxury after La Coustète. I still hoped

François would come and I was determined to do things well, even in face of the Apocalypse. It was there that our cousin, Gabrielle Pieyre de Mandiargues, found us. Papa had received a telegram recalling François at the same time as he received a letter from me announcing the glad tidings of his arrival and our journey to Nîmes. He had telephoned to these cousins in Nîmes asking them to break the news to us. I must send François back as soon as he arrived.

At 9.30 p.m. I met François's train. Henri was worn out with the day's emotions and was sound asleep in bed, but I had promised to wake him as soon as his father arrived. I found the station crowded. All leaves had been cancelled and the men who had been recalled were accompanied to the train by their anxious families. At first when the Paris train came in I could see nothing of François in the crowd. Then suddenly over the heads of the people on the platform I saw his radiant smiling face. He was waving to attract my attention and as soon as he was within speaking distance he called triumphantly, '*Tu vois! Je suis passé entre les gouttes!*' I had to disillusion him and tell him that he was recalled. He pointed out that at least we would have a few hours together. It would be only a few hours. We looked up the next train to Paris and found it left in the small hours of the morning.

In the meantime we went back to the hotel. We tried to wake Henri but though we even hung him up by his feet he slumbered on. Even when the time came for his father to leave for his train we were unable to rouse him. It was a bitter disappointment to him the next morning.

The next day I woke with a heavy heart, but the Pieyre de Mandiargues family left me no time to brood. They were round at the hotel first thing in the morning to fetch us, and Henri and I spent the day with them in their lovely Provençal home on the outskirts of Nîmes. The family consisted of Robert and his wife Gabrielle and their four small daughters, and a calm cheerful lady who had been nurse to all the children and who still lived with them. Sole man of the household except the chauffeur, who had been his orderly in the First World War, Robert set the tone for them all. There was no word of discussion or speculation as to the turn events might take, no hanging over the wireless to hear the latest news. He managed to convince me—wrongly, as it turned out—that at that very moment Alice and her family were certainly in a boat on their way over to England. He said the war would be all the shorter for being more active. We then spoke of other things.

The luncheon was one of the best I ever ate. Robert maintained that the morale of a nation depends on what it eats and that it was our duty to eat accordingly. When the remains of an excellent melon were removed, he told the maid in an aside to keep the seeds for re-sowing. The melon was followed by a couple of his own rabbits cooked *à la provençale*. They had the exquisite taste of the wild rabbits bred on the *garrigue* and he explained to me that this was because he had them fed exclusively on the herbs that grow there, thyme, sage and rosemary. We had coffee afterwards in the drawing-room and then Robert led me to the pianoforte and asked me to play. I was never more surprised in my life. I doubt whether music or any of the arts play much part in his life, but he is a man of great delicacy of feeling and he had guessed that to play would help me.

We spent the rest of the day in the garden, among the oleanders and the giant geraniums. The four little girls kept Henri amused while I sat peacefully in a deck-chair. We left for the station in the early evening in better spirits.

Pont-d'Hérault, where we changed into the Valleraugue bus, was decorated for Joan of Arc Day. The decorations had a hollow look and my spirits began to flag once more as we approached Valleraugue. The sight of La Coustète all bedecked with wild flowers was almost more than I could bear. To make matters worse, we were scarcely back but the weather broke. Our part of the Cevennes has the highest rainfall of the whole of France, or so Papa tells me, but it all seems to fall in what are virtually two periods of monsoon, one in the spring and the other in the autumn. It was therefore quite according to rule that we should be washed into the sinister tunnel that led to our defeat on streaming rain. As I stood looking out of the window through the tender green of a young walnut-tree I could see sheet upon sheet of rain. It fell from the lintel, it fell from the roof, it fell from the leaves of the trees, from the low grey clouds; it blotted out the mist-capped mountains. The stream that flows from our grotto behind the house became a torrent and the thunder of the waterfall made conversation impossible from one room to another through an open door. And as the Hérault rose to danger level, so the news grew steadily worse in a rising crescendo.

At this point the full disadvantage of having Odette in the house was brought home to me. One of the first sounds I heard in the morning was her rising wail as she ran her eye over the headlines before bringing the newspaper up to my room. It was one of the most hair-raising sounds I ever heard. Amy managed to keep calm though her look was wan and tragic. Odette simply let herself rip. Altogether the strain was intense. Not only the children looked to me for support and comfort—that was normal; nor only Amy and Odette. The peasant women, too, with whom I came in contact expected me, as the only member of the educated classes within reach, to know more about what was going on than they did and to be able to interpret events favourably and give them ground for hope. They expected me to keep a cheerful face and relied upon my doing so. It was Esther Laune who came running to announce that the Dutch had laid down their arms, and she expected *me* to reassure *her*. The whole situation was beyond me. All my life I had been accustomed to lean upon others, and what I really wanted as badly as any of them was a shoulder to weep on. And when one evening I came home from the village just after dark and heard the sound of Odette's rising wail before even I had crossed the Hérault, when I found her sitting on the grass in front of the house, the image of noisy despair, and she greeted me with the announcement, in Cassandra-like tones, that France was betrayed by her generals and that voices were telling her to go forth and save her country, I felt I could bear no more. If Odette was all that stood between France and disaster, then it was high time that I once more took refuge under Papa's sheltering wing.

I decided to go back to Mandiargues, and the next day we were off. Not even the prospect of the arrival of a friend,

Geneviève Petit-Dutaillis, could hold me back. She had sent me a telegram a few days earlier to ask me to find her a house in the valley because she was forced to flee from her holiday house in Normandy by the advancing Germans. I remember I was in the garden replanting young leeks in the rain when her telegram came (these leeks were another of my attempts to win the war by doing unlikely and unpleasant jobs). I abandoned my leeks and hurried over the bridge to the Launes' to ask Esther whether she knew of any house that I could rent for the Petit-Dutaillis. She said she thought she could take it upon herself to let them have the house of the Lévi-Strauss family. It was standing empty and she it was who had the keys. She thought it unlikely that Monsieur and Madame Lévi-Strauss would reach Valleraugue from Paris now, and if refugees continued to pour into the valley there was a danger of the house's being requisitioned; it might as well be my friends who got it. So she argued with herself, thoroughly enjoying the prospect of newcomers to provide material for gossip, for she was a lively and intelligent woman who had far too little to occupy her mind. She suggested a rent which she thought would satisfy Madame Lévi-Strauss and which seemed to me eminently reasonable. I closed with it and she set about preparing the house.

But I had no idea when I could expect Geneviève and her family to arrive, and I was convinced that if I stayed another week in the same house with Odette I would go stark staring mad. In record time we made everything as welcoming as possible for the Petit-Dutaillis, and we beat a hasty retreat back to Mandiargues. It was not in any sense a glorious retreat. I left all my bucolic ventures at a critical stage. The baby rabbits were born, but the rabbit-hutch had not yet arrived. Nor had the beehive, but Amy had absent-mindedly opened the shutter that sheltered the swarm which was making honey in my living-room. It had fallen to the ground outside the window, and before I had time to call someone to my help in capturing it, Amy and Odette in their terror had poured a pan of boiling water over it. Before I left I begged Esther Laune to look after the rabbits for me. There were only the mother and the babies left. The father had disappeared one dark wet night. All I heard was a heart-rending shriek. No doubt he had escaped from the woodshed where I kept them, pending the arrival of the hutch, and had been carried off by a fox.

Papa proved the rock I had hoped he would be. He saw the war in terms of 1914–18, and according to his calculations we were about ripe for the Battle of the Marne. He had been in the trenches for two years in the First War, and what his generation had done he was confident the next generation would achieve. As for Maman, she was naturally anxious for her children, three of whom were mobilized, but her confidence in France was total.

Under their wing we settled down once more to a tolerably normal life. I found my friends again and we did what we could to keep each other's spirits up. It was at this point that Papa planned to teach me painting as a diversion. But this phase soon came to an end. The day we learned that Belgium had laid down her arms it was as though Papa dissolved before my eyes and re-formed into a different man. Everything he had believed in, every ground he had had for hope, all, it now seemed to him, had been illusion. He had always had a weakness for monarchical government; in the old days he would jokingly quote whoever it was who said that the ideal form of government is monarchy tempered by regicide. He no longer joked. He spoke of our democratic institutions as *les institutions qui corrompent les hommes* and held them responsible for altering, as he believed, the very stuff of which the French are made. It took him years to recover, much longer than the war lasted. It was only when he had fought through to serenity on quite a different level that he became himself again, and that was when he was already an old man.

In spite of the fact that one part of him had to all intents and purposes died, his immediate reaction was a generous and a practical one. A number of Belgian refugees had recently appeared in the region and two of them had been engaged to work in our vineyards. The moment Papa turned off the wireless after hearing the news about Belgium, he went out and told his own men to say nothing that could be offensive to the Belgian workers. He need not have been afraid; it was the Belgians themselves who were railing against King Leopold, comparing him bitterly to his father. They left the same day to enlist in the French army.

From then onward Belgian refugees came pouring into the little town of St Hippolyte-du-Fort, and the problem of lodging and feeding them became acute. We soon learned that the clergyman's wife was calling an undenominational meeting to discuss the possibilities of pooling private enterprise and coming to the help of the official municipal effort to deal with the situation. Maman asked me to go to this meeting in her place.

At five o'clock that afternoon I went up to my room to get ready. Swallows from their nest in the honeycombed roof were darting to and fro across the high narrow window. Beyond, through the great lime-tree whose fragrance filled the room, I could see a panel of blue sky and the vineyards stretching peacefully away to the first slopes of the Cevennes. In front of a looking-glass so old that my face appeared in it crooked and tragic, I set about making myself neat but not gaudy, as befitted such a meeting. Undenominational, I had been told, included everything from the Catholic curé and Reformed Church clergyman to a couple of representatives of the Salvation Army.

Suddenly the twittering silence was torn through by the shrill voice of Anna, Brunel's wife, crying: '*Boodioo! Y a une alerte!*' It seemed improbable. I went to the window, but Anna had disappeared. The wind rustled in the lime-tree; a cock, though Gallic, cried, 'Cockadoodledoo!' and bowed to me through an open gate.

I went down to the enclosed vineyard behind the house, the *enclos*, where Papa was standing with some of his men, watching the bee-man prepare a hive to receive a newly-captured swarm. They told me the air-raid warning had actually sounded from the village three hours earlier and that the *alerte* was not yet over. Papa explained that when the Catholic church and the Home for Old People rang together it meant an air-raid warning. When the Protestant church rang alone (except presumably on Sundays) it meant a fire. I had never troubled to trace the sound of any bell to its source; besides, as we were some distance from the village I had noticed no ringing of bells at all. I set out across the vineyards to St Hippolyte-du-Fort. Here and there a refugee boy lay basking in the sun. Aged peasants (all the young men were, of course, mobilized) tramped to and fro among the vines, copper-sulphating them in glorious streaks of lapis-lazuli.

Suddenly the slow clanging of bells began to ring out across the plain, very soft, very slow. Yes; two bells, on two distinct notes. It must be the end of the warning. I felt singularly relieved.

In the large cool dining-room of the vicarage I found various black-clad ladies of St Hippolyte sitting round the table on stiff-backed chairs. Through the window that opened on to the garden came the smell of green leaves and the sound of trickling water. The curé had been too overburdened with work to come but he had delegated a voluble lady to represent him. She sat next to the half-blind old Protestant clergyman who was doing the work of the local man, now mobilized. Madame Mas, the young Swiss wife of the absent vicar, sat at the table with lists and notes laid out in front of her. She looked tired and not a little discouraged. I knew that her health was delicate and her first baby on the way.

The party was completed by two Salvation Army bonnets and the clergyman of the Chapel. I am afraid I can give no satisfactory explanation of the difference between the various Protestant sects that flourish in the Cevennes. As far as I can make out, the Reformed Church is about equivalent to our Presbyterian Church, and the Chapel nearer to Episcopalian.

The Mayor of St Hippolyte-du-Fort had not yet arrived, but Madame Mas suggested she might give a rapid account of the situation while we waited for him. She read aloud from the notes in front of her, punctuated by cries from the black-clad ladies of '*Eh oui, pechère!*' or '*Eh non, pechère!*' as their warm hearts were wrung with pity for the refugees.

She explained that there were two types of refugees which the little town had been called upon to succour, the families, destitute of everything, which must be fed, comforted and housed, but were not to be billeted upon the population; and the isolated men and boys, of whom there were some two thousand, ranging in age from fourteen to thirty-five, and who must be organized on a communal basis. The majority of the second group had joined the French army the day Belgium laid down her arms, but some five hundred remained. These were most of them in such rags that they scarcely dared show themselves in the little town. All these refugees, of both categories, lacked even the most elementary utensils—spoons, forks, plates and so on. Moreover, though the municipality provided them with the raw materials for their meals, none of the male refugees knew how to cook. Madame Mas's idea was to organize mending and cooking committees with the help of the women of St Hippolyte-du-Fort. She was on the point of developing her plans on the subject when the Mayor arrived, and we all rose respectfully to our feet.

A little grey-haired man with a tired face, he began in a slow, soft, gentle voice to tell us what *his* plans were. My admiration grew as I listened, and little by little I felt the burden of my share of responsibility fall from me, to my intense relief, like a cloak. I began to wonder what we were all making such a fuss about. This little man, who had lived all his life on a vine-filled plain where water is scarcer than is easy to conceive of in Britain, seemed to have a keen sense of the needs of a people from the rain-sodden north, presumably lovers of hygiene. He told us his plans for their washing facilities, he went further; under our nose, as it were, he disinfected the barracks that had been built to house the Spanish refugees; before our eyes he drew two hundred brand new beds from his sleeve and capped them with two hundred spotless mattresses. Out of the air he conjured two trained male cooks—I could see them with their high white caps, brandishing wooden spoons and chopping onions with flashing knives—who ruled over a two-kitchened refectory and under whose direction young Belgian lads ran to and fro, making themselves useful; an infirmary sprang up in the Old People's Home for those who arrived exhausted and shaken; our excellent but already overworked doctor found miraculous leisure to examine each new arrival and decide what treatment he required. Last but not least, the Mayor showed us our vineyards, no longer at the mercy of the oldest inhabitants, but vigorously worked by young Belgians in the true spirit of Baden-Powell. All he asked of the population, the warm-hearted, generous population, was that each family provide a spoon, a fork, a knife, a soup-plate and a drinking-cup, and five francs per head to form a little capital for exceptional cases.

A murmur of relief went round the room and the black-clad ladies relaxed. I emerged from the dream the Mayor's words had spun about me and I was a little surprised to see that Madame Mas looked more discouraged than ever. We rose to go. As I said goodbye to Madame Mas I made an enthusiastic remark about the Mayor. She looked hesitant and murmured something about his ideas always being very good but that nothing ever came of them. I went away feeling a little sour. I felt she was too critical in the way the Swiss are apt to be, a moralizing way. But I am afraid that she was right and that I was influenced by the pleasant feeling of euphory that comes when all responsibility is taken from one's shoulders. I was unwilling that Madame Mas should put it back where it belonged.

What came of all these plans I never heard. The Belgian refugees were soon to seem as remote in interest as the Spanish refugees, as remote in time as those other Belgian refugees I was taken as a small child to visit in a hospital in Aberdeen—because I spoke French.

Nor do I know whether this was the Mayor the *Maquis* executed three and a half years later for his betrayal of a number of *maquisards*, or whether the accusation was justified.

It was shortly after this meeting in the vicarage that we returned to Valleraugue. What decided me to leave and where I found the necessary firmness of purpose I do not know. I only know from my diary that some time early in June I took the plunge. Perhaps—I hope—my conscience pricked me at not having been there to receive and sustain Geneviève Petit-Dutaillis and her family. More probably the prospect of their company and that of the other friends and members of the family that had trickled through from Paris gave me courage. In any event, it must have helped that it was now summer weather.

So back we went, but it was to quite a new way of life, for we had left Amy and Odette behind with their friends in St Hippolyte-du-Fort. My breakfast was no longer brought up to me in bed; when guests came no secret message told me waffles were being made; no one sang hymns, no one mended my sheets. I had all the housework to do myself, and in very difficult circumstances as I soon discovered. It had seemed to me no great hardship that water must be carried up to the house from the *béal*; I soon changed my mind. When I attempted for the first time to wash our sheets I found myself in serious difficulties. I had neither expected them to be so unwieldy nor to require so much water. I knew they should be boiled but neither how nor for how long. In the end I did as I had seen the village women do, I washed them as best I could in the river and left the rest to the sun. But there were the floors as well as the linen to wash, and their rough tiles were harder to keep clean than I had realized. There was the cooking to do, there were the dishes to wash, and only a wood fire to heat the water. There was the wood to fetch and carry. Worst of all, since sleep was my only respite, the children woke me with the lark.

On the other hand, even at the time I knew it was lucky I had so many material difficulties to contend with for they got me through the day. Besides, I had now company and support and was no longer isolated between children and peasants and expected by both to be a rock of ages. Best of all, there was no Odette to wail like a mourning Arab over the headlines.

Geneviève Petit-Dutaillis and her sister Mimi Lauer were now settled with the children at Cancabra, the Lévi-Strausses' house, only a few minutes' walk from La Coustète. You cross the Hérault by our high rickety bridge and then, a hundred yards or so along the road to L'Espérou, a path turns off to the left and leads between the river and the vines to where two typical Cevenol peasant dwellings stand, side by side. These houses had been bought some years earlier by two friends, one Raymond Lévi-Strauss, a Paris painter, and the other a banker from Brussels called Cahen. The friendship between these men was doubled by a similar friendship between their wives, and every summer they all met in these twin houses. At the time I am speaking of I knew neither the Cahens (Monsieur Cahen died shortly before the war and only his wife and sons remained) nor Raymond and Emma Lévi-Strauss, whose son, Claude, is today one of the most famous of French ethnologists. It is suggestive of the change that was taking place in our standards even so early as that first summer of the war, that it seemed to me a natural thing enough to have rented the Lévi-Strausses' country house without their knowledge. I never gave the matter a thought, and Cancabra soon came to be almost as familiar to me as the house of Oncle Ernest in Valleraugue.

Looking back on that period of nightmare, I cannot believe it was all crowded into so short a space of time. Each day was such a struggle and so charged with emotion that months seem to have elapsed between our return to Valleraugue and the final collapse of France. I cannot even remember who of our friends and relations besides Geneviève and Mimi had reached Valleraugue at the time of our return. At the point where my memory picks up the thread of events I know that Oncle Ernest and Tante Berthe were at L'Espérou and that their daughters Germaine and Lucienne were in the Valleraugue house with Germaine's two young sons, Jean-Pierre and Dominique. Paul Sarrut, another painter from Paris, had also arrived with his family, and another family of friends, the Bargetons from Marseilles, were in their house, La Coste, in the Vallée de l'Hérault. The presence of all these people was comforting, but what came as something of a shock was when, about a week after we reached La Coustète, Raymond and Emma Lévi-Strauss themselves arrived. They appeared one day out of the blue, thankful to reach at last a refuge and a moment of respite in which to take stock of a situation which for them was even more tragic than for us because of their being, like the Cahens, Jewish. They found their once peaceful house bursting with women and children. It was a blow, but they decided to leave things as they were and to camp in an outhouse they had fitted up in happier days as an overflow for guests. I think they already had the tragic fear that it might be dangerous to assert themselves. No doubt they had, too, the same feeling of responsibility for the Jewish race that I had for the British. One of the most tiring things in the years that followed was the never being able to act as a private person but always feeling that as you behaved so your people would be judged.

The next to arrive was Madame Cahen. Luckily for her, both her sons were abroad, one in French Africa and the other in Switzerland. Close on her heels came a host of Belgian relatives who, like herself, had escaped from Brussels before the invading armies. Last came the wife and three young daughters of Marcel Griaule, the ethnologist. Altogether we were becoming a hotbed of ethnology. Germaine Dieterlen is herself an ethnologist. She had been working in collaboration with Marcel Griaule and it was with her that his family now took refuge.

There was no lack of company. But the news grew steadily worse. I had no wireless and it was often my fate to hear bad news through an open window as I went through the village. I know few such unpleasant experiences.

It was at about this time that an absurd incident took place which I relate only to show my deplorable state of mind. Early in the war I had bought at a local antique shop some crystal champagne glasses of the form called *flutes*. These glasses had been for sale in a lot of thirteen. Because they were beautiful I quashed my superstitious fears and bought them for the victory celebrations. It must have been on June 5th or 6th that I tried to avert disaster by throwing one of them out of the window against a rock. That, I think, was my most heroic effort to come to the aid of my adopted country. It was not successful. Soon I was to be seen sitting in a limp heap on the steps that lead down from the living-room to the mulberry-grown terrace behind the house. I had just learned that Italy had declared war on us. Beside me stood Henri with on his face a new sombre expression. I remember he said, '*C'est tout de même un peu beaucoup, tu ne trouves pas?*'

I did.

Nor was that all. By almost imperceptible degrees the situation was narrowing down for my children and me from a national disaster to an acute personal tragedy. We were without news of François. There was nothing yet positively alarming about this since no letters were coming through at all. But I knew that the Germans had by now swept down beyond the part of the country where he had been stationed when we last heard of him, and though there was every reason to suppose his company had retreated in time to escape being encircled—his was not a fighting unit—yet there was room and ample room for the sharp wedge of fear to insert itself in one of the many weak places of my moral armour. For some time I managed to keep my fear on the level of an undercurrent. I was only too ready to listen to those about me who assured me that there was no real cause for anxiety: no one so far had news of her husband. But what with one thing and another, I was beginning to feel once more that I had had enough of living alone, even with friends so close at hand. I wanted to be in a house full of people, and more especially I wanted to be with Germaine, with her high standards of behaviour to bolster me up. Lucinde too drew me, but I had long ago discovered that, like the austere enduring mountains that bred her, Lucinde could help you only if you were prepared to help yourself; she was not a

prop for the weak but rather a guide for the strong. I so
definitely did not want to have to bear dreadful things that
I found it cold comfort to be told the Lord would give me
the strength to carry me through them. Germaine, I knew,
would neither moralize nor bolster me up with illusions, but
would set me a standard of everyday behaviour that would
help to stiffen me. I badly needed to be stiffened, and when
she suggested we occupy her parents' room I accepted with
enthusiasm. It was in Oncle Ernest's big old-fashioned bed
that I learned one morning that Paris had been occupied.
Henri and André had crept into bed beside me and were
lying one on either side. For the first time since the outbreak
of war Henri burst into tears.

After the fall of Paris, the wheel of disastrous events
turned faster and faster. The first thing that happened was
that a number of officers, wretched remnant of our army,
began to trickle into our valley in the hope that a last stand
would be made in our mountains to allow the government
time to escape to Algeria. Germaine had to find room for
several of them in her house because the village was now
overflowing with refugees. The next thing was a telephone
call from Marcel Griaule. He was on the General Staff of the
French Air Force. They had reached Le Puy and because
they too hoped a last stand would be made in the Cevennes
he telephoned to advise us to take to the cellars. We did
not take to the cellars. Germaine had long since ceased to
consider the war from a personal point of view as a matter
of her own or even her children's safety. She hoped a last
stand would be made in our mountains, but she was beyond
taking precautions.

As for myself, to be honest the prospect appalled me.
If I took no interest in Oncle Ernest's capacious cellars, it
was for no better reason than that I had faith in no cellars
as a protection against war. I knew that however deep I
went underground fear would follow me. Under a calm
exterior—a British upbringing dies hard—I hid a bosom
more panicky than ever.

It was, I think, at this point in the ill-starred proceedings
that a telegram arrived from my sister Letty suggesting that
I ship my children to her in New York. It put me in a perfect

fever. Should I? Should I not? If yes, then how should I go about it? I put my problem to Madame Paul Sarrut whom I met in Valleraugue by chance. Her answer came at once, 'Never, whatever happens, separate from your children!' My deepest instinct told me she was right.

As regards my British upbringing, I was shortly to have proof that it was cracking at the joints. I used to go up the valley to La Coustète every day, mainly because of a puppy, Catou, which old Laune had given to Henri. I had been unable to keep it in Oncle Ernest's house because, like all Cevenol sheep-dogs, it was an arrant thief. Food was growing scarce for lack of transport, and the day we found Catou on the dining-room table wolfing the children's tea I knew he would have to go. I installed him in the stables at La Coustète and brought him food and took him for an airing every day. On the particular morning I am speaking of I had taken Henri and Dominique with me and had left them playing by the river while Catou and I paid a visit to Cancabra. On my way back to join the children towards the end of the morning I heard the roar of an aeroplane overhead and was suddenly seized with panic. I remembered the accounts we had heard of refugees being machine-gunned on the roads of France and I imagined that the sole purpose of this aeroplane was to machine-gun Henri and Dominique as they played by the river's edge. I started to run. And as I ran, with what little breath was left me, I suddenly found myself shouting for the children, but shouting in a voice I had never before heard issue from my lips, the voice of panic, fury and hysteria. I could see no sign of the two little boys. I ran up and down the river, still shouting, while the aeroplane zoomed overhead. Then all of a sudden, from a tuft of willow, their happy unconcerned faces emerged. The smile froze on their lips and they gazed appalled at the stranger I had become. It was over in a moment; the aeroplane was gone, the children were safe, reason reasserted itself. But it was a shock to me to see what overwrought nerves could do to me.

I often hopefully wonder whether my reactions would have been different if I had been in Scotland and had been told that we were to be the last bastion of England's stand

against invasion. Surely I would have shown more courage.
Certainly I would have found it less of a strain keeping up
appearances in a land where people hide their fears behind
the homely mask of everyday life, and make a cup of tea
to keep their flesh from creeping. I was disconcerted by
the French, and more especially the Parisian (and I was
surrounded almost exclusively by Parisians) capacity for
keeping a cool head and unshaken nerves while lucidly
expatiating on the worst that is likely to befall them.
Besides, in spite of my international habit of mind, sheer
instinctive patriotism must have come to my help.

The deep feeling I have today for France quite obviously
is not instinctive; it is the fruit of the long years during which
she has been about her insidious work of assimilating me,
a work that in 1940 was scarcely begun. The war and the
Occupation certainly hastened the process and brought to
the conscious level much that was still unconscious; but it
continued for long afterwards, and the artisans who wrought
my assimilation were above all my children. It was through
them that I came to know not merely the history of France
but all history seen from the French angle. They taught me
French standards of behaviour and made me aware of certain
qualities of the French mind, their passion for intellectual
integrity, their belief in the creative power of words, their
gift for taking what they do seriously but themselves not
at all. I came to identify France with a climate, a scale of
spiritual values, rather than a country whose boundaries
may be traced on a map. I believe now that in that sense,
and quite independently of the myth of patriotism, France
is worth dying for.

Little by little my feeling for France has grown up inside
me like a tree. Its roots go deep and are knitted up with the
roots of that other tree whose seed was sown long ago in an
Aberdeen nursery. Over the memories, still crystal-clear, of
my childhood in Scotland are other memories that are not
really mine but which seem as much mine as though I had
had two childhoods, one in Scotland and one in France. Not
only have I, through my sons, been trained vicariously in a
French Lycée, but I have so often heard my little daughter
and her friends sing, as they bounced a ball or hopped in

and out of a pattern chalked on the nursery floor, songs so rich historically that they cease to be mere nursery rhymes and become a thread that links us to the past. Timidly and respectfully, under cover of my children for whom the songs are a birthright, I would stretch out my hand and touch the thread and little by little the knowledge came to me of what it means to the French to be French. But I have never dared speak the proud exclusive words, '*Nous autres français*'. I might have earned the right if at the outbreak of war I had known what I know today of France and the knowledge had given me the peculiar and outstanding form of courage that the circumstances of the Occupation required and that can never, I think, have its roots in mere private life. But I doubt it, I doubt it. I am not at all sanguine that it would have done more than give me an added awareness of the extent of our catastrophe.

It is true that I was not the only one who suffered from a certain degree of panic in June 1940 after Griaule telephoned that we should take to the cellars. Geneviève and Mimi were haunted by the thought that if the Germans came to our valley they would be found in what they insisted upon calling their 'ghetto'. They used the term from no contempt for the Jews. They told me—it had never occurred to them to mention it earlier because before the war it would have seemed irrelevant—that their maternal grandmother had been Jewish. Normally they should be in no danger. Their fathers, fathers-in-law and husbands were all 'Aryan' and well-known in academic circles. But if they were found in a house owned by Jews, and next door to another house packed with Jews, would they not have to produce proof that they at least were pure 'Aryan'? What would happen to their children? That of course was the question I too was asking myself. Would it make things worse for mine that they were half British? We were horribly afraid, all three of us.

We cannot have stayed long in Oncle Ernest's house. I know we were back at La Coustète before June 17th. Catou and our vegetables made it difficult to be long absent—it is the small, foolish things of life as often as not that determine our course of action. Germaine had, as I expected, kept me up to the mark so long as I was within her zone of influence. She never faltered. I remember how once when we were shopping in the village she cut me short when I showed signs of discussing what was uppermost in our minds while we waited our turn in the shop. She said to me in an undertone, 'Not in the village. No one must see we are upset.' It was a language I could understand. My own grandfather would have used no other.

It is characteristic of Germaine that all through this dreadful period I saw her only once with dishevelled hair and never with untended nails, and that with her world falling about her ears she went on caring for the silkworms she was breeding as an interest for her children. Whatever the news, whatever the weather, out she would go to gather mulberry-leaves for their food, and she brought them through to the butterfly stage at about the time of France's final collapse.

The final blow fell, of course, on June 17th. I was busy in the kitchen when suddenly I heard Geneviève calling me and I hurried out to meet her. She came running towards me with the tears streaming down her face. We fell into one another's arms and she said, 'I'm so ashamed I can hardly bring myself to tell you. Pétain has asked for an armistice!'

Her first thought had been for me when she heard the news on the wireless, and she was determined I should hear it from someone who cared almost as much as I did about the fate of Britain. I had of course known we were in desperate straits. I had heard Paul Reynaud's speech in which he said he believed France would be saved even if it required a miracle to save her. I knew no Frenchman lightly confides his future to a miracle. But I had not when it came to the point expected defeat. The worst I expected was that war should come to the Cevennes, and that seemed to me bad enough. We sat down on the kitchen steps and let our tears flow. Geneviève was not one to take defeat easily. Her grandfather had been the heart of the Resistance in Lille during the First War, and her father, Professor Pierre Jouguet, the Director of the French Institute of Archaeology in Cairo, was to be the voice of the Gaullist movement in Egypt. I did what I could to comfort her. I never for a

moment believed Britain would be defeated, but I tried
to convince her that France could do no more and that
probably no other course was open to her. Surely we could
trust Pétain. Gradually we fell silent as the knowledge took
root in our hearts that this was the end and that we were still
there to face it. It never occurred to either of us that it could
be anything but the end as far as we were concerned. In that
moment no world beyond France had reality or substance,
nor any time beyond the present day.

But tomorrow came, and tomorrow and tomorrow, and each
in its turn had to be faced. I think I reached my lowest
ebb in the hours that elapsed between our being told that
Pétain had asked for an armistice and the publication of the
armistice conditions. My memory here is very confused. I
thought till I looked up the dates that days had elapsed
between the two announcements; I think that in fact we
were given the conditions very shortly afterwards and on
the same programme as a translation of Hitler's speech to
the French people. Was it a speech or a message? I cannot
remember. It was at Cancabra with Geneviève and Mimi
that I heard both. I am afraid we grasped very little of
what we were told. We were convinced when we turned the
button of the wireless that the same fate awaited us as had
befallen so many people in occupied territories; we believed
the Apocalypse had been loosed upon us and that we would
all be torn asunder and deported separately to concentration
camps. We listened with beating hearts, and of what we
heard one fact and one only penetrated our frantic minds:
a part of France was to be left free, the part we were in. We
thought that this meant what it claimed to mean—though,
to be honest, it would be too much to say that we thought at
all, for our minds were numb. It seemed to us that although
on the national level everything was lost, at least our private
lives were being restored to us, though whittled down to
bare essentials. In that moment nothing seemed to matter
but that we keep our children and our husbands. I must
confess that we fell in one another's arms with tears of
relief. Moreover, the conciliating tone of Hitler's speech
(or message) bewitched us into believing that perhaps after

all he had been maligned, for it had on us the very effect it was calculated to have on the French people. We dreamed for a moment that he was after all human enough to respect all that France stood for. Had we not been too battered by emotion to reflect at all, we would have known that in view of the fate of Poland and Czechoslovakia such a hope was necessarily dishonourable.

This moment of euphory was short-lived. I was shaken out of it the next morning by Oncle Ernest, only to be plunged into another illusion, scarcely more honourable. He motored down from L'Espérou and stopped where the path leads off to La Coustète, just long enough to give me on the spot a short and realistic account of what we had to expect. His point of view was that of a businessman; of a man, that is to say, who is accustomed to facing facts however unpleasant, and respecting contracts however unsatisfactory, and for whom nothing one cannot see and touch and prove and measure is a fact at all. He looked broken and old; his world too had come to an end.

He said to me, 'We're done for and we have to face it. England is done for too. She can't stand up to Germany alone. They'll force us to use our navy against her, and there is nothing we can do to prevent it because we have not an atom of freedom left. It's lucky for us that we have a man like Pétain at the head of things. If anything can be done, he'll do it. We must try to pull the country together. Pétain has good men with him. There's Baudouin. I know him and he's a man you can trust.'

That is the gist of what he said. He believed, as so many people did in France at that time, that England's defeat was now only a matter of weeks. For years the French had been told that their army was the best in the world; its overthrow was to them incomprehensible. They were forced to the conclusion that no country could stand up against the strength of Germany.

I murmured some protest against Laval's presence in the government. He answered, 'Oh! Laval is a sly fox. He'll outwit the Germans.'

That I did not believe. Even at that stage I knew Laval to be so sly a fox he would always overshoot the mark. Nor till

Oncle Ernest spoke had it so much as occurred to me that Britain could be done for. I had so far taken it for granted that she would ultimately win, but I felt it would no longer concern us here in France, for we would be long since dead. But at the thought of France's navy being used against my own country, it was as though a cold hand were squeezing the blood from my heart. For the first time I felt afraid with a fear that had nothing to do with my own or my family's safety. I began to look ahead beyond our own straits and to ask myself what Hitler's next step would be. I told myself that defeat was not possible for Britain; I reminded myself of my father's last words when I left Edinburgh, that America could not afford to let us be beaten. But it seemed to me that this altered no whit of the fate that lay in store for us in France. My horizon shrank once more to our immediate straits. I saw nothing for it but to clutch at the only straw that Oncle Ernest had offered me when he said we must work at pulling the country together, whatever that might mean. I wondered whether that straw could serve to build me a new world.

I went back to the house feeling pretty desperate but clinging to my straw. It has often struck me what a wonderful thing is the will to happiness and how hard it dies. Again and again I was to feel it rear its hopeful head at the most unlikely moments. Scarcely more now than a will to escape disaster, it was yet rooting around for some way out of the darkness back into the sunlight. Soon it had bolstered me up with all sorts of illusions. The prestige that surrounded the name of Pétain, Oncle Ernest's assurance that good men were rallying to him, all this combined to allow me for at least a few hours to believe that there might yet be something to live for. In moments of great stress the unheroic ask only for strength to live till night falls and sleep comes; we seize upon any attitude of mind acceptable to our conscience that can help us to do so. Sometimes, though never for long, we camouflage it to get it past our conscience. I had barely succeeded in achieving a precarious equilibrium, just sufficient to allow me to face the everyday round of cooking and cleaning and keeping a fairly calm face in front of my children, when another visitor appeared. It was Jeanne Nick, the eldest of Pasteur Nick's children, and though the sight of her was as welcome as only the sight of such a friend could be, in what was then my state of mind it was about as *comforting* as would have been the vision of an angel with a flaming sword.

Poor Jeanne! Not for a moment do I doubt that when she crossed the perilous bridge that leads to La Coustète she felt certain that here at least she would find support and understanding. The world as far as she was concerned had shrunk to a few ardent souls; she took it for granted I must be one of them by reason of my very origins. Alas! She came to me when my courage was at its lowest ebb. The worst had happened and not only were we faced with a future I expected to be compounded of every horror I associated with Nazi rule (as for the Jews and the brave so it was), not only was I cut off from my native country, but it looked as though my choice now lay between condemning France or renouncing my loyalty to Britain. It was a thought I could not face and so had fashioned for myself a middle way. I told myself that without renouncing my solidarity with Britain I must suspend my judgment of France and try to see things from the French point of view. Moreover, as I myself had reached the end of my tether and could bear no more, I persuaded myself the same was true of France and that no more should be expected of her.

As for seeing things from the French point of view, so far I had only Oncle Ernest, Geneviève and Mimi to go by. The immediate reaction of Geneviève and Mimi had been pretty much the same as mine. In the first moment of shock we scarcely saw further than our own, our husbands' and our children's safety. I cannot say we any of us considered what things were going to be like for our husbands. Our one concern was that they be preserved to us. The whole situation was beyond the pale of our experience. We did not know that though a woman may at a pinch build her universe, as a bird builds its nest, out of homely bits and pieces, a man worth his

salt requires freedom as he requires air, whether or not
he takes advantage of it.

As for Oncle Ernest, he was an old man and life had
already given him a good deal. He could more easily than
a young man renounce the rest. Besides, no other course
occurred to him but the one Pétain had chosen. Somehow I
knew that neither of these points of view would carry much
weight with Jeanne or any of her family.

Our kiss of greeting was scarcely over but Jeanne began
to pour out her overflowing heart. She gave free and furious
vent to her contempt for Pétain, her horror of Laval. The
pure burning flame of revolt that inhabited her blasted my
illusions and reduced them to ashes. To say that my heart
sank is to put things mildly. Battered by the tempest for
so many weeks past, I had found at last a temporary haven
in which to lick my wounds, and here was an angel of
God come to warn me in no ambiguous terms that it was
an ignoble haven and that I must rise up, go forth, and
once more face the blast. It was almost more than I could
bear. I remember that as I listened to Jeanne it occurred
to me that never before had I grasped the full meaning of
the word 'Protestant', nor realized that it corresponds far
more to a human type than to a member of a Christian sect;
and though I shut the lid of my mind precipitately on the
thought, it occurred to me too that they are on the whole
a troublesome lot. It only made matters worse that I knew
my place was on Jeanne's side of the barrier. And so it was
with a rather quavering voice that I yet sought to convince
her (and myself) that Oncle Ernest's was a valid point of
view. Her indignant start when I suggested that in view of
Pétain's record we should, perhaps, give him the benefit of
the doubt, was no more than I expected. I knew she had
won and my voice trailed away into silence.

At last she left me to toil her hot steep way up the stony
shortcuts to L'Espérou, and she left me shattered, not least
at having disappointed her.

And so began the new phase of our lives, the Occupation,
which in the free zone was fraught with the same demoralizing ambiguity as was the cock-eyed war. The race we ran
had now no goal but had become the Red Queen's race whose

object is not to lose ground. We had strained our strength to break in a door which suddenly had burst open of its own accord, displaying an abyss beyond, and the energy that had lashed us forward must now be jerked into reverse. There followed a short period that was strange indeed, in which we clung to foolish things to get us through the day. Germaine's instinct as a hostess (she had still a number of officers in the house as well as her other guests) led her to organize the life of her household and take them bathing and walking to keep them from brooding. The will of youth to wrest some happiness from life, whatever the circumstances, was at work in us and we co-operated most willingly. But there was more to it than that. The French generally speaking consider it bad taste to talk freely of what lies nearest the heart, and courage to them is courage only if it is lightly worn. They accordingly split their personalities with surprising ease. On one level they played bridge and bathed and mountaineered and were very social. On another they brooded secretly. Even Germaine had bouts of brooding. I remember going to her room one morning and knocking. A few minutes passed before she let me in. For the first and only time I found her with her hair dishevelled and her face distraught. She apologized and was obviously distressed at being caught out in a moment of *laisser-aller*.

I admit that the presence of all these strangers had a salutary effect upon me. It forced me to pull myself together and take some trouble about my appearance. Neither disaster nor despair can ever quite quench in me the feminine instinct to look my best before strangers of either sex. And the moment a woman begins to take trouble about her appearance her morale is pretty sure to mend. It is an example of the saving grace of any discipline whatsoever.

I received support of a different kind at about this time. One morning when I was picking tomatoes in the vegetable garden under a broiling sun, I looked up and saw coming towards me Raymond Lazard, one of our greatest friends. He arrived from Cannes, near where he had been mobilized. He came to ask whether I had any news of François. He told me that his own plan had been to escape in a yacht to Gibraltar with two other men, but that the others had

Janet Teissier du Cros, about 1938

left

Janet (centre) with friends at
Laxenburg, Clara Wittgenstein's
country house, 1924

right

Sir Donald Tovey, composer and
pianist, who offered to take Janet as a
pupil

below

Clara Wittgenstein's salon in Vienna,
where Janet often played the piano

left

François's cousin Germaine Dieterlen, 1930

right

Valleraugue: a pre-war view.
On the left is the River Hérault and the quayside; on the right is the Protestant temple and behind it the spinning mill where the silkworm cocoons were unwound. La Coustète is a little further up the valley

below

François's parents (centre) between his Oncle Ernest and Tante Berthe (Germaine's parents)

François Teissier du Cros, about 1931

Janet in the 1930s

Janet, Henri and André, with François's mother, 1938

backed out when they heard the armistice conditions. It was impossible to sail the yacht single-handed so now Lazard's intention was to organize his departure for England by way of the United States. Failing that, he proposed to buy a house and a plot of land in our region and transform himself into a peasant. He was the first person I had met since our world collapsed who had decided on a constructive line of action and was not simply marking time and waiting upon the event. I saw a good deal of him in the weeks that followed.

The first I heard of de Gaulle was when one day—it must have been June 18th—I looked in at Oncle Ernest's after doing my shopping. Germaine was in the garden, and on her face was a new and purposeful look. Standing under the cascade of a wistaria that pours from the first-floor balcony, she told me about his broadcast from London. It was the first time I had heard his name and I knew nothing of his broadcast. I realized as I watched Germaine that for some time past she had been as though stunned, an automaton driven by the sole force of breeding. Now she had come to life again. The thing that in her bewilderment she had been waiting for, expecting, the unknown thing whose existence one was certain of only because one felt its lack so cruelly, that thing had now happened. France was showing her true face. Germaine had kept an open mind about Pétain out of respect for her father, until she heard the broadcast speech in which he told the French people that the defeat was the wages of their sins, or words to that effect. That any man should so speak within hearing of the victorious enemy was a thing that, although Pétain had excellent biblical precedent, revolted her. As far as she was concerned he stood condemned. What had stunned her was that no other voice should be raised and no alternative offered to those who could not in their hearts accept the conditions of the armistice. Now there was such an alternative.

And so at this point France divided herself into two parts. On the one hand were those who prefer injustice to disorder and who would no doubt call themselves 'realists'; on the other side were those who prefer disorder to injustice and who believe in the intangible values. Pétain satisfied the 'realists' because he was reassuringly unheroic and seemed to take a compassionate interest in the fate of the man in the street—provided he be Aryan. In actual fact, his concern was less for the civilian population than for the prisoners of war, and the real purpose of every concession he made was to spare them suffering or gain them some advantage. By his practical standards he may have acted rightly, but his standards were not those of de Gaulle. The air of the 'realist' world is unbreathable to a man of de Gaulle's temper. The magnificent absurdity of the course he chose, setting out with for sole baggage France's honour, and only his two unauthorized hands to shelter it from the blast, was to him the only conceivable course. And it was some such magnificently absurd action that so many people were waiting for in the land that bred Joan of Arc. He was, as it were, the crystallization of the aspirations of a whole part of the population. From then on, that part of the population led uprooted lives, owing allegiance to none of the legitimate powers in France, whether French or German, but bound over to the spirit of revolt.

During the remainder of the month of June my undercurrent of fear for François gradually rose to the surface and blotted out everything else. For so long as none of us had news of our husbands, I kept fear at bay. I joined in the bathing parties, I was often with Germaine and her guests in Valleraugue when they sat round the wireless in the evening listening to the nine o'clock news and *Les français parlent aux français*. It was I who had the idea of the party at La Coustète in mock honour of the Vichy government. We bought up all the *toile de Vichy* in the local shop, a cotton material in variegated checks of every sort and colour, and we spent a feverish day concocting each in her secret privacy a full-length dress for the occasion. But I backed out of the great expedition to see the sun rise from Mount Aigoual. Marcel Griaule had arrived, Pierre Dieterlen had arrived, another cousin, Pierre Chazel, had arrived. Everyone but myself had at least news of her husband. My friends no longer said to me, 'He'll turn up quite suddenly, just as the others did'; they said, 'Don't worry! There have been very few casualties and he's not in a fighting unit. He's probably a prisoner.' Don't worry! In the good old days of the cock-eyed war when we could still allow free rein to our imagination, the fear that most haunted me was that François should be made prisoner. I was honest enough to admit to myself that with his delicate constitution and sensitive nature that would be the worst thing that could happen, better for him he should be killed outright. I now found myself praying that very thing had befallen him. When it came to the point I could not face the idea of his death nor the prospect of life without him.

The advent of Pierre Chazel roused new hopes, for Pierre had in fact been made prisoner. His account of his last days in the Maginot Line was tragic, but he told it in a spirit of high comedy, and the story of his escape was pure farce. The French convention—it almost amounts to that— of telling a tragic story in the language of comedy is akin to the Japanese convention that requires the person to laugh when announcing the death of a near relative. Pierre's description of how during the night German soldiers parachuted on to the surface of the Maginot Line, tampered with the revolving cannon so that they no longer revolved, of how the next day when fighting reached their part of the Line they could aim in only one direction with the result that the German tanks sailed over their heads, reduced us to tears of laughter; but it came back to haunt us in the years to come, shorn of the laughter. His escape was frankly comical. He was sent somewhere under escort, I forget for what reason. His escort was simply a German soldier. At the station where they were to take a train Pierre invited this soldier to drink a glass of Calvados. The man accepted. They went to a café and Pierre asked to be given a bottle of Calvados, a wine-glass and a liqueur-glass. He put the wine-glass in front of the German and the liqueur-glass he took for himself. In rather a shamefaced manner he told his companion that the French are a puny race who can drink spirits in only small quantities. Simulating a sigh of envy, he filled the man's glass and his own liqueur-glass and drank to his escort. When after a couple of drinks the German fell into a doze, Pierre boarded the first train and by easy stages tacked his way to Bordeaux and thence to Valleraugue.

This story made me hope that François too might escape, if he was in fact a prisoner.

The fall of France and my ever-growing fear for his safety had stripped my world of everything but the humblest essentials. All I now asked of life was that François and Henri and André and I be safe together under the red roof of La Coustète. A peasant life would be enough, or so I thought, forgetful of Papa's axiom, that fortune is always the double of what one has. In the tragic setting, on the dark stage, the actors were no longer for me nations, but the homeliest figures. The issue at stake had shrunk from man's spiritual heritage to our own household gods. And as I listened to Pierre's story I began to dream that the play was not to be tragedy but light comedy.

Then on July 3rd I received a letter from François's commanding officer. It ran as follows:

Madame,
    Captain Teissier du Cros left us on June 16th some kilometres from Montargis to reconnoitre the canal, since when we have had no news of him. If by any chance you too are without news, I advise you with all my heart to quiet your fears, for he must certainly have been made prisoner, as has so often been the case with officers separated from their men by the enemy's rapid advance.
    As Military Commissary for the Navigation Commission at Meaux, your husband was so good as to honour me with his friendship. I had occasion to appreciate his high sense of duty and his patriotism. But the privilege of age and my experience of the last war enabled me to give him certain advice which he has always followed. I am certain that he has committed no imprudence. However great my sorrow at no longer having him beside me at the present time, I am convinced that we shall soon have news of him. When I return to Meaux I shall leave no stone unturned to discover his whereabouts, but my firm hope is that you have heard from him and are reassured as to his fate. This being so, I am going to ask you, not to show courage, for I know you to be

worthy of him, but to have all the patience that may be necessary.

This letter was dated from Avignon. I had scarcely taken in its contents when Papa arrived from Mandiargues. He had received a similar letter and had come at once so as to be with me when I learned the news. Now the extraordinary thing is that the letter had in a sense reassured me. Pierre's account of his short experience as a prisoner of war had left me with the impression that this time it was no serious matter; no doubt François too would escape, or so I told myself, and strove to silence the awful fear that lay in wait for me at zero hour when the chattering monkey in my head fell silent. If such dubious optimism was what Captain Bernard meant when he said he knew I was worthy of my husband, then he was right; but I am afraid it was not at all what he meant. And mine was not Papa's point of view, which fortunately he concealed from me. For him the letter had read like an obituary notice; yet he put so much heart into convincing me that François was certainly still alive and that Hitler could never keep so many prisoners, that he succeeded in his purpose. If I sat mingling my tears with his it was out of pity for what François must be enduring, and not because I had lost hope.

I am not going to pretend that my mind was set at ease either by Captain Bernard's letter or by the few hours I spent with Papa, but between the two I kept afloat. Fortunately for me only three days later, on July 6th, I received a telegram which François had managed to have sent to me. It told me he was a prisoner of war. I say that it was fortunate I got this telegram because close on its heels came the official war office announcement that my husband was missing, and that he had been awarded the *Croix de Guerre*, in terms which almost amounted to saying that his decoration was posthumous. It was little Jean-Pierre Dieterlen who came running to La Coustète with the telegram, radiant at being the bearer of what now seemed to us good news. Once more my standard had slipped.

Actually François's disappearance had other effects besides causing us all acute anxiety. Since he was missing I had

received no income; that is to say since the beginning of
May. No doubt it was due to the general confusion, but
I like to think that a frugal government was suspending
payment rather than dole out a captain's pay where only a
widow's pension might prove sufficient. When Papa came
to Valleraugue he left me some money to carry on with,
but as by that time I had debts it did not last for long. I
remember that I invited Lazard to luncheon with the last of
it; fortunately he guessed how things might be and offered
me a loan to tide me over till François's survival should have
reached official ears.

And so life went on. I had more leisure than I had
latterly had and could spend more time with my friends.
Germaine and I had decided that, cataclysm or no cataclysm,
something must be done about the children's education.
Normally they would be at school till July 14th. We
felt that it was bad for them to lead such disorganized
lives. I accordingly wrote to Mademoiselle Rouveyrol at
St Hippolyte-du-Fort and asked whether she knew of
anyone who would come to us as governess. By great
good fortune a brilliant sister of hers who was studying
at the École Normale in Paris, had escaped with the tide of
refugees and was now with her family. She declared herself
willing to come as governess to our children and glad of an
occupation to take her mind off the situation. She proved an
excellent teacher and a pleasant, quiet companion to have in
the house, and she took the children almost completely off
our hands. We opened up the huge schoolroom at the top
of Oncle Ernest's house which had stood closed for years.
There they all gathered every morning round a big table.
Each child was set a task suited to its age and capacities,
and they soon settled happily down to a routine. In the
afternoon they would all come up to La Coustète to bathe
and have tea on the terrace.

I spent a good deal of my time at Cancabra. I found its
atmosphere comforting, in spite of the intermittent fear of
Geneviève and Mimi of being identified with their 'ghetto'.
Our conditions of life were very similar. Like me, they had
no maid and not much money, and lived in a peasant house
almost as devoid of convenience as La Coustète. Like me,

they were putting off to a later date the coming to grips with the deeper issues involved, and struggling on as best they could from day to day while recovering from the initial shock. And like me they seized upon any and every occasion for laughter. Actually at the time I am speaking of they were up to their necks in an orgy of dressmaking, a wonderful comfort to the female mind in any crisis. I am no adept at making clothes and I watched them with envious eyes. Geneviève had discovered a small hand sewing-machine in a cupboard in the living-room at Cancabra and she was now neither to hold nor to bind. She even at last volunteered to help me to make myself a backless summer dress, and every afternoon would find us gathered in the chequered sunlight that filtered through the vine-trellis in front of the house, moaning together over our country's fate or laughing over some absurd joke, while snippets of gay material flew from Geneviève's scissors.

It was Germaine's example that first opened my eyes, but it was during those long hot afternoons that it really dawned on me what fortitude French women learn in the seemingly frivolous school of elegance. The qualities of mind required always to look one's best whatever the circumstances will, I was more and more to discover, take charge when occasion arises and see one through most of what life can do to one. It is with deep respect that I look back and see with my mind's eye Geneviève and Mimi bending over their bright material, their hair well groomed, their nails neatly varnished, a sign to their children that though their world was rocking it still clung to its base. It is with shame that I remember how years later when Germaine was describing our anguish of mind during that terrible summer, she summed the situation up by saying, 'Janet no longer had a recognizable hairstyle!'

In the meantime summer had come to stay, and summer in Valleraugue means day after day of sun so hot you feel it as a direct and burning sensation on your skin. Towards evening the air fills with moisture and the grass turns soaking wet, the sky in the east dims to a smoky blue and in the west pale yellow chills to paler green, then blossoms to a rose. The hills flatten and turn deep blue, like the hills in a Japanese print. The nights are almost cold though the stones of the terraced hills hold the heat long after the sun has gone.

On July 11th I went and dined at Valleraugue with Germaine and her household. During dinner we listened to Pétain's declaration about the change of constitution. It was followed by the Marseillaise. Germaine sat frankly weeping into her plate. We were all suffering in various degrees from the overwhelming emotion the playing of the Marseillaise was to arouse in us each time we heard it during the Occupation. One of the things it was so hard to forgive Pétain was that he should so have cheapened that emotion. There was to come a time when, though we still found it impossible to control our tears, they were in part tears of rage that we should be fools enough to be moved by what seemed to us a travesty. It used to bring to my mind a story Tovey told me of his childhood, how the first time he heard I forget which of the Mendelssohn trios he wept with emotion that was part fury at being so moved by what his critical sense condemned.

After dinner I went through to the billiard-room and sat down at Oncle Ernest's little pianoforte. I remember that I found myself staggering as I walked as though I were slightly drunk—and while they discussed this new turn of events I began to play Chopin's F sharp minor Polonaise, disguising my misery with a ribald, 'Don't ask me to mourn for the Third Republic!'

Little Mademoiselle Rouveyrol came and stood beside me, her eyes full of tears. She said, 'Was it for this that we had so many revolutions, to be dictated to by Laval under the thumb of Germany!'

I stopped playing. I realized that what for me was bad enough was for them far worse. My life was up against a dead wall, but Britain was still intact. But for them, everything they believed in had been wiped off the slate and the Rough Beast was preparing to leave its mark in its place. I knew I had no right to speak or to play even that Polonaise.

But ordinary life went on, as I was to discover it always does. Who was the French diarist whose only remark about the Revolution was that his aunt continued as usual to receive on Fridays?

Not long after this episode I was invited to spend the day with the Bargetons. Their house, La Coste, stands some four miles from Valleraugue and I planned to go there on my bicycle. It is a downhill run all the way there but a weary toil back. It was so hot, I was tempted to wear Geneviève's backless dress which was now finished. I had a long struggle with myself. On the one hand was Lucinde's interdiction with regard to shorts and sunbathing dresses in the village, on the other was the pitiless sun. Ostrich like I decided to wear the dress but to rush through the village so fast, so fast, that not a soul would have time to recognize me or take in what I had on. I shot through the village like a meteor so that at least I did not see people seeing me, but a mile beyond it I was caught out. As Lucinde herself would have said, I spat in the air and it fell back on my nose. Not a mile out of Valleraugue I ran into a funeral going the same way as myself. There was nothing for it but to dismount and follow at the tail-end of the cortège till it turned aside from the main road. Never in my life have I felt so foolish as I did following along behind such a procession of black-clad respectability.

I found the Bargetons' house full to overflowing with a family that branches off into subsidiary lines of lively children like a many-tailed mouse. We all went bathing in the broad deep pool they have coaxed the Hérault to cradle between the great boulders in its bed. After luncheon we drank our coffee on the terrace and I talked with the wife of the eldest son, Edith, an extraordinarily beautiful Rumanian Jewess with glorious red-gold hair and long mysterious velvety eyes. It was the first time I had met her and I fell under her spell. She was like a breath from Central Europe that brought memories of lilac and Schubert's music and talk that takes no count of time. Before leaving, in a burst of reckless euphory, I suggested to the family at large that as many of them as cared come and lunch with me the following week. And I mounted my bicycle and toiled home to Valleraugue.

At La Coustète I found a telegram. Routledge wanted to know if my translation of the book on Finland was finished. Finland! Nothing could have been further from my thoughts.

It was, of course, bad luck on Routledge that the Germans should have started their western offensive before the book came out. Finland was no longer news. I had forgotten all about the book. The telegram came as a salutary shock. I wired back that I had not quite finished and prepared to get down to work.

My first problem was a typewriter. I managed to hire one from the wife of the director of the École Communale in Le Vigan, our nearest market town. The next problem was to find enough time to justify my statement that the book was 'not quite finished'. I began hatching plans to send the children up to their grandparents who were now at L'Espérou for the summer. I went and discussed the matter with Germaine and we decided to send all the children up, Germaine's to their grandparents and mine to Papa and Maman. The Griaules had left by this time and Mademoiselle Rouveyrol agreed to accompany the rest of them and continue the lessons.

The moment they were off I plunged into work. The first morning of solitude I spent cleaning the house thoroughly so as to have less to do in the time to follow, and I was sitting in my tin tub enjoying a much-needed bath when I heard voices at the door. I flung on a bath-robe and ran to see who it was. I found Edith Bargeton on the doorstep with two other members of the Bargeton family and an echo rang in my ears of my own voice inviting as many as cared to come and lunch with me on this very day. I had forgotten all about them in the flurry in which Routledge's telegram had plunged me.

On the whole, I carried the situation off well though in fact I deceived no one. I told them about the translation and said I had planned to take them to lunch at the hotel, though the mere thought of it struck death to my soul, for I was short of money. Jacqueline, one of the Bargeton daughters, set my mind at rest at once. She suggested we round up the contents of the larder and cook a meal for ourselves on the terrace. We spent a pleasant couple of hours grilling egg-fruit and mixing salad and talking nineteen to the dozen over our improvised meal, washed down with the acid rose-coloured Coustète wine. They tactfully left at an early hour and I got seriously down to work.

For a short space my life fell into a regular rhythm. I would clean the house briefly and then take a small table out to the shade of an apple-tree within sight and sound of the river. I would set my typewriter on the table and laboriously copy out what I had translated the afternoon and evening before. I was still at the stage of typing if not with two fingers certainly not with more than four, and I still instinctively began by feeling with my feet for the pedals.

There the postman would find me when he came with an occasional letter, and there the carpenter found me when he called one morning about some work he was doing for me. He asked if I had news of my husband, and when I told him François was a prisoner he sighed and then said in more cheerful tones, 'Well, well, we can only hope they'll make short work of the English!'

I burst out laughing. He looked taken aback till I explained why to me that would be cold comfort. Then he laughed too and told me he had always thought I was Swedish. He added that he had no ill feeling towards the English; he only wanted to console me with what seemed to him the best prospect of my prisoner's return.

I was gradually getting into the swing of my translation. Most fortunately, though I had left almost all my clothes to my English nurse in Edinburgh—I thought I would need no clothes to face the Apocalypse—I had taken my French dictionary and my Roget's *Thesaurus of the English Language* with me. Why I brought them I cannot imagine. Even so, it troubled me that no English person should be at hand to look my work over for me; I had a nasty feeling that my English was going French on me.

Germaine would come up to La Coustète at about tea-time for a swim in our deep pool in the Hérault, and bring whatever friend had found her way up to Valleraugue at the time. They would come up to the house after their bathe, with damp hair and a great show of discretion, but I always caught in their eye a hopeful gleam that something in the nature of tea would be forthcoming. Actually, after a day of work I was always delighted to have their entertaining company.

Griaule had been succeeded by another ethnologist from the Musée de l'Homme, Jean-Paul Leboeuf. On one occasion we invited the Lévi-Strauss couple and their son, Claude, who had arrived at that time from occupied territory. Tea of course there was now none, but in the early stages of the occupation there was no shortage of wine, and that was what I was going to offer them. Lucienne, though she was too busy painting to come herself, had sent a cake that she had made for us. The rest of the food was to consist of some very delicious melons. I had set the tea-table under the apple-tree where I did my typing, and when Germaine and Leboeuf arrived we settled round it on deckchairs to await the arrival of the Lévi-Strauss family. The bathing and my strenuous typing had made us all hungry, but there was no sign of our guests. I have never lost the English habit of drinking tea at about four o'clock, though in France five is a more usual hour; and so when half-past four went by and then a quarter to five and still no one was in sight I suggested, the hungry wish being father to the thought, that our guests had probably forgotten and we had better begin without them. With a glorious pop we opened the first bottle of sparkling wine and we fell to, throwing our melon skins recklessly into the river. Soon we turned to the cake. We started by cutting it in half and then divided one of the halves equally and carefully in three. These three slices we ate. We waited another ten minutes—it was well past five o'clock—and then Leboeuf picked up the cake-knife and looked at us with raised eyebrows. We gave our willing consent and with extreme care and loyalty he cut the second half in three. He had just straightened up from his bending position over the cake and was on the point of gallantly passing the plate to us when suddenly I saw his jaw drop and his eye fix a point beyond me with an expression of horror on his face. I turned round. There were the three Lévi-Strausses, carefully picking their way along the narrow path beside the *béal*. We rose simultaneously to our feet, babbling unacceptable excuses, and handed them what was left of the cake.

On the whole my translation was progressing well, but it was ill-starred from the first. One afternoon when Geneviève had come over from Cancabra and Lazard had turned up from Avignon and we were all three sitting on the terrace, a message came down from L'Espérou that little André was ill and I must go up at once. I mounted my bicycle and rode off in the broiling heat. Not that I intended to bicycle the twelve miles uphill to L'Espérou. I was never in better training than I was then, but I knew it would be impossible. My gears were out of order, and as they were English gears there was not a hope of having them repaired. I rode to La Penarié where the steep short-cuts begin which reduce the last nine miles to some six or seven. There I left my bicycle under a vaulted outhouse, assured that in that valley of honesty I would find it again when I came down, whenever that might be, and I set out on foot.

I am still proud of that climb. No mountain goat could have sped faster up paths that are sometimes sheer static torrents of stone. The sun was merciless and I had only occasional relief on the few paths that run between high bracken and broom with shady trees overhead. In all, from the time I left La Coustète, I took one hour and three-quarters. I crossed the threshold of Oncle Ernest's Espérou house, where I had been told they were all staying, at exactly a quarter to seven, in time for dinner at the half-hour, to Oncle Ernest's huge satisfaction. But I was not interested in dinner. I found André in high fever and very wasted.

A terrible fortnight followed. The doctor came up from Le Vigan on his bicycle, a weary climb of about twenty miles. He diagnosed a violent attack of coli-bacillosis. The members of the various families rallied round me. I was then and still am an inefficient and inexperienced nurse. Solange de Lapierre gave the saline injections, Madeleine Nick did the wrapping in hot wet towels to bring down the temperature. Both had done their Red Cross training and were of invaluable support. André could keep no food in his body and he seemed to be melting away before my eyes. The doctor made the awful journey at first every two days. There was now no petrol so he had always to come by bicycle. At night I slept with André's little burning body in my bed, so afraid was I of not waking when he called me.

For all day, between feeding and tending him, I sat in his room working at my translation and by evening I was worn out. The harrowing thing was that he was so hungry. He lay in bed repeating over and over again in the broad southern French he had lost no time in acquiring, '*André veut des sardines! André veut du pain grillé!*'

Sometimes he fell asleep towards morning, but our room was immediately above the dining-room and Oncle Ernest was an early riser. At seven o'clock each morning we would hear a loud banging of doors and an authoritative voice calling for breakfast to be served. Then André's ritornello would change to, '*André veut qu'Oncle Ernest se tienne tranquille!*'

How I agreed with him! But though Oncle Ernest had a heart of gold, it never occurred to him at any stage of his career to keep quiet if he had something to say.

At last the worst seemed to be over. The fever had fallen though André was still so weak he could not stand. By this time everyone was leaving L'Espérou. Helena Scob had left some time before to settle in a house the Nicks own in common in Le Vigan. We had heard that she was making financial ends meet by running a sort of restaurant in her home for the officers who had trickled into Le Vigan as they had done in Valleraugue. By this time her husband had managed to join her. He had served as a private in an all-foreign regiment, most of them White Russians like himself. Now he would have to start his career as an architect all over again from scratch, for he had no intention of returning to Paris.

Madeleine too had left. Her husband had been killed, the only one of our group. By a strange chance the armistice had found him fighting in the very corner of Alsace which had been to him and his brothers and sisters what L'Espérou was to his wife's family. He and his men had agreed to reject the armistice conditions the moment they heard them and to go on fighting. First François Dieterlen had been wounded. He had got his men to prop him against a tree and had gone on till he was killed. The Germans buried him with military honours. Now Madeleine must make a living for herself and her two little girls. She had been offered a job in Valence and to Valence she had gone, leaving her children with Helena.

Soon André and I were all alone with a maid who had been left to clean the house. Oncle Ernest and Tante Berthe had been the first of the family to leave, taking Jean-Pierre, Dominique and my Henri with them. Then Papa had come up from Mandiargues in his little car to fetch Maman down for the vine harvest. He had still a very little petrol left, enough, he told me, to make the journey once again when André was fit to travel.

I felt horribly abandoned, but a little relieved. During our time at L'Espérou I had come to be aware that an intangible barrier had grown up between my parents-in-law and me. It had its roots of course in the tragedy of Mers el-Kébir. I have come to that horrible event out of its real chronological place. It had been one of the worst shocks and no doubt was one of the greatest psychological mistakes of the whole war. Its effects were to be incalculable. Yet it was a very excusable mistake. Probably the English imagined they were making things easy for the French by holding a knife to their throats and providing them with an excuse for turning their backs on Pétain. No doubt they knew nothing of the turmoil of emotion to which the French navy was a prey. The navy had not been beaten; it had come creditably out of what encounters it had had with the enemy. It was intact. The collapse of the army was a bitter pill for the navy to swallow. Her army was to France what her navy is to Britain; its collapse cut the ground of prestige from under the feet of the French navy, never quite sure of itself at the best of times, for throughout the years it had been constantly made to feel its inferiority to the British navy; the best places in foreign harbours were always kept for the British ships, the best of other harbour attributes had shown preference for British sailors because they were better paid; and the French sailors themselves had always taken the rather self-conscious behaviour of the English in foreign parts for high-and-mightiness. When the French army went down all over France like corn in a hailstorm, and the British navy summoned the French ships at Mers el-Kébir to surrender on pain of destruction, the smouldering feeling of resentment that had been no more than an undercurrent so long as the two countries were fighting side by side burst into the open like a geyser and drowned in bitterness all rational feeling. The French navy had wanted to go over to Britain of her own free will or not at all. Britain could obviously not afford to risk the alternative. The whole situation was of the very essence of tragedy.

Certainly Papa and Maman had no feeling of hostility towards me, but they were bitter against England—it is harder to forgive a friend than an enemy. At the same time they were determined not to discuss Franco-British relations in front of me; they had no wish to hurt me. The atmosphere had been strained. I saw them go with anguish because of what had been, with relief because of what it had become.

And so late September found me alone at L'Espérou. September in L'Espérou! The rowans are scarlet against the still blue sky, there is a feeling in the air as though one had reached a sort of oasis in time when everything stands still and catastrophe and even anguish are held at bay. When after the first inevitable downpour of rain the sun returns, it seems it has come to stay forever. The peasants emerge from their granite houses and take possession once more of their village, as though the rain had washed it free of the pollution of 'summer visitors'. There are shouts of laughter as jokes are bandied in front of the butcher's cart about how they let themselves be frightened away by the rain. Real life in L'Espérou has begun again. Nostalgic smells waft hither and thither about the village, wood smoke and drying mushrooms and the pungent trail of a flock of sheep that has passed through on its way to the valley pastures, which lingers on the air long after the tinkling bells have become part of the silence.

After about a week Papa came back to fetch us. I carried André down to the terrace in front of the house and set him on the ground while Papa turned the motor-car. He tried to walk but his knees knocked together and his feet slithered away on either side. All the way down the hairpin bends to Valleraugue I held him on my knee, gazing ahead of me into the grim future, blind to everything but the thought that my magnificent baby was now a live version of a photograph that used to haunt my childhood from the pages of a medical book on my mother's bookshelf, the photograph of a rickety child. The protuberant belly, the knock-knees, the solemn eyes gazing sadly back at me, all were there.

During all this period communication was possible between prisoners and their families, and between occupied and unoccupied territory, only by means of printed cards which the German authorities had put into circulation. Gaps were left in the printed matter to be filled in by the sender, as for example: 'I am in . . . health', or '. . . is a prisoner'. I therefore knew only the bare fact of François's being a prisoner and still in France. I could see there was now little chance of his escaping without incurring very great risk. As for ourselves, I had no clear notion how we were going to live nor where. My small allowance was coming in regularly once more, but it would cover our expenses only if we stayed in Mandiargues or Valleraugue. I decided I had better make up my mind to try to spend the winter at La Coustète. Oncle Ernest in the meantime had generously insisted that we come to him from L'Espérou till André recovered a little of his strength. I decided to take advantage of this opportunity and have some sort of kitchen made in the stables of La Coustète. I knew the living-room would be impossible to heat in the winter, and that I would be glad to have a warm kitchen to retreat to when the children were in bed.

We had to do things very cheaply, and to this day I regret that I could afford only a cement instead of a tiled floor. But I had a real window made in place of the rough opening and the walls plastered and white-washed. I got the builder to make me a stone sink (though for lack of water it had no tap) and a white-tiled charcoal stove. I had discovered that charcoal is almost as convenient as gas to cook on, though not nearly so clean. For the cold weather Maman had sent me an old cooking-stove in which we could burn our own wood.

In all we were probably about ten days at Oncle Ernest's. I spent most of my time up at La Coustète watching the work progress, or reading on a deck-chair on the terrace. Towards evening I would wander back and join Germaine and her husband Pierre for a drink in Oncle Ernest's garden, for though food became every day more scarce, wine was still plentiful. I find a note in my diary, written under its mellowing influence:

'You would think now that everything is lost that life would be unbearable. France is under Germany, England is being bombarded night and day, and I have no news of my family. Worst of all, François is a prisoner. And yet . . . and yet . . . happiness has a way of creeping back unawares in the wake of apparently unquenchable hope. In these glorious September days you feel yourself open out like one of those hard dry pellets which in water gradually unfold and blossom into a bright and curious Japanese flower.

'I sat in the garden with Germaine and Pierre. Beds of begonias, pots of scarlet-flowering cacti, of shocking-pink geraniums, lemon-trees in great stone jars, all culminate in the sophora-tree that gives point to the garden. It stands in melancholy grace at the far end, facing the house, and its leaves hang down over the village square like ropes of greenery woven for some sacrificial ceremony. We lay back in the Indo-Chinese basket-chairs, a glass of muscatel in our hands, and we felt ourselves slip back once more into bliss. How is it possible? And yet, how could it be otherwise when your mind grows so confused between the autumn sunlight and the wine that so resembles it, that you no longer clearly know whether it is the wine you are drinking out of a crystal glass or the September day.'

We settled into La Coustète shortly afterwards. Germaine and Pierre had decided to return to Paris with their two young sons. Germans or no Germans, they could ill conceive of life elsewhere, and besides both had their work in Paris. Oncle Ernest and Tante Berthe stayed on for some weeks and then left for Nîmes. They had no wish to live within sight or sound of the Germans. They rented a huge flat in the beautiful fossil that is Nîmes, more fossil than ever during the Occupation. I think that Oncle Ernest had brought his personnel south at the time of the *débâcle*. He installed the offices of the Compagnie Générale d'Électricité d'Indochine

in the larger part of the flat while he and Tante Berthe
set up house in what remained. Only old Lucinde stayed
on in the house at Valleraugue. As soon as everyone was
gone, she took possession once more of the kitchen and I
found her putting everything back in the order to which she
was accustomed and which had been disturbed by Oncle
Ernest's town staff. She explained to me that she could
find her way about and keep her independence though
practically blind from cataract only if she knew exactly
where everything was.

My translation was coming on apace. I worked in the
evenings between eight and midnight, when the children
were safe in bed and I had the warm kitchen to myself.
One third of the book had already gone off to London
and to New York and had arrived safely. In spite of this
I had instructions from Routledge to send the rest through
an address in Switzerland. I did as I was told, but nothing
sent this way arrived and two-thirds of my work was lost.
Fortunately I learned this only much later.

For company I had Lazard's occasional visits and as time
went on I began to see more of the Lévi-Strauss parents, Raymond and Emma. They had recovered Cancabra:
Geneviève and Mimi had gone to settle temporarily with
an uncle in Montpellier. Madame Cahen's Belgian relatives
had gradually melted away. She herself lingered on for a
few weeks and then also went and made a home for herself
in Montpellier. Sometimes when Lazard came we would
bicycle over to Le Vigan and spend some hours with the
Scobs. More often we scoured the country hunting for a
peasant house with some land where he could settle if his
plans for leaving the country came to nothing.

The most exciting event that occurred after our return
to La Coustète was that I received a letter from my father.
I found it where the postman had shoved it under the
kitchen door while I was shopping in the village. When I
saw his handwriting I was so excited I could scarcely open
the familiar little English envelope. I had written to him
several times, much as I might have cast a bottle containing
a message into the ocean, and with about as much hope of
getting an answer. And now here it was! It was the first news

I had had from home and it was not all good news. The letter
was dated July 31st and had therefore been two months on
the way. It told me that my father had had news of my sister
Alice in Holland through my other sister Letty in New York,
and that they were well. But it also told me that Tovey had
died on Wednesday July 10th. His death was such a loss to
me that I believe I could hardly have borne it at any other
time. I sat in the kitchen looking inward at the pain in my
heart with strangely detached eyes. Through my head ran
the words of the sonnet in which Shakespeare begs for the
exact opposite of what I was experiencing. I was thankful
this shock had come after all the others. I knew that nothing
short of the tragic events of the last months could have made
this latest blow so strangely bearable.

October brought the first cold weather. Though the sky was
still blue and the sun almost as bright as ever, an icy wind
blew the first red leaves under the rough doors and made it
impossible to keep warm, even in the kitchen. Lazard did
what he could to block the gaps in the doors by nailing old
blankets over them. Though I knew I would soon have to
desert the big living-room, for it would be impossible to heat
when the real cold came, I tried to hold on a little longer by
hanging also in front of the door a curtain which François
and I had bought at a Polish exhibition in the early days of
our marriage. It was hand-woven of red and fawn-coloured
linen and it looked like cloth of gold. The size and beauty
of the room did my cramped spirits good and the roaring
naked flames in the high primitive fireplace, though they
heated only one half of my body, warmed the heart of me.
I remember one late afternoon when I was sitting there in
front of the fire. There was only one small weak lamp and
the flaming of the shifting fire to light me. The high rafters
and most of the room were in shadow, and the cold wind
whistled under the door. I had been re-reading *Emma* but
had laid the book aside, overcome by an irresistible longing
for a teaspoonful of chestnut jam. At the best of times
chestnut jam is heart-breaking work to make. For the few
pots I had put away in a cupboard I had had to go without
sugar for a couple of months and more. I knew it would be

a crime to touch it, but I told myself I would take only one small teaspoonful. But when I had done so a sort of madness seized me. Just as I finished the pot there came a knocking at the door. It was already pitch-dark outside. Who, I asked myself, could have found his way over our crazy bridge in the dark and up our crazy path, from terrace to terrace by steps that are mere stones jutting out from the terrace walls, and along the narrow edge of the *béal*, without an accident? I opened the door and there stood our local clergyman. He was doing the round of what no doubt he optimistically thought of as his parishioners, and he had included me among them. I never in my life felt such a lady: here was someone, and no mere summer visitor, who took me and my house seriously enough to pay me an official call. While he blew out the candle in the lantern which had made the visit possible, I furtively put this and that between him and the empty jam-pot. We then sat down and talked of I no longer remember what, not I think anything connected with the church. I know I found his visit comforting; it made me feel I was not merely a war accident, nor even a foreigner, but a member of a community. After that day I did sometimes find my way down to church with the children and I became quite friendly with both the clergyman and his wife, and my children with their children, though I doubt if I ever made the status of parishioner.

The pot of jam was, of course, symptomatic. The food problem was becoming more and more acute. Butter had disappeared from the market and we were reaching the stage when our subsistence was to depend not on how much money we had, though that counted too, but on the extent to which we could make ourselves liked. During the years that followed, years that for me were nothing less than an education in human relationships, I was often haunted by the fear that my link with people was not affective but had its roots in the need to get something out of them. It was a very nasty sensation. At this early period, though, things did still come to one without a tooth-and-nail struggle.

My first experience of what we later came to call the grey market, that is to say the procuring of food not through paying exorbitant prices but by exploiting friendship, occurred one dank October evening. I had gone down to Valleraugue just after dark and was starting for home when Fabre, the hairdresser, whom at the time I scarcely knew but who was very pro-British, stopped me and invited me into his shop. There he asked if I would like him to pass on some butter to me at the normal price. His only son was ill with tuberculosis and he spent his spare time scouring the countryside for food to give him. He had been up to Aire de Côte, a forester's house high up in the mountains, and had brought back more butter than he needed. I was profoundly grateful, and was carrying my butter, two half-pound packets, carefully concealed in my shopping-bag, when I saw Raymond Lévi-Strauss coming towards me on his bicycle. He dismounted when he saw me. He looked old and tired and infinitely sad. He told me he was trying to find butter, but that there was none in the village. I offered him half of what Fabre had given me. It still seemed easy and natural to share what one found, as it did (except in moments of madness) to keep the best of everything for the children. As time went on and one's whole system cried out for lack of essentials, it became more and more difficult. I never regretted that butter. From it sprang a friendship which was to be my mainstay during all the time I eventually spent in the valley of Valleraugue.

All news was not bad news that autumn. There had been a rumour that certain categories of prisoners were to be returned to civilian life. Of these the *Ponts et Chaussées* department of engineering was one. As it had been my husband's branch of engineering before he turned aside to do research, I began to feel very hopeful. There seemed every reason to suppose that the rumour would prove well founded; in the interest of the Germans themselves, it would be necessary to repair the bridges that had been destroyed during the *débâcle*. And indeed at long last the news reached us that François had actually been liberated and was in Paris recovering from this period of captivity. He was to go on shortly to Meaux where he had been appointed to a post as engineer and where he would be working under the same Captain Bernard that had written to tell me he was missing. I would be able to join him as soon as the necessary safe-conducts had been issued by the German authorities.

This altered my whole outlook. There would be no need now to continue the struggle against wind and water. I would soon be leaving La Coustète. But the time passed, and passed slowly, and no safe-conduct reached me. I was finding it harder and harder to keep warm without the winter clothes I had left behind in Edinburgh. Even if I had had the money to buy new ones, I had no clothes coupons. They were issued, a few at a time, only to children, refugees and pregnant mothers.

In November the rain came back, not the autumn monsoon but a real Scotch drizzle. The wind fell and the temperature rose, which was all to the good, but in the south the peasant houses are built with small windows to keep out the sun, and now that there was no sun it was very dark and very depressing inside La Coustète. I decided to hasten on the safe-conduct by means of a little magic. I began to reorganize the living-room as though I were to spend the whole winter in the valley. I dragged the huge sofa, part divan and part bookcase, till it stood in front of the fire. It was a herculean task and at first ill-rewarded. The rough floor was so uneven that in its new position the sofa rocked to and fro like a seesaw. I had to prop it in place with wedges of wood. I next drew up two armchairs, one on either side of the chimney-piece in true English fashion, and I piled wood till the fire roared. The temptation to go one further and have a bath up there by the fire was so great that I put water on to boil on a couple of tripods and I fetched up my tin tub. Soon my spirits began to soar as I sat facing the dancing flames, pouring hot water down my back. But once more I was caught out. Through the gentle rustle of the rain came the sound of approaching voices. Next there came a knocking, first down below at the kitchen door, then higher up at the first-floor door. Then the voices came closer and the knocking was at the door of the living-room. I had sprung from my bath at the first sound of voices and I was drying myself as fast as I could by the time the visitors announced through the door that they were Helena and Lazard come over from Le Vigan on their bicycles to pay me a visit. Lazard went to Le Vigan about as often as he came to Valleraugue, for both the Nicks and the Scobs were old friends of his. It was, in fact, through him even more than through Madeleine that I came at this time to be intimate with Helena. When I first met her I found her a little intimidating because of her great beauty and her aloof look of dreamy violence. Lazard brought us together during the weeks that followed. She became and has remained one of my greatest friends.

I explained through the door that I had been taking a bath and they patiently waited in the rain till I was ready. Soon we were all three sitting round the fire and I felt justified in my new arrangement of the furniture, though I deplored the presence of the tin tub. Lazard was a little silent, but Helena and I talked and I found myself confessing what so far I had not admitted even to myself, that in spite of my joy at the coming reunion with François, I was haunted by terrible misgivings at the prospect of deliberately introducing my children into occupied territory.

The magic worked and the safe-conduct arrived within the next few days. I was packing our trunks on what I expected to be our last day in Valleraugue, my heart torn between happy expectancy and the anguish which all uprooting causes me when it comes to the point, when the postman brought me a letter. It was from Lazard. In it he said that though he had balked at telling me so outright, he thought me a fool to go into occupied territory. He said I was giving the enemy a means of putting pressure on François, and he suggested I reconsider the whole matter before making a final decision. As I had in the meantime had a second letter from my father in which he besought me not to take the children into the occupied zone, I was rather shaken. But we were expected the very next day at Mandiargues where we were to break the journey north. It was too late to turn back and I decided the best thing would be to leave the decision with Papa and Maman; I felt incapable of making it for myself.

And so at last on a grey November afternoon we left Valleraugue in a bus that now ran not on petrol but on charcoal. It went very slowly and it smelt horrible, but it got us at last to Pont-d'Hérault where we took the train. At St Hippolyte-du-Fort we got out and I left most of our luggage at the station, still convinced that we would be leaving for Meaux in a couple of days. I embarked the children in the horse-cart Papa had sent for us, and I myself set out on my bicycle with Catou the dog running behind. We had scarcely left the station when Catou vanished into the gathering darkness and I never saw him again. Lucinde afterwards told me that a Cevenol sheepdog will always smell its way to the nearest shepherd and I need not trouble about him. At the time we were very much upset at losing him.

I laid my problem before Papa and Maman as soon as I was alone with them. They were very taken aback and obviously thought Lazard's point of view absurd. By choosing to stand by Pétain they were committed to believing in the good faith of the Germans, and since, so Papa argued, I was French by marriage and the Germans were on terms of legality with the French government, obviously I ran not the slightest risk, and the same applied to François. It did not occur to me that I had nothing to prove I was French; my marriage certificate was in Edinburgh, and by some error my marriage had not been registered in France, though this I discovered only later.

I realized as I listened to what Papa said that though he was perfectly honest in believing that we ran no danger, his opinion was not the outcome of serious reflection but the result of his political position. For the first time I began to ask myself whether Lazard was not perhaps right after all. I was at a loss what to do.

The next day Lazard came himself to explain his point of view to Papa, who remained unconvinced. He even told me that he disapproved of Lazard's decision to leave the country. Papa knew nothing of the treatment that was being meted out to the Jews. He knew nothing of the concentration camps, and at the time would certainly not have believed it if he had been told. He had lived all his life in a world in which such things would have been impossible. In his youth both he and Oncle Ernest had been passionate Dreyfusards. He knew that anti-Semitism could cause injustice; but it took the Eichmann trial to open his eyes to what had actually taken place under Hitler. We were so poisoned with lies during all the years of the Occupation that he soon formed the habit of disbelieving everything as pro- or anti-German propaganda. His considered opinion in 1940 was that the Jews had only to lie low and wait upon the event. It had not, I think, occurred to him that the only event which could justify such behaviour on the part of the Jews would be British victory.

At last I thought I saw how I could cut the Gordian knot. I decided to delay my departure long enough to allow me to go to Marseilles and consult François's old chief, Monsieur Gourret, the Director of the Marseilles Harbour. He was an eminently practical man and as a member of the Armistice Commission he would surely be well informed. Nor was he the man to advise against taking a risk unless it was serious. I rang him up and asked for an appointment. Lazard, whose sister-in-law had just escaped from occupied territory and was in Marseilles, decided to go with me.

I was rather nervous of the coming interview. Gourret was not only a very important person, he was a most outstanding personality. He had the tremendous intellectual and physical vitality which I associate with a certain type of Frenchman. His job as Director of the Marseilles Harbour was more than a mere job to him; it was a passionate interest. He had a piratical side which hugely enjoyed the political game that was the heart and soul of Marseilles public life. François, like Gourret a Protestant, was handicapped by a tendency to balk at any dubious action however trivial. Gourret ignored the motes and balked only at the beams and he attained his ends. Nothing could be done, even by so important a man, without taking into account the foibles of the local politicians. But it troubled Gourret not a whit that human nature is a sow's ear; with the unlikely material it offered him he went his tranquil way, making a silk purse of it.

He had been a good friend to us in Marseilles, never standing on his dignity with his younger colleagues. He had no need to stand on his dignity. Though he was in no sense a good-looking man (he looked as though he had sucked his thumb till of an age to switch over to cigarettes), though he forgot to cut his hair and cared not at all what he wore, he was a great man.

One vivid memory of Gourret carries me back to before the war. We were travelling to England and so was he, and we met by chance in the corridor of the Paris train. He was dressed in loud checks and his hair lay neatly over his collar. He beamed at me and said, 'Vous voyez, Madame, pour aller dans votre pays je me suis habillé à l'anglaise!'

On another occasion he came to my rescue in a difficult moment. I was going back to Edinburgh to play in a concert and I suddenly noticed that my passport had expired. There was no time to get it renewed through the normal channels. François rang Gourret up and explained my problem and he said I must come to his office with my old passport. It was the first time I had visited harbour headquarters. I was taken up in the lift and ushered into a large room with a magnificent view over the Joliette. Gourret rose from behind a colossal desk and waved me to an armchair. He took my passport from me and picked up the telephone. As he waited for his number he cocked an eye at me and said, 'Now, Madame, you shall see in what way I am superior to your husband!'

He gave a brief order and I had my passport the same day.

It was into the same room that I was ushered when I came to ask his advice about venturing into occupied territory. His answer came at once and was categorical. He said that for so long as François remained in a town as small as Meaux it would be madness for me to go and join him because the Germans made arrests quite arbitrarily and my having a French passport would be no protection. He said that François should aim at being transferred to a much larger town, preferably Paris, where I would pass unnoticed. I left him with my heart in my boots. I never saw him again because he was killed not long afterwards in an air crash.

Lazard and I dined that evening with the sister-in-law, Sonia, whom he had come to see. Sonia was an odd person, Lithuanian-Jewish by origin, remarkably intelligent, almost effusively friendly, and not at all a bad person with whom to laugh, an important point in my eyes. She entertained us vastly over a black market dinner in an Italian restaurant much haunted, we afterwards learned, by the occupying forces—in civilian clothes since we were not supposed to be occupied in the south. She told us her adventures when crossing the line of demarcation between occupied and unoccupied territory. She had studied in Berlin before her marriage and she spoke perfect German. She offered her services as interpreter to the harassed German official whose job was to sift the travellers and pick out the Jews and suspects. She managed to convince him that none of the people whose papers he examined were Jews. When at

the end he thanked her, without even a glance at her own
papers, he remarked what an odd thing it was that so many
French people looked Jewish. 'Ah!' she replied, 'but then
you aren't used to the Mediterranean type!'

I returned to Mandiargues the next day to break the news
of Gourret's decision. Papa and Maman resigned themselves, but they obviously disapproved. I was in something
of a quandary. I felt I could not bear to face the cold of La
Coustète again, nor the awful problem of getting Henri to
the village school. I said nothing about this in its right place.
He had been going to school for only about six weeks when
we left Valleraugue, but those six weeks had marked me.
School began at eight in the morning and Henri had only
a toy bicycle on which to do the mile or so to the village.
When the rains came in November it was no longer merely
a problem of getting up in time, bad enough in itself; by the
time he had got from the house to the road through dripping
grass and sometimes, when the river flooded, even through
water, he was soaked through and through. We had none of
us either stout boots or waterproofs and we had small chance
of procuring them. What it boiled down to was that when it
rained Henri had to stay at home. I remember that for the
first time in my life at Valleraugue I began to rejoice when
it rained because it meant we need not rise early. When I
woke in the morning, from where I lay I could see Henri's
head protruding tortoise-like from his blankets, anxiously
waiting while I lifted the curtain to hear my verdict on the
weather. Our hearts would rise when we saw the dripping
window-panes and we would sink back into an ecstasy of
sleep. But obviously this was not a good thing from the
point of view of his education.

What was I now to do? Papa suggested that we settle
once more at Mandiargues. There seemed no other solution. I toyed with a wild notion of taking the children
to live in Marseilles where I had a number of friends.
I even went the length of writing to the place where
Sonia was staying and which was cheap, but they had
no room. Besides, it was a student hostel which was
stretching a point by taking in refugees from occupied
territory but could not stretch it sufficiently to take in

children. I could afford no other solution so I gave up the idea.

In the once congenial atmosphere of Mandiargues spiritual isolation was to be my lot. In fact, it was during this period that I took to dreaming in *les Robinson*. The very real affection that bound me to my parents-in-law remained, but it was as it were in suspense. Still, better, or so I told myself, isolation within a group than isolation pure and simple. I had lost faith in my own inner resources. I knew their precarious burgeoning took place only in fine weather. I could no longer count even on Lazard's fortnightly visits, for he was soon to leave France. Ever since he came to Valleraugue and found me picking tomatoes in the sun, we had been in correspondence with my sister in New York about an affidavit she had agreed to provide to allow him to go to the United States. His intention was to make arrangements from there to join the Free French Forces in England. It had been a long business and before any affidavit arrived his position in France had seriously deteriorated. It was now urgent for him to leave the country. The Vichy government, obedient to its German masters, had sent round a questionnaire to be filled in by all government employees, which in France covers a wide field. Lazard like my husband was an engineer in the service of the state. He had to fill in this questionnaire whose real purpose was to eliminate Jews. Only such Jews as had been decorated in active service would be kept on, and it would be in the lower ranks of their service. With fierce enjoyment Lazard stated that two of his grandfathers had been Rabbis and he filled in the rest of the form in the same spirit. He added in conclusion that as he had never been within sight of the enemy, he had had no opportunity of winning a decoration and that there could therefore be no occasion for degrading him in his service. He then sent in his resignation. His boats were burned. He was now without a job and openly declared a Jew.

To return to the affidavit, before I even left Valleraugue we had sent my sister Letty a night letter telegram asking whether she could send it by cable. Lazard had allowed for a very long pre-paid reply in the hope that it would be used for that purpose. Unfortunately it turned out to be impossible to send an affidavit by telegram, but Letty wasted so few of the precious words at her disposal in explaining this fact that that part of her answer was almost incomprehensible. Instead of concentrating on the matter in hand she took advantage of what seemed to her a unique opportunity to send me a nice long chatty communication. Poor Lazard was a little taken aback and though I, very naturally, was delighted, our problem remained unsolved.

Just before I left Valleraugue Letty did send us another cable to say that the affidavit was under way. The question was, how long would it take to arrive? Lazard was growing impatient. It was then that I had an idea which I thought might bear fruit. Shortly before we left Marseilles François and I had been to a dance given by some people we scarcely knew in honour of the children of the French Ambassador Charles-Roux. We had been taken to this dance by our friends the Zafiropoulos and had been introduced among other people to the American Consul. We had not even stopped to talk to him and he would certainly not remember us, but I had subsequently met his wife on several occasions and my children had been to a party at their house. I decided to write and ask him to give Lazard his exit permit on the strength of my sister's cable. There was one difficulty. In saying I had met him it would have been useful to be able to mention the name of the people at whose house we had met, but for the life of me I could not remember it. I decided at last to say that we had met at the house of the Zafiropoulos. I was not certain he had ever been there but I told myself that he would be flattered that I thought he had, for they are one of the Greek families that form the élite of Marseilles society. In any event, I knew they would vouch for me. I could not count on the Consul's wife, though I mentioned that I had met her; it was unlikely that she had stayed on in France.

Armed with this letter, Lazard left once more for Marseilles. He came back triumphant. It had worked and he had been able to make arrangements to leave France before Christmas, in a tent on the deck of a cargo-boat if I remember rightly.

I give the details of my dealings with the American Consul solely because they were to have a sequel.

And so at last came the time for Lazard's departure. He was to sail from Marseilles, and I went with him as far as Nîmes, meaning to buy the children's Christmas presents there, for there was nothing now to be found in the shops of St Hippolyte-du-Fort. In the train on our way there Lazard suddenly handed me two cheques, making in all a total of the equivalent of about eighty pounds. He said I could consider the money as a loan and pay him back after the war. I had serious qualms about accepting it, but he found the right argument to convince me when he said that as a Jew he would lose any money he left behind. He then advised me to use the money to help me to a life of independence and suggested I settle at Le Vigan near the Scobs. He knew I would do better at that time away from Mandiargues.

In Nîmes I did my Christmas shopping. The cheques had made me reckless and I bought the best toys available in the rather barren toy-shops. I remember the stuffed camel that ran on wheels which I bought for André, congratulating myself that thanks to a Jew neither Hitler nor Laval was going to prevent my children from having a real Christmas.

But the shadow of Lazard's departure was heavy on me. It brought me face to face with the future. The door for him was open. He would escape. We must remain in the static present, thankful to see no further than the coming Christmas Day.

We spent the evening devising a code to allow us to correspond freely for so long as he was in the United States. Lazard promised to transmit it to my sister Letty. We then bade each other goodbye as casually as though we were to meet again next day, for the occasion paralysed us. He was scarcely out of the room when the realization came that my best prop was gone. I burst into floods of tears, the last tears of self-pity I was to weep until the liberation of Paris, and those were retrospective.

I returned to Mandiargues with a heavy heart, but with so many parcels of Christmas presents that presently my spirits began to rise. I had even found a *pâté de lièvre* for Papa. There were now so few days to go, and the weather that year was colder than it had been for years in the South; I was certain it would keep.

All Papa and Maman's children who lived in unoccupied territory were expected for the Christmas weekend. Only François and his sister Claude, married in Geneva, would be absent. Roger, a naval officer, had recently married an enchanting girl, half French and half Laotian, and they were living in Toulon. So was the third brother, Jacques, a naval engineer, with his Swedish wife Karin and their small son Yann. The youngest of the family, Rémi, was studying law at Montpellier. If I had not been such a skeleton at the feast it would have been, in spite of everything, a happy enough occasion. The old house is an ideal setting for a family gathering, and in spite of the bitter cold the sun shone brightly. But though Roger and Jacques were not really Pétainists, they brought with them a breath of the Pétainist air of Toulon, and it was blasting to all my hopes and beliefs. In justice to Jacques, I must say that he had chanced to be in Casablanca when the tragedy of Mers el-Kébir took place. He was sent on by the Vichy government to report on that lamentable event, so saw everything immediately after it occurred. It would be more than anyone had a right to expect that he should remain objective. He had nonetheless the generosity not to tell me then or at any time that he had been a witness to the destruction caused by the British navy. I learned it only recently from another source. At the time all I was aware of was a strain in our relations.

Our most immediate concern, however, was the cold. During the first winter of the war the weather had been so mild and sunny that it had been possible to work in an unheated room till late in December. This winter was very different. Roger and his wife Déva complained that though they kept a fire going in their bedroom, by morning their damp towels were stiff and frozen on the towel-rail. Theirs was one of the coldest rooms, but all of them were icy. We could no longer use the central-heating for lack of coal, and I know I never found the courage to remove my dressing-gown, one of the few warm garments I possessed, before going to bed. It took me all of the fortitude I possess to strip it off the next morning and don clothes which were not merely inconsistent with the temperature, but had gathered to them in the night all the cold air that hung about the room.

And so dawned the second Christmas of the war. I was now sleeping with both my children in my room, for with so many extra people in the house we could no longer monopolize the two best bedrooms. On Christmas Eve I went up to our room as soon as the children were asleep. I brought out the toys I had carefully hidden in the cupboard and prepared to fill their stockings. I brought out, too, the presents for the various members of the family which were to go on the Christmas tree (no fir but a young Mediterranean pine). It was then I discovered that the whole of the pastry had been eaten off the top of the *pâté de lièvre*. Long afterwards André told me that he clearly remembers eating the pastry off the pie and that what is more he had played every evening, before his brother Henri came to bed, with the toys I had so carefully hidden, and more particularly with the stuffed camel. I guessed about the pastry, but I had no notion when I filled his stocking, setting aside the camel for the Christmas tree, that the toys were already his familiar friends.

Christmas Day passed pleasantly enough. It was towards evening that shadows began to fall. I forget how the subject of politics came to the fore, for we were usually careful to avoid it. I know I had a slight passage of arms with Roger and Jacques after Papa and Maman had gone to bed, and that one of them said to me, 'It is time you made up your mind whether you are French or English!'

I fought back, but as soon as they had all gone up to their rooms I fell a prey to the awful fear that, partly because I have so little faith in my own judgement, secretly haunted me, and was most acute at Mandiargues where we lived cut off from all news of the Allied world. Was I an apt judge, I asked myself, of what was or was not the right course for France? Was I objective? Was Pétain perhaps the saint and martyr his admirers took him for? Did I identify de Gaulle with Britain or with France? What, above all, did François think? Would he agree with his brothers or with me? Little by little I felt my confidence weaken. After all Lazard as a

Jew was perhaps no more objective than I. As for the Nicks,
they were born fighters, not to say anarchists. Always and
inevitably they would be on the side of dissidence. To whom
must I turn to 'see things from the French point of view?' I
felt that I was reaching the end of my tether and must either
give in or go away. It was only then that I remembered the
words Lazard had spoken in the train. At the time I had been
thinking especially of Christmas presents and had paid little
attention when he advised me to settle in Le Vigan. Now
the idea began to take root. I decided that the very next
day I would go and consult Helena and her husband. As
an architect, Scob might know of some cheap place where
I could stay.

I piled wood on the fire; those evenings after everyone
was gone to bed were my best moments. I surreptitiously
turned the button of the wireless till I got London. It was
never easy but that evening I was lucky. Loud and clear
came a voice, and what a voice! It was the voice of Desmond
MacCarthy. For me that evening, racked as I was with doubt
and lonely as never before, it was the last straw. I sat on the
floor by the fire with my head on my knees, remembering
the last time I had heard that voice. He had come to stay
with us in Edinburgh on the occasion of a lecture he was
giving, and the usual party had been given at home in his
honour. I remembered how when all the guests had left he
had come through to my music-room with my sister Letty
and me. There in front of a roaring fire of good Scotch coal
he had reclined on the sofa with his feet up, while Letty
and I admired the neat line of exceptionally decorative braid
down the side of his evening trousers. Letty told him that
none of our father's guests had ever played the lion as well
as he. He purred like a cat and set about entertaining us with
stories of London literary life, delightfully malicious stories
of people many of whom we knew only through their books.
He described, I remember, how artfully 'Elizabeth' of the
German Garden prepared as she talked to you a pedestal
for you to step on to, and when candidly you mounted it
how sharply she knocked it from under you.

I forget what his subject was that evening when I listened
in Papa's drawing-room by the glowing embers of vine-root

and mulberry. But the effect his voice made on me I shall
never forget. It was literally a voice from another world,
the world of youth and freedom in which Europe alone
counted and frontiers had no real existence, and where only
intellectual and spiritual values mattered. Above all, it was
a world bathed in the light of a magical future. For the first
time I really faced the fact that there was now no future. I
must get used to living from day to day with no help from
a hypothetical tomorrow—we could no longer even afford
to dream for fear the shock of the awakening be too rude.
Then suddenly the voice was gone. I sat there on the floor,
feeling as though a knife had only now brutally severed me
from the past. One thing was clear; I could no longer stay
at Mandiargues. Lazard had been right. Tomorrow, beyond
any possible doubt, I would go and prospect Le Vigan. Firm
in this resolution, I tore myself away from the warm fire
and made my chill way up the bare stone staircase, with
icy blasts blowing about my ankles. And so to bed—in my
dressing-gown.

I went to Le Vigan the following day and I spent a couple of nights with the Scobs. With their help I found and rented an unfurnished flat. It was in the medieval part of the town in a very old house, not without charm. It contained two good-sized rooms and a silkworm-nursery, but that could be used only for storing. The bigger room had two spacious alcoves, one with a window. It would make a small bedroom for the children. The room I chose as my bed-sitting-room had a pleasant view down the narrow street to a thirteenth-century bridge shaped like a camel's back. On the other side the windows looked out over a tiny vine-trellised garden which belonged to the first-floor flat, now occupied by Judith Paley, Scob's secretary. There was neither gas nor electricity in my part of the house and the whole place needed repainting. Scob undertook to have all this put right at a very small cost, and as the rent of the flat was absurdly low, I closed with the offer.

To this day it amazes me that I should have gone to so much trouble to settle into a flat I was to occupy for only a few months. I did have a notion that François might take some time to find a post in Paris: above all, in my joy and relief at being with people who were of my own generation and who shared my views on all essential matters, I was tempted to settle down in the moment of time that had brought us together. Besides, living as we now did without a future, the present came to seem eternal. This incidentally was one of our chief sources of despair.

I had still to find furniture. I bought a beautiful desk and a kitchen-table for a song at the local junk shop, and Helena lent me three divans. Obviously I would need more than this. My mind began to be haunted by memories of the '*grand salon*' at Mandiargues. Maman has always had a '*grand salon*' but it has never served its true purpose. In the old house of Mandiargues it was used as a dump for a quantity of old and very valuable furniture which had found no place in the rest of the house. Maman was always more interested in people and gardens than in houses and furniture. I had some hopes of borrowing what I lacked.

Back in Mandiargues Papa and Maman raised no objection to my going to live in Le Vigan. They knew it was difficult for me in Mandiargues, and it must have been something of a strain for them having me. I was a permanent thorn in their hard-won, precarious and only very relative peace of mind. They were so honest in their beliefs, they were so warm-hearted, they suffered very much that I, of whom they were genuinely fond, should have been so led astray in my political opinions. One has to bear in mind how deeply-rooted in the past the mutual distrust between French and English is, how easily brought to the surface. To Papa, whose only view was through the distorted glass of the Vichy press and wireless, the worst of his suspicions seemed to be being confirmed. It was easy work for the Nazis to inject their poison into the popular mind with whispered rumours of how the RAF rushed back to England the moment the German troops broke through, and French soldiers were left to die on the Dunkirk beaches because the English ships would take only the English.

It is a fact, too, that Papa in his Mandiargues isolation knew far less than I did about Nazi Germany. As I said earlier, he knew nothing of the concentration camps. He thought the anti-Semitism would blow over and had no notion what it meant in Nazi Germany and occupied territory. He lived in the past, and when something occurred to shake him out of it he took refuge in disbelief or laid it at the door of democracy, and it was difficult to deny that under the Roi Soleil Hitler would probably have had to stick to his house-painting. Looking back I can understand Papa's being a Pétainist: he was never at any moment a collaborator.

Before I finally moved with the children to Le Vigan several things occurred. One was a visit. My brothers-in-law and their wives had left by this time and I was once more alone with Papa and Maman. I spent a good deal of my time reading or writing in my room, and it was there a message was brought to me that someone was asking for me downstairs. I went down to the drawing-room; Papa and Maman had tactfully withdrawn at the sound of my visitor's accent and I found myself alone with an unknown clergyman. It was Donald Caskie, the chaplain of the Presbyterian church in Paris. He told me at once that he was an old student of my father's, which made him automatically an old friend. As we drank our *ersatz* tea, he told me it was the English prisoners at St Hippolyte who had told him I was in the neighbourhood. I had only recently made contact with these prisoners who were living at the police barracks on parole. I sometimes joined them for a drink in one of the cafés when my morale was at a low ebb. They were a real cross-section of the nation, as an army always is. There was a little of everything. A small red-haired Scot had told me how he had looted a travelling clock and some toilet requisites in what he had taken for an abandoned farm while escaping through occupied territory, only to be warned by the farmer's wife, who turned up just in time, that they belonged to the commanding officer of a German unit that was stationed there. He kept his loot when he fled. There was a Cockney who told me all the latest plans of escape over a glass of beer and ended by saying, 'We'll get away all right if only the boys don't talk in the cafés'. There was a quiet man with a patient face who always looked as though he saw something just beyond you. He told me he had been wounded in the head and would have to be operated on as soon as he got home. He added, quite simply and making no bid for sympathy, that he would be quite blind in a very short time. All these men had made their way through occupied territory with the unfailing help of the French population. All of them had imagined they would be safe when they reached the free zone. All were arrested. Most of them afterwards escaped with the help of the population of St Hippolyte-du-Fort.

I discovered that the prime mover in these escapes was the Reverend Donald Caskie. I wish I had seen more of him, but my time in St Hippolyte was drawing to a close. In any event, I believe his fleeting visits, whose ostensible purpose was to hold religious services for the British prisoners, soon came to an end. The Gestapo was on to him and he had to escape by way of Spain.

Before I left for Le Vigan with the furniture Maman had generously lent me, I had to go once more to Marseilles. Lazard's affidavit had arrived, and I had promised the American Consul that I would bring it to him as soon as it was in my hands. It occurred to me that it would be a good opportunity to collect some of our belongings from where they had been stored, in a warehouse on the Vieux Port which our friends the Borellis owned. Blankets, linen, pots and pans, and our vacuum-cleaner would be useful in our new flat.

A porter carried my suit-case from the Gare St Charles to my hotel, and on the way we had a heart-to-heart conversation. He told me that what most stuck in his throat under our new regime was the anti-Semitism. The best bosses he had ever had, so he said, had been Jews. It made him sick to see them treated as though they were sub-human. Marseilles, I know, had the reputation of being what we then called *mal-pensant*, and it may to some extent have been true of the middle class. In my experience it was not true of the working people. My contacts were slight but they were revealing. None of us was at all cautious in our speech. Caution is a thing you cannot easily learn when you have grown up in a free country. In Marseilles as elsewhere I spoke my mind freely and I met with nothing but kindness and sympathy. In one shop I was even given a knitted suit for André at half-price because I was '*anglaise*'.

The first thing I did after I arrived was to call at the American Consulate. It was crowded with people trying desperately to get out of the country. I was shown into the Consul's office. I recognized him at once: he was a well-known figure in Marseilles—but he obviously did not know me. As obviously he was suspicious. Poor man, I do not blame him. Those were suspicious times. We met cordially enough, but he very quickly set me a trap. At the far end of his office was a chimney-piece on which stood a number of photographs. He suddenly pointed to one of them, a large studio portrait, and asked me whether

I recognized it. Now I must explain that I am short-sighted but far too vain to wear spectacles. I hesitated for a moment. I had a strong suspicion that it must be his wife but had no wish to commit myself. After all, it might, for all I could see, be a signed portrait of Franklin D Roosevelt. As I am too vain even to admit that I require spectacles—or was then—I was in a dilemma. I thought my best course was to say quite honestly, 'No'. Triumphantly the Consul exclaimed, 'It is my wife!'

I crossed the room and looked at the photograph and said, 'Of course!' But our interview came to a hasty close, and I left the consulate feeling not merely a fool but also a very suspicious character. I knew that if when he returned to the United States he told his wife the story she at least would remember me. In the meantime I could only hope that our paths would never again cross each other. Unfortunately they did.

There were three other contacts to be made while I was in Marseilles, the Borellis, Sonia, and my old friend Margaret Grey.

I went first to the Borellis. They are a delightful and very original Provençal family consisting of Jerome and Juliette Borelli and their four daughters and one son. The son, François, was later killed in the American bombardment of Marseilles. Jerome was the most curious blend of distinction and bohemianism I ever met. He was too much the gentleman of leisure to lead a regular professional life, yet too much of a Bohemian to be at all distressed at having, by reason of a change in his fortunes, to earn his bread and live in narrower circumstances than had been his custom. He solved the eternal problem once put to me very neatly by a friend in Paris, the problem of how to earn one's living without giving up one's time to it. He let the flats of the house he owned and lived in, in the Rue Sylvabelle (we had lived in one of them ourselves), and he vaguely did business in antiques of which he had an enormous quantity. These antiques used to be a godsend to us when we lived in his house. When we had a big party he would lend us chairs and crystal glasses which put our own to shame. He had no shop, but the ground floor and basement of his house were stuffed with furniture. He would keep no maid at a time when most people kept at least one, because he hated strangers about the place. He would have no fixed hour for meals but expected a running buffet to be kept going in the kitchen by his devoted wife and daughters.

It was at this house that I was now invited to lunch. Jerome was present and we ate in proper order round a big dining-room table in the kitchen, a beautifully furnished room where everything that could offend the eye was kept behind a decorative antique screen. The daughters did the waiting. They also entertained us with their talk, for they were children of exceptional intelligence and vitality.

After lunch Jerome and Juliette took me down to the warehouse on the Vieux Port where our furniture was stored. I found that 'parked' would have been a more suitable term, for it simply stood grouped in a corner of an enormous depot and the Marseilles rats had wrought havoc among our mattresses. Seeing my distressed face, Jerome waved a lordly hand, as much as to say that it was a small matter at a time when Europe was tottering on her base, and assured me that he would have everything put to rights. I extracted some of our blankets, our linen and whatever else I could lay hands on, and arranged for them to be sent to Le Vigan by rail. I felt that it was lucky I had come. So much would be saved from the Old Harbour rats.

The same evening I dined at our Italian restaurant with Sonia. We could no longer blind ourselves to the fact that it was bursting with Italians and Germans, but the Chianti had such a magical effect on our spirits that this seemed to us an enormous joke. There we were, a Jewess and a Scot, chattering away in French in the middle of our arch-enemies. We had a hilarious dinner and parted rather unsteadily on the Canebière, swearing eternal friendship.

The next day I lunched with Margaret Grey, a delightful Englishwoman who had taught dancing in Marseilles ever since she was a young and timid girl, fresh from her training. She had been brought over by Madame Rodokanachi, the wife of our Greek doctor and a member of the aristocratic Greek set which, as I said earlier, rules over Marseilles society. Under such a sheltering wing, and thanks to her own gifts and tact, she rapidly rose to the top of her profession and at that time no one would have dreamed of studying dancing with any other teacher.

I was so unaccustomed by now to eating normally that a black market lunch on top of a black market dinner finished me off. I woke the next morning with the first of the three liver attacks which are all I can boast of so far. But Margaret and I had arranged before we separated to spend the following day at the house of Colonel Peter Teed, Château Fontcreuse near Cassis, just along the coast. Colonel Teed was well known to most English people who haunted the Côte des Maures before the last war. He had, so I was told, retired from the Bengal Lancers and settled in France for love of Jean Campbell who lived at Château Fontcreuse with him. It was a delightful house to go to. One never quite knew to which of the two one felt more drawn. The place itself had also great charm. Round their lovely Provençal castle they had made an English garden which had a curiously exotic air in the middle of the vineyards. They entertained a number of English writers and artists as well as their many French friends. Peter Teed took an active part in the work in the vineyards and would receive his friends in his working clothes. It was a curious contrast when he took you up to his study on the first floor to show you the silver cups he had won in India with his polo ponies. As often as not, he would afterwards take you down to taste the various vintages of his wine. In the cool twilight of his vaulted cellars, a sip here and a sip there would seem to be having no cumulative effect. But the moment you stepped out into the torrid sunlight the wine would rush to your head and send you staggering through the garden to the open-air tea-table where Jean Campbell sat behind her tea-cups, surrounded by the odd assortment of English ladies whom life had cast up on the shores of the Mediterranean.

I had been astonished to learn that Peter and Jean were still in France and delighted at the prospect of meeting them again. And now here was I, a limp heap in my bed, with aching head and eyeballs. The mere thought of the cellars of Fontcreuse sent a wave as of seasickness over me. Nothing, I felt, could stir me from where I lay. I raised my head painfully from the pillows, just sufficiently to reach the bedside telephone and ask for Margaret Grey's number. I told her that Cassis was out of the question for me in the state I was in. 'Nonsense!' she answered briskly, 'the fresh air will do you good and the Teeds expect us.' The thought of fresh air had much the same effect on me as the thought of the wine. I moaned but to no purpose. Margaret had the firm English belief in the therapeutic effects of bracing fresh air.

I dragged myself out of bed and bathed my aching eyeballs in cold water. What a waste, I told myself, what an appalling waste! There was nothing I would better have liked than a day at Fontcreuse in my normal state, and now all I wanted was to lie limp in bed.

Margaret was a little staggered when she saw what I was looking like, but she still hoped the fresh air would cure me though she was less categorical. We boarded the little train that then ran along the coast, and my head throbbed in time to the rhythm of the wheels. Yet I remember that it was the sort of glorious January day which I associate with Marseilles, the sort of day that would soon bring the mimosa out in downy clusters all along the shores of the Mediterranean. Again and again I was tempted to raise my heavy head and peer through the parasol pines and the steely sunlit air till I caught a glimpse of the dancing sea. At the mere sight another wave of nausea would submerge me.

How we got from the station of Cassis to Fontcreuse I cannot remember; it is quite a long walk. But we got there. The moment Jean Campbell saw my face she hurried me upstairs to her bed and there I lay for the rest of the day, feeling more and more of a fool as my condition improved. I never even saw Peter Teed. I got up in the late afternoon when he was back in the vineyards and we left immediately to catch our train.

On the following day—it was January 4th, 1941—I returned from Marseilles to Le Vigan, with only the briefest halt at Mandiargues. I find in my diary:

'The odd thing about my present situation is that on the face of it nothing has changed. Last spring when I looked the possibility of defeat in the face it seemed the end of everything, a tearing asunder of every tie and the loss of all the people I care for. Now the worst has happened and we are all exactly where we were a year ago. François in Meaux, my father in Edinburgh, Alice in Holland, Letty in New York, Molly and Flora in England and I in France. And everything is dead and broken. I can only forget in the train where an anachronistic feeling of happiness keeps breaking through in spite of everything. In spite of the snow like a shroud on the countryside beyond the windows of the train, something in me stirs and remembers that soon the mimosa and almond-trees will flower on the Mediterranean shores. Even here the sun will come back again and it will be enough merely to be alive.'

I still harboured the illusion that it could sometimes be enough 'merely to be alive'. But then, we deliberately cultivated our illusions during the Occupation.

As soon as I reached Le Vigan I left the children with the hospitable Scobs and bicycled over to Valleraugue to fetch what I still lacked for my new installation. There are traces of that visit too in my diary:

'The worst of the cold has broken. A wild wind is blowing from the north, not a cold wind but one that smells of snow. There is still snow on the mountains and spread thin across the valley. The road is slippery with ice, but though every step put me off my balance, the wind, for all it was blowing against me, filled me with such crazy enthusiasm that it spurred me on. When I boarded the train to leave St Hippolyte I was still sunk in lethargy and despair. The Christmas atmosphere, with everyone still brooding over Mers el-Kébir, had been stifling. Now I feel free. Everything here is simple. The peasants listen to no propaganda. As long as there are Germans on French soil the war for them is not over.

'As I crossed the village I met the draper, drunk with Roosevelt's latest speech. He told me to look in on my way back as he had twenty pounds of dried chestnuts for me. I was the more touched that I knew he had laid them aside chiefly for Britain's sake. The next people I saw were the Launes. I found them sawing logs in the cellar under the vaulted terrace of the Mourgues' house, our neighbours on the other side of the valley. By the light of the pale wintry sun shining through the open door I could just distinguish them. We stood in the chill half-light like three conspirators, exchanging war news and optimistic forecasts.'

From Valleraugue I joined the children and we settled into our new home. The kitchen-living-room had been painted a gay yellow and my bed-sitting-room a sober white against which the few good pieces of furniture from Mandiargues showed to great advantage. We improvised a bathroom in one of the alcoves, with basin, water-jug and tin tub. When all was ready I started looking about me for a maid. I was sick to death of housework.

It was rash of me to send to L'Espérou for one of the Reilhan girls, a grand-daughter of old Pierrelette about whom I had heard innumerable stories when I first came to the Cevennes. Paulette Reilhan, my new maid, was one of ten brothers and sisters and true, as I was soon to discover, to the family tradition of amiable dishonesty. She was delighted to come. The fact that there was nowhere for her to sleep except a corner of the silkworm-nursery troubled her not at all. It may have been because of this inconvenience that I decided on a girl from L'Espérou; hygiene and modern conveniences had never then entered their lives. One thing and one only counted in the eyes of Paulette. She was in Le Vigan, a large town by her standards and full of amorous possibilities.

My engaging a maid at all was really a piece of foolishness since I had to shop and cook myself in order to make both food and money ends meet. But Paulette cleaned and washed (everything except herself) and she took the children walks between school hours, gathering young men in her wake as a magnet gathers pins. Both my boys were now at the local communal school where the Scob children, Michel and Edith, were both pupils. There they speedily forgot what was left of their English and learned to speak their native tongue with the broadest of southern accents. They soon picked up the usual schoolboy repertory of unspeakable words and I one day heard my son André, then aged three and a half, and Michel Scob, aged seven, greet each other in the street with a friendly: '*Bonjour*, *putain!*' They pronounced it 'putang', that being the local accent.

The communal school was a good school as regards teaching and the teachers were good-natured, friendly men. I got some entertainment from the copy-book phrases in use in the writing class. I particularly remember one of these. It well illustrates the Mediterranean genius for diluting moral uplift with a dash of worldly wisdom. The sentence was, '*L'argent ne fait pas le bonheur, mais il y contribue.*'

There was a good deal of imposed sentimentality with regard to *notre Maréchal*. The children had to write a letter to Marshal Pétain and they had to draw his portrait. The Scob children were perfectly clear in their minds as to their parents' and teachers' real attitude to Vichy. Mine tell me that they were horribly confused all through the war.

Helena and I spent a good deal of our time scouring the country round for food and paying court to the local shop-keepers in the hope of behind-the-counter extras. Looking back, it seems to me that we spent the intervals lying on a divan in the sun in the Scobs' living-room and talking for all we were worth. The one luxury we had at that time was service. Helena had her own maid and Madeleine's maid, for Madeleine's children were then living with the Scobs. I had Paulette. We made the most of the situation.

Our circle in Le Vigan consisted of one other person, Judith Paley, a Russian Jewess of British nationality and French education. I mentioned her earlier as occupying the flat under my own. She was Scob's secretary and I found her excellent company. Scob's position was rapidly improving. The peasants in the Cevennes were earning money for the first time in their lives. Hitherto, tilling the narrow strips of soil on the hand-built terraces of the hills, where no machinery, and not even a donkey, can be used for lack of space, they could ill compete with the cheap production elsewhere and the cheap transport that brought food to the Cevenol villages from the rest of France. Now they very sensibly spent the money they were earning, thanks to the present keen competition for food, on improving their houses both inside and out. City dwellers, too, with houses in the Cevennes where they used only to come in the summer but which they were now inhabiting all the year round, were having them overhauled and made more comfortable. All this was grist to Scob's mill. He was the only architect in the region. He had tided over the first difficult period before money began to come in by making bicycle trailers to a model of his own invention, the innovation being that they ran on a single ball-bearing wheel. Bicycles were our sole means of individual transport, and soon there was not one in the whole region without one of Scob's trailers. I invested in a trailer myself and found it invaluable on our food expeditions and for transporting André, a heavy proposition.

Before I had been long in Le Vigan I had grasped the general picture of the population in terms of their political opinions. They fell simply and naturally into two groups, black and white, sheep and goats, Pétainists and Gaullists. To this day I am incapable of seeing them in any other light and continue to choose my tradesmen accordingly. Our grocer, Vivens, was a particular favourite with Helena and me. He was an enthusiastic Gaullist, always optimistic. He was also unfailingly kind about selling us any extras he could, never at black-market prices. We chose our butcher for the same reason. He had a Belgian refugee at the cash-desk who was as well-informed as we as regards people's political opinions and who treated them accordingly. He had also an astonishing flair for smelling out plain-clothes policemen on the look-out for illegal food traffic. I remember one occasion in particular. We had stopped at the cash-desk to pay for our meagre weekly ration of meat, when suddenly he cocked an eye at us and asked whether we would like a leg of mutton. A leg of mutton! Our ration was three ounces per head and per week. We gasped assent and he put his hand back to seize a particularly large one that hung on a hook behind him. Then he as suddenly recoiled and went back to his accounts with a curt, 'Good morning!' We left the shop in unutterable amazement and considerable disappointment. On our next visit he explained that he had seen a plain-clothes policeman coming into the shop. We got our leg of mutton a week late. There was a rumour that this Belgian was an army officer who had fled from Belgium with the Gestapo on his tracks.

We gave little credit to this romantic story; it seemed too good to be true. We were wrong, and we were later to meet Georges le Belge, as they called him, in very different circumstances.

Another source of comfort to us was our plumber. He was a member of the Communist Party and of course a rabid anti-Pétainist. He was the mildest and kindliest little man imaginable, but he kept a black list, more to relieve his feelings than for any practical purpose. He made no use of it at the liberation. But he would hint to us which of the 'wrong-minded' were set down on the list for retribution on a day in whose dawning we had almost ceased to believe, and if we had cause to complain of anyone he would murmur darkly, 'Never mind; he's on the list!' The fishmonger too would make desperate efforts to serve the right-minded in preference to his Pétainist customers, if not in fish, for there was none, then in frogs' legs and an occasional egg.

When I look back on the months I spent in Le Vigan my heart rises on a tidal wave of gratitude to Scob. It was he who set the tone of our little circle and filled our evenings round the fire with delight by making us laugh as no one before or since has ever made me laugh. He spent his days on one or other of his building sites, dressed in clogs and corduroys to which he gave a royal air. In the evenings he was always relaxed and high-spirited. He entertained us with stories of his student life at the Beaux Arts in Paris and cloudy fantastic memories of the splendour of his Russian childhood. I remember seeing him depressed only once. It was when the Vichy government decided to withdraw the naturalizations accorded since the outbreak of war. Life had been so easy for foreigners in France in the old days that it never occurred to the Scobeltzine parents to apply for French naturalization. Even when Scob grew up, he had been perfectly satisfied with his *apatride* passport. But during the first year of the war French nationality was offered to all foreign recruits. Scob had taken advantage of the offer and now was furious at its being withdrawn. 'When a general came to inspect our regiment,' he would tell us, 'they used to put me in the front row to show what a fine race the French are. And now they are giving me back my *apatride* passport. There's gratitude for you!'

And so the evenings passed. Towards ten o'clock hunger would begin to gnaw our vitals and Scob would go rooting round for what he called a *chaterie*, in other words something that tasted good. As often as not we were reduced to cold boiled dried chestnuts. When there were none left Judith Paley and I would rise to go. We would pick our way through the pitch-black streets and hasten to bed before hunger returned and made sleep impossible.

I had not been long in Le Vigan before a letter came from Sonia asking me to come back to Marseilles to help her; she was having difficulties with her papers and especially her entrance permit to the United States. She made references to my influence with the American Consul which made my blood run cold. I knew that her whole purpose in coming to Marseilles had been to arrange to join her husband who had left France at the time of the *débâcle*, either for Britain or for the United States. It seemed she had had news of him and that he was in America. Lazard, who had reached New York, had also written asking me to do what I could for his sister-in-law.

All this made me feel very discouraged. One of my worst weaknesses is that I am apt to bite off more than I can chew and expect more of myself than I am capable of giving. It is a form of vanity. It would have been quite simple to write and explain to Sonia that my name was now mud with the American Consul. Instead of this, though I did tell her that I was unwilling to face him again, I did not definitely refuse to do so.

It was the time of the Greek campaign and our spirits were very low. Greece had done more than almost anything else to keep us going lately, and we had come to believe she could beat not only Italy but Germany too, alone. It was one of the illusions we cultivated during those years as more fortunate people cultivate flowers. There had been endless jokes, all detrimental to the Italians and excellent for our morale. But it was beginning to look as though there would be no more jokes. The news of the German advance into Greece cast a black shadow over my visit to Marseilles.

This time I stayed with Sonia in her hostel. We got along together pretty well, but it was becoming perfectly clear that her firm intention was to make use of me, and I had the depressing presentiment that I was going to be made use of to no purpose. I knew only too well that the American Consul was a lemon I personally could no longer squeeze. I told Sonia quite honestly that I thought he was deeply suspicious of me, and that just because I knew he was suspicious I was going to look horribly suspect. She looked through me and said would I try all the same; her departure was being held up by the fact that she could not obtain the entrance permit from the American Consulate. In fear and trembling I set out, accompanied by Sonia, and we found the Consulate even more full of would-be emigrants than it had been the time I came there with Lazard's affidavit. The hall was a seething mass of people and it had apparently become a very difficult thing to get through to the Consul. What made matters worse was that whereas Lazard had something about him, something that no doubt people acquire only if they live and have always lived in a free country, Sonia seemed every moment to dissolve a little more and melt into the general type of the incipient refugee.

I sent in my name to the Consul. I thought I would be shown into his office and was preparing an ingratiating speech, when I saw him coming towards me, head and shoulders taller than the seething mass of anxious candidates for entrance permits to the United States. His face was icy. By the time he reached me my nerve had virtually gone and Sonia was looking so like a displaced person, though the term had not yet been coined, that I felt I was going to get little support from her. As soon as our rather strained greeting was over I broached the matter that had brought me once more where I had hoped never to come again. I asked the Consul whether he could do for Sonia something in the nature of what he had done for Lazard. He looked down at her as though she smelled; she looked up at him as though she expected him to clap handcuffs on her. He then turned to me and said that he could see no reason why she should not wait her turn like everyone else. As neither could I, we took our leave. And that was the last I saw of the American Consul, as it was the last I saw of Sonia, for although she had to bide her time she got away in the end.

Some weeks later I made yet another journey. Captain Bernard wrote telling me that he was in unoccupied territory for a few days on a visit to his wife's family at Tournon. He suggested I come and spend a couple of days there so that he might give me news of François and a real letter from him, and so that he might take a letter back to François from me and tell him how I was looking. This was an exciting prospect. Helena offered to keep an eye on Paulette and the children. I was still unaware that my maid was filching all my less noticeable possessions or that she was *au mieux* with most of the lads of Pétain's local Youth Camp. She had suggested that her elder sister, Yvonne, come down from L'Espérou to help her mind the children and I had agreed to this plan. Our connection with Paulette's family goes back three generations and I was—I am—fond of them all. I knew, and there I was right, that they would be kind to the children. It was not till a good deal later that I was told by the neighbours that Yvonne had been seen parading in my clothes and Paulette in my costume jewellery. Knowing them as I now do, I have not a moment's doubt that they were out on the tiles as naturally as a couple of cats in the spring as soon as the children were asleep. But I am still convinced that they took good care of them according to their lights. There was nothing wrong with the Reilhans' hearts. When Yvonne came down from her mountain fastness she brought me eggs and sausage and even a little butter as a present, and she was perfectly sincere in saying she was delighted to be of service to me; she and Paulette were willing girls in more ways than one.

And so once more I took the train and I travelled up the right bank of the Rhône with a singing heart. At Tournon I took a room in a modest hotel and there Captain Bernard found me and took me to join his brother and sister-in-law for lunch in a restaurant run by an old schoolfellow of his brother.

Captain Bernard proved to be a man after my own heart. He had reached the rank of chief engineer in the *Ponts et Chaussées* department of civil engineering without having the privilege of going through Polytechnique or any other of the Grandes Écoles, not at all an easy thing to do. He was a vigorous upstanding man, deeply religious but having great zest for life and no narrow moral code. He had no need to worry about the right or wrong of a thing for, like the Nicks, he carried in his heart a sort of mystical compass that unfailingly pointed to the north. He was a Gaullist from June 18th onward, and he it was who organized the resistance movement of Meaux, though I knew nothing of this at the time I am speaking of. My heart went out to him at the mere sight of his broad, laughing, fresh-complexioned face under its shock of grey hair. He gave an impression of exceptional moral and physical strength lightened by gaiety and intellectual vivacity. He looked the rock he was, but it was a pleasantly mobile rock.

In the restaurant we were shown upstairs to a private dining-room and there we were served a real black market lunch which beat our Marseilles dinner hollow. It was only when I came to Tournon that I realized how poor a part of France I had been fated to settle in. Food was a problem all over France, but there were degrees of difficulty, and Tournon seemed to be favoured.

Everyone was vastly amused at the amount I ate, and I myself was profoundly grateful that life in France had cured me of the notion that it is well-bred to restrain one's appreciation of good food. While I ate (and drank), Captain Bernard gave me a picture of life in occupied territory. He told me I would be far happier there because everyone was Gaullist. He also gave me good news of François and a letter from him.

I think I stayed in Tournon for only a couple of days. Bernard left before I did and knew nothing of the awful blow that fell upon me the last morning, just before I went to the station to take my train. On packing my suitcase I discovered that my bread-card had been stolen. As it was the beginning of the month this was a major catastrophe. I remembered the hungry eyes of my children when their meagre breakfast ration of bread was doled out to them, and a wave of despair broke in my heart. I knew quite well that my card had been stolen by the chambermaid, but I was incapable of accusing her. I told her I was desperate at losing it and begged her and the woman who ran the hotel to help me find it. They looked at me with cold indifferent eyes and told me I must certainly have left it behind when I came. I did not know then what I later came to know very well, that honesty walks hand in hand with a full stomach and that my own standards were on the downward path. I boarded the train with bitter feelings and a heavy heart.

Not long after this journey I had a visit from François. He crossed the line of demarcation between occupied and unoccupied territory disguised as a workman in a group of peasants who were allowed through to and from their fields. The journey from Meaux to the south of France took him three days. He was with me for only a very few days, and they were not nearly as happy as they should have been. Something in me seemed to have broken and I could no longer rise to an occasion. The whole of his visit was overshadowed by his imminent return to occupied territory and my heart was harrowed because he looked so worn out. He told me something then of his captivity. He had been made a prisoner on the banks of the Loire. He had stayed behind on his own initiative when his company retreated south. He wanted if possible to save some petrol barges from falling into enemy hands, but the river was bottled up with boats and the enemy advance too rapid.

During the very first day of his captivity he heard the German sentries who guarded the prisoners discuss what the latters' fate would be when the German army moved on farther south. Some of the sentries thought that the best thing would be to shoot them, others said that this would be illegal. At length François, as the only officer in the group of prisoners, was informed that if the French army continued to shoot down the German parachutists who were being landed in the region, the prisoners would all be shot. As there was no reason why the French should spare the parachutists, it seemed likely enough that this would happen. François there and then made up his mind that it would be too stupid to let oneself be shot in cold blood without making any effort to escape. He decided to kill his particular sentry some time that night and he looked about him for some sort of arm. All he found was a bottle, but he felt that should be sufficient. When night came he took his bottle out of its hiding-place and sat for a moment nerving himself for the task. It took him very little time to realize that he was utterly incapable of killing even a German in cold blood, merely to save his own life. He lay down again and faced the prospect of being shot. Next morning he was told that orders had come through that the prisoners were all to be sent elsewhere. What followed was what all prisoners at that time had to go through, the long marches day after day with blistered feet and very little to eat.

François's liberation three months later had been due to a stroke of luck. The news went round the camp where he then was that several categories of prisoners were to be set free on parole and were to resume their normal occupations in occupied territory. Among them were the civil engineers. At the same time he discovered that one of his former chiefs was at the head of the *Ponts et Chaussées* department of engineering in the nearest town. To be liberated he would have to take some action; he had not been serving as an engineer at the outbreak of war, so there was no post standing empty for lack of him, and there was a risk that no spontaneous demand would be made for his liberation. The other prisoners helped to smuggle him out in a fatigue party. Once in town he called at the office of his former chief who agreed to ask for his liberation. He then returned to the camp to wait on the event. He had not long to wait, but he told me it had been harrowing saying goodbye to those who stayed behind and with whom he had been through so much, and who would now be sent to Germany. He also said that he had no notion how exhausted he was till he reached Paris. Thence he went on to Meaux, where he had been given a post following a request made by his friend Bernard.

And so time passed, each day like a heavy disc that you must always cast anew; but it did pass and spring came again to Le Vigan. It came as it always does in the Cevennes with day after day of torrential rain, disastrous for our morale. Looking back on those early spring days I see the Rue du Vieux Pont where we lived under a deluge of rain that flows in muddy torrents underfoot. I see the dustbins standing by the doors, full of sodden refuse (which is unfair of me since they were emptied regularly enough except when there was a funeral—the dustmen did double duty as undertakers) and I see the small dark medieval shops in whose windows nothing was displayed but tight-rolled strips of liquorice, bottles of *ersatz* liqueur, their necks adorned with fly-blown bows of ribbon, and a great portrait of Marshal Pétain.

Even in the dreary days of our spring monsoon, Judith Paley and I had two sources of comfort, although neither could be indulged in with any frequency. We would sometimes squelch our way through the mud, unfearful of wet feet thanks to our made-to-measure wooden clogs, but with the rain from the roofs spurting down our necks, and we would wend our hopeful way to the Café des Cevennes on the main square of the little town, the Canourgue. There we would settle in the darkest corner and in husky tones implore the waiter to give us 'coffee' with milk in it. He never refused, though it was forbidden to serve milk in public places. Milk was strictly rationed and reserved for children. No drink I do believe, not even my native whisky, could so have warmed the cockles of my heart as did that horrible *ersatz* coffee, thanks to the milk. They gave us large breakfast cupfuls and we sat sipping in a state of bliss. We dared not come often; we felt it would be unfair. Our other orgy was when, armed with a towel and our monthly ration of green clay soap, we paid a visit to the public baths, the *bains-douches* that are to be found in most French towns. I forget what a bath cost; it must have been little enough though the place was kept very clean and the water was boiling-hot. But we had neither soap nor money to squander on such luxuries. I doubt whether we had more than one bath a month.

The rain made a deep impression on my mind, so deep that I have still a panic fear of the spring and autumn in the Cevennes, though once the ten days or so of downpour are over they can be the loveliest seasons of all. How often have I gone to bed to the monotonous sound of rain, to wake next morning to a strange silence and see a shaft of light piercing the shutter of my room. I would spring out of bed and throw the shutters open and find that instead of sheet upon sheet of rain, my window framed an arabesque of green leaves, leaded with blue and flecked with gold. The new day was there like a gleaming sparkling jewel, and I knew it was no isolated jewel but the first of a long string that would slip through my fingers, one by one, till the September rains came some three or four months later.

It was, I think, in the early days of the fine weather that Pasteur Boegner, the head of the French Protestant Church, came to preach at Le Vigan. The last time I had seen him had been when I was introduced to him at Principal Sir Thomas Holland's party that evening long ago in Edinburgh. I went to church to hear him preach solely because I wanted to speak to him after the service, as though contact with him could somehow link me with all I had left behind. What I thought he could do or say to lighten the load on my heart I do not know. I expected a miracle.

I went round after the service to the room where he was shaking hands with a few friends. I timidly approached him and reminded him that we had met in Edinburgh. He was polite and quite pleasant, but he never spoke the open sesame at which the doors of a lost world were to spring open. Poor man! He had other and graver things to do than to pour balm on the wounds of a lonely Scot. It could serve no useful purpose for him to become involved with a person of whom all he knew was that she was born British and had married into a family he was acquainted with. I see that now, but at the time I 'went weeping away'.

CHAPTER THIRTEEN

We were drawing near the turning point of the war though we had no notion that it was the turning point. We were bogged down in the wood and saw nothing but the endless trees.

June 21st is a date I shall love all my life. It was on that day we learned that Russia had entered the war, and it was to be on that day a year later that my third son, Nicolas, was to be born. On that particular June 21st I wrote in my diary:

'This morning we learned that Russia had been attacked and forced to join the dance. Every face in the streets and cafés was radiant with scarcely-suppressed joy. Vivens stopped Helena and me as we passed his shop on our bicycles and shook our hands with silent fervour. At a sign from him we followed him into the garage where he stores his wares. Broadly smiling, he slipped a tin of *cassoulet* into my shopping-bag for the celebration dinner. He took it for granted there would be such a dinner, and he was right. We have celebrated so many phantom occasions, bubbles that burst before the feast was over, that such an event must leave its mark.'

We decided to have dinner in my flat and we co-operated over the menu. There was the *cassoulet*, a small tin for four hungry people, but I had also a little rice, one of the most difficult things of all to obtain. We remembered that there were snails at the fishmonger's; the Scobs' washerwoman was a master hand at preparing them. The Scobs also undertook to bring a great deal of white Bordeaux.

That afternoon I had a visit from an aunt of Paulette's, Maria de la Baraquette she is called, to distinguish her from the other Reilhans. The Baraquette is an old tumbledown farm she owns in the Vallée du Bonheur, but Maria is a real woman of the woods, with matted hair and a wary eye, to whom a house is no more than a shelter for the night, and who spends most of her time walking from place to place on some purpose known to herself alone. Since our defeat she had taken to black-marketing as a duck takes to water, and could be seen now here, now there, with a sack across her shoulder. She would come into your kitchen, casting a wary look behind her, plunge her hand into the sack and produce a lump of butter wrapped in a sheet of writing-paper, or half a dozen eggs and a small piece of bacon. Actually she never asked black market prices of Helena and me, but she expected something in exchange, preferably and rather surprisingly soap, for which she was prepared to pay. Sometimes there would have been a clandestine kill at the Baraquette and she would have in her sack a hind or fore-quarter of mutton. On these occasions, delightfully steeped in secrecy, she would not even expose the contents of the sack but would plunge in a sun-baked arm that tapered off in a long wicked-looking knife and would hack off blindly whatever cared to come. On this particular occasion she brought a piece of bacon and half a dozen eggs. I planned to lay them aside for the children and on no account to sacrifice them to our rejoicings over Russia's unwilling aid.

The dinner was a huge success. Scob was radiant and bursting with Russian patriotism. He even talked of going over to the Communist Party. Wine flowed, our talk rose higher and higher like soap-bubbles opalescent with rosy dreams of victory. When everything was eaten we took what was left of the wine and gathered round a log fire to finish it. By eleven o'clock hunger was once more making itself felt. Reckless with wine, we decided to make an inroad on Maria's eggs and bacon. One small rasher each and one egg. There would still be something left for the children. I was drunk, drunk with Bordeaux and happiness when I swayed my way into the kitchen to prepare them. My hand shook when I was breaking the first egg and it slipped and fell on the floor. I stood helpless with laughter as I watched it crash and then dissolve into a still-life on the rough red tiles. The next four I broke neatly, each on its rasher of thick salty bacon, and as soon as they were cooked we fell on them.

At about midnight Scob and Helena left for home, but Judith and I were too excited for sleep. I opened the window over the narrow street and I heard a sound that made my heart leap. Far off, too far off for the words to reach me and destroy the illusion, some of Pétain's Youth were singing to the tune of Auld Lang Syne. Too foolishly moved for speech, I leaned far out of the window and drew a deep breath of the warm night air. It was then that a thought rose to the surface of my mind; this was St John's Night, the night fraught with divine magic. *Johannisnacht*. Auld Lang Syne died away and the air seemed to fill with the smell of lilac. In my mind rose another and very different music, wave upon wave, drowning the present in heart-rending memories. Then the braying of an ass broke through the song of an old man in love. Midsummer Night! Surely *Johannisnacht* and Midsummer Night were one and the same thing? Shakespeare and Wagner interwoven. Anything might happen on such a night. Perhaps the youth of Le Vigan (the real youth, not Pétain's Youth Movement) were celebrating the occasion with the old pagan rites forbidden by Pétain as unsuited to what he bleatingly referred to as '*La France meurtrie*'. Tonight France for a fleeting magical moment was no longer *meurtrie* but *en liesse*. We decided to go out and see whether anything was on foot.

Still a little drunk, though not with wine, we picked our way over the cobbled stones of the Rue du Vieux Pont, between the old houses with their blind windows. We went as far as the Canourgue, the big square where our *café au lait* orgies took place. No one was about and the cafés were all closed. We took the direction of the *Mairie* and at a turning found a small café open and in it some men deep in a penny-in-the-slot game of question and answer. We ordered some red wine and sat watching the play. It consisted in putting a coin in the slot, asking the machine a question, and then pulling a handle that set a ball spinning. The answer to your question depended on where the ball came to rest, a matter not only of chance but also to some extent of skill. We soon discovered that the men were asking the machine which country would win the war. We drew closer and became an integral part of the group. When at last after several disappointments England turned up trumps, by common consent the game came to an end. We all sat down round one of the tables and ordered each another glass of *gros rouge*. Two of our companions were railwaymen from the north; the other two were local workmen. They told us we had come too late for the celebrations but that they had actually taken place. There had been the traditional bonfire and the ritual game of jumping over it when the flames began to burn low. Afterwards they had all sat round it singing songs, not the songs of Pétain's Youth Camps but the far older songs of which France has such a store. Now everyone but these men had gone home to bed. One of the railwaymen rolled me a cigarette from his own tobacco, a generous gesture, for tobacco was now severely rationed—two packets of cigarettes a month and one of tobacco—and courteously held it out for me to lick the sticky edge myself. He then gave me a lesson in rolling my own cigarettes. He asked me how I managed since women were given no tobacco-card. I explained that Chanel, the Valleraugue tobacconist, had made capital of the fact that my name, Janet, has in French a masculine look and had given me a tobacco-card. But I took advantage of his lesson in rolling cigarettes to smoke the tobacco from my own fag-ends.

Our midsummer madness was short-lived. On June 26th I was woken by a loud banging at our front door. I leaped out of bed and opened the shutters to see what it could be. I saw a very unpleasant sight and one that I would never have expected to concern me. Two policemen were standing looking up at me. It was they who had been knocking. They called out that they wanted to speak to Madame Teissier du Cros. My heart missed a beat. I bade them wait while I dressed and then went down and opened the door to them. I led them upstairs—there was no sign from Judith Paley's flat as we passed—and ushered them into my room. They announced that they had come to arrest me. I asked for what reason and they answered that they had orders to arrest all Russians. My heart ceased to flutter. This was obviously sheer nonsense. I produced my identity-card. They remained unconvinced (rightly, since it was a false one); they said an identity card proved nothing nowadays. They had been told that I was a Russian; they wanted to see my passport. I explained that my passport was at La Coustète—I was beginning to lose my temper. I pointed out with considerable acerbity that they could if they would refuse to accept my identity card as proof that I was French, but the fact remained that if I was not French then I was British, not Russian. They made no reply but their faces stiffened to the 'orders is orders' look behind which officials love to take refuge. I took a firm line. I told them they must give me time to go and fetch my passport since they were willing to take that as sufficient proof. I swore that I would bring it straight to the police station as soon as I got back. They went grumbling away. I followed them down the street with my eye and an inner voice queried, 'What is more absurd than a policeman?' To which echo answered, 'Two policemen!' Then suddenly anger surged in my bosom, the furious anger of one who has always lived within the law, whose habit of mind has its roots in Habeas Corpus and who deep in her subconscious carries the conviction that no foreigner has the right to pass judgment on the British. But anger was soon washed away on a wave of laughter when I remembered that lying low on the floor beneath me was a genuine Russian, and not only was she Russian but she was also Jewish. The thought that it was she and not I who was counted as British because her father had been naturalized when he lived in London and she had a British passport, made the situation only more gloriously absurd.

But anger re-emerged and it sustained me during the long bicycle-ride to Valleraugue. I was in wonderful physical form in spite of under-feeding. The amount of uphill bicycling I was obliged to do to provide my family with food had turned the little flesh I had into steel muscle. Almost the whole of the ten or twelve miles from Le Vigan to Valleraugue are uphill, yet I had still breath in me to fan my fury. Nor had it one whit abated when I sailed back the next day with hardly a turn of the pedal, and made my way to the police station. There I demanded to see the lieutenant himself, with true Protestant scorn for intermediaries. I was shown into his office and before he could say a word I had

opened wide the dams and was giving vent to my fury. I
told him what I thought of a service which, believing me to
be a foreign national and undeclared as such, had waited so
long to make inquiries. I stigmatized him for not taking the
trouble, in a country where my husband's family was well
known, to find out something about me before going the
length of rousing me from my bed like a criminal. I listened
to my own voice rise with an eloquence I recognized quite
lucidly as being a good echo of my father at his angriest and
most eloquent. I wound up by handing over my passport
with a dramatic gesture and saying that I would go quietly
the day they came to arrest me as a British subject, but that
I refused to be put in prison as a Russian. I was so angry that
I never noticed till he handed me back my passport with a
low bow, without having so much as looked at it, that the
lieutenant was trying his hardest not to laugh. 'Madame,'
he said when I reached the end of my rodomontade, 'I
have no need for your passport at all. Your accent is to me
sufficient proof of your origins. As for arresting you as a
British subject, there are so many Germans to be arrested
first that I doubt whether we shall have the time!'

I think that was the last time I ever felt the proud bubble
of British moral indignation swell in my bosom. He pricked
it once and forever. I went humbly home.

But though I was safe, the police had been busy elsewhere.
When I hurried round to the Scobs to tell my story I found
their house in a turmoil. Scob had actually been arrested
and was now in prison. After he had been taken away the
police had remained behind to search the house. It had
been a very unpleasant experience for Helena, yet even this
lamentable occasion had had its funny side. The police had
gone through all the papers in the house and this included
a number of letters that had nothing to do with Scob.
Helena had found one of the policemen giggling over a
packet of letters my sister Letty had written years before
to Madeleine. They were composed in her very picturesque
French and their contents, so Helena told me, were more
than picturesque, they were frankly Rabelaisian. Helena had
been greatly relieved to see the man side-tracked by such a
disarming quarry. Her terror was that they should read her

father's letters. Pasteur Nick was already deeply involved in the resistance movement of Lille, and his house stood open day and night to any and every Jew, friend or stranger, who cared to take refuge there. The letters Helena received from him were sent through the medium of friends who passed from one zone to the other clandestinely, and in them he made no bones about his activities. Fortunately the police had been favourably impressed by a portrait Helena had of her father in full uniform, painted during the First War. At the sight of his beautiful face, of indisputable grandeur and command, and of the ribbons of his many decorations, they had paused respectfully to inquire who he was. And so, when they did at last lay their hands on a packet of his letters, Helena had only to say rather coldly, 'Those are my father's letters', for them to lay them down unread.

But Helena's anxiety for her husband was extreme. Fortunately she heard that Pasteur Boegner was in Nîmes for a few days. She went there at once to ask him to use his influence to have Scob liberated, which Pasteur Boegner immediately did. Scob was set free after only a weekend in prison. Actually I think that in any case the lieutenant of the *Gendarmerie* would have done his best for Scob. According to Scob's own account he had had quite a gay time in prison. He had also heard the lieutenant taking a telephone call from the St Hippolyte police, warning him that some of the English prisoners had escaped. He waited for a couple of days before taking action so as to allow them to get clear of the region.

When our emotion at last subsided I found that I had other difficulties to contend with. Henri and André had caught what looked like a bad cold. They threw the worst of it off fairly quickly but went on coughing in a rather alarming way. I sent for Dr Clarou who told me it had been no cold but a mild form of whooping-cough. I thought little more about it at the time, except to give them the prescribed medicines. I had no notion that even mild whooping-cough can have bad after-effects.

In the meantime I developed toothache for the only time in my life. I had to make up my mind to visit the local dentist whom I deeply mistrusted. He said the tooth must come out. I demanded a respite, and as I thought things over I gargled with the lotion the dentist had given me. The lotion did me more harm than good so I decided I would go to Lasalle and consult a Paris dentist I had heard Papa and Maman speak of. Like so many of us, he had taken refuge in his country house.

It was a long slow journey to Lasalle, which is about forty miles from Valleraugue. First you took a bus to Pont d'Hérault and another to St Hippolyte. There, after waiting for about an hour, you got another bus to Lasalle. It was to be the first of many visits I paid to Dr. Étienne, Professor of Stomatology at the Paris faculty of Medicine. At the beginning of the month I would make the journey by bus. At the end of the month, when my money was running out, I would bicycle one way. Fortunately for me it never even occurred to Dr Étienne to draw the guilty tooth and I have it to this day.

I got Dr Étienne to examine the children's teeth too, and one of the first things he remarked upon was that Henri was suffering from the after-effects of whooping-cough. He advised me to have him X-rayed. He suspected that the glands along his bronchial tubes were swollen (if I understood him rightly—I have no knowledge at all of anatomy), and that if he were left in that condition he would fall an easy prey to tuberculosis. He advised me, in view of his extreme thinness and general lack of tone, to send him to some mountain school at an altitude of at least three thousand feet to recuperate.

I admit that this was a shock. Living as we were doing from hand to mouth, where would I find the money to send Henri to a mountain school? But the problem was not immediate. We would soon be going to L'Espérou for the summer. In the meantime I had him X-rayed and Dr Étienne's diagnosis proved correct.

It is a miracle to me that I needed to be told all was not well with Henri. The fact is that all children at that time were so thin and unflourishing that there was no point of comparison. When I look now at the photographs taken of Henri at this time I am appalled. At the time I was blind. Much later, immediately after the liberation, when I took my third son, Nicolas, born in 1942, to stay with one of my sisters in Woodstock, and playing with him one day by the lake in Blenheim Park I met a young English mother with a small boy of the same age, the scales fell from my eyes and I hurried home and hid in my bedroom to weep.

CHAPTER FOURTEEN

We had learned to live without ever looking ahead, taking each day as it came; but now Henri's failing health showed that a sinister thread linked them. Even in the event of victory, the children would pay for what was being done to them, if only in their bones and teeth. This knowledge was like a grim relentless ground-base over which we wove the passacaglia of our uncertain lives, celebrating every possible and impossible occasion and enjoying what little there was to enjoy. Fortunately we were blind to the real extent of the damage that was being done.

Our official rations were so small they would scarcely have fed us three days in the month. Actually it was the fat shortage that taught me one of the secrets of French cooking. The first time I was asked how I now seasoned my food I was surprised; I had always thought of seasoning as a matter of salt and pepper. I now discovered that the French use their fats with a definite eye to the taste they give the food to which they are added. Butter is a universal fat, but bacon may be advantageously used in certain dishes; arachide oil is best for deep frying, olive oil must be kept for specifically Provençal dishes. And so on. At the time I am speaking of the fat shortage was such that I was haunted by an obsessional longing for bacon and eggs; but the lack of bread was a more immediate problem. The harm done when you lack fats is insidious; the bread shortage, when you are really hungry, is felt immediately. The French especially can taste their food only if they have bread to eat with it. Lucinde once told me a story of the First War. Bread had been rationed then too, though less severely. One Sunday when she was coming out of church a woman she knew stopped her and told her she had been given a recipe for something that made a good substitute for bread. Lucinde begged for the recipe, but as soon as she had grasped it she cried, 'But, Madame! to eat that I would require bread!' I too tried out a recipe I had seen in the local newspaper. It was for making pancakes out of flour and beer. The flour I had to grind in the coffee-mill from wheat bought illegally. The beer I bought in a café and it was thin and bitter, but I was nothing daunted. I mixed it with the flour and hopefully set out to fry the pancakes in an ungreased frying-pan. The mixture disintegrated and when the children came home from school there was nothing for their tea. I had run out of dried chestnuts which, boiled, was what I usually gave them.

But though we had little enough to eat that spring, we had almost a surfeit of flowers. It was the necessities of life we were denied; the superfluities sometimes came to us in a very curious way. That month of June my room was so full of lilies and roses that I had every evening to set the vases out on the staircase lest I wake with a headache. Helena and I had been given them by a woman who had a garden on the outskirts of Le Vigan. I remember sitting in my room one day and breathing in their fragrance with an intoxicated appreciation of its luxury. I turned the button of the little wireless set I had recently been lent by Edith Bargeton. She had come south from Paris where her husband worked, and was now living at La Coste with her small daughter, because as a Jewess she was safer there. Helena and I occasionally saw her and I had once stopped to dine and spend the night with her on my way from Valleraugue to Le Vigan. It was on this occasion that she had lent me the wireless set. I turned it on and the voice of Pierre Bernac singing Duparc's *Invitation au Voyage* swelled out till it filled the room and blended with the smell of roses and lilies. It was in such moments when memory came to haunt one of what a glorious thing life can be that it was hardest to bear what it had become.

But our time in Le Vigan was nearly at an end. I knew now that André and I would have to spend the next winter at La Coustète to save money, since Henri would be going to a mountain school. I felt that the sooner I got to work making the house comfortable with the furniture I had acquired, the better. Besides, the holidays were at hand and it would be foolish to keep the flat on while we were at L'Espérou. The time had come to break up the ephemeral home I had been at such pains to create.

The problem was to find transport for my belongings. Lorry drivers had risen in rank since France collapsed and were now the cocks of the roost. I knew one, a man called Boisson, and I had been told the name was no misnomer. He was earning so much with his *gazogène*, as the lorries that ran on charcoal were called, that apparently he was seldom sober and when drunk was inclined to violent language. I remembered him as a huge, friendly creature who had been recommended to us by Lucinde before the war to bring some furniture from Marseilles to Valleraugue. As soon as he had carried everything up to the house he had rolled up his trousers and gone down into the river, to reappear some minutes later with two gleaming trout which he had given to me. It was the first time I ever saw anyone tickling trout. My own sons were soon to become experts at this illegal art.

I had some difficulty in finding Boisson at home. I called again and again, and when at last I found him he may not have been exactly drunk but he was far from sober and was, in fact, very violent in his language. Still, he agreed at length to transport our things at a reasonable price the next time he went up to L'Espérou for wood; but I could not pin him down to a day. I had Maman's furniture taken to the station in a horse-cart and it went back to St Hippolyte. We then sat perched on our few remaining belongings till Boisson thought fit to come for what he contemptuously referred to as our *fourbie*, or worthless possessions.

There was no trout-tickling this time, nor did Boisson bring our furniture over the bridge and up to the house. I went down to the village for old Pieyre, the scavenger and my good friend. He carried everything over without help. I shall never forget the sight of him crossing the bridge with my tall Empire desk on his back, steady as a rock though bowed with age.

And so we were once more back at La Coustète. It was the height of summer when only to be alive was to have been enough; and for the first few days it did seem as though it would be enough, so lovely the valley was. Each new day that greeted me when I opened the door on to the terrace before making my way down by the outer steps to the kitchen, was like a gift. Sometimes I woke very early and was out on the terrace just as the sun flooded the Lusette, the mountaintop that is the first to catch its rays (hence its name) when all the other hills are still in shadow. The grass would be drenched in dew, a bird would be singing down by the river, giving point to the silence and seeming a part of it. The line of Lombardy poplars along the path that leads to the Mourgues' house opposite would be a shimmer of silver where the northern breeze caught and turned the leaves. Gradually the sheet of liquid gold would spill over from the Lusette and flood the valley, and a new fresh-faced sun appear above the eastern hills. The moment of silence was over and the cicada were tuning up.

Tante Berthe, Oncle Ernest and Lucienne were already in their house for the summer, with Lucinde. As of old, I would look in on them when I went shopping in Valleraugue. Tante Berthe's proud spirit was in a turmoil of revolt. She was much more of a fighter than Oncle Ernest and from the first she had very little patience with Pétain's passive attitude. She always made us welcome when we came and would regale us with winter pears baked without sugar in the oven. The huge garden they own on the outskirts of the village, le Mas Mouret, provided them with plenty of fruit and vegetables and Tante Berthe often invited us to a meal. I remember the day when, shaken back to normal standards by the still ceremonious atmosphere of Oncle Ernest's house, the scales fell from my eyes as regards the level our own behaviour had sunk to. The children were eating their dessert and had reached the point when they could scrape no more off their plates with their spoons. Simultaneously they raised them to their faces and licked them clean. I gave a gasp of hypocritical horror. They lowered their plates and gazed at me with round eyes full of reproach. 'But, Maman,' they said with one voice, 'you always allow us to lick!'

Betrayed. So indeed I did.

It seems strange to me that I should remember so well the happy moments in Valleraugue and have let the details of our struggles sink underground. I remember as clearly as if it were yesterday a morning when I threw the shutters back after a night of rain and thunder-storm. One of them caught the branch of a mulberry-tree that grew outside, and a shower of raindrops fell glittering from its broad green leaves. Beyond, the hill rose terrace after terrace to the sky. The mass of clouds was wearing thinner and thinner, allowing deep blue to break through broader and broader gaps. It was heart-breakingly lovely, an intimate loveliness that assails not only through the senses but through the very pores. Almost perpendicular against an apple-tree stood an old, crooked, hand-made ladder, seeming as organic as the tree itself. Ladder and tree became the focal point of all the beauty that saturated the morning air and shouldered responsibility for the emotion that surged and broke at their feet. Timeless they stood, the tree and the crooked ladder, safe from the grim shadow that lay on all our lives.

That I remember clearly. Yet it is only now, in writing about our return to Valleraugue, that I recall the struggle we had to find, for example, milk. At all times Valleraugue is poor in milk because there is little pasture for cows. Long before the war I had to learn to drink goat's milk, and I discovered that it is really very good if you drink it immediately after milking. I discovered, that is to say, that it is good with coffee but that, as Esther Laune once remarked to me, it does not 'marry' with tea. But even goat's milk was impossible to find; it was all booked for earlier comers than ourselves. I complained loudly at the *Mairie* when I found I could not obtain the children's legitimate ration, but as Monsieur Adgé, the secretary of the *Mairie*, pointed out to me, there were now more children than milk in the valley, and, as with the goat's milk, it was first come, first served. I succeeded in the end in procuring a couple of pints a day, but it came from a neighbouring village and I had to go to Valleraugue every evening at ten-thirty to fetch it when the cans came in on the bus. It was maddening to know that up at L'Espérou there was all the milk we could need and more, but so unhygienically produced that it was sour when it reached you if you had it brought down by *gazogène*.

Wood was another problem. We had nothing else to cook

on since liquid gas, coal, and paraffin were all impossible to obtain. During the first autumn of the Occupation we cut down our evergreen oaks for fuel. We should have to wait nine years before we could cut them again. There were still enough logs to get me through the summer, but then the struggle would begin. First I would have to buy a cart-load of tree trunks, then find someone willing to bring them down on his lorry, and some other person to carry them over the bridge and up to the house and chop them into logs that would fit our small stove. Each of these proceedings would add to the cost.

Just as the taste of walnuts eaten with honey carries me back to Mandiargues, so the combined smell of wood-smoke and stewed apples (our substitute for jam, and they were stewed without sugar) plunges me back in the atmosphere of La Coustète during the year we spent there. I remember one of the many summer mornings when I rose early and stole out of the bedroom so as not to wake the children, in whose room I slept. I did so not from any particularly kindly motive, but because the moments when I was alone, when there was no sound of quarrelling, when no one was falling into the *béal* and shrieking for help, or imploring me to hook a worm on his fishing-rod, such moments were so precious. To comfort myself in view of the menial tasks ahead of me, I had put on a pair of black satin pyjama trousers and a blue Chinese coat, all that remained to me of pre-war glory; and as I stepped on to the sunlit terrace I murmured to myself, 'I am Duchess of Malfi still!' This thought sustained me while I battled with the fire and suffocated in the smoke that always filled the kitchen when the fire was newly lighted. I flung the door and window wide open, allowing the smoke to escape, and I went out and sat on a stone till the air was clear. Then I prepared our 'coffee', dried roasted chestnuts ground in the coffee-mill, and I put on to boil the dried chestnuts which were the basis of our meal. While I was absorbed in this task, with my back to the door, a shadow fell on the kitchen stove and a voice, a hearty friendly voice exclaimed, '*Alors! Toujours sans homme, ma pauvre dame!*' '*Toujours sans homme!*' I automatically replied, and turned to see who had spoken. It was Audibert, the man who had supplied a swarm of bees for my hive (which had arrived in the end), and who made me periodic visits to see how they were progressing. He himself kept bees at his farm half way to Pont-d'Hérault. He was a man of liberal principles and a stout defender of the underdog. At that time I could claim in his affections the status of underdog since I was in at least theoretical danger from Hitler and the Vichy government. As far as Audibert was concerned, I had only one rival and that was Edith Bargeton, who as a Jewess was actually one up on me. He brought me news of her. His farm was just over the river from La Coste. He also brought me a sack of potatoes, and my heart soared at the sight. Nothing was more difficult to find. I was as usual short of money but I paid him one hundred francs down and he said the rest could wait. We wandered out and sat on a wall in the sun. I was waiting for an opening to broach the subject of his own honey.

I knew honey was worth its weight in gold and that I could expect none from my own bees for another year; would he sell me some at a price I could afford? I casually asked him what the price was this year. He said fifty francs the kilogram. My heart sank. It had been seven francs fifty before the war. He asked whether I wanted any; I said I doubted whether I could afford it and I hastily changed the subject. I knew it was a kindness to sell me honey at any price; more precious things may be had for it than money, tobacco for example. We returned to the subject of my own bees. He said I must plant flowers for them and drew me a glowing picture of what my garden would be like with bees to bring beauty to the flowers. He also conjured up visions of the honey that would flow from my hive in a little over a year if the bees were properly fed and the winter were mild. As he spoke I gazed at my poor stony terraces where only vine, mulberry and wild flowers grew. I gazed, and as I gazed they blossomed. They flowered in geraniums and hydrangeas and rhododendrons. Bees hovered over bright begonia-beds; butterflies settled on deep damask roses. I was busy training the twisted trunk of a wistaria along the front of the house when shrill noises off warned me that the children were awake and I must leave my garden of

Eden. We rose to our feet and Audibert bade me farewell. He took my hand in both his and told me he would bring me twenty pounds of honey and that I should pay the price I could afford.

Next day something very exciting happened. The postman brought me a letter from a friend of my youth, Cathy Gower, who had become the wife of Augustus John's son Romilly. The last time I had seen them had been in Edinburgh in 1938. Cathy's letter told me that she had had my translation of the book on Finland to review and that she had got my address from Routledge. Apparently the book had been finished by someone else. I was so excited at having a letter from her that to his great astonishment I tipped the postman twenty francs. This left me with thirty to last me till the end of the month, but it was July 27th; we could eat vegetables from the garden. Then I remembered that I had an appointment the next day with the dentist at Lasalle and I fell to calculating whether if I bicycled both ways I would have enough for a meal at the little restaurant there. Definitely not, as it turned out, for that afternoon old Pieyre came to consolidate the vine-trellis in front of the kitchen and I paid him twenty francs. When the time came I also gave him two cigarettes from an extra packet Chanel had let me have. I meant only to give him one, but when I looked over the wall to where he was cutting our brambles, and said, 'Pieyre, do you want a cigarette?' he gazed up at me with such fervour in his innocent blue eyes, saying, '*Madame François, j'en bave!*' that I handed him down two.

My last ten francs went the next day to pay the woman who came every morning for a couple of hours. All my money was gone. I would have to bicycle to and from Lasalle and go without food for the whole day.

I went across the river to fetch my bicycle from the Mourgues' garage where, rather from custom than with any definite permission, I kept it sheltered from the dew. Just as I was mounting it I saw in the distance Lucienne coming along the road towards me. She was on her way to do some painting up the valley, as I could see from the material she carried with her. A saving thought struck me. As soon as our greeting was over I asked her whether, oh whether, she could lend me one hundred francs. She could. She did. With an overflowing heart I mounted my bicycle and sailed off down the road. A voice in my bosom was recklessly singing, 'I'm afloat! I'm afloat!' Now I could lunch at the Lasalle inn! Now I could charge my bicycle on the bus instead of pedalling the long climb home!

Uphill and downhill I rode, but more downhill than uphill on the outward journey. Into the blazing sun I sped, then back into the shadow of the chestnut-trees, cool as a plunge into water. Every inch of the road as far as Pont-d'Hérault was familiar to me in its minutest details; on my left the great black rock that stands like a bathing elephant in the Hérault, then on my right the Bargetons' house and then the village where I visited a house with Lazard when he was planning a return to the simple life. On, on past the great sleepy house, pale pink with green shutters and slow steps curving to the front door, the first house I fell in love with when the country was new to me. Eight miles to Pont-d'Hérault, another eighteen or so to St Hippolyte-du-Fort and about eight more to Lasalle. The ground was less familiar after Pont-d'Hérault and I was beginning to flag by the time I reached Ganges. I stopped at a café to slake my thirst; there was nothing to be had but *ersatz* lemonade sweetened with saccharine, tepid and unappetizing. Soon I was passing through St Hippolyte-du-Fort with a heavy heart at the thought of Papa and Maman only a mile away. How happy had once been my welcome in the peaceful old house! They would still make me welcome but it would be because they have good hearts and not because they could possibly be glad to see me.

From St Hippolyte the road to Lasalle runs through friendly, intimate country. There are the same chestnut groves as between Valleraugue and Port-d'Hérault, the ups and downs are shorter and more frequent, but the road has the same twists and turns. The end was in sight and my spirits began to rise. The last landmark before the village is Le Campet, the de Billy property which I visited with Papa in that first arcadian-seeming year at Mandiargues. No doubt some of the family would be there for the summer, but I knew nothing of their present political opinions. In my experience 'sterling qualities' often ran to seed in Pétainism. I hurried on.

I went straight to Dr Étienne's house where I was shown through the cool kitchen to the little waiting-room. There I relaxed, which seems a strange thing to do in a dentist's waiting-room. There are worse things than the dentist's drill; besides Dr Étienne had the delightful habit of spraying his patients with some sort of narcotic before inflicting pain. I would be spared here what I dreaded even more than pain, the having my frail incongruous props knocked from under me. On the contrary, my batteries would be re-charged. I was like a virginia creeper, always reaching out for some support, and I had found one in Dr Étienne.

And so I relaxed, and not only in the waiting-room but also in the fatal chair. Dr Étienne had improvised a consulting-room in what had been the conservatory, a glassed-in terrace that opened off the sitting-room and overlooked a garden ablaze with sunlight and hydrangeas. Through a narcotic mist I gazed out over the mass of pink and blue flowers that are characteristic of the region, to the terraced hills beyond, whose sweeping line was broken here and there by a blue-black cypress-tree. The splinter of ice in my heart that dated from the downfall of France and grew apace as the months dragged on, melted and dissolved as I sat listening to Dr Étienne's metallic voice rise and fall, swell and retreat, and its place was taken by a feeling of deep peace.

At the little inn where I could lunch without giving up a meat-ticket, the innkeeper stood over me while I ate and entertained me with his talk. He showed me through the window his little Cochin-China cock and hen and the stream of tiny chickens running in their wake, and he boasted of their intelligence. The hen laid all her eggs on the kitchen dresser and was such a good layer that their number made up for their lack of size. At last, hazy with wine and food I slunk out into the torrid sunlight. As I waited for the bus I saw what looked like chocolate buns in the baker's window. It seemed unlikely, but I am an incurable optimist and I went in and bought one for each of the children and one for myself. I ate my bun in the bus. It was not a chocolate bun at all but was made of dark millet flour, unsweetened. Even at such a time it was uneatable.

On my way home I had an encounter which left me for days and weeks with a heavy heart and undid all Dr Étienne's good work. I was sitting in my usual café in St Hippolyte, waiting for the Valleraugue bus, when suddenly seven English officers came in and sat down at the next table. I mentioned earlier the British prisoners from the neighbouring barracks whom I used sometimes to meet in this very café. So far I had met no officers; my cronies had been privates. Most of them had the Cockney accent I find so difficult to follow. Our contacts had been friendly, sentimental even in a sense, but limited. At the sight of these officers who spoke the same language as myself and could probably tell me the things I wanted to know, I sat paralysed with emotion. I am naturally shy of addressing strangers, and it was some time before I plucked up enough courage to speak to them. They were surprised to meet a compatriot in such an out-of-the-way spot, and I think that at first they were a little suspicious of me. But they invited me to join them at their table. It should have been for me one of the great moments of the Occupation. Somehow it was not. To begin with they were so very English they brought on a violent attack of my Scotch inferiority complex. At least that is what I thought it was, but I think it was rather that for the first time I became aware that I had become something that was neither fish nor flesh nor even good red herring. I was in a very vulnerable condition. I had begun to grow the roots that were to bind me closer and closer to France, but I was unaware of it. I only knew, and I only knew it now, that I had shed my native skin. The seven officers started as one man to criticize the French, as taking it for granted I must share their point of view. Soon our talk turned to Mers el-Kébir. God knows I had risen in defence of what the English had done when my French friends deplored it—how much more mildly!—in front of me. I had explained to them everything that these officers explained to me. Now I was on the other side. I tried to make them understand how different things might have been if the English had shown more understanding of the deep humiliation suffered by the French navy. Round the little iron table we sat, but it was no round table conference. I was the prisoner in the dock and these seven men were my judges. To all my arguments they answered as one man, 'You are a civilian. You cannot understand the military point of view'. I felt foolish and hurt, foolish at having imagined the feelings of the French could possibly have been taken into account, and hurt at being thus excluded and reduced to the status of outsider.

Years later, when one of my sons said to me that he considered the 'you cannot understand' type of argument as of all types the most dishonest, I remembered that day and I agreed with him. At the time there was nothing I could say and I felt as though my heart would burst. With relief I suddenly noticed that the bus was ready to start. I rose to go. The seven men rose with me. One, a Major Gibson, wrote his name on a piece of paper and they all asked me to look them up when I came that way again. The bus was already full; I had argued too long. As I got in, one of the officers fired his Parthian shot. He said, 'Get in. You'll see, no one will give up his place to you!'

I got in and it was as he had said. I had expected nothing else. It is not the custom in the good-natured but ill-bred south, it is exceptional even in Paris, for a man to give up his seat to a young and able-bodied woman. On the other hand, no Frenchman would ever have spoken to me as these Englishmen had spoken, and it struck me that I had come to prefer consideration to gallantry. Yet that day I would have given all I possessed for one man to offer me his seat. Deeply humiliated, and trying to conceal the fact that I was in tears, I waved my judges goodbye.

CHAPTER FIFTEEN

Of what followed that summer I have less memory than of any other period of the Occupation. My diary, which I never kept at all assiduously, is a blank from January to December of that year. I cannot even remember whether or not I spent any of the summer at L'Espérou, though the children must have, in view of Dr Étienne's advice about Henri. I know I had another visit from François and that we met at La Coustète. Audibert turned up while we were there, with the promised honey. As he dumped it on the kitchen table he remarked to my husband, 'I'm bringing your wife honey because she is English!'

François, too, brought food with him. Through Captain Bernard he had made contact with a pork-butcher who did some clandestine killing and sold on the black market. He provided François with a veal-pie and some sausage which we ate with a sense of awe. I was beginning to discover what a refiner of the palate austerity can be. It is not, where austerity is a euphemism for underfeeding, that one becomes difficult; obviously not. But one comes through to a deep appreciation of the pure unadulterated flavour of things, even the simplest things. Illogically enough, it was austerity that taught me the underlying principle of French cooking. For French cookery does not seek to disguise but to enhance. It takes a thing, whatever it may be, with a deep respect for its inherent flavour. It mounts that flavour as you mount a jewel, it may be against a sauce woven of ingredients whose purpose is not to improve but to give point; or it may be that, eaten after this, before that, and together with a wine grown and matured in just such conditions and precisely long enough to arrive at its predestined *rendez-vous 'à point'*—the hour, the place and the loved one all, at last, together—it takes to its own wings and soars. Indiscriminate blending of tastes may blunt the palate till we miss the point. The lash of hunger, though it could, would and often did drive us to eat anything, yet willy-nilly brought us back in the end to first principles. We had so little; we must extract from it so much. We needed no sauce to recover man's primitive sense of taste. The Innocent Eye. The Naïve Listener. Why not the Pristine Palate?

In the course of the summer the great decision had been taken: Henri was to go to school at Le Chambon-sur-Lignon, in Haute-Loire. Maman had offered to help to pay the expenses involved. Our problem was to fit him out with the long list of clothes required by the children's *pension* where he was to stay. I ran my eye down it with desperation when it reached me, wondering whether these people had heard that there was a war on. Nothing could be bought without coupons, and they seemed to be reserved for the bombed-out, the pregnant and the newly-born. I cut down my skiing-suit to fit him. I mended and patched and adapted whatever came to hand, while Maman knitted jerseys and socks from the rough unwashed Cevenol wool. The wife of one of François's colleagues sent me a pair of skiing-boots that no longer fitted her son. In the end I could at least say that Henri had all the garments on the list, but in what a state!

When Henri was gone, André and I went and spent a few days at Mandiargues. Karin was there with her little boy, and François's sister Claude had come from Geneva. It soon transpired that we were all three pregnant, Karin obviously so, Claude imperceptibly so, and I only just certain that I was. I lay low about my condition except to Claude. I was afraid of a fuss. It was late September and the weather was beautiful and everything went smoothly. Once Ernest's son, Jean, came over from Meyrueis for a couple of nights with his wife, Ginette, which may in part account for things going so smoothly. They live in an eleventh-century castle on the far side of Mount Aigoual. It stands on an upland plateau of the kind called 'Causses', and they run it in summer as an hotel. It was such a hotbed of resistance that it was to come to be known as the *Château de la Résistance* and was awarded the Resistance medal at the end of the war. I did not know this at the time, but it was obvious that Jean and his wife saw eye to eye with me on all essential matters. I promised to spend a weekend with them some time in October.

François came back in the course of the autumn, this time on a regular mission in connection with the *Ponts et Chaussées* department of engineering. Out of the mist there rises the memory of a grey damp evening. We are walking arm-in-arm on the village square below Oncle Ernest's garden and I have just told him that our third child is on the way. I had hard work convincing him that the prospect, far from alarming me, delighted me more than it ever had before, though I had always been glad. He was glad too, but afraid for me. No doubt he saw more clearly than I did the reefs ahead of us. As I said earlier, I no longer looked ahead.

I think my memories of that autumn and winter at La Coustète are vague because I had no occasion to laugh. I had, however, one solid cause for gratitude. I had acquired the services of the daughter of a neighbouring farmer, a delightful girl called Gillette Boisson. She came every morning in time to bring me breakfast in bed and dress little André. She left at the end of the morning, having cooked our meals for the day. Better still, she declared herself willing to take André to stay with her parents any time I wanted to go away. This meant I could occasionally visit the Scobs in Le Vigan without trailing André along behind my bicycle. It also allowed me to spend the promised weekend at the Château d'Ayres with Jean and Ginette.

I went there late in October. The season was over and there was only one guest staying in the hotel, a French officer home from Syria where he had fought against de Gaulle's troops at the time of their landing. I did not meet him at once.

During my brief stay, and to make up for what they knew were the conditions of my life at La Coustète, Jean, Ginette and Madame Roussel, Ginette's mother, treated me like a queen. I was given the best bedroom, and every morning my breakfast was brought me on a tray by a chambermaid with a frilly white apron. I had forgotten such things existed.

It was on the second evening that I met the French officer. We very quickly got into an argument. He was reticent about the English and bitter against de Gaulle. He believed, and like Passemard he really did believe it, that the attack on Syria was part of the old Intelligence Service policy with regard to the French in the Near East; a taking advantage of their misfortunes to eliminate them as influence from that part of the world. De Gaulle was to him a traitor who was sacrificing French interests to his own thirst for power. He was sick with horror at having had to fight against his own people, and sincerely convinced that the Vichy forces were right in opposing de Gaulle. He was shaken, too, by what was probably his first experience of real warfare; it seemed to him that its inherent cruelty was the cruelty of France's old enemy.

I had no real arguments to oppose him. I was not even aware that I needed any. I was so naïvely certain that the British Intelligence Service was incapable of behaving as he said that I soon became as worked-up as he was himself. We walked up and down the immense monastic-looking vaulted dining-room arguing. His fury was directed especially against de Gaulle, but illogically enough I found myself identifying de Gaulle with Britain and taking everything he said as an insult. Madame Roussel, Jean and Ginette got into a huddle in a corner and every time the officer's back was turned to them they made me desperate beseeching signs to keep calm. But I was beginning to be carried away by what I took for my own eloquence. Besides, I had no notion how dangerous a guest he was in my hosts' eyes. I knew nothing of their clandestine activities, nor how unimportant it seemed to them—and how useless—to try to convince this man that he was wrong. There were more urgent matters on foot. They could not refuse to take a guest in because of his opinions; after all, they ran an hotel. But they could see to it that discretion was a screen for their own valour.

In the end we both calmed down and we bade each other goodnight courteously enough. We avoided meeting again.

Another visitor arrived while I was at Meyrueis, Madame Roussel's brother, whose name was Harrison. They were both of English descent, tracing their ancestry in some vague way from an Earl of Bridgewater whose arms were on some of their possessions. I went walking in the castle grounds with Monsieur Harrison. He told me he was doing the same sort of job as Donald Caskie. In occupied territory everything was well organized for helping British prisoners to escape. The difficulty began when they crossed the line of demarcation into unoccupied territory. He had come to the south from Paris to try and organize something. He wanted to find people willing to give a night's shelter to escaped prisoners and then direct them to the next address on the list he was trying to establish. He sounded me as to whether I would be willing to let La Coustète figure on the list. I heard myself answer that I would, in a voice that quivered with fear and excitement. He then inquired what my immediate plans were, and it was at this point that the fact of my being pregnant came to the fore. He at once clamped down and changed the subject. I realized that he had decided I must be kept out of the circuit because of my condition. I was uncertain what I ought to do.

I left Meyrueis that same evening. Madame Roussel gave me a packet of real coffee; Monsieur Harrison handed me privately an address in Nîmes and an ordinary air-mail envelope with nothing written on it. He said that if ever I felt that I was in a position to be of help I was to go to Nîmes, to the address he had given me. I was to hand the air-mail envelope to the person who received me and leave the rest to him. He added, and on this he insisted, that I was not to do so before very mature consideration.

I never was in Nîmes except when I passed through on my journey north to Paris. Even if I had had occasion to go there, I doubt whether I would have done as he suggested. I suspect that sheer shyness would have prevented me. I cannot see myself walking into the flat of an unknown man and handing him an air-mail envelope. I would be too afraid of being made to look an utter fool. I admit, too, that mature consideration is not my path to glory. I might in an expansive moment let myself in for that sort of thing, and once in I might, I hope I would, live up to what I had let myself in for. But mature consideration must always remind me of one awful fact. All that would be required to make me talk would be a glass of some alcoholic liquor. A couple of glasses of wine, and I would be confiding some seemingly

insignificant but probably essential fact to anyone who gave
me the drink. Torture would be quite unnecessary—though
certainly effective. I would like to add that maternity doth
make cowards of us all, except that I know it to be false.

The Scobs and I were now separated by some dozen
miles. but they remained my greatest source of comfort.
There was a new bond between Helena and me, for she too
was expecting a baby. We spent one cold autumn weekend
in the Nicks' house at L'Espérou and scoured the country
round for food for our hungry families. We set out from
L'Espérou on our bicycles the very first afternoon and rode
along the valley of the Dourbie, We meant to go as far as
the village of Dourbies to see whether we could find some
meat, but we never got there. We were tired, evening began
to fall before we were halfway there, and one of our tyres
punctured just before Les Laupiettes. We had to turn back
and before we reached the first village on our way home,
night had completely fallen. The country round us was cold
and wild and a little frightening. We could see nothing but
could hear the sound just beneath us of the Dourbie which
had gaily gleamed like a ribbon of liquid steel between the
red bracken and the gold and russet beach-trees on our
hopeful outward journey, Helena suggested that we stop
at Les Laupies. She knew a family of peasants there. Her
mother used to buy their butter and cheese at a time, long
long ago, when they found them hard to sell. We stopped
and knocked at their door. A white cross was painted on it
to indicate that they were Catholics. The door was opened
by one of the loveliest old women it has ever been my good
fortune to see. Her hair was quite white, but she had a pair
of the youngest and most undisillusioned eyes I ever saw in
any face but a child's. She made us welcome and set chairs
for us by the fire. Her husband and daughter came in. Both
were very deaf but they showed by their smiling faces that
they too were glad to see us. It occurred to me then, and
nothing in all the years of our subsequent friendship ever
caused me to change my mind, that these people really
were what children imagine the grown-ups they love to be,
completely and naturally serene and good.

We explained our troubles to them and they invited us

to *manger la soupe* with them, using the popular French expression that is equivalent to the biblical breaking of bread. We gathered round the table and the soup was set before us, a real peasant soup made of potatoes and other vegetables straight from the garden, and whose secret is the piece of bacon which is boiled with the vegetables and removed before serving to be used again the following day. After the soup came a piece of home-made sausage, home-made butter and the family's ration of bread. Old Madame Passet was so anxious to make us welcome that she suddenly rose and went to a cupboard in the wall. With a slightly defiant glance at her husband, she produced from it, holy of holies, the home-cured ham. I think that in her generosity she would have given us the house itself if the thing had been possible.

That evening meal has remained stamped in my memory as one of the great moments of my life, and not merely because of the food and the good red wine we drank with it. It was to be the first of many visits and its spirit has presided over them all. I never found any of the three Passets other than we found them on that first occasion, loving, generous, confiding and poor. During the Occupation they had their brief moment of relative prosperity, for they had then a steady market for their milk and butter and cheese, but it was only very relative prosperity. They never sold at black-market prices.

They would have had us stay for the night, but we knew that Tante Berthe, who was also food-hunting at L'Espérou, would be anxious if she heard we had not returned. We left on foot, each having bought some half-dozen little cheeses and a small packet of butter. They had moreover made us a present of something almost as precious as butter, a couple of pounds of potatoes for our next day's luncheon, and a small bottle of oil in which to fry them, an unheard-of luxury.

We set out with our hearts in a glow of happiness, but the way was long, the wind was icy. When the lights of Les Laupies were far behind us we suddenly remembered that a Spanish prisoner had escaped from the Valleraugue police station. The wretched Spaniards, refugees from the Spanish war, had many of them been arrested on suspicion of communism, and though in our hearts we knew what kindly creatures they were and how harmless, the shades of night were working on our nerves and we soon came to imagine this poor fugitive grown evil through fear. We saw him lying in wait for us at every turn of that twisting road. I do not know whether we laughed or trembled most, for every time a rustle in the bracken set our hearts beating and then proved to be but the wind, we were shaken with helpless laughter. I do know that we were glad when at last we saw, far ahead of us, the faint twinkling lights of L'Espérou. Poor Tante Berthe we found in a fever of anxiety. She had stirred the whole village up and had drawn a piteous picture of us two pregnant women fallen down a cliff somewhere on the road between Dourbies and L'Espérou We felt extraordinarily foolish. No one had known that we were pregnant and we felt it was too soon to broadcast the fact. But it would seem to be the fate of town folk to appear foolish among country people.

Even so, our day's emotions were not yet over. When we reached the Nicks' house we lit a roaring fire and sat down on either side of it to talk, talk endlessly, as we did whenever we were together. And when the hour of midnight was waning into the first hour of morning and the fire was smouldering at its hottest, it seemed to us that someone softly tried the door. Soon we were so worked up that we thought we not only heard the door-handle move but even saw it turn. We sat for a moment with our hearts in our mouths, scarcely even daring to speak. In view of what were to be the respective attitudes of Helena and of myself in face of danger when danger really came, I am amazed at what followed. For it was I who suddenly rose to my feet and determinedly seized the poker. It was I who advanced towards the door with no uncertain step and flung it wide. There was nothing there but the blasty autumn night, nothing but the mountain scene which we had always associated with a summer sky. The sky was starry, but wild clouds blew ragged beneath them and it was bitter cold. We closed the door, filled a couple of wine-bottles with near-boiling water and clasping them we crept upstairs to our chill beds.

I wish I had sufficient mastery of words to give a true

impression of L'Espérou as it appeared to us when we awoke the following morning. It was cold and blowy but gloriously sunny. The garden was gay with red and gold beech-leaves blown there by the wind. A lorry had come up from the plain to fetch a load of the mushrooms that spring from the rich moist beds of dead leaves in the beech forests after the autumn rains. All this was familiar, but there was an exotic note which no one in his wildest imaginings could have expected to find anywhere in the Cevennes. A group of Indo-Chinese conscripts whom it had not yet been possible to send home to Indo-China had been lodged in temporary barracks some few hundred yards from the village, and against the blowy October sky we saw silhouettes as familiar but as fantastic as would be the silhouette of a stork carrying a baby in its beak, or an Arab seeking refuge behind a kneeling camel from a rising sand-storm. For the silhouette of an Indo-Chinese peasant, bare feet in wooden-soled sandals and carrying water from the fountain in pails slung from a yoke on his shoulders, was for us as much a part of an illustrated book of legends as either of these. Yet, coming and going from our homely village fountain we saw just these fantastic figures, and for the first time in my life I experienced for myself the species of malaise that is caused by the presence in a primitive population of an ethnic minority. One Indo-Chinese, two even, L'Espérou could have digested, but not—how many were there? Thirty perhaps, certainly almost as many as there were adult male members of the Espérou population. They clung together, as was normal; they knew very little French and certainly no *patois*. For us they were the foreign element from which anything might be expected. We bore them no ill-will, but we feared they might—must, in view of the circumstances—bear *us* ill-will. Our days were strange and our nights hostile. In view of all that has happened in the world since that autumn of 1941 I am filled with remorse to think that we did literally nothing for this stranger within our gates. But I do not know what we could have done, for lack of a common language. The only contact Helena and I had with them was when in the course of the morning they came to our kitchen window with pieces of soap which they held out, repeating the single word, 'Onions!' We soon discovered that what they wanted was to exchange soap for onions. Soap was a thing we never got, not real soap, which this was, provided no doubt by a grateful government. They seemed to have little use for it and an insatiable longing for onions. Was it honest to exchange unrationed onions for soap that would have fetched a high price on the black market? We scarcely stopped to pose ourselves the problem. We poured onions into their bag and pocketed the soap.

When François came to visit me that autumn, food was not the only thing he had brought me. He brought, too, a couple of volumes of Dickens which he had bought in Paris: *Our Mutual Friend* and *Martin Chuzzlewit*. Any laughs I had that winter I owed to Mrs Gamp and to the Rooshan Empire. But though I drugged myself with Dickens, even borrowing French translations from Oncle Ernest's library, it was Jane Austen who saved my soul. Dickens's laughter rings out against a background as sinister in its way as that of Europe under German occupation; Jane Austen lives, and makes you live, in a luminous world whose characters are never evil and where even the vulgar are civilized. Not only during the winter of 1941 but throughout the whole of the Occupation she was the gauge I used to plumb the abnormality of the world as we then knew it, a world which tended to impose itself as normal. Gradually, as in Poe's story, the walls were closing in on us, cutting us off from everything beyond and driving us towards not one but three pits, between which we could choose. We could be martyrs, torturers' accomplices, or cowards. But at Jane Austen's touch the walls sprang back, the pits vanished and the world beyond appeared. You had only to establish a link at any point between Jane Austen's England and the world Hitler was forging to know that Hitler's world was a nightmare which could never last. My favourite link was to imagine Miss Bates being roused from bed at five in the morning by the Gestapo. I have lived the scene again and again, from the alarmed opening of the door by a round-eyed Patty in her nightgown, to the appearance of Miss Bates in curl-papers, volubly thankful that her mother is a little deaf. At the mere image my world would right itself. I knew then that there was another path out of the nightmare forest—to endure without dishonour, the path of the shorn lambs.

I had need of books to keep me going that winter, for it was both cold and lonely. Its memory is so bleak that even in imagination I can hardly bear to go back into it. I missed Henri, and he wrote me unhappy letters. He found it difficult to adapt himself to communal life. He begged me to send him a 'friend', by which I knew he meant some toy that smelled of home and could be taken to bed. But his toys were all in Edinburgh. I scoured the Valleraugue shops but could find only a wooden painted bird which must have served his purpose indifferently.

My nearest neighbours in the valley were the Lévi-Strauss *ménage*, and we were becoming fast friends. When André was safe asleep, I would pay them short visits and we would listen to the BBC and to the American programme when we could get it. I did not know at the time that their son Claude had escaped to the United States and was speaking for the American radio. They apparently heard his voice from, I think, Washington, every day. It was a state secret which they wisely shared with no one.

Cancabra was then a more comfortable house than La Coustète. Raymond had done the plumbing himself when they first bought the house. He had also had a rough wooden interior staircase put in, whereas I had to go out every time I went from one floor to the other. They had had the primitive front door replaced by one that kept the draughts out, and as they had a good stove the house was much warmer than mine. To me Cancabra seemed a very haven, but I dared never stay long because of André. Once when I had gone down to the village as usual at ten-thirty to fetch the milk I saw as I rounded the bend of the road on my way home La Coustète ablaze with light. As I had left it in darkness I was very alarmed. I knew that André must have woken up and be searching the house for me, and I was terrified lest he should set out for Valleraugue in pursuit of me and fall through one of the many gaps in the bridge into the foaming river. Clinging to my precious milk-can, I began to run down the narrow stony path towards the bridge. It was so dark I could scarcely see where the bridge began. I felt my way from plank to plank—I could just see the reflection from the water below—almost as afraid of falling in myself and never reaching André as of his having fallen in. I stumbled from terrace to terrace up to the house where I found André sound asleep in bed. He told me afterwards that when he realized that I was gone he had decided that the best thing he could do would be to go back to bed. I date his subsequent independence from that day.

My chief trouble throughout the autumn was that I felt very sick. This was normal enough, but I thought I would see whether the St Hippolyte doctor could do anything for me. He diagnosed low blood pressure and prescribed injections. I recovered so quickly that I had to use only one of the two boxes of ampoules he made me buy. But though I no longer felt sick, I remained miserable from cold and hunger. I made up a bed for myself in the alcove where the kitchen used to be. There at least I escaped the draughts from under the doors; but for lack of sufficient blankets and warm clothes I lay shivering all night long, reading and re-reading Dickens. It was that winter that I took to sleeping in an ermine cape inherited from the Mactavish grandmother whose father helped to found the Hudson's Bay Company.

Christmas brought François and Henri. Henri came first; François was to spend a couple of nights with his parents and then bring them to lunch with us on Christmas Day. In preparation for the event I spent a day at Le Vigan with Helena, and we trekked about the town together hunting for food and toys. We found some brightly painted wooden toys, but food there was none. We were wandering disconsolately through the streets when we were brought up short before the pork-butcher's shop by an incredible sight. The window was empty of all the normal appurtenances of a pork-butcher's shop; in their place was a heap of truffles, marked at some absurdly low price. We hastened in, fearful of some misunderstanding; but no, the truffles were being sold at just that price. Truffles do grow in our part of France. Perhaps the difficulty of transport had prevented their being sent to their usual market; perhaps some patriot-philanthropist had recklessly decided to pour truffles like

balm into the wounds of his poorer fellow-countrymen. We
did not stop to inquire. We bought each a couple of pounds
and made for home, trailing behind us the most glorious
smell in the world—that of fresh truffles.

My problem was to find something with which to eat
our truffles, for I had never heard of *truffes à la serviette*.
It was only on Christmas Eve that I managed to persuade
a Valleraugue shopkeeper to kill one of her rabbits for me.
No rabbit before ever was in such royal company.

The same evening, with a light heart, I decorated my
Christmas tree. I had written a week earlier to Yvonne
Reilhan asking her to have one of her brothers cut me down
a small fir and put it on the Valleraugue bus on Christmas
Eve. Though I got no reply, I never doubted she would do
as I asked. I went down to the village on the appointed day
and when I saw two Christmas trees being unloaded and laid
by the roadside, I took for granted that the small one was for
me. I charged old Pieyre to drag it back to La Coustète and
set it up on a table in the big living-room.

When Henri and André were safe in bed, I lit a roaring
fire and spent a glorious evening decorating my tree. In
spite of the fire it was bitter cold, for the north-west wind
was blowing. The middle rafter of the sloping roof is quite
eighteen feet above the ground and the room itself measures
about thirty feet by twenty. Under the door is a three-inch
gap through which the cold wind swept the floor. No fire
can heat such a room, but I was so happy that I scarcely
felt the cold. At nine o'clock I turned the button of the
wireless. It was possible to get through to England only
from nine o'clock onward, and usually the programme was
violently disturbed. That night I got the news so clearly that
I had no need to hang over the instrument, but could go on
decorating my tree while I listened. Before the news was
given, the national anthem of every country that had fought
or was fighting Germany was played. At each new anthem
the lump of sentiment swelled bigger in my throat, but I held
out till it came to the Greek anthem, with its rapid tempo and
lively rhythm, expressive not of self-righteous patriotism but
of the defiance of a fighting-cock. One of my oldest and
dearest friends is an Athenian, and the thought of her and

of my other Greek friends now rose to the surface. Before even the anthem was finished I was weeping floods over a wooden gardener pushing a wheelbarrow full of wooden fruit, my present for André. Then it occurred to me that no doubt my sister Alice in the Netherlands was decorating *her* tree* to the sound of the same programme, and the thought comforted me because it brought her so near.

I was still busy with my tree when, as once before, a knock came at the door. Again when I opened it I found a clergyman, this time the Methodist minister of Valleraugue. He apologized for disturbing me and explained that he was in search of his Christmas tree. I then learned to my horror that both the trees lying by the roadside were his. He had himself gone up on foot into the mountains to cut them down, one for his chapel and the smaller one for his family. He had left them by the roadside to be brought down to Valleraugue on the bus. While he was speaking he looked past me and saw his tree standing in the firelight, all decorated and ready for the morrow. He melted at the sight and said that I must keep what in fact I had stolen. I felt very ashamed, the more so that I found it impossible to make my voice sound sincere when I protested. He assured me that he thought nothing of going up again early the next morning to fetch another. He looked such an epic figure, so much the hero of a Brontë novel, that my voice trailed away into silence and I kept the tree. When I look back I wonder at myself; but so I often do when I look back on my behaviour during the Occupation.

On Christmas morning François arrived with his parents, and he brought me two parcels. I opened the first and found, nestling in tissue paper (at that time a treasure in itself) a tiny, cherry-coloured hat, elegant beyond all belief, and a perfect sample of the new wartime Paris fashion. Carefully following François's instructions, I perched the cherry-coloured absurdity over my left eye and went and looked in the glass. I saw, gazing back at me in wonderment a face I had not seen for a long time. At the sight, hope and youth rose in my veins like sap. Only a Frenchman, I

---

* I was wrong; the Dutch have their tree on St Nicolas Day.

reflected, would have known what a hat can do to a woman. Then suddenly I caught sight of the rest of the picture, the old jersey and skirt, the bare legs, the wooden clogs. I remembered the life I was living, sawing wood, drawing water, cooking, cleaning. I remembered my condition. I sat limply down on a chair and I laughed and I laughed. In that one long gust of laughter I made up for all the days I had lived that winter without laughing out loud once.

It was then that François suggested I open the other parcel. In it I found a cherry-coloured three-quarter length coat to go with the hat. It was of the thinnest material but it was beautifully cut with balloon sleeves.

It was with all my old zest for life restored that I went down at last to the kitchen to prepare our Christmas luncheon. I made strange pastry out of little more than home-ground flour and water and I converted the rabbit and truffles into a pie. Emma and Raymond Lévi-Strauss were our guests and they brought an apple-tart. Papa and Maman brought wine and I forget what else. We were a very gay party, and when everything was eaten we went up to the living-room for the Christmas tree. There we were joined by Tante Berthe and Oncle Ernest. When all the presents were distributed I left the grown-ups huddled over the fire and went down to prepare something in the nature of tea. Oncle Ernest followed me down, but he stopped on the first floor to watch the children play with their toys. I spread the children's ration of bread with condensed milk, of which as a pregnant woman I was allowed a small monthly ration. On top of the condensed milk I put unsweetened apple-sauce. I left them each a plate thus garnished on the kitchen table and prepared a tray for the rest of us, which I carried up to the living-room. Oncle Ernest was still downstairs so I went back to fetch him. What was my horror to discover that in my brief absence he had cleared the contents of one of the children's plates! I was not the only one who was losing grip as regards food.

CHAPTER SIXTEEN

That Christmas night François and I made a last attempt to sleep in the *magnanerie*. We dearly love the great room with its high raftered roof, where squirrel-dormice come and go at twilight and at dawn; we were unwilling to admit defeat. How bitter cold it was! Not an ounce of my flesh nor the marrow of a single bone but holds to this day the icy memory of that Christmas night. Though we piled wood on the fire, though defying the stringent electricity restrictions we fixed our feeble radiator so that its heat fell on our heads and shoulders, though we filled an old champagne bottle with hot water for lack of a real hot-water bottle, still we shivered. Finally François put on a couple of jerseys and I had again recourse to my ermine cape, and so we slept at last. When François's few days of holiday were over and he returned to Meaux, taking Henri with him to deposit him on his way at Le Chambon-sur-Lignon, I regretfully closed the living-room for the winter and returned to my downstairs alcove.

It was by the stove in the downstairs room that every evening I gave André his tub. One January evening we were going through the usual ritual when I thought I heard a faint knock on the door. I opened it, but there was no one there. Then suddenly I looked down. There on the stone step sat the enormous toad I often met when going to or from the spring behind the house. It was looking up at me with something closely resembling a smile. It was a strange moment. I was certain it had knocked because it knew that we were lonely. In truth I suppose it had seen the ray of light under the door and, moved by some instinct peculiar to its kind, had jumped against it. But standing there under the starry winter sky, with a crescent moon shining down on me, I expected every moment to see it dissolve and re-assemble as an enchanted prince. For a moment we gazed at each other, the toad and I, but nothing happened. At length André broke the spell by asking who was there. 'Only a toad', I said in doubtful tones, and closed the door. But ever afterwards when we met on the path to the bathing-pool, I greeted it as a friend.

Day by day the cold increased. As our house is on the sunny side of the valley, we had about three hours a day of warm sunshine, but all the rest of the twenty-four hours were iron-cold. When the first morning rays reached us we would see, little by little, the hoar frost melt on the grass and turn to glistening dew. At last a clear-cut line divided our side of the valley from that of the Lévi-Strauss house which the sun never reached and which remained silver-white. One morning I went down the path at the back of the house to fetch our drinking water, and was stopped short by an unnatural stillness. The roaring of the waterfall had ceased, and the sight of it, petrified to silence, was the more breathtaking, the more hallucinating, that the impression it gave was not of motionlessness but of violent motion suspended. The frozen water still poured foaming over the rock that overhangs our bathing-pool, but time, it seemed, time had ceased to flow.

During all this period of intense cold I had neither stockings nor socks; we had followed the Scobs' example and had clogs made to measure by the *savetier* of Le Vigan. But my clogs and my dressing-gown were my only assets. Everything I owned—and it was little enough—was gradually becoming too small and I had no real winter coat.

On one of the brightest but coldest days I mounted my bicycle and rode to Notre-Dame-de-la-Rouvière to visit an Englishwoman whom by an odd chance I had met. It had happened one day when I was sitting in the bus on my way home from a visit to the Scobs. A woman with a small boy got in at one of the stops, and she looked so unmistakably English that my heart missed a beat. When she addressed the driver in fluent but very English French, I surmounted my dislike of speaking to strangers and asked her, superfluous question if ever there was one, whether she was in fact English. She almost fell on my neck. For both of us it was a moving moment. The last thing we either of us expected was to meet a compatriot in that region of all regions, at that time of all times. Soon she was pouring her story out to me. She had been a masseuse, and one of her patients, a retired General, had left her a little money, enough to allow her to spend a holiday on the Riviera. There she met and married a Bulgarian. The boy was their only child. It had been a late marriage; she told me that she was then fifty-four years old and that her son was the same age as Henri. In a breathless undertone she confided that her husband was pro-German and that she was not even allowed to listen to the BBC She was starved for news of the outer world. She begged me to come and visit her, but specified that it must be during one of her husband's many absences. She promised to write to me. It was in answer to a written invitation that on January 8th I set out for Notre-Dame-de-la-Rouvière to spend the day with her.

Notre-Dame-de-la-Rouvière stands on the brow of a hill high over Le Gasquet, the first village on the road from Valleraugue to Pont-d'Hérault. You reach it by a road that branches off at that point and climbs the hill by a series of hairpin bends. In the far-off happy days before the war it was a favourite place to which to take visiting friends on moonlight nights. There was a café where, if warned in time, they would give you dinner. In those days we motored up, but since the war I had been up the stiff climb several times on my bicycle. On this occasion the icy north wind was so strong that it blew me up the steep ascent, and for once I found the going easy. My English friend lived higher still, at Le Puech-Sigal. As the road took me no farther, I did the last part on foot. On the highest crest of the hill I found a little white concrete cube of a house and my friend waiting at the door to welcome me with open arms. She explained to me that her husband had built the house with his own hands, carrying all the materials up from below on his back. It was for their son's health that they had decided to leave their home in Nîmes and settle in the country. The Bulgarian had scoured the Cevennes to find a suitable place in which to build their new house. Why he hit upon Le Puech-Sigal I have no idea. It is hard to imagine a more isolated, or in winter a more wind-swept, spot. Over an excellent meal cooked by my friend herself in a kitchen that stood outside the house and consisted of three walls and a tin roof, she told me that she had had to learn to cook the French way because her husband liked good food and ate a great deal of it. In spite of the restrictions, he managed to supply her with plenty of raw materials. He spent his time roaming the countryside, buying up the tobacco-cards of such peasants as did not smoke (she said he had always plenty of money) and bartering them for whatever he could get. He had even bought a cow so as to have milk and butter and cheese, and it was his wife who milked and churned. Her hands were red and chafed with the rough work she had to do (my own were bad enough) and she told me that what she found hardest was having to stand the churn in the icy water that flowed from their spring, and churn in the open air.

Inside the house it was warm enough. She showed me over. There were just two fairly large rooms, separated by a smaller one for the boy. One of these rooms was her husband's private lair. She insisted that I look inside, though I was most unwilling. He had begun to assume ogre-like proportions in my mind and I felt much as Bluebeard's wife must have felt when she unlocked the fatal door. Not that there was any untoward discovery to make, but I was brought up sharp against the personality of an unknown man, and I felt as indiscreet as though I had been reading his correspondence. It was an ugly utilitarian room, and in spite of being fairly full of furniture, it gave an impression of barrenness and left me no desire for further acquaintance. This brief insight into the nature of the Bulgarian, acquired even more from his wife's tone of voice when she spoke of him than from his room or anything she actually said, made me feel all the more respect for her that she should have remained so essentially and even absurdly English, that she should be so cheerful, and that she should have succeeded in bringing up so normal and so well bred a boy, and one, like herself, so English. He was helpful about the house and devoted to his mother. At the same time, she told me that he fitted in with no difficulty at all among his companions at the village school, and could speak the local *patois* as well as any of them.

In the middle of the afternoon I left for home, after having extracted a promise that she and her son would one day come to La Coustète, which they later did. Outside, the wind was still bitterly cold, but the sky overhead was oddly still. When I reached La Rouvière I stopped for a cup of *ersatz* coffee at the café where we used to dine. I had a long conversation with the woman who kept it. She knew my Englishwoman well and liked her immensely. She told me that the little boy had his midday meal with her every day between morning and afternoon school. About the Bulgarian husband she was reticent.

At last I summoned up courage to face the blast outside. I could see through the windows the terraced hills; they had the hard still look that intense cold gives to a landscape. Far down in the valley a frozen stream lay motionless, except where the sun caught it at a turning and it sparkled back, pure gold, to life. The mulberry-trees with short-lopped branches stood out like so many black gallows, impervious to the wind. But wind or no wind, I must go.

It was not long afterwards that a cousin came to stay with Oncle Ernest and Tante Berthe, who were spinning out their Christmas holiday at Valleraugue. This was Loyse Bouteiller, a remarkable woman who devotes her time to politics and social work. I found to my relief that she and her husband, Pierre, were passionately Gaullist and pro-British. At the end of the visit she suggested that André and I come and spend a week in their house near Sète at the end of January. By way of inducement she mentioned that, as her husband was directing engineer of the local gasworks, they could ignore the gas restrictions, and that both their central heating and hot water system were run on gas. I would in any event have accepted her invitation; the prospect of being with people who shared my point of view was irresistible.

In the last days of January we set out. We took a bus to Montpellier and another thence to La Peyrade where the gasworks are. André found Montpellier very exciting. It was the first real town he had seen since he had been too small to take much in. He stood on the pavement jumping for joy at the sight of the electric tramways, and I could scarcely tear him away.

The atmosphere in the Bouteillers' house was congenial in every way. Loyse is one of the most hospitable people I know and her house is always full. While we were there we had the company of Pierre's father, a small man with a pointed beard who, though one of his nephews had been killed in command of his ship at Mers el-Kébir, was staunchly pro-British and Gaullist; a young war widow with her two small daughters; and a Spanish cancer specialist, a refugee from the Spanish Civil War. Everyone who came near the house was Gaullist, and we all sat round the wireless listening to the London news each evening punctually at nine o'clock.

I doubt whether I have ever lived within the aura of less mystical but more practising Christians than Loyse and Pierre. Loyse invited all and sundry to meals, although the country round La Peyrade is composed of vineyards and salt-marshes and produces nothing but wine and an occasional eel. I remember a day when we were to be twenty-two for lunch. In the middle of the morning I went into the kitchen to see whether Loyse needed help. Not only was she not there; there was nothing in the kitchen to cook as far as I could see. I was standing disconsolate in the middle of the room when Pierre wandered in from his office next door. I asked him what I should do. He laughed and said not to worry. Loyse would turn up and somehow or other would produce a meal. She did turn up, at about half-past eleven, and she did produce a meal at about two in the afternoon. Some one of the many people to whom she had shown kindness had come round with some clandestine beef or a tangle of eels. This often happened, and on each occasion Loyse would cock an eye at me, a rather triumphant eye.

When our week was up, Loyse very generously suggested that I come back to them for the last weeks of my pregnancy. I could leave André with some member of the family and have a complete rest. I accepted with a thankful heart.

Valleraugue was still in the grip of winter when we returned from La Peyrade. The waterfall flowed once more but the grass when the hoar-frost thawed in the morning sun showed yellow and lifeless and the earth was iron-hard. On my birthday, January 26th, the sun 'leapt the rocher de Gache', as the peasants had told me it would do; in other words, it rose above the hill which in November and December casts its shadow over the valley. It now shone all day long, but with little strength. The air remained cold and the house icy.

Towards the end of February I left André with Gillette's family and went to visit Henri at Le Chambon-sur-Lignon. I had had some difficulty in making myself look presentable enough to face strangers. My red coat was not warm enough for the season and I had none other. Lucienne, who turned up in Valleraugue for a few days, made me a present of an old antelope coat of her own. At the best of times it would have been too small for me; in my present condition it would not even meet in front. I wore it open and pinned my faith to my red hat. It was so elegant I trusted it to divert attention from the rest.

Le Chambon-sur-Lignon made a delightful impression on me as soon as I stepped off the train. The station was full of pink-cheeked children, all wearing clogs enamelled in bright colours. It was some time before I spotted Henri. He too had pink cheeks and clear eyes. I had grown so accustomed to seeing thin, pale children that it was a surprise to me to see them under their normal aspect. Even as Henri and I fell into one another's arms I knew that his immense joy at seeing me was tempered by a certain feeling of dismay caused by my Paris hat. I said nothing but bided my time.

I had heard a great deal about Le Chambon-sur-Lignon before coming there. It owes its reputation to an international and co-educational school which was founded there before the war, and which at that time was at its zenith because its staff included many Paris Lycée teachers who had fled the contacts of the German occupation and the necessity, since Lycée teachers are state employees, of swearing fidelity to Marshal Pétain. As a result, Le Chambon was a hotbed of resistance.

The village itself stands in the middle of forests and undulating fertile country, at about the same altitude as L'Espérou. The school-buildings are in the forests outside the village, but their presence has influenced village life. There are good hotels, and as I passed through the streets with Henri I noticed an excellent bookshop and, in spite of the restrictions, two good cakeshops.

Henri was as yet too young to attend the Collège Cevenol. He lived with a family who ran a *pension* for children, and he attended a juvenile school run by an Alsatian refugee. Before taking me to visit his *pension* he showed me where my hotel was. The snow still lay in patches on the ground and the air stung every inch of exposed skin and filled one's lungs with vigour. As we walked I broached to Henri the matter of my hat. I asked him to say quite honestly whether he would rather I left it at the hotel before we went to call on Madame Barbier-Comte, the lady he lived with. He looked a little shame-faced and lowered his eyes as he admitted that he would indeed prefer it. With a secret sigh I resigned myself to facing strangers in my dowdy clothes, unalleviated by any frivolous breath from Paris.

The *pension* stood outside the village in a garden full of pine-trees, and the children went to school and to church on skis. I soon realized that Henri was not nearly so unhappy as he made out in his letters and that he was very fond of the daughter of the house, who was in charge of the younger children. I went back to Valleraugue feeling much happier about him, and especially as regards his health.

Back in Valleraugue the frost had broken, but soon the rains were on us, the interminable diluvian rains that blot the world out and leave you a prey to despair. No Scotch rain, mere mists and drizzle, can give any idea of what falls from the skies when storms come down from the Rouerg, or the wind blows up from the Mediterranean, carrying its moisture to be poured down at the touch of Mount Aigoual. Nor can a Briton, whose country's colours grow more vivid in the moist air, easily imagine what rain can mean in a land whose every beauty seems to go out like a snuffed candle when the rains fall. The weather becomes an obsession; the memory of the long blue days and the hot summer sun are like the memories of a lost paradise. It seems as impossible that they should ever return as that, when they are with us, they should some day cease. I find in my diary:

'March 4th. Rain.'

'March 5th. Rain.'

'March 6th. Grey all day and in the evening wild wind and rain.'

'March 7th. Fine with a strong cold wind.'

'March 8th. Wind still cold.'

'March 16th. After March 8th there came two days of lovely weather, and then the rain came back, implacable.'

There is no mention of anything but the weather for as long as the rains lasted, except for a reference to a visit Helena and I paid to our doctor in Montpellier. Usually so colourful and lively, the little city was grey and damp and cold. The shops were empty and in the cafés, where only a few years earlier my sister Molly and I, in an August heat-wave, had absorbed ice-cream after ice-cream while awaiting the incredibly delayed birth of my son André, nothing remained but *ersatz* coffee, with no milk, and sickly *ersatz* lemonade. The bill of fare from bygone times, headed by *croissants* and *brioches*, still lay beneath the glass that topped the little tables. Nostalgically I read it through wondering whether my sister and I had been more heroines or fools not to have eaten everything with which it now taunted me. The cheerful waiters of old, in captivity, or hiding, or working in Nazi Germany, were replaced by limp waitresses whose zest for life seemed to have vanished with the waiters. It was all very depressing.

The one bright spot was our doctor. He settled down for conversation when our consultation was over. He gave us a fiery dissertation on the political situation, striding up and down the room as he talked, tall and gaunt with bushy white hair and eyebrows. He blasted Pétain and Laval with his scorn, and he brought Helena and me back to life with his high confidence that sooner or later England would win the war and France find some means of helping her.

I returned to Valleraugue on a new wave of optimism. André in my absence had had a great time with Gillette's family. He had had no difficulty in adapting himself to a peasant life, and at our first meal he cast a critical eye over the table and asked where the *pinard* was, the rough red wine the peasants drink at table. At bedtime he informed me that

Gillette said one should not wash in hot water; it opens your pores and you catch cold. I asked whether he would rather I washed him in cold water. He looked doubtful and I realized that he hoped not to be washed at all.

Soon after my return, Raymond Lévi-Strauss fell ill. At first no one knew what was wrong. He seemed simply to be wasting away. The only definite symptom was that his temperature rose every evening and fell below normal in the morning. Emma was anxious, but the only doctor Raymond would consult was the old and incompetent Valleraugue doctor, who was obviously at a loss. But he was their friend; there could therefore be no question of calling in Dr Clarou from Le Vigan. It was all of a piece with Raymond's whole attitude towards life, an attitude that made him extraordinarily lovable but that must sometimes have been trying to his wife. For example, if Emma suggested they might kill and eat one of the rabbits which they bred far more successfully than I had done, his face would cloud over and he would say, 'Surely you don't want to eat a rabbit that looks so like your own daughter-in-law?' or whoever it was that in his eyes the rabbit resembled. The result was that the rabbits thrived and multiplied to no practical purpose. He was a tender-hearted man whose nerves were permanently exposed to shock: he had never learned to grow even the semblance of a shell. It occurred to us that perhaps he was wasting away for no better reason than that he was psychologically unfitted to the circumstances of life in the year 1942.

But in this we were wrong. The doctor at last diagnosed Maltese fever. For the first time I learned that there was a good deal of the fever in our valley. I had been a little reckless in my attitude to goat's milk and cheese. Gillette told me that her father had had the disease, and she described its symptoms as *une lassitude et une longitude*, which seemed exactly to fit Raymond's condition. She added that she had never known the fever to be fatal.

It seemed however in Raymond's case as though it were going to prove fatal. I went round one evening after André was in bed to inquire after him. It was a pitch-black night in March, the blackest night we had yet had. There was no moon, and the stars were masked by heavy clouds. As a rule when I crossed the bridge I could see a faint glimmer reflected from the sky in the water beneath, and it helped to guide me. That night there was none and the river was as black as the banks on either side. It was the only evening on which I had to cross on all fours.

When I reached Cancabra Emma took me up to the room where Raymond lay in bed. There was a young Jewish doctor with him, Dr Bernard, a friend of their son, Claude. He was living in hiding as were so many Jews who could not leave France. I think that he had heard that Raymond was ill and had come to see if he could help. Raymond himself lay in his bed unconscious, and his face was the waxen colour of a corpse. It was a most disturbing sight. Dr Bernard said that his blood pressure was so low that, though the illness itself should not be mortal, he was afraid his strength would simply peter out. I asked whether anything could be done to raise the blood pressure. He said that in theory it could, but that in fact he could do nothing; as a Jew he had not the right to make out prescriptions. It was then that I remembered the second box of ampoules I had been given to raise my own blood pressure and had not used. I mentioned them to Dr Bernard, who begged me to fetch them. Back I went along the pitch-dark road, running and stumbling till I reached the bridge which again I had to cross on all fours. The moment I got back to Cancabra, Dr Bernard put the contents of four ampoules into his syringe and injected them into Raymond's fleshless arm. With extraordinary dexterity he carried the whole operation out with only his right hand, for he had had poliomyelitis as a child and his left arm was paralysed. The results of the injection were immediate. Standing round the bed with our hearts in our mouths, we watched the colour of life seep slowly back into Raymond's deathlike face. At last he opened his eyes and recognized us. He was over the worst and from then on he gradually improved, but he never recovered normal health.

CHAPTER SEVENTEEN

It was that year that for the first time I became aware of the miracle that spring is. All my life I had, like so many town dwellers, preferred the autumn, the real season of renewal in a city. But when one fine morning I felt the ground soft underfoot instead of iron-hard, I woke at last to the full wonder of spring. From then on, gradually the dead yellow grass made way for the young green growth, and soon I was to see Gillette wandering about the terraces of the hill with a salad basket in her hand and her eyes fixed on the ground. Every now and then she would bend down and pick something off the ground and put it her basket. When she came back, triumphantly she showed me the first salad of the year, that they call *doucette*; I believe we call it corn salad. All winter we had lived on the sort of large pale-yellow carrots they use to feed animals, dried chestnuts, dried mushroom and onions; and I came to have a horror of onions from having regularly to sort from our store those that were rotting. Those first spring salads are unforgettable.

The next sign that winter was over was when I found a bed of violets down by the *béal*. I remember it was Easter Day and Henri was with us for his holidays. I had dyed some eggs which Maman had sent us for Easter, golden yellow with the skins of our rotting onions. We took a picnic with us to *a point de vue* in the grounds of Les Angliviel, a circular stone bench with a low wall round it and tall pines to lend their shade, very nineteenth-century and on the whole very pleasant. It was when I was hiding the eggs that I found the violets. We picked a bunch for our picnic decoration. The river below our *point de vue* was swollen with the spring rains, the sky over our heads was blue, the air we breathed was the mild air of spring. We had come through the winter and survived. It felt like victory.

François came that spring for another of his brief visits. I spun it out by accompanying him as far as Montpellier, where we called in on Dr Roque. He said that he thought our baby would be born at latest at the end of May, and that I had better settle with the Bouteillers on about the twentieth. And so, on May 18th I left André at Mandiargues, where Jacques was to pick him up and take him to stay with his family in Toulon.

I felt very low at leaving André, but when I boarded the bus at Montpellier that was to take me to La Peyrade, my spirits rose. Here on the plain it was already almost summer. I felt the unhappy self that had struggled with cold and damp, with getting up early and carrying weights, with solitude and despair, dissolve and re-assemble as an individual with a life of her own, and with hopes and aspirations other than the purely material ones of providing food for her family.

I was made very welcome at La Peyrade. As usual the house was full. The Spanish cancer specialist was still there, and Loyse's old father and mother, Oncle Charles Eggyman and Tante Adèle, had come on a visit. Tante Adèle was the sister of Grandpapa-de-Genève, an intelligent woman with a great heart and lively sense of humour. Oncle Charles was also Swiss by birth but French by adoption, and his profession was that of a rare book expert. He was a white-haired, white-bearded old gentleman with piercing blue eyes, very distinguished in appearance. He spoke the pure classical French that one so rarely hears spoken, but Tante Adèle told me that every morning at about five she would hear him turning about in his bed and muttering to himself: 'Ah! Les cochons! Les cochons!' at the thought of the Germans. They had fled from Paris at the approach of the enemy, and were then living in Montauban where they had the congenial company of a number of Paris intellectuals, all of them Gaullists.

Altogether there was a pleasantly conspiratorial atmosphere at La Peyrade. There were two wireless sets, one in the drawing-room and the other in a secret cupboard in a small upstairs room. The possibility of our wireless-sets being confiscated was always suspended over our heads. It had happened in the north, and Jeanne Nick had told me how in Lille, when the order went round that all sets were to be handed in to the *Mairie*, people had flowed in with brown-paper parcels of every size and shape. It was not till everyone had gone that one of the largest parcels toppled over and fell rattling to the ground. It turned out to be no wireless-set but a bird-cage. The other parcels were immediately opened and not all were what they claimed to be. The Bouteillers took their precautions in advance, and it was in the upstairs room that we gathered in the evening to listen to the BBC news. There was no real need for caution; a garden with a high wall cut us off from the outer world. But it made us feel safe and secret, which heightened our enjoyment.

Soon after our arrival we were joined by a new guest, a friend of Loyse who was librarian at the municipal library of Toulouse. She told us exciting things about arms hidden in the cellars of the library. She firmly believed, as many people did, that a clandestine army was being organized under the auspices of the Vichy government, and that it would come into action should the German army cross the line of demarcation. I believe it was true that the army was secretly becoming organized, whether or not with the connivance of the government I do not know. I have been told that the army was let down by Pétain and Laval when later the Germans did cross the line, and that the only man who followed out what had been his instructions, in defiance of their having been annulled, was General de Lattre de Tassigny who marched his men out of Montpellier, to our general surprise, and was immediately arrested. We had our first echoes of that great Frenchman at this time. Another young friend of the Bouteillers who came at this time was our source of information. He was on leave from the École de Cadres at Uriage, whose real purpose was to breathe a new spirit into the army and prepare it—so he maintained—for the struggle to come. He was the first to speak to us about de Lattre de Tassigny, who had not yet joined de Gaulle, but neither had he accepted defeat. The Bouteillers' young friend was full of enthusiasm and we found it infectious. De Lattre de

Tassigny became for us a rising star to which to yoke our hopes.

Our circle at La Peyrade was widened by the presence at Sète of a labour camp where German Jewish refugees were employed by the Vichy government at various jobs about the harbour. Loyse and Pierre made these refugees free of the house and garden, and they sometimes came and joined us in the evening when their work was over. They were a very mixed lot and an excellent illustration of the absurdity of anti-Semitism. One was a distinguished physicist who had worked with Professor Born when he was still at Göttingen before Hitler came to power. Another of the refugees was a rabbi whom I found especially interesting, though he spoke no French and my German was rapidly going. At the other extreme there was a Viennese who looked like a full-blooded Austrian and not at all like a Jew. There was also an insignificant little man from Berlin, rather vulgar and very sure of himself, who might have been anything, racially. Only Friedmann, the physicist, spoke fluent French; with the others conversation was rather heavy going. But although we lacked words to express what we felt, we scarcely needed them. We were bound together by an affective tie of a sort one rarely experiences in normal life, a feeling of profound solidarity. It was what chiefly sustained and nourished us during all those dreary years, and it is the one thing whose loss has left all those who knew it with a strange insatiable nostalgia. As we all sat together in the twilight, under an umbrella-shaped tamarisk in the garden, it hung on the air and mingled with the smell of the night-stock that grew near by.

We had entered into a period of intense and heavy heat. I led a completely lazy life. Loyse, in the goodness of her heart, brought me each morning my breakfast in bed. Late in the morning—I had an incredible capacity for sleep during the month I spent at La Peyrade—I would wander down to the garden and sit in the shade of the tamarisk; or I would make my slow, heavy way through the village to the salt marshes and sit gazing out to sea.

The house we lived in used to rouse in me wave upon wave of homesickness. It was the official residence of the chief engineer of the local gasworks, at the time Pierre Bouteiller, and it stood in a huge garden. By some odd chance the first engineer appointed to the post was an Englishman, and the house was built in accordance with his tastes. Except for the mosquito-netting in front of all the doors and windows, it was, in fact, an English house. As I wandered through the corridors I could clearly see what the underlying intention had been in planning it. One part of the house was obviously set aside to contain the nurseries, another for the service rooms; and the part that included the dining-room, drawing-room, master bedroom and guest-room, was planned so that no noise should filter through to it. There may not actually have been a green baize door, but in spirit it was there.

The Bouteillers were gloriously unaware of all this. To them it was simply a large house, not quite convenient because of its being, in some intangible way, cut in two. The French have no notion of living in any sense isolated from their children. In a French family the hour of family meals is sacred to the children's education, in the French sense of the word which is nearer to 'upbringing'. It is at table with their parents that they learn how to eat and how to make conversation; it is at table that they acquire their general knowledge. The Bouteillers would have been no doubt shocked if they had understood their house's thwarted purpose. But I was haunted by the ghost of English family life, just as the house was, and I was often homesick.

In spite of this, the first fortnight passed happily enough. I enjoyed having hot baths again, and I revelled in the right to do nothing, which the Bouteillers accorded me as the normal thing for one in my condition. But as I never went to bed without a hope that I would be wakened in the night by the first pangs of childbirth, each day brought me new and increasing disappointment. On June 2nd I went in to Montpellier to consult my doctor. I had a secret hope that he would tell me I could go straight into the nursing home where he had booked me a room. He said nothing of the sort. He told me that no one could predict the exact time of a baby's arrival till the pains have started. I pointed out that if mine delayed much longer, then evil tongues would be able to cast doubts on its father's identity. He was not to be moved, but told me the law itself allows for a maximum of ten months. I found this talk of ten months very discouraging; a month is a long time to wait when the sirocco is blowing.

I boarded my bus feeling very low, but as we were crossing the city I noticed a poster announcing a concert to be given by Paul Casals in the municipal theatre. I noted the day and determined that somehow or other I would hold the baby back till after the concert. My whole outlook had changed. Was it possible that Casals had stayed on in France? Had he not gone to America as so many other great musicians had done? Had I dreamed what I saw?

The moment I reached home I told the Bouteillers what I had seen. They seized a newspaper and found that there really was going to be such a concert. We determined all of us to go. Actually I had a secret hope that the excitement of the moment might bring my pains on, and that I would kill two birds with one stone.

Even such shattering emotion as I felt on the night of the concert was without effect, beyond giving me a general and intermittent impression that the baby was trying to put its umbrella up. Even to that I soon paid no attention. I had often heard Casals play; I had even met and heard him at the house of Sir Donald Tovey in happy bygone days. I doubt whether I ever heard him play more beautifully than he did that night. Round, pure and true the sound rose from his instrument, as though at the mere touch of nicely adjusted bow on taut strings a door was opened through which the music flowed of itself. It struck me what an extraordinary thing it is that the greatest music played in the purest style should find its way to every heart. That such an artist, so little the virtuoso, so much the musician should have reached such a height of popularity increased my respect for the human kind. Each phrase flowed out so perfectly formed, that the beauty of line was even more breathtaking than the beauty of colour. As he sat there playing quietly and almost selflessly, he seemed to me to symbolize everything which our European civilization has contributed to the world, and which makes nonsense of our present sense of guilt. How could I ever have thought that Casals would go to America? There are rare indigenous plants that you cannot uproot.

We had one more visit at La Peyrade before the strain of waiting became too much for me and I took matters into my own hands. Loyse had a friend, a young woman who had taken orders and volunteered to go as chaplain to the Camp de Gurs, a sinister place in the Pyrenees where Pétain interned the German refugees escaped from occupied territory into the 'free' zone. She had lived among the prisoners, doing what she could to help them, until her health gave way and she was carried out of the camp on a stretcher. It was while she was still convalescent that she came to stay with the Bouteillers. She gave us an appalling account of conditions in the Camp de Gurs. Not that the internees were up against the deliberate cruelty of the German concentration camps; but they suffered extreme and unnecessary discomfort and were even more miserably fed than the rest of the population, since they had access to nothing beyond their rations. Even their rations were often kept from them by dishonest guardians who sold them for their own profit on the black market. The roofs of the barracks where the prisoners slept were not even rain-proof, and some of the internees trained themselves to sleep without moving so as to keep in place the small receptacles they placed here and there about their beds to catch the rain from the leaking roof. The sanitary conditions were such that there were several cases of typhus. Worst of all was her account of how, on Pétain's agreeing to hand over to the Nazi authorities a certain number of the prisoners, she had spent the last night before the Gestapo came to claim them in trying to comfort them. She told us how one woman had sat up all night breathless with asthma, a thing that she had never had before. It was brought on solely by fear of what she knew was in store for her. I remembered that Pasteur Nick once said to me that the thing he never would or could forgive Pétain was his handing over to the Nazi authorities of Germans who for political reasons had taken refuge before the war in France.

In the meantime my static condition was getting more and more on my nerves. The Bouteillers never so much as hinted that I was outstaying my welcome; but I knew that I had not been expected to stay so long. The food problem was appallingly difficult even for Loyse, for whom miracles were almost daily events. But what troubled me most was that I was really beginning to fear that my baby would never be born. Too often I had gone to bed full of hope and woken to despair as the knowledge came with the early morning light that there was no change in my condition. I always expect the pangs of childbirth to take me in the night. If dawn finds me as day left me I give up hope till the morrow. It was now so hot that exercise was impossible, yet exercise seemed my best hope of precipitating events. I felt an utter fool every morning when Loyse appeared with my breakfast. Putting myself in her place, I could not but feel that had she known what she was letting herself in for she might not have formed such an enslaving habit. It was no use my making up my mind to get up before she came; I woke at dawn only long enough to bewail my fate, and never stirred again till I heard her knock. I sometimes wondered whether I had not contracted sleeping-sickness, so deeply and so long I slept.

By June 17th I was desperate. It was one of the hottest, muggiest days of that hot muggy spring, but I told myself that I must brave the heat and go for the longest walk I could bear. I trailed my weary way down to the salt marshes, and walked far out along one of the dykes. When I reached the end of it I sat down to rest on some stone steps that led down to the water. Sadly I gazed out to sea. Before me, in the direction of Sète, was a stretch of grey water, the salt marshes, and beyond was the open sea. Like the water, the sky was greyish white, merging here and there into palest blue. Everything was very still except for the movement of the cranes in the harbour away to my right, and the lapping of the water at my feet. Little by little the constant movement of the water cast a spell over me. It carried me back through time to Glenuig Bay, on the western coast of Scotland, where I used to stay with friends. It brought back the smell of seaweed, of moss, of peat-smoke; the memory of the little low grey cottages, the beauty of line and colour which no dullness of climate can dim, the sound of the sea, the real sea, the sea that has a tide to wash smooth the rocks and feed the seaweed on whose beds you may walk barefoot. Suddenly I hated the Mediterranean from whose shores of cruel treacherous rocks that cut your feet you view eternally heart-racking unattainable beauty. I was homesick for the smell of oatcake and home-made bread and kippers, and I lost myself in a dream of memory as it all came back to me in more and more intimate detail. Again as once before came the mocking thought that it had not in the old days been merely the smell of peat-smoke that intoxicated, nor the sight away out to sea of the blue, pointed hills of Mull. It had been the prospect of a marvellous future. Now I was in that future, and where was happiness? In looking back. Would one never put salt on its tail?

On June 19th I decided I could bear waiting no more. I told my kind friends that I was quite certain my time had come. I was going into Montpellier while I could still travel by bus. I packed my luggage and left La Peyrade for Montpellier, determined that come what might I would return no more.

CHAPTER EIGHTEEN

However we may dread the event beforehand, when our hour strikes we all come to childbirth as a soldier comes to battle or a student to his examinations. This is to be our trial of strength and we must mobilize every atom of courage and resource that we possess. This time, in point of fact, I must do more, for by some means or other I must not only bear the pains but bring them on. How this was to be done I had no idea, but I had a hope of persuading Dr Roque to precipitate matters with an injection. In the meantime the instinct that drives a cat to seek out a convenient hatbox was at work in me. Dr Roque had early booked me a room in a private nursing home run by the midwife he worked with, but I could hope to go there only once the pains had started. Even if they could have taken me earlier, which was doubtful since there was a shortage of rooms in hospitals and nursing-homes, I could not afford to go till it was necessary. I must find something else for the night, perhaps for two nights, and I was determined it would be nothing mean or sordid. I went straight from the bus station to the best hotel. Just because it was the best hotel, part of it had been commandeered by the German High Command. I knew this before I went there, but I scarcely gave the matter a thought. In my experience there was a tendency in the south to take the prevailing untoward circumstances as an excuse for letting slide the standard of cleanliness in hotels; I was pretty certain the hotel I had chosen would be an exception to this rule. With the possibility hanging over me of the baby's taking me unawares after all, and being born in an hotel, I considered the German High Command as a lesser evil than dirt.

I took the smallest and cheapest room there was. It was papered with the inevitable wallpaper in imitation of

Provençal chintz, but it was perfectly clean and it had the toilet facilities I lacked at La Coustète. My spirits began to rise. As soon as I had unpacked my belongings, I sallied forth to visit Dr Roque, fully persuaded in my new state of optimism that he would decide my hour was at hand. He did nothing of the sort. He said that one thing and one only was clear to him—labour had not yet set in. I murmured something about bringing it on with an injection. He told me to go back to my friends and be patient. It could not be very long.

But that was what I was determined not to do. On the other hand, I had not money enough to stay more than a night or two in such an expensive hotel. I was at a loss. Finally I made up my mind that I had better call at the nursing-home and try to persuade the midwife to do what the doctor had refused. I dragged my hot weary way through the town, hopefully carrying a small suitcase containing the baby's layette. The nursing-home proved to be simply the midwife's flat, fitted up to receive three or four patients. I rang the bell, feeling that never, oh never would I have the courage to go back the way I had come, carrying my suitcase in the heat. Somehow or other I must persuade her to take me in and bring on labour. The door was opened to me by the midwife herself. I introduced myself and explained my purpose. Her face fell as soon as she heard who I was. She explained that I was at least three weeks overdue, and that as the patient who had booked the room after me was ten days early, she had had to take her in. There was no room for me. No doubt Dr Roque had known this fact and it was the real reason he had refused to give me an injection. He had said nothing, not wanting to upset me and calculating, very probably, that if I hung fire a little longer the room might once more be free. Small wonder he advised me to go back to my friends.

Seeing my look of mute despair, the midwife said that if the worst came to the worst and labour set in immediately, she would give her own room up to me and sleep in the sitting-room.

But obviously I could not require her to precipitate events which were going to cause her so much inconvenience. I must go back to my hotel, but she agreed to let me leave my suitcase.

Back I went. As things were, I dared not even spend money on a meal in a restaurant. I ate my ration of bread with some fruit in my hotel bedroom. For a while I sat disconsolate; then, partly to pass the time and partly to calm my nerves, I set about altering a skirt that no longer met about my waist. Those were the reasons I admitted to; but in truth my superstitious mind was once more at work. Deep down it calculated that if I spent the eleventh hour in altering clothes, I would deceive the mysterious being with whom superstitious people play their eternal game of chess into believing me resigned, and he would slacken his attention long enough to allow the baby to get under way. Nor did I miscalculate. Suddenly as I sat sewing I felt the first faint pains low down in my back. I stopped and listened, so faint they were. Was it my imagination? I went back to my sewing. After about twenty minutes I felt the pains again, faint and far-off like the first off-stage trumpets in the Leonora Overture number three. This time there could be no mistake and my heart leaped with joy. I told myself that if the baby was after all to be born on the hotel premises then the German High Command would get not a wink of sleep. Not even a British upbringing would prevent me from letting myself rip.

Just then there came a knock upon the door. It was the midwife. She said that she had been worrying about me and had come to tell me what to do should the pains start. I told her they had actually started but were coming only every twenty minutes, and that labour with me was apt to be a long business. She advised me to time them carefully, and when they were only ten minutes apart to send the night porter for a taxi and come straight to her. In some astonishment I asked her where the taxi was going to come from. She said that in emergency cases some sort of vehicle could be found. I must leave that to the night porter. With these hopeful words she left me to my fate.

And so I still sat sewing (I dared not stop for fear of a disappointment) and paused to look at my watch each time the trumpets sounded. By midnight they were fairly strong and coming every ten minutes. I decided my hour had struck and, feeling very exhilarated, I packed my weekend case with my immediate needs and went down to the hall to find the porter. There a disappointment was in store for me. The porter told me he was not allowed to leave the hotel, nor did he seem to have the slightest notion how a taxi could be obtained. I felt that the midwife might have done a little more to smooth my way. From the start I had mistrusted her hard face, but because it had softened a little in sympathy with my difficulties, I suspended final judgement. The porter advised me to go over the way to the police station and throw myself on the mercy of the police. He said that if anyone could get me some sort of a vehicle it would be they. It was only a short distance to go. By now the pains were coming every six minutes and were fairly strong. They overtook me on my way to the police station and I stood beside my little suitcase in the silence of the night with clenched teeth, waiting for them to subside. At the police station I explained my situation with considerable embarrassment. The man on duty said he would do what he could, and bade me sit down. He indicated a bench on which a number of people were already sitting. I soon realized that I was part and parcel of the night's bag of prostitutes, drunks, pickpockets and what-not. I sat among them, enormous with respectability, the butt of veiled jokes between the policemen and the shady characters on the bench. I was seized with a fit of giggles which was interrupted by a wave of pain. I turned my face to the wall and silently ground my teeth. I glanced at my watch. Five minutes now, and still no sign of a vehicle. I went to the desk and told the man in charge that I doubted whether I could hold out much longer. He said he was doing his best to find me a velo-taxi, a sort of bicycle rickshaw manned by a stalwart southerner, the usual and costly equivalent of a taxicab. I reflected that he would need to be stalwart who hauled me over the cobbled streets in such a vehicle, and I nerved myself to face the expression the man's face would certainly assume when he saw the client that the police were imposing on him. I need not have worried. No velo-taxi was to be found. The policeman suggested that perhaps

I could walk to my nursing home. I explained that my pains were coming every four minutes and that it would take me an hour to reach my destination at the speed I could make, carrying a dressing-case and a handbag and stopping every four minutes in the moonlight to grind my teeth. He saw my point, and again sent a man out to comb the streets. This time his efforts bore fruit, though it was strange fruit. He came back triumphant with an old station-omnibus. I climbed in with some difficulty—it stood high off the ground—and off we went, bumpety-bump over the cobbled street. I felt like a salad being shaken about in a salad-basket, and I speculated between giggles and groans what the chances were that my baby be born in a disused station-omnibus. But no; I stayed my course, though I think the rough drive hastened my labour, for which I was to be grateful.

In the nursing home I found the midwife and her room all ready waiting for me. I sank into the best bed I ever lay on, after assuring the midwife that I had still some hours to go. Thankful to be at peace at last, I turned out the light and settled into what was to be the most relaxed confinement of my life. No one disturbed me, no one hung anxiously over me, no one forced me to speech. The pains were hard to bear, but I was so peaceful and relaxed that even when they were only two minutes apart I fell asleep during those two minutes. At six o'clock in the morning the midwife came and examined me, and peace was at an end. I became taut and nervous and impatient of her presence. Soon the doctor was there too, scolding me for not having sent for him at once. He said he could have spared me several hours of pain, and he accused me of having *la vocation de la douleur*. While he talked he was wheeling me through to the operating-room and hoisting me on to the operating-table. From that moment began one of the most extraordinary experiences of my life. I had the impression of being in the hands not of a doctor but of a conjuror. It was not so much that he made some use of such contemporary aids to childbirth as were available to him; he was blessed with what almost amounted to a sleight of hand such that I had the impression he did half the work and I hardly suffered

at all. Deliverance came as a glorious hard-won reward for
months of misery.

When I opened my eyes after a moment of repose,
Dr Roque was unrolling and laying with pride across my
stomach a long thin baby. Nicolas was born. It was once
more June 21st. St John's Day, Midsummer or the first day
of summer according as you looked at it. At the thought I
remembered to ask what news there was. When I left La
Peyrade things had been going badly in North Africa. 'My
poor child,' said the doctor, 'Tobruk has fallen. But never
mind; they may lose Egypt, they won't lose the war!' Back I
was cast into the nightmare world that I had almost forgotten
during the last two days, preoccupied as I was with my own
minor troubles. Never, it seemed, would we emerge from
the mists of gloom and despair. I saw the Nazi occupation
spreading like a pool of filthy oil on a lovely patchwork
counterpane. One after another the patches of beautiful
faded cretonne that represented in my mind the countries of
Europe had been stained and had lost their character. It had
become the turn of the more brilliant patches of the North
African countries. Even if Germany should end by losing the
war, the harm done would be lasting. Traces would subsist
of the anti-Semitism, cruelty and corruption they brought
wherever they went; the dishonesty that had become a part
of patriotism would linger on as a habit. What sort of gift
had I given Nicolas? An overwhelming desire for François's
presence came over me. We were allowed to telegraph from
one zone to the other in the event of a birth or a death. I
arranged for notice to be sent him of his son's birth, and
from then on I lay with my eyes glued to the door, hoping
each time it opened that it would be he. But no: it was
the maid disguised as a hospital nurse; it was the doctor
on his daily rounds; very occasionally it was a member of
the family; most rarely of all it was the midwife. The doctor
assured me that it was wrong to wish him to come so far for
so few days and in such terrible heat. Far better he should
wait and use the pretext to cross the Line openly for his
summer holiday. I knew the doctor was right, but I went
on hoping.

In the meantime I had to decide under what name our

son was to be registered. We had agreed upon Nicolas as a first name, but I knew that François intended to give him as a second name that of Captain Bernard, who was to be the godfather. For the life of me I could not remember what Captain Bernard's first name was. I fell back on his surname, and the long thin baby was registered under the name of Nicolas Bernard. Bernard was in fact a family name: my father's Irish grandmother had been a Bernard. My father would be delighted to have the name remembered.

Papa and Maman came to visit me. They brought me eggs and *crotillons* to eat with my bread. Friedmann, the German physicist, sent me a bunch of pink carnations. Françoise, the wife of Pierre Chazel, the only member of the family who lived in Montpellier, brought me cold boiled chestnuts to eat when hunger gnawed my vitals, which was continuously. The eggs I had to hand over to the midwife. I had no means of boiling them in bed, and even if it had occurred to me to suck them I would not have known how to proceed. She kept at least the half of them for herself. She was a woman I was coming to like less and less. I resented the fact of her being seldom there, being too busy with outside confinements; and also her leaving all the work to an already overworked maid. Nicolas never once had an all-over wash, and I was expected to set my internal processes to an alarm-clock. The maid brought me a bed-pan morning and evening; if I rang for her between these times she was most displeased. The food was well prepared, but there was so little of it that it served only to whet the appetite. As I fed Nicolas myself, it was a disastrous state of things.

I did not blame the midwife for the lack of food, but I felt I had a right to all my eggs; and I heartily disliked the way she would honour me with one of her rare visits immediately after someone had called to see me, and inquire with a smiling face whether there was anything I wanted her to put away in a cool place. Looking back, I blame the woman less than I did at the time. We were all so hungry that our finer feelings were fast disappearing. Actually most of my anger was directed against myself; I despised my being too weak-minded to protest openly. My great comfort in all this was that I was allowed to keep Nicolas in my room, with his cot so near my bed that I could gaze at him to my heart's content. He was an enchanting baby from the first. He never cried, but lay there peacefully sleeping, or waving his hands and feet in the way the French call 'knitting', for the heat was so extreme that there was no need to cover him.

I have one outstanding memory of the fortnight that I spent in the nursing home. I was lying in bed, one broiling afternoon, unable to bear even the sheet that covered me; I was hungry and lonely and hot; and I had given up all hope of François's coming south and altogether I was nearing the end of my tether. Suddenly through the open window came a sound that made me sit upright. It was still far off but was rapidly drawing nearer. It was the sound of singing. Some schoolmaster, obviously, was taking a class of young boys out walking and making them sing as they marched, and singing with them. It was very different singing from that of the Pétain Youth Camps, with their back-to-the-earth songs of Germanic inspiration which they sang half-heartedly and out of tune. These little boys and their master sang with all their heart, beating out the quick rhythm with rapid marching feet, and the song they sang was as French as it could be. It was *Il était un petit navire*. The sound swelled as they drew near, and as the song passed under my window I burst into uncontrollable tears. It was the more moving that there was not an ounce of sentimentality either in the song or in the way it was sung. The voices were rough, high and shrill, but they sang with verve, and the volley of rapid, clear-cut syllables that are characteristic of French songs rang out on the hot sleepy afternoon air, the subtle rhythmic phrases of the music as closely fitted to the words as a glove to the hand that wears it. It was a shout of defiance, and like everything French, their courage, their love-making, and even, *dixit* Jean Dutourd, their cruelty, the form it took was gay.

Before going further I must tell of Friedmann's tragic end. Shortly after I left La Peyrade he attempted to escape from France into Switzerland, with the help of the Bouteillers. Loyse and Pierre made all the arrangements, procured false papers for him, and provided the money for the journey. They had planned things very carefully, and there was only one danger spot in the whole scheme. Friedmann must spend a night in Lyons before passing the frontier. I was never told what the plans for crossing into Switzerland were, but Loyse later told me they had been foolproof. Pierre and Loyse had no contacts in Lyons, and if Friedmann had been sensible he would have spent the night in the station waiting-room, ready to take cover at the slightest alarm. But he was tired, and like all of us he was utterly unaccustomed to living in an atmosphere of clandestinity. Like the rest of us, he found it difficult really to grasp the fact that the Germans did behave as we had been told. It all seemed too inhuman to be true. Relying on his false identity card, he took a room for the night in the nearest hotel. That night all the hotels were raided, Friedmann's false identity came to light and he was arrested. He was never heard of again. I learned all this only much later.

It was Tante Berthe who came and fetched me home to Valleraugue, and there at last François came and joined us. The first few days we spent in Oncle Ernest's house. I had been given food cards for the new baby and I went the round of the shops, collecting the few articles of food to which they gave me a right. I had some trouble over the fat coupons. When I presented them to the corpulent, red-faced grocer, a man I heartily disliked and seldom dealt with, but who at the time was better provided than any other, he told me that he could give me nothing; I should, or at any rate the owner should, have registered his cards at the correct time, which was in January. I pointed out that this would have been difficult, in view of the fact that the owner had not then been born. He blandly replied that, that being so, the owner must count as a summer visitor, and as such should have brought his fats with him *d'où il vient!*

After a few days rest we decided to go up to L'Espérou. Jacques and his family were in the Maison Noire with André, whom we longed to see again. We set out on foot, I with Nicolas slung over my shoulder in a sort of haversack. He fitted in very neatly, with only his head and feet sticking out. With a small pillow to support his head, he was perfectly happy and cried only when I sat down by the wayside to rest. We created quite a sensation when we walked into the village with our new baby in a haversack. It was an exciting moment. Not only was there the prospect of seeing André again. There was also the Scob baby to see. He had been born on the same day as Nicolas. This was a thing that Scob had not foreseen when once he generously offered to let me have my baby in his house, instead of going to a nursing home, adding that he would walk Helena and me out in the last days, one on either arm, to show what a White Russian was capable of. Thirdly, there was Jacques and Karin's seven-month-old daughter Catherine, whom neither François nor I had so far seen. On the whole I would have preferred there to be fewer calls on my enthusiasm. I would have liked to devote myself solely to André, who looked disconsolate and wan from our long separation.

We stayed only a few days at L'Espérou. We went down to Valleraugue to welcome Henri, taking André with us. Soon afterwards François returned to Meaux, and the children and I were once more alone at La Coustète. Nicolas's presence helped to reconcile me to my return to what was now normal life. I had had a lovely basket cradle made for him in a neighbouring village where they still did basket-work. It stood on a table in the living-room, and the moment you crossed the threshold, before even you caught sight of it, you sensed that there was a presence, an unaccustomed presence, for the perpetual motion of his hands and feet stirred the room to life, much as does the shifting of a fire in the grate. Even when he slept there emanated some magic from his cradle which filled the room as though with music. I never tired of standing over him, watching the busy bicycling movement of legs that, to be honest, closely resembled Gandhi's. I remembered how I had envied my rabbit when it lay in its bed of straw, with all its babies round it, the picture of happy fulfilment. I wished I were capable of the same emotional simplicity. I longed, as so often in those years I longed, for my horizon to shrink, not only externally but internally too, till it included nothing beyond the hills that encircle Valleraugue. Again and again glimpses came and went during all that period of what I can only describe as a latent poetry in village life, a deep-flowing current which I with my town mentality could never quite reach. Suddenly an incongruous word, an insignificant encounter would tap the source and a flow of peace well through. It might be Esther Laune, complaining at having to don her corsets to go *en ville*; or I would pass in the hot streets of Valleraugue a neat little old woman clad in black, with hat and widow's veil. For a moment of transient illumination it seemed that I too would be absorbed into the peaceful stream. But it never lasted; city life had blunted my perceptions and I could never feel for a narrow environment the respect implicit in those corsets, that hat and veil, whose essence is humility. I came nearest to it in the company of an old woman called Lydie who, like Lucinde, had known and worked for François's great-grandmother. She was very old and a little foolish, but she had never lost her feeling of love and respect for the great-grandmother I had never known, and for whose sake she made me welcome. She would lure me up to her flat on the Quai, and indulge in an orgy of remembering, her mind wandering back and back, from one person to another, none of whom I had known. Every now and then as I listened some image would take hold of my imagination and the feeling would come. I remember in especial her telling me how one evening, early in November, when she was still young, she had gone out to the garden and was gathering parsley for the fish she was to cook for dinner, when they called her in because the old woman who was then her mistress was dying. Everything was still alive in her memory, the misty November twilight, the parsley bed, the fish, and then suddenly the presence of death, as though by opening the door into the garden she had let the blight of autumn into the house. It carried me back to the world of my childhood, a world where it had been safe to dream, and where even my old enemy, death, came, not with an accompaniment of hypodermic needles and the smell of anaesthetics, still less with instruments of torture, but carrying familiar homely objects in his hands, and trailing after him the breath of slow-burning autumn leaves.

CHAPTER NINETEEN

Our time in the south of France was drawing to a close. François had been appointed to a post in Paris, and there could be nothing unreasonable in our going to join him in occupied territory. Once more we were marking time till the German authorities should think fit to send us a safe-conduct. In the meantime matters were complicated for me by the fact that I had to go regularly to Montpellier for treatment. Dr Roque had been shocked at the damage done by my first confinement. He insisted upon treating me by cauterization. It was no easy matter finding transport to Montpellier. The bus service was slow and irregular, and inconvenient with a baby because of the crowding, yet it was impossible to leave Nicolas behind since I was feeding him myself. Dr Roque would have liked me to come twice a week, but he had to resign himself to condensing into a single weekly treatment what should have been done in two.

Late in October Oncle Ernest and Tante Berthe left for Nîmes. Before they went they offered to lend us their house for the week or two that we would probably still have to spend in Valleraugue. I accepted thankfully; the autumn rains had revived the waterfall and I had to dive under it to fetch our drinking water. Besides, it was comforting to have the company of Lucinde. She cooked our midday meal and she kept my spirits up by assuring me that even if the Germans were to come to Valleraugue, which at the time seemed of all things the most unlikely, she never doubted our winning the war in the end. 'And afterwards?' I would ask her, 'how shall we avoid a third war?' She stood for a moment, holding both my hands in hers while she reflected. Then she looked up at me very earnestly and said, 'Madame François, the Germans are like everyone else. There are good ones and there are bad ones. What we need is someone who can sort them out!'

Her greatest delight was when I wheeled Nicolas's perambulator into the big kitchen and asked her to mind him while I went out. To Lucinde, minding even so young a baby was a whole-time job. She would settle down in a low, high-backed chair, and with one wrinkled old hand on the edge of the perambulator and the other folded in her lap, she would rock him gently to and fro, singing as she rocked some lively song in *patois*, usually one about the *Petit Chaperon Rouge* meeting the wolf in the *Plaine de Montrouge*, which has become a populous suburb of Paris. I knew as I watched them that I was storing up trouble for myself; a happy gleam in Nicolas's eye showed me that he wholeheartedly agreed with Lucinde's attitude to baby-sitting. But no man or woman could ever have persuaded Lucinde that to curb your love for a baby could serve any useful purpose. Nor could anyone have resisted the happy expression on her face—and it was a moot point whether the wrinkled old face or the unwrinkled young one looked the happier. I never regretted having waived my principles; Nicolas never saw Lucinde again nor Lucinde Nicolas, for she died in the course of the following year. She died, I am certain, before her true time, for all she died at the age of eighty-six. Lucinde had so fine a palate that she could never accustom herself to eat what we had to eat. I have seen her dine off a scrap of bread and a lump of sugar, because that at least was honest food. She would rather have gone hungry, a thing she often did, than admit that the word *ersatz* had become a part of the French vocabulary. She fell one winter day in the village square and, though she lingered on for several months, she had to keep to her bed and she gradually lost her strength.

Every evening when Nicolas was safe asleep, André and I went out for a modest dinner. In a house on the outskirts of the village, a house that had stood empty for several years, a mother and daughter had opened up a *pension de famille*. They were not local people—rumour had it that they were Russians—but they were generally liked and their prices were within my reach. Actually, as I discovered later, the

left Nicolas with grandparents, and *right* family (minus Henri) at Longpont, the Dieterlen's house, both in 1943

Janet, Henri and André, Edinburgh, 1939

left
La Coustète:
the terrace and the *magnagnerie*,
and *below left* lunch under the
vine

right
looking across the valley

below
a side view of the terrace

Madame Laune, Janet's neighbour at La Coustète

Lucinde, Oncle Ernest's housekeeper at Valleraugue

Janet at her piano in Paris, about 1970

Janet in Germaine's garden at Valleraugue, about 1980

Janet and François at Mandiargues, June 1990

mother was only half Russian, and the daughter was born and bred in France. They were refugees from occupied territory and, under cover of their *pension de famille*, they gave temporary hiding to young men who were taking to the mountains to escape being sent to work in Germany. They kept the young men for a couple of nights to allow them to rest, for many of them had come a long way; then, late at night, the daughter would take them high into the mountains to a forester's house called Aire de Côte. Some two hundred yards from this house there was a cabin where they were given shelter. She kept them regularly supplied with food, carrying it up by night on her back, a climb of several hours. I knew nothing of all this at the time, but there was a strong aroma of resistance about the place and I found it very livening. I soon made friends with the daughter, though our time together was too short for intimacy, and she often borrowed English and American books from me.

There were never many guests when André and I arrived, but as there were only two tables we usually had a table companion. I made some interesting contacts in this way. On one occasion we dined together with a travelling locksmith who had reached our part of France by way of Corrèze. He gave me my first accounts of the Resistance as an organized movement, and told me exciting stories of arms parachuted in the mountains of Corrèze.

On another evening we dined with a couple of lorry-drivers. They told me they were taking a load of wood to Montpellier, and they offered to take Nicolas and me along with them. I jumped at the opportunity. I had my last appointment with Dr Roque the following day. I ran home and put André to bed. I returned with Nicolas and we set out at eleven o'clock by bright moonlight. The lorry was enormous and was heavily loaded with tree-trunks brought down from L'Espérou. Nicolas and I sat in front between the two men, who immediately set me at ease by telling me that I had only to say the word if I wanted to stop to feed Nicolas or 'for any other reason'. During the journey they entertained me with stories of the Spanish war in which they had both fought. They said that I must never mention this fact because under the Vichy regime it was counted as a crime to have taken the republican side in the Spanish conflict. At the height of our discussion a rabbit suddenly darted out from the *garrigue* on to the road in front of us. It hung for a fraction of a second poised where the glare of the headlights caught it, then darted zigzagging down the road ahead of us. The men's reaction was immediate. Hunger had made hunters of us all. For a few hair-raising moments the huge lorry lurched forward in incongruous snipe-like pursuit of the terrified rabbit. I clung to Nicolas while we swayed to and fro between the shouting men. Then suddenly the rabbit was gone.

At about one in the morning we drove into sleeping Montpellier. The immediate problem was to find me a room for the night. Montpellier was full of refugees from occupied territory and I foresaw some difficulty. Fortunately there was a room in the very first hotel we tried. It was strange enough alighting before the hotel by bright moonlight, from a lorry laden high with tree-trunks; it would have been fantastic if I had had to fall in with the men's suggestion and taxi with them through the town from hotel to hotel till I found somewhere to sleep. I bade my friends farewell; I was to go home the next day by bus as they were going on elsewhere. I remember nothing more of that last visit to Montpellier, but I remember only too well the dire consequences of having to condense my treatment into four instead of eight sessions.

These overtook me a few days after our return to Valleraugue. We were invited, André and I, to tea with two elderly sisters who lived up the valley at a distance of two or three miles. Lucinde was to take charge of Nicolas during our absence. We left them happy together in the big kitchen full of copper pans, Lucinde rocking Nicolas in time to one of her songs, and we set out, I on my bicycle and André in the trailer.

The Misses Laporte had prepared us a warm welcome and an unforgettable tea. Not that we actually drank tea, for I doubt whether there was any in the whole of the Cevennes. I forget what we drank, but I clearly remember what we ate. There was the chestnut jam for which the Laporte ladies are famous in the valley, and there were *rillettes* made from their own pig; there was honey, there were walnuts and chestnuts, and there was even bread. I had eaten no such meal for a long time nor had André. Our hostesses were delighted to see us so happy and they pressed us to eat as much as we could, for which we were grateful. Towards the end of the meal I began to have a strange feeling as though suddenly my inside had begun to weigh abnormally heavy. I told myself that I had eaten too much, but that was not at all what it felt like. When our hostesses rose to their feet I rose too but with difficulty, and the moment I was upright I had the awful sensation that the whole of my inside was falling out. At a shout from one of the sisters I looked down and saw to my horror that I was standing in a pool of blood. Our kind friends hustled André out of the room and came to my rescue. I soon found myself lying on a bed while they ran to and fro with hot water and towels. To my considerable embarrassment it dawned on me that they took for granted that I was in the throes of a miscarriage. I disliked this idea intensely, but when I assured them that I was only suffering from the consequences of too violent treatment by cauterization, I saw they were unconvinced. As soon as I felt capable of standing I persuaded them as best I could that my troubles were over and I mounted my bicycle once more, with André in the trailer. I was so ignorant of all things medical that it never occurred to me that it might be dangerous even to walk. Fortunately it is a downhill run all the way from the Mas Méjean, where the Laportes live, to Valleraugue. As soon as we reached home I made some excuse to Lucinde and retreated to bed.

The next day I telephoned to Dr Roque for advice. The telephone was working so badly that we could scarcely hear each other. I half caught the name of the medicine he told me to take, but I had no pencil at hand to write it down. It escaped my memory as soon as I put down the receiver. I went back to bed and let nature do her best for me. I was unwilling to alarm Lucinde, and so I got up every evening and dragged my weary way with André to the restaurant.

Nature pulled me through in time, but only just, for my journey north. The German safe-conduct had at last arrived and there was nothing to prevent our joining François. He had even found us a flat after weeks of house hunting. Not that at that time it was difficult to find accommodation in Paris; so many Parisians had fled to the free zone that you could borrow a flat as easily as you could rent one. The difficulty was to find one in good condition. It was essential to do so since it was impossible to redecorate.

Our journey north was epic. We had suitcases and hampers and hold-alls, eleven pieces in all, for we had to take with us every garment we possessed, in whatever condition, and every atom of food we could lay hands on. One huge hamper was full of the dreary jam called *raisiné*, which you make by substituting grape-juice for sugar. I had also pounds and pounds of wheat bought illegally, to be ground in the coffee-mill and made into porridge, or roasted and ground as a substitute for coffee. I had dried chestnuts and dried mushrooms and even earthenware jars full of salted mushrooms. The salt had of course dissolved into brine, which made transport difficult, but somehow or other they too must be brought to Paris.

The first part of the journey we made in the familiar Valleraugue bus. It took us to where we joined the train at Pont d'Hérault. All my memories of long-distance travel with luggage during the Occupation are sheer nightmare. Every time you had to board a train or bus, till the last moment you were in panic fear of not even managing to get inside. Everything was overcrowded; everyone had an incredible amount of luggage, for the excellent reason that most people's purpose in travelling was to find food. When your luggage was too heavy or too voluminous for you to carry yourself, there was the fear of finding no porter, or of having the bus driver refuse to hoist it on to the bus-top. Often you had only a few minutes in which to board long-distance trains, and while you struggled to fight your way in at the bottlenecks that formed at all the entrances, you saw agile youths wriggling in at the windows, and by the time you had got inside, they had booked the vacant seats for the members of their families.

We reached Pont-d'Hérault late because of the innumer-able halts on the way to take in new passengers with new loads of belongings. By the time we drove up to the station

the train was already signalled. Hysterically I started pulling
my affairs out of the bus, shouting frantically to the driver
for his help. But he was busy collecting fares and was unable
to come to my rescue. I seized what I could carry, and rushed
towards the platform with little André panting in my wake
and Nicolas under one arm. The train was drawing into
the station and we just barely managed to rush across in
front of the engine. Horror of horrors, as we emerged on
the other side André shouted to me that he had lost one
of his shoes. Nothing worse could have befallen us, short
of losing our lives. Real leather shoes were impossible to
procure in France, and these were real leather. They had
been sent from Switzerland by a compassionate aunt. They
were brand new and rather too large, which was why André
had lost one when he had to run. The moment it went round
that a small boy had lost his shoe a general hunt-the-slipper
was started. Men and women ran feverishly up and down the
train, peering between the wheels of the carriages. Everyone
had grasped the full drama of the situation. At last a man
fished it out from under the engine and we boarded the train
in a general rush just as it whistled and began to move. I
had still only the luggage I had been able to carry. I hung
out of the window shrieking appeals to the guard to hold
up the train, and to the bus-driver to bring my luggage.
While the guard stood with his whistle to his lips and
the engine-driver fumed, the bus-driver panted to and fro
with one incongruous package after another. But the train
would wait no longer. One object was missing still, Nicolas's
basketwork cradle filled with various articles of food and
clothing. The driver promised to send it after us, and with
this promise (which he kept) I had to be content. The train
steamed out of the station. Our new adventure had begun.

That was November 11th, 1942. It was in Nîmes, where
we were to take the night train, that I learned about the
Allied landing in French North Africa. I remember that I
was with Maman, though what she was doing in Nîmes I
cannot remember. She was very upset. She firmly believed
in the theory exposed at length in the Vichy press, that this
was a new attempt the English were making to annex the
French overseas possessions. I tried neither by word nor

look to betray my ecstatic happiness; but Maman sensed what I tried to hide. She spoke what I do truly believe was the only hard word she ever addressed to me in her life. She said I cared nothing for France and thought only of my native country. I bowed my head, at least metaphorically. It was no use quarrelling at the eleventh hour. Besides, I knew that nothing I could say would convince her either of my love for France, or that Britain's purpose was not to annex Algeria. I bottled up my bitterness, and that is never a good thing to do.

But still . . . but still . . . The train was no sooner out of the station of Nîmes than my heart began to soar, as it always did once the journey was really under way. There was the excitement of the North African landing, there was the prospect of reunion with François, there was the unwonted luxury of travelling first-class, for François was now working in the Ministry of Public Works and we could all travel first-class without paying. How could I help being happy? I had no notion as our train thundered through the night on its northward journey that the German army was pouring south to occupy the whole of France, or that by doing so they were clearing the air and making honest Pétainism almost impossible.

Some time in the middle of the night I made my first contact with the occupying forces. At Moulins the train stopped and the German check took place. When at last we moved out of the station, it was as though heavy gates had closed behind us. There would be no more letters from my father, or from any of my friends in Great Britain. I was going to experience for myself what I had so often heard described by refugees from Germany before the war, or in novels and newspapers. I would be in Occupied Territory. Already the Rough Beast had ceased to be a visionary image in a poem of W B Yeats, and had taken on a face, a uniform. I knew him at last for what he was, a monster of mediocrity, a suburban frog inflated to such inhuman proportions that even his bureaucratic shadow cast a chill.

Part Two
'...What rough beast...'

CHAPTER ONE

When we reached Paris, François first took us to stay with
a Swiss uncle. Dreamy, unworldly, a little vague and very
gentle, but with a mind critical enough to feel at home in
Paris, Oncle Robert is a philosopher, luckily possessed of
some private means. He is one of Maman's brothers, the
fourth of Grandpapa-de-Genève's seven children. He has
retired since to Geneva, but he spent most of his adult
life in Paris, doing a little coaching, translating books of
German philosophy, and working quietly away at, among
other things, the philosophy of rhythm. He was one of
the few members of our immediate circle whom tragedy
overtook in the early stages of the war. In the exodus from
Paris at the time of the invasion, he and his younger son
were somehow separated from his wife and elder son. Those
two were caught by a bombardment at Poitiers, and Tante
Renée, Oncle Robert's wife, was killed by a bomb in full
view of her son, Philippe. As soon as the fighting was over,
Oncle Robert made his way back to Paris, to the big old
flat he owns in the Rue de Tournon. There he settled down
again as best he could, with his two sons.

Deep affection bound François to Oncle Robert who,
when François had been a rather delicate child, had taught
him Latin and Greek and roused in him a lively interest in
philology. When François was appointed to a post in Paris,
his uncle offered to take him in till such time as he should
have found a flat of his own. This invitation was extended
to include André, Nicolas and me, for, though we had a flat,
our furniture was still in Marseilles at the mercy of the Old
Harbour rats.

The morning after we reached Paris, François took the
three of us to visit the flat he had rented for us. I had my first
bitter taste of Occupation as soon as we left Oncle Robert's

house. At the top of the Rue de Tournon, on the edge of the Jardin du Luxembourg, stands what before the war was the Senate House. This building was occupied by the German air force, and an enormous Nazi flag had been hoisted over it, the first I had seen. It floated there in all its hideous symbolism, against the luminous changing sky of the Île de France. White hoardings had been put up to prevent the Paris population from coming within bomb-throwing distance, and German sentries with closed hostile faces were mounting guard.

The Rue du Cloître Notre Dame, where we were to live, is only about half an hour's walk from the Rue de Tournon. We went on foot, wheeling Nicolas along with us in his perambulator. It was an exciting moment for André and me when François turned the key in the lock and opened the door of our new home. We were a little damped to find waiting for us Lucie, the maid François had engaged and who had come to show us over. A very respectable-looking woman of about fifty much better dressed than myself, Lucie had divorced a hairdresser husband. As her only child, a daughter, was married, she had decided to go into domestic service, of which decision we were to have the benefit. She was already familiar with our flat, for she had come there several times to do a little cleaning in preparation for our arrival. She led us from room to room, announcing in authoritative tones the purpose of each: dining-room, drawing-room, *petit salon*, master bedroom, children's bedroom, etc. As I followed her about, rather disheartened, I felt that she was forcing me into a mould not made to fit me for, though I fell in love with the flat the moment I saw it, I suspected that I would never be able to live up to its standards as interpreted by Lucie. What had we to do with a *petit salon* and a butler's pantry? But these were problems that could wait.

Of the time that we were still to spend in the Rue de Tournon, what I most clearly remember is the cold. It was November, a bitterly cold November, and there was no question of central heating or of hot water, for there was neither coal nor oil to be had, and gas and electricity were rationed so severely that we could count on them only for a minimum of cooking. A small quantity of briquets, imported from Germany, was doled out to us every winter, but for all practical purposes we had to depend on wood, and wood, expensive at the best of times, had risen to such a prohibitive price that we were lucky when we could heat a single room. Even that would have been impossible if the inventive French had not devised wonderful slow-combustion wood-stoves which gave out an even heat and used amazingly little fuel. Oncle Robert had one of these in his sitting-room, but as this served him also as a study, and even at that time as a bedroom, for he was an elderly man who suffered badly from the cold, we were a little hesitant about invading it. In our own room there was an old-fashioned stove; it would have burned more wood than we felt would be fair to Oncle Robert. It was difficult to find wood, not merely to pay for it, and could be done only through some contact in the country. It was difficult, too, to find a lorry to bring it into Paris once you had bought it. We lit a fire in our bedroom only the first evening, to celebrate. The rest of the time we suffered, in my case not always in silence. Not only am I no Spartan; I was terrified for Nicolas. He had few warm clothes and the room he shared with us was so cold that I was afraid to undress him, afraid to wash him, almost afraid to change him. I kept him in his cot, rolled up in layer upon layer of old cut-down blanket, with a wine-bottle full of hot water at his feet, but even so his little hands always looked blue, and the sight of him lying so good in his cot made my heart ache. It was, illogically, the more harrowing that he was always gay.

It was during that cold autumn and winter in Paris that I discovered what courage it can require merely to keep clean. At La Coustète we had for our washing facilities the primitive comfort of our ancestors: I had to draw the water from the stream, carry it up to the house and heat it in the water-tank of our wood-burning stove. But at least when all was done we could take our tub in front of an open fire. In Paris there were no tubs; there were fine but useless baths in icy bathrooms where icy water flowed from real taps. How I envied the people, and in France there are many, who have never had a bathroom and have learned from the start to keep clean in difficult circumstances. It was in 1942 in Paris that it occurred to me for the first time that it is perhaps because we Anglo-Saxons are lazy that we take for granted that a people with few bathrooms must be a dirty people. And when I hounded myself into the chill bathroom and forced myself to wash, inch by inch, with cold, cold water and green clay soap (I pass over in silence the occasions when I refused to be hounded), how I resented having to use up good courage for no better purpose.

As regards food, we were rather better off than in the Cevennes for as long as we remained with Oncle Robert. It was not that he could afford to buy on the black market; for that you needed to be rich. But he had lived long years in Paris and was a regular customer in the shops of his *quartier*. This gave him access to what extras were being kept under the counter. Besides, he had a Breton maid who had been with him for years and who arranged for monthly parcels of butter and bacon to be sent from Brittany by a member of her family. It was no large amount, but it meant that there was a rasher of bacon to 'season' our evening vegetable soup, and a minute pat of butter to put on our meagre breakfast ration of bread.

As soon as our furniture arrived I began to spend most of my time in the flat. Moving house is at the best of times a discouraging business; in those days, when nothing could be repainted or repaired for lack of materials, it was heart-breaking. Even cleaning materials were not to be found, and our furniture had suffered from three years in the Marseilles warehouse. The mattresses had been patched, but it had been impossible to replace the wool the rats had stolen for their nests. They were thin and therefore cold. But for all this I found some comfort in the joy of recovering my Steinway pianoforte which a friend had sheltered in his Marseilles flat. Besides, it was exciting unpacking the food that came with me from Valleraugue. The salted mushrooms had survived the journey, and only a pot of *raisiné* had burst its bonds and leaked over André's modest wardrobe.

I think it was when I was wheeling Nicolas home from one of these unpacking expeditions, with André trailing in our wake, that an incident occurred which stands out in my memory as the most painful of that winter. We were walking along the Boulevard St Germain, just beyond the Place de l'Odéon, when it took place. It was not in fact an incident; it was a man. As I said earlier, I am short-sighted but never wear spectacles except when I really have to see, as in the cinema. It was not till he was close upon us that I saw the man. He was little and elderly, with bowed shoulders and poorly dressed. I doubt whether I would have noticed him at all if it had not been for the sinister distinguishing mark on his left breast, the yellow star with *Juif* printed across it. It was the first I had seen; in unoccupied territory the star was not worn, and in occupied territory only from June 1942. I stopped dead in my tracks, stunned. He passed us by without looking at us, but it was a full minute before I recovered the use of my legs. In all my life I have never felt so deeply humiliated. The full impact of our defeat came home to me in one stunning blow, the terrible difference between knowing a thing intellectually and feeling it emotionally. If Nazi Germany had reduced France to this, then truly she had cause to feel humiliated.

This matter of France's humiliation was one to which I was only now awakening. So far I had not thought of our defeat in those terms. But the *pauvre dame* had ceased to be *sans homme*, and it was curious how her values shifted and her vision changed. In a sense, men and women taken separately are incomplete. I am aware that this may seem to Anglo-Saxons a very French point of view. I think the notion of equality or inequality between men and women is foreign to the French. I think they see them as complementary, each having an essential contribution to make and lighting truth up from a different angle. This is not really irrelevant to my point, that men and women are incomplete taken separately. It was a French abbé who pointed out to me that the word 'man' in the sentence in Genesis, 'God created man in his own image . . . male and female . . .' should be translated by an equivalent of the German word *mensch*, for its sense is not exclusively masculine. What he had in mind is confirmed on one level by the findings of psychology. But it goes further. Not only the unequal doses of male and female in the two people involved add up to form a composite personality which makes nonsense of the arithmetical concept: $1 + 1 = 2$; but each gains as an individual.

However that may be, it was through my renewed daily contact with François that I came to understand just what defeat meant to men in France. It affected women more indirectly. Theirs was the cumulative humiliation of being little by little degraded to an exclusive preoccupation with material things; the humiliation daily renewed of having to beg even for what they bought; and they shared with the men that other humiliation whose fierce thrust I had just felt, of seeing to what treatment of the Jews Vichy had agreed. But the actual fact of military defeat is, I think, harder for men to bear than for women and, so long as German troops remained on French soil, the wound was kept open. In spite of what the Nazis found it politic to say at the time, which served especially to enhance their own valour, no Frenchman felt that France's defeat had been glorious. Most had accepted the armistice as inevitable, but the country as a whole found it impossible to subscribe to the policy afterwards followed by the Vichy government. When it came to the point, it was intolerable to see their army disbanded when the struggle could well be continued in France's overseas territories; intolerable to know that Frenchmen were taking up arms to defend those territories, which should have served as a base against the enemy, against their Allies. It was clear to all but the collaborators, clear even to what I call the honest Pétainists, that our one hope lay in Allied victory. It must have appeared to all our friends that we were running with the hare and hunting with the hounds in the wake of Pierre Laval. It was from the feeling of revolt to which these reflections gave rise that the Resistance movement grew, as naturally as a mushroom grows among dead leaves. In its beginnings it was no organized movement; in town, village or countryside, those in whom it burned soon came to know which of their neighbours shared their views, and with no clear notion how their feelings could be translated into action they forgathered, at first simply for moral support. Heroism crept upon many of them like a thief in the night. But even those who never became organized found opportunities in

the exercise of their profession that enabled them sooner
or later to thwart and flout their German masters. Their
efforts were not spectacular and were soon forgotten, but
they were effective. There were the slow strikes of the miners
of the north and of the workers who had been forced into
the *Todt* organization; there was the deliberate delaying of
transport in German service; the suppression by the police
of documents incriminating suspects; the sheltering of illicit
transport under their uniformed wing by the *gendarmes*;
the spontaneous passing on of information useful to the
Resistance by postal authorities; the help given to Jews by
the man in the street. In fact, though the actual members of
organized Resistance movements may not have been many
in relation to the total population, they were numerous who
had some act of effective resistance to their credit.

The *Maquis* itself was an arm unwittingly forged by
the Germans against themselves. When they disbanded the
army authorized by the armistice, a number of officers went
underground. When they extorted workers for Germany
from the Vichy government, thousands of those who were
scheduled to leave France for enemy country took to the
forests and hills. By rounding up Jews and by practising
reprisals on the members of resisters' families, the Germans made the *Maquis* inevitable. By hunting down and
massacring the unarmed *maquisards*, they forced them to
take up arms.

Even among those who were neither collaborators nor
even Pétainists, but were with all their heart for some sort
of resistance against the enemy, some are to be found to
this day who condemn guerilla warfare and terrorism as
disloyal. I know honest and very Christian Frenchmen who
deplore the *Maquis*. I am easily convinced by anyone who
argues well and states his case with clarity, because I have
little respect for my own intelligence. I have often been
argued into agreeing with this point of view. But it never
lasts. The moment I am alone again the pendulum swings
back to where it stood before. I believe it was right that
people should combat Nazism actively and by every means.
Besides, I think that we who benefited by the heroism of
others have no right to pick holes in their methods. They

took terrible risks, and not only for themselves but for the people they most cared about, and their selfless courage cauterized and left the Resistance movement pure. I mention the conscientious objector attitude to the Resistance to show that it was no easy matter for anyone in an occupied country to decide what action he was justified in taking. It was not a simple matter of deciding whether one was pro-Vichy, pro-German, pro-British or pro-de Gaulle; people had to bore through layer upon layer of habit of mind and solve for themselves the problem of what does or does not justify violence.

If I felt only now, and through François, the humiliation of military defeat, it was partly because I was still British enough to feel that it did not concern me. But even after I experienced it vicariously, some inner voice told me there was no cause for it. Whose but the Nazis' was the humiliation, when their victorious soldiers invaded the shops of Normandy, buying up everything they could lay hands on, and eating butter by mouthfuls straight from the packet? No one who saw the Germans in the streets of Paris, with their uniforms of an ugly grey-green (which, as Jacques Perret points out in *Le Caporal Epinglé*, were meant to blend with nature's colours, but in France clashed, for nowhere in France had nature made greens of that sickening shade) and their unthinking faces, could feel that their imposed presence in that city of all cities humiliated any but themselves. That by force of arms they achieved only because they sacrificed to it everything that gives life meaning, that the monstrous stupidity of the Nazis should have vanquished humane, civilized, peace-loving France, was surely no more humiliating than the fact of their having, as they had done, vanquished their own élite. But that was not how men saw our defeat.

They had another problem to solve that most women were spared. They suffered continuously from the fear that the work they were doing might be of value to the Nazis. It was not always easy to tell; Germany took such a high percentage of all France produced that it was difficult to know what was or was not of indirect use to them. The work that François found when he came to Paris was from this point of view completely satisfactory. It was even a magnificent gesture of optimism, for you could take it seriously only if you believed that France had a future. His headquarters were in the Ministry of Public Works, and his job was to make the plans for a motor-highway between Lille and Paris, the *Autoroute du Nord*, which would certainly never be built while the war lasted, and in fact has not been completed to this day. I think that it was as much because it was a job that could be of no conceivable service to the German war effort, as because it enabled him to bring his family north, that François accepted it.

But François had a more immediate and vital problem of which I knew nothing. At the time I am speaking of he was still a prisoner on parole. When he was allowed to leave the prisoners' camp he had first to sign a promise that he would commit no act hostile to the German army. He had also afterwards to present himself at regular intervals before the German authorities. The fact of having found work that was of no service to the Nazis was small consolation for feeling, as he did feel, that he must keep his word and take no active part in the Resistance till he could obtain his full release. Since the end of the war, and in the light of later experience, he has admitted to me that if it were all to live over again he would have no scruples about breaking his word. It was difficult at the time to see clearly where his duty lay, and difficult to shake off the habits of a lifetime. He told me nothing then of the struggle that was going on inside him. I would certainly have encouraged him in thinking that his promise was binding. My reasons would not have been his. As I said earlier, I am not the stuff of which martyrs are made, and when I was young I was good at refusing to face unpleasant facts.

Late in November we settled into our flat in the shadow of Notre Dame. I had once more, and in new conditions, to tackle the problem of providing food for the family. The official rations were insufficient to provide so much as one meal a day. Roughly they were as follows, counting the ounce at thirty grammes:

Our meat allowance was three ounces each a week. There would besides be an occasional distribution of sausages that exuded a sinister liquid when fried, or some equally disquieting galantine. Shellfish was unrationed, but we got fish only about once in three months. I think that we were supposed to get an egg or two a month, but we seldom got them. We would go for several months without any and then suddenly be told, perhaps in March, that the November eggs were 'out', as they said, not a reassuring thought. We got one pound of sugar a month, and babies two and a half pounds. Adults received half a pound of jam and children a pound. Children also got four bars of chocolate-coated fondant a month and a small bag of boiled sweets, at which the adults gazed with ill-concealed longing. Our fat allowance, and this covered all fats, was ten ounces a month, but it dwindled to two ounces in the winter of 1944. Adults got no milk, children under six a pint and a half a day, and over six theoretically half a pint, but it vanished after 1943. We had a very small allowance of fatless cheese. When the vegetable season was over we would each receive half a pound of macaroni (or its equivalent) and a small tin of vegetables. Once or twice in the winter there would be a distribution of a quarter, sometimes even half a pound of dried peas or beans, and about four pounds of potatoes. We received a small packet of coffee substitute a month; children could have instead the same amount of Banania or Phoscao—if you could find it. Our bread ration was six ounces a day, but often on some pretext or another, reprisals or what-not, it was less. Children under five got five ounces, but what we called the J3s, that is to say adolescents, got eight ounces. I noted these figures at the time and I think they are correct.

It was impossible to subsist on these rations, eked out only by such carrots, Jerusalem artichokes, Swedish turnips and an occasional cabbage as we could wrest from the market by dint of long queueing. We were all of us driven to some form of dishonest practice. It was no small hardship having to throw our moral scruples to the winds and settle down to a dishonest way of life, in full view of the children and in contradiction to all we were striving to teach them. Not but what my practical Scotch mind made a clear distinction between what is immoral and what is merely illegal; but such distinctions are not easy to explain to a child. Besides, there was a haunting feeling that this was the thin end of a wedge and, as such, not a good thing for the nation.

What were we to do? There was no alternative. The rich bought on the black market, and quite rightly. The only people who suffered deprivation through them were the Germans; however much food France produced, her people were not going to receive more than starvation rations. Those of us who could not afford the black market bought on what we came to call the grey market. We got in touch with country people who would sell us their produce at a reasonable price out of friendship, or because we had been recommended to them, or had something to barter. We never obtained much, and the grey market was as illegal as the black. It was only less shocking because the working people had as many contacts as, or more than, the rich, and it was not money that caused injustice.

Those who suffered most from this state of things were probably elderly people living alone on a small income, and certain communities. In January 1946 my daughter was born in a convent nursing home in Paris, and the nun at the head of the maternity section used to tell me about the various ailments caused by under-feeding from which they had all suffered. One of the symptoms, caused especially by the lack of fats, was that the skin dried and cracked. She herself had worked throughout the Occupation in the maternity section of the nursing-home and she said it had been agony for her every time a new-born baby was handed to her to be cleaned after birth. The glaireous matter on a new-born baby's body is apparently acid to the touch and it burned her deeply chapped hands.

It took us some time to get into contact with the grey market, and our early stages in the Rue du Cloître Notre Dame were very disheartening. I used to comb the neighbourhood hopefully and come home at last with a few green peppers, small and rather wizened, or a couple of pounds of carrots or Jerusalem artichokes, and, of course, swedes, which the French were eating for the first time. To this day swede, or *rutabagas* as they are called in France, are remembered as the very symbol of the Occupation, and their being reduced to eating them was counted by the French as a major German victory. One of our friends looked the word up in the Larousse Encyclopedia. He firmly maintains that the swede is there described as a root vegetable which is given to animals in time of famine. I kept to myself the fact that I had eaten them every winter of my life in Scotland.

It was especially through François's new job that help came. For one thing a sort of co-operative had been organized in the Ministry, and every now and then he would bring home a cauliflower or a war-gingerbread, or some other unexpected addition to our menu. He also made contact through one of his new colleagues with a market gardener north of Paris. He would visit him on his way back from Lille, where he had to go fairly often. Lucie and I gathered round on his return, and watched with excitement while he unpacked his rucksack, and potatoes and beans and even occasionally eggs were laid on the table. Lucie remarked that we were like a robber's womenfolk waiting to inspect the loot. In Lille, too, François sometimes had luck. The people of the North of France are dogged, courageous and generous, and very ready to help one another. His *Ponts et Chaussées* colleagues in Lille did what they could to help, and he usually brought either chicory or bacon fat. The chicory was smuggled over from Belgium, and though it was of no value as food, it was popular as a substitute for coffee and could be successfully bartered for more useful things.

Every time François went to Lille he spent the night with Pasteur Nick. From him he would get what was as precious as food, the latest optimistic rumour and some accounts of Resistance action. Above all he came home happy from the welcome he always found, and comforted by the assurance that a man he considered as something of a spiritual father was as rabid an anti-Pétainist and as ardent for the Resistance as any of us.

In the meantime we were gradually renewing contact with our friends and little by little weaving the web that was to bear us up through all that dreary period. Soon after we settled into the flat we were invited to dine with one of François's oldest friends, Janine Delpech, a writer and journalist, and with her husband, Bob Teissier. This invitation posed me a nasty problem. We had dined with them already, but it had been informally, whereas this was a dinner party. My problem was that I had nothing to wear, not only by Paris but by any standards. Without exaggeration, all I possessed was an old pair of slacks, a skirt cut down from a dress of Tante Berthe's (who was smaller than I am) and a jacket she had knitted for me to wear with it, out of the very bad wool which was all one could obtain even with coupons. Some clothes coupons had been doled out to me during my pregnancy, and I had bought some black woollen material for a dress and coat, but had not been able to have them made in Valleraugue. Now there was no time. I had a vague hope that perhaps it would not really matter; in my innocence I thought that perhaps the other guests would also be at a low ebb, after two and a half years of Occupation. I was wrong. The women in Janine's drawing-room were almost as elegant as before the war. I was to learn that Frenchwomen, and especially Parisians, sensed the Germans' deliberate wish to humiliate them by forcing them to dress badly. They considered elegance an essential part of resistance. The Paris dressmakers had, in the same spirit, plied their wits. Like Racine and Corneille before them, out of the restriction imposed by Authority they had forged a new style. It was soon clear to me that I was not going to be allowed, as I had half hoped, to slack off. The

new style laid the accent especially on hats and shoes, but
coats had a sort of bustle effect at the back which seemed to
defy the Nazis so to reduce us that we could no longer waste
material. The novelty of the shoes was in their soles. Leather
there was none, and I imagined when I came to Paris that
we would be allowed to wear our clogs, perhaps enamelled
as at Le Chambon-sur-Lignon. Not a bit of it! Only the soles
of shoes were of wood, and instead of attempting to disguise
the fact fashion underlined it by making them several inches
thick, but tapering to half an inch in front. The uppers were
made of a variety of materials. I have seen evening shoes
whose soles were of opaque glass, their uppers by contrast
mere twists of cherry-coloured velvet, and the effect for all
their weight was Cinderella-like. These thick soles, in fact,
gave an added elegance to the legs above them. Many of
those legs had no stockings (I had none, and I remember
that we managed to persuade ourselves it was not the lack
of stockings that made us feel so cold), but the owner stained
them the fashionable shade and it was no easy matter getting
the colour to look even.

The dresses made no concession that I can remember
to our straitened circumstances. Where the material came
from was nobody's business. Those who could bought on
the black market; those who started the war with a capital
of clothes adapted as they went along; those who had suitable
curtains or bedcovers cut them up: others fell back on ances-
tral remains. Once Tante Berthe brought out of a drawer
yard upon yard of crocheted lace and got her dressmaker
to make me a beautiful blouse by sewing the strips edge to
edge to fit a paper pattern. No one without actual experience
of the thing can imagine the effort and ingenuity this
surface elegance represented; the unpicking and unravel-
ling, the adapting and piecing together, the re-making and
contriving. Only the dressmaker who did the latter part of
the work knew what it hid. I remember my shame the first
time I shed my outer skin and stood before my dressmaker
in underclothes worn to cobwebs. She set my mind at ease
at once. 'Madame!' she said, 'Everyone is the same!'

But hats were the thing with which they chose chiefly to
taunt the Nazis. Hats can be made of this and that and still

make a good show, for the maker's art is everything. By making a joke of the restrictions, the tiny hats of last winter, of which François had brought me such a lovely sample to Valleraugue, had led to trouble. I was told at the time that after his dress-show one of the famous dressmakers was informed by the German authorities that unless he did something about the hats, he would have to close down. There is no denying that they had a frivolous, impertinent look, not at all the right thing by Nazi standards for a beaten people that owed its defeat to its very frivolity and should be wearing only ashes on its head. These hats were cast aside and a rush was made to the other extreme. The bigger and absurder the hat, the more the Parisian women felt that they expressed their determination not to suffer the to them extreme humiliation of being dowdily dressed. Geneviève Petit-Dutaillis, who had also returned to Paris, told me at about this time that she had seen such an extraordinary hat in the underground that she had tried to work her way through the crowd to get a view of it from behind. The front was a mass of flowers and she wanted to know what the back was like. The underground during the Occupation was the only means of public transport. The carriages were so crowded that you could scarcely get out once you were in. She found that she was making no headway. But a man who was better situated saw what she was about. Over the heads of the intervening people he murmured, '*Derrière, Madame, il y a des fruits!*'

I have strayed from Janine's dinner party. The standard of clothes I found in her drawing-room was not the only thing that disconcerted me. I had imagined that when we invited friends to the house it would be to share the *rutabaga* or whatever it was that we would normally be eating, and that it would be the spirit of the thing, sustained by the wine that was only now beginning to disappear from our tables, that would count. I should have known French hospitality better. When guests were expected— and I think there was more entertaining on a small scale among intimate friends during the Occupation than at any other time—those who could would go all out on the black market; those who could not would exploit their connections on the grey market, even at the cost of depriving their family. The result would be a tolerable meal, and sometimes a really good one. This was a good one. Janine and Bob, who own a place near Paris, had managed to procure a turkey. I think that we were ten at table; I know there was plenty for everyone. We had been told about the turkey over the telephone, for it was really the pretext for the party. Even so, I was so haunted by my own difficulties that I dared take only a very little. I thought that perhaps Janine was counting on its doing duty for the family the following day. I was in a state still bordering on innocence, the country cousin come to town.

And in more ways than one. I discovered with some embarrassment that I could hear almost nothing of what my neighbour said to me at table. I had grown so used to silence and to solitude that the noise of ten people speaking all at once with the verve habitual to the French, and which only the French expression *brouhaha* aptly describes, so confused my ear that I was incapable of concentrating on the one of those ten voices which was addressing itself to me. It was a curious and disconcerting experience.

Another person with whom we renewed contact at this time, and who was to be one of our greatest supports and best sources of information during the Occupation, was Louis Armand. Louis Armand, who at that time was one of the three directors of the *Société Nationale des Chemins de Fer*, is one of the great men of contemporary France. The qualities that make men great are blended in him in proportions that are, I think, specifically French. His mind is as universal as is ever possible, and he has that immediate grasp they say Napoleon had of unfamiliar matter, as though there were always at the back of such minds some knowledge which by analogy can throw light on a new problem or technique. He has the gift that Tovey had of lifting you out of your naturally mediocre context and letting you share in what lies beyond your normal scope. He has great courage, both physical and moral, and his integrity is such that to his friends he is a touchstone on which they test their beliefs, whether or not they share his opinions. He is like some dense, very rare metal whose contact tarnishes whatever is false. He is one of the most brilliant talkers (and one of the worst listeners) in a land that breeds brilliant talkers (and bad listeners); but he is essentially a man of action. His intellectual formation is scientific, but his approach to scientific matter is that of a poet, though his language is such that any intelligent schoolboy would feel at home in it. Though he cannot fail to know by how far he out-tops most of his contemporaries, he never plays the lion. No; that is not quite true. He does play the lion, but it is the lion he is, amiable, entertaining and generous.

François came home one day from his office and told me that Armand had telephoned an invitation to lunch with him at the restaurant of the Gare de Lyon. I was glad. Our friends were not only our chief source of comfort, they were, with the BBC, our best source of information. They told us what was being said in the *coulisses* of the Ministries, what René Payot had written in the *Journal de Genève* and what the new date was on which we might confidently expect the Allies to land. They also told us the latest jokes, the endless stories of Hitler at the gates of Paradise, in which St Peter was credited with a strong dose of French wit; the definition of collaboration: 'Give me your watch and I'll tell you what time it is'; of democracy: 'A system under which when they ring your bell in the early morning it's the milk'. I knew that Armand would have more reliable information than anyone else, and probably funnier stories.

When I reached the Gare de Lyon I was shown up to his office, where François was to join me. There a shock was in store for me. I was the first to arrive, and when Armand came to meet me with outstretched welcoming hands he spoke words that in the mouth of a Frenchman always fill me with misgiving. He said, '*Quelle bonne surprise!*' I realized at once that François had made a mistake and that it was a men's party. I would have given anything to beat a hasty retreat, but it was too late. He soon put me at my ease as far as that was possible; but he struck a chill to my heart by saying he thought it courageous of me to come back to Paris when so many people were leaving because they were afraid the food situation might become such that we all starved. It was a double chill. I am instinctively suspicious of anyone who says I am courageous, and I was disheartened at the thought that the food situation might grow worse. To prove his point, Armand began to open ledgers and show me the figures of what the Germans were taking out of France. He showed me that the cattle the SNCF was being forced to ship to Germany was no longer counted by the head but by the trainload. There was a danger that milk would disappear altogether. He gave details of much else that I have forgotten. Then the other guests and François arrived (they were, in fact, all men) and we went through to the station restaurant where a table was being kept for us. By that time I had forgotten both my embarrassment and my fears. Armand's vivid personality has the effect upon one of a blood transfusion. I remember no detail of what was said, though Armand told us something of his contacts with the German authorities. He spoke his mind so freely, scarcely even lowering his voice, that I remember thinking that he at least could not possibly be a member of the Resistance. In actual fact he belonged, I believe, to three distinct resistance movements, and was also working for the British Intelligence Service.

But these contacts were the highlights of our existence. The rest was hunger, cold, and a sort of chronic despair. Looking back I see our Paris life as a dreary monochrome, a film whose greys vary only from the muddy greys of the Paris winter pavements to the luminous greys of the Paris winter skies. Sometimes we would take refuge in a cinema, hoping for a moment of forgetfulness, but whatever the film, we were never spared at the end a view of the German Atlantic Wall with its huge fortifications, its gigantic cannon and its well-armed, warmly-clad sentries. The bubble of the latest incandescent rumour would burst on their bayonets and all hope of an Allied landing vanish in the sea-mist that wrapped the Atlantic Wall about. In our inmost hearts we had never really believed a landing possible. We believed in our liberation as something so remote it scarcely concerned us, much as one believes, when one does believe, in an after-life. We pretended to believe so as to survive; it was a sort of game to pretend. But when we emerged from the cinema it was a game we could no longer play. And when we reached home with the last underground, in a fevered rush to be off the streets before midnight on pain of spending the night at the police station, we had still to roast and grind the wheat and put it to soak for next morning's porridge.

Before we had been very long in the Rue du Cloître Notre Dame I fell ill. I was run down with the effort of feeding Nicolas. It was foolish of me to persist in feeding him even partially, which was all I was capable of. But I was haunted by Armand's talk of Paris being deprived of milk, and besides I gained such advantages for the rest of the family in extra rations of milk and sugar, which I was given as a nursing mother, that I could not make up my mind to wean him. The result was that, as I had no resistance to the cold, I went down with bronchitis.

We called in a young woman doctor recommended to us by Lucienne. She prescribed for the bronchitis and she added to her long list of medicines a malt product whose purpose was to improve my milk supply. She then examined Nicolas, who lay in his basket cradle by my bed. She said that I must give him fruit juice. I asked her how you procured fruit in Paris. She murmured something about getting one's friends to send apples from the country and making tea with the apple-skins. She might as well have suggested that our friends send us *foie gras*. She then went through to see André who, though not properly speaking ill, was pale and wan. She turned him round with his back to her and diagnosed curvature of the spine. She said that he must at once start remedial gymnastics and that he too must have fruit juice and good food. And with these encouraging words she left us.

As soon as the prescribed medicines had been bought, I opened the packet of malt product and found that it contained saccharine-coated granules. Hopefully I took the prescribed teaspoonful. It tasted wonderful. Before I knew where I was the packet was empty. I had pains that night and my milk supply remained static. I dared not tell the doctor what I had done.

I had recovered only long enough to arrange for André to have remedial gymnastics at his convent school when Nicolas in his turn caught bronchitis. We were well into December and Christmas was drawing near. I transferred him from our icy but luminous bedroom to the living-room, on which Notre Dame's shadow fell, but where we had a stove. I did my best to carry out the doctor's instructions, but he made slow progress and could seldom be persuaded to take any food other than what he got from me. On Christmas Eve he was feverish. The doctor was out, but I left a message asking her to come as soon as she could. On Christmas Day I rose at six and went into the kitchen to peel potatoes. The food problem made it necessary for me to shop and cook myself. That Christmas morning I peeled seventy-two very dirty potatoes. We had invited Oncle Robert and his two sons to lunch with us, and as Henri was home for the holidays there would be eight of us to eat the duck which François had triumphantly brought back from his last visit to Lille. There would be nothing else, so I calculated that we would need nine potatoes each. Every now and then I left off peeling and went through to the living-room to look at Nicolas. The moment he saw me he would coo and wave his arms and legs. I persuaded myself that there was probably nothing much wrong with him, and went back to the kitchen.

In spite of an undercurrent of anxiety, the party was a success. Just as we were finishing, Oncle Ernest and Tante Berthe, who had returned to Paris shortly after I did, called to wish us a happy Christmas. We all gathered round the stove with our *ersatz* coffee. Gradually the room filled with laughter and tobacco smoke, in spite of the rationing, and I began to feel anxious that Nicolas should be in such an atmosphere. It was at this point that the doctor looked in. She had got my message only late the night before. She examined him and announced that he had a touch of congestion of the lungs. That was the end of the party. Oncle Ernest and Tante Berthe and Oncle Robert and his sons went home, and we were left with our anxiety.

But Nicolas recovered, though he continued to have so little appetite that his brothers used to hang round while I was giving him his milk-pudding in the hope that he would refuse it and it would fall to their share.

In the months that followed other problems began to raise their heads. When late in January or early in February the family pig was sacrificed at Mandiargues, Maman took advantage of its now being possible to send food parcels from one zone to the other to make us a present of a round of bacon. Nicolas was nearly eight months old, and I kept this bacon for him and gave him a small rasher for breakfast every other day. As no one else got any of it, I was surprised to notice that it diminished by leaps and bounds, and that these leaps and bounds took place on Saturdays. At last I was forced to face the fact that Lucie was taking large slices of it home when she left on Saturday evening for her Sunday off. In the end I had to have the matter out with her, and we had a rather harrowing scene. She told me that her daughter was expecting a baby and that it was for her she took the bacon.

Nor was this all. One of my worst memories belongs to this period. I went one day to the fishmonger to buy our three-monthly ration of fish. I stood in the queue for a long time in the cold, and then went to the cash-desk to pay for what I had got and show my card. For fish we had not coupons but a card that must be signed each time we bought something. On this occasion, when I produced my card a terrible scene took place. The woman behind the cash-desk accused me of having bought my ration the day before and then scratched out the signature with a penknife. She showed me the card and when I looked close I could see that it did look as though the signature had been scratched out. I knew that I had done nothing of the sort; I was so certain of my innocence that in the end I burst into tears. The whole thing was unspeakably painful. Contemptuously, the fishmonger let me keep what I had bought, but I knew that he and all the people waiting in the queue thought me dishonest. I went home seething with revolt and feeling my humiliation to the full. The same afternoon I was sitting over the stove doing some mending when the door-bell rang. Lucie was out so I opened the door and found myself face to face with the very woman who had accused me. She was obviously as taken aback at seeing me as I was myself, but she asked if she might come in. She followed me into the sitting-room and there explained to me that the day before Lucie had come to the shop and had told her we were commercial people and that it would be in their interest to serve us extras behind the counter. Her purpose in calling was to discover whether what Lucie had said was true. She had no notion that Lucie worked for the person she had that morning accused of dishonesty.

As she spoke, it dawned on me that there were wheels within wheels of which in my innocence I had no notion. Apparently shopkeepers rendered each other these services, using their wares to obtain from other tradesmen what they themselves lacked. I explained to the woman that, unfortunately for us, we had neither a shop nor any sort of business that could in any way be profitable to her. She looked as though she wanted to add something to what she had said, but she changed her mind and took her leave. It was only some weeks later that it occurred to me what it must have been. The scales suddenly fell from my eyes and I knew it had been Lucie who, when she went to the shop the day before, must have used the card to buy fish for her daughter and then scratched out the signature. I had not the courage to take the matter up with her, but I knew it would not be possible to keep her beyond a few months. I clearly saw that in our present situation where it was essential that any maid we engaged should have not only the normal qualities but also honesty in the face of hunger, and a loyalty we had no right to expect of any stranger, it would be wiser to manage without a living-in maid.

But that could wait.

In the meantime we were gradually learning the abc of life under enemy occupation. In other words, we too were learning to be dishonest, though we called it by another name. Through our friends we heard that it was possible to obtain false bread cards, and through the intermediary now of one, now of another, we bought one every month. There were real false cards and false real cards. The first were counterfeits of the real thing. The second and more expensive were genuine bread-cards sold in the towns by

country people who could obtain wheat illegally and make
their own bread. We bought the first kind, and the best of
them were a pretty poor imitation of the real thing. I never
entered the baker's shop and handed my false coupons
over the counter without trembling. I always expected to
be denounced and hauled off to prison. It took me some
time to grasp the fact that no one cared less than the baker's
buxom, flirtatious, warm-hearted wife, on duty behind the
counter, whether or not our cards were genuine so long as
we produced coupons of some sort for her monthly accounts.
Nor did I know then how little it is in the French character to
denounce at all. The baker's wife sometimes batted an eyelid
when our coupons were a particularly bad imitation, but she
never showed by the shadow of a sign that she had noted
my accent and drawn her conclusions. It was only when I
returned to Paris after the liberation that she greeted me
with a broad smile and said, '*Maintenant on peut le dire,
Madame, que vous êtes anglaise!*'

Procuring our official cards was a longer and more
exhausting business than buying our false cards. You took
your place in the long queue that overflowed from our
local food-office, and streamed along the pavement with
no protection from the rain. During the long wait, as the
queue moved forward inch by inch, conversation was soon
joined with the other grumbling women. We all spoke our
opinion without restraint and I never even attempted to
conceal the fact of my origins, for it only made them more
friendly. When at last my turn came and I was inside the
building, going from counter to counter, from queue to
queue, for the various cards, I was always in a fever lest
some mistake be made and I come away with less than my
due. How I hated the women behind the counters! They
were not nearly so friendly as the women in the queues.
They were most of them tasting power for the first time
in their lives; they were also certainly as underfed and
overworked as the rest of us; but I took no account of
that. I told myself that these were the women who knitted
at the foot of the guillotine; what I forgot to remember was
that they no doubt were thinking, 'Here comes the English
Miss!' Our mistrust was mutual. When I had wrested my

full batch of cards from their unwilling hands, my suspicions were unabated. I would count them over and over till I was certain I had everything; then scuttle home, clutching my handbag to my bosom, convinced that every passer-by was bent on snatching it from me.

I never dared use my tobacco-card in Paris. I would have had no scruples but I lacked the courage. I think it would have been more difficult to get away with than the bread-card. Now that tobacco was rationed, except among friends most men bitterly resented women's smoking, and any tobacco-card handed over the counter by a woman would have been carefully examined. The ration was two packets of cigarettes a month and one of tobacco. As François smokes very little at the best of times, he allowed me to keep his cigarettes. But what are two packets of cigarettes a month to a hardened smoker? Soon he found himself giving up his tobacco too. To this I added the tobacco from my own fag-ends and I bought a little machine that made my cigarettes better than I could make them myself. Sometimes François brought tobacco back from Lille. Like the chicory, it was smuggled over the frontier from Belgium. There was a joke going about at this time about Gallant Little Belgium striking her breast and saying, 'As long as a blade of grass remains in Belgium, our sister France shall not lack tobacco!' But none of this got me very far and I was soon looking round for other things to smoke. I remember an evening when François asked me to make him some lime-tea. I had to confess that I had smoked it all during the week.

All that year, but especially in the spring, when we were not too tired to fight our way in and out of crowded trains, we spent our Sundays and sometimes the whole weekend at Longpont with Germaine and her family. Longpont is a village south of Paris, where a great-uncle of François's owned a beautiful eighteenth-century house standing in a large park. This great-uncle, Oncle Jean Darier, a famous skin specialist in his time, died during the first year of the war and left this property to a Swiss nephew. The house had been standing empty at the time of the invasion and had been promptly occupied by a group of German officers. Germaine, who never knew fear and who can wield at will a manner compounded of such highhandedness and so much charm that it is difficult to resist her, went straight to Longpont the moment she heard that it was occupied, and firmly told the German officer who received her that the house belonged to a Swiss banker and must immediately be evacuated. She soon had the officer eating out of her hand. He promised to evacuate the house, and when he saw her out across the park, he gallantly lowered the branches of the cherry-trees to allow her to eat the cherries. Oncle Emile Darier, the new owner of Longpont, was so grateful to her for saving his house that he wrote and told her to make what use of it she cared for so long as the war lasted.

As the park contained an immense fruit and vegetable garden, though uncultivated since Oncle Jean's death, his offer was thankfully accepted. Soon not only Germaine, Pierre and their two sons now spent their spare time digging and planting in the garden, but also Oncle Robert and *his* two sons. The next to join the colony was Marcel Griaule. We too were given a plot of ground to cultivate and a couple of rooms to sleep in when we could. As often as possible we came out on Saturday afternoon. We dined all together off vegetable soup and a large dish of carrots, or whatever vegetable was ready, and we spent the evening round a roaring fire, for here there was no shortage of wood. On Sunday mornings the men worked in the garden. In the afternoons Germaine and Griaule got down to the files of their last journey in the Niger Bend, while the rest of us sat round the fire, reading.

In the evening, heavily laden with rucksacks full of vegetables, and carrying branches of whatever tree had started to flower, we walked the mile or so to St Geneviève-des-Bois and fought our way on to the crowded evening train. It was not unlike old days in Austria when, at the end of a Sunday spent in the Wienerwald or by the Danube, my friends and I would board trains teeming with Viennese excursionists weighed down under similar rucksacks and be borne back to a spring night in Vienna—green domes against a peacock-blue sky and the smell of lilac. Then our hearts had been light and our hands empty except of flowers, and we were only half aware that the Viennese went abroad as much for food as for pleasure. Now the tables were turned.

It was that same spring that I met May Kalf. She called on me one morning and introduced herself as a friend of my sister Alice in Holland. I had often heard Alice speak of her, but did not know that she was in Paris. She was a woman of well over fifty, so like a distinguished-looking man in appearance, with her white hair cropped short and her masculine cut of clothes, that she herself later told me she often had difficulty in gaining admittance to the women's section of the Turkish baths she visited regularly. She told me that morning among other things that she was a member of the Communist Party. She also said that she had come to see what she could do for Nicolas.

I told her my difficulties, shame-facedly since they were everyone's difficulties. I soon saw that she thought me feckless and a bad manager. 'Listen!' she said, and I had not been ten minutes with her before I discovered that she had two favourite words: 'Listen!' and 'Nonsense!' 'Listen!' she repeated, and proceeded to explain to me that she had lived in Berlin during the English blockade of Germany in the First World War; that things at the end had been worse there than they now were in France, and that with energy and good management one could get along all right. By bicycling about the country round Paris she had made contacts with several Dutch farmers who had settled in the region before the war. She went her rounds every week and brought back a certain amount of food. She said that I could count on her for four eggs a week for Nicolas. I sensed that she felt I should be bicycling about myself, and the fact that so far as I was concerned the farmers would have to be Scotch if the right chord were to be touched was obviously to her irrelevant—and my being born Scotch in the first place a matter of bad management. But though May's manner was downright and a little impatient, her heart was a heart of gold, and her chief purpose was to cut gratitude short.

She was a good friend to me all through the Occupation, as she was to my sister during all her life in the Netherlands.

She began to lecture me on what in her eyes was responsible for my difficulties. Obviously our ideas about food were all wrong. I should be feeding my family on raw vegetables cut up fine and on *Bircher Muesli*, the recipe for which she gave me. In rather quavering tones I spoke my doubts of getting a French family to eat raw vegetables however finely cut, and *Bircher Muesli* even if I could find the ingredients. 'Nonsense!' she cried, 'The French are fools about food. They don't know what is good for them. They must learn!'

She then told me how to keep warm without heating. She lived in a studio which had been central-heated and had no fireplace. This meant that she had no heating at all. She told me I must do as she did—open all my windows to create a nice draught which would clear the damp, and that damp is the only real inconvenience of the lack of heating. We then compared notes about our experiences at the time of the invasion. She had left Paris on her bicycle with the flow of refugees when the Germans were at the gates of the city. As a member of the Communist Party, she had no wish to make contact with the Nazis, though she spoke German, as she spoke English, like a native. Before she was out of the Vallée de Chevreuse she realized that the enterprise was hopeless and stopped at the first village she came to. There she noticed an old peasant in his garden and watched to see whether he lived alone. When she was certain of this, she went and asked him if he needed a charlady to cook and clean for him. He said that perhaps he did, but that he could not afford one. She told him (probably beginning her sentence with 'Nonsense!') that all she wanted was food and shelter, and that in exchange she was prepared to clean and wash and cook for him. I gather he was not enthusiastic, but he let her in, and she was as good as her word. Whether or not she managed to convert a French peasant of nearly eighty to raw vegetables and *Bircher Muesli* I never dared ask. I do know that the first thing she did was to set about cleaning the lavatory at the foot of his garden. For either of these achievements she would deserve a medal. I imagine that most people know or can guess what a peasant's outdoor lavatory is like. May, whose father in his time had been the European representative of Westinghouse, and whose husband was still curator of Dutch historical monuments and picture galleries (they had parted temporarily though still good friends; I gather he objected to the raw vegetables), took a scrubbing-brush and pail after pail of water and went down on her knees and scrubbed that lavatory till it would have done honour to her country of origin. She then turned to and washed the peasant's socks. She won his deep respect, and no wonder. They settled down together, May cooking and cleaning and washing, till all hope of French recovery was gone. She then bicycled back to Paris, where she would escape notice more easily than in a village.

I have a last memory of that first year in Paris, the memory of the only dinner party I ever gave that was an out and out failure. We wanted to return Janine's and Bob's invitation, and François managed for the occasion to get a small shoulder of black-market mutton and some haricot beans. The shoulder was only a quarter of the size of those that used to appear on our table in Scotland, and the beans filled only a small dish; but I triumphantly turned to my mushrooms to provide an entrée.

From the very start, everything went wrong. We invited the wrong people to meet Janine and Bob, people whom I had never met before but who had been kind to François when he was alone. Our guests turned out to have nothing in common. In Paris as a rule guests come prepared to do the entertaining. All you have to do is provide the food and drink. For a tired hostess, it is extraordinarily pleasant because she can relax as soon as the first couple arrives. I have been to dinner parties where the talk was so deftly and lightly kept going that you seemed to see rising above the dining-room table a magical construction of airy bubbles that was the work not of one specially gifted guest but of them all, each adding his or her bubble and yet helping it to form a homogeneous whole and never allowing it to sink or even to cease developing. Janine and Bob are adepts at this game. The other couple were pleasant people, but they had no idea the game existed. François did his best, but I still trailed my bucolic clouds, and anyway, I was soon too worried to make much effort. To begin with, the table looked

all wrong. With native Scotch honesty, I had weighed out to
the best of my ability the couple of ounces of bread which
was all our rationing allowed us at each meal. It had not
been easy and the result was a rather sordid arrangement
of bits and pieces beside every plate. I knew my guests
would give me coupons and I was determined not to cheat
them, but I suddenly realized how odd it looked. But that
was not the worst. What went wrong with the mushrooms I
cannot imagine. I had soaked them before cooking, exactly
as Esther Laune told me I must do. When I tasted them
before going to dress they seemed perfect. Perhaps as they
cooked they went on giving out their accumulated salt.
Certainly when Lucie handed them round and we all fell
to hopefully, there was a moment of aghast silence. The
mushrooms tasted of nothing but brine. The guests fixed
appealing eyes on me, but I knew it was no use saying they
need not eat them. They *had* to eat them for there was too
little else. I have learned since, but I did not know it then,
that most French people would rather go hungry than eat
something that is not really good. I myself have such a liking
for salt that, though I quite saw this was going a little far,
I was not fully alive to their dilemma. I apologized, but
I set the example of eating them. I shall never forget the
expression on Bob's face when he realized that his fate was
sealed—sympathetic concern, extreme distress, determined
heroism.

That summer and the summer that followed I left Paris before the end of the school term and took the children south to Valleraugue. French schools—and this was especially true in those less crowded days—are not adamant in these matters provided the children hold their own in class, and on the whole parents in France are still powerful. The Lycée Henri Quatre raised no objection to my removing Henri early. For André it was easier still; he was in the infant class not of a state but of a convent school. It was a good school, but we chose it especially because it stood in a quiet street just round the corner from where we lived, and even a child of five could go there alone. It will seem an irresponsible reason for sending a Protestant child to a Catholic school. The truth is that we were so weary, we seized upon every opportunity of lightening our burden. I never had cause to regret our choice.

Before we left for the south, May Kalf on one of her visits asked if I would care for her to come and join us in the Cevennes. She said she would do the cooking in exchange for her keep. I accepted her offer joyfully. Not only would I have her lively company, but I would have a much-needed rest from cooking.

On the journey south something occurred the shock of which stands in my memory as analagous to what I felt when I first saw the yellow star. It was somewhere round midnight and the train was standing in the station of Lyons. I opened the door of my compartment and was looking down the corridor when I saw someone come lurching towards me, as though drunk. He was an elderly, very civilized-looking man, with the ribbon of the Legion of Honour in his buttonhole. He staggered past me with wide staring eyes that seemed to see nothing. As he disappeared down the corridor there burst from his lips with hoarse passion the words, '*Ah! Les salauds! Les salauds!*'

I took it for granted that he was, in fact, drunk. I was surprised, because he looked more like an elderly intellectual than anything else. Besides, drink was then hard to come by. The shock came later when another traveller told me that some young *maquisards* loaded with chains had been hounded into the luggage-van at Lyons.

When I reached Valleraugue, one of my first visits was to Emma and Raymond Lévi-Strauss, who were still living at Cancabra. We spoke of this and that, and they mentioned the possibility that always hung over their heads as Jews of their house being searched, and their anxiety at having in their keeping a part of their son Claude's library, which included a good deal of communist literature. They were asking themselves whether they ought not to destroy these books, but hated the idea of doing so. I suggested they hand them over to me. No one, I felt, would be likely to take so unpolitically-minded a person as myself for a communist. Besides, François's family was too committed to property in the eyes of the local people to be suspected of Marxism. Anyway Raymond gave me free leave to burn the books in case of need. I therefore carted over pell-mell to La Coustète a nice selection of communist authors and stacked them on one of my bookshelves. I then forgot all about them.

After we had been settled at La Coustète for about a fortnight, May Kalf turned up one evening on her bicycle, with a minimum of luggage strapped on behind. She explained that she had not ridden all the way, but that since foreigners living in Paris had not the right to leave the city without the permission of the German authorities, and as she had no intention of drawing attention to herself by asking for such permission, she had quietly bicycled out by the Porte d'Italie, exactly as though she were going on one of her food-hunting expeditions, and had then boarded a suburban train that took her to the first halting-place of the Nîmes express. I learned later that François stood in a queue from five in the morning until eight to buy her ticket and book her a first-class sleeper. May knew the German mentality well. She rightly calculated that their immense respect for wealth and authority would prevent them from disturbing the *wagon-lit* passengers at the line of demarcation. It was for this reason that she travelled by sleeper.

We spent the rest of the evening on deck-chairs on the terrace in the warm dark, watching the fireflies and talking English to our heart's content. When at last we decided to go to bed, May asked whether she might go to my room to choose a book. She came down again looking very alarmed and told me that as a member of the Communist Party, who had left Paris illegally, she simply could not risk living in a house so full of communist literature. After a short discussion we decided to find some hiding-place for the books that seemed to us of particular value or interest, and to take advantage of Raymond's permission to burn the rest. The next day I filled a couple of shopping-bags with bound volumes of Marx, Lenin and Engels, and I took them down to Oncle Ernest's library. There in the glass-fronted bookcases that surround the room I inserted them here and there, between such respectable French authors as adorn the shelves of a normal French private library. In fact, I hid them so well that I have never to this day been able to lay hands on them to return them to their owner. I cannot remember even their titles. I felt no guilt towards Oncle Ernest in doing as I did; I knew no one could suspect him of communism. I kept a few of the remaining books on my own shelves, in such disarming company as von Bülow's Memoirs and a life of Mussolini which some guest had left behind in pre-war days. We then lit a roaring fire in the kitchen stove and set about our work of destruction.

I would never have believed that books could be so diffi-cult to burn. It took only a very few volumes to extinguish the fire, and they were barely consumed. We gave up in despair, raked their charred remains into the dustbin along with the other condemned volumes, and groped our way down to the *béal* in the dark, and along it by the narrow path that runs between it and the Hérault, which flows some fifteen feet below. There in a spot well hidden by trees, and seemingly above a particularly deep and swift-flowing part of the river (judging by the sound) we emptied our dustbin and then made for home. Fortunately for our peace of mind we never troubled to go back by daylight to see whether the place had been well chosen. I discovered years later that the books must have caught among brambles and roots of trees till the autumn rains washed them free. The truth is that I could never take danger seriously at La Coustète until the very end. I felt safe the moment I was over the bridge, so certain I was that no German would dare cross it—their courage is of a different sort.

We went up to L'Espérou soon after May arrived, and it was there that the news reached us of the massacre at Aire de Côte, the forester's house I mentioned before in connection with the early *Maquis*. This *Maquis* had been a haphazard assembly of young men gone into hiding by twos and threes, directed to Aire de Côte by a couple of *résistants* in Alès, and shown the way by my friend of the *pension de famille*. It had disintegrated and been partly absorbed into a more stable *Maquis* organized on a military basis. A Belgian spy had been introduced by the Germans into their midst and he had informed the *Schutz-Staffel* authorities as to their exact position, their habits and so on. A detachment of SS was sent up one evening and the *maquisards* were encircled just as they were on the point of changing camp after a warning they received that they were in danger. Half of the young men were massacred and the rest deported to concentration camps in Germany. A handful escaped and fled to Ardaillès, where another *Maquis* was being formed. According to the account given by the few who survived deportation, all the Germans were raving drunk. The forester himself, who had taken no active part in organizing the *Maquis* but had merely closed his eyes, was deported along with the *maquisards*. He survived, but he committed suicide shortly after his return to France.

But life went on with its day to day struggle to find food. The Scobs had stayed on at Le Vigan when we went to Paris, and Helena and the children were now at L'Espérou. Helena and I renewed our endless talks and our food-hunting expeditions, while May stayed at home with Nicolas, whom she kept in a wooden tub on the kitchen terrace for lack of a play-pen. She had brought two brand-new pre-war men's shirts with her, and a piece of pre-war soap, for me to barter for food, but I proved a poor hand at bargaining. I gave one of the shirts to a peasant-woman in the hope that she would sell us butter regularly, which she never did. I did no better with the soap. Helena and I went off one day to visit the Borie du Pont, a big farm some six miles from L'Espérou. Helena's mother had always made a point of buying what she could from the local people, long before the war, when they had great difficulty in selling their wares. The country people never forgot this, and Helena was made welcome in a number of farms where something was always kept for her. La Borie du Pont was one of them, and she hoped that Madame Fadat, the farmer's wife, might extend her goodwill to me, especially with a cake of pre-war soap to back me. The farm was one I had never visited. It stands in a grassy hollow, but as you approach it the grass is trampled into mud by men and beasts, and only a few pots of flowers on the stone terrace wall give grace to the place. They were very few. Much more striking was the great heap of cows' dung by the kitchen door.

Helena introduced me to Madame Fadat and I made a rather hypocritical attempt to win her good graces by admiring her flowers and her farm. She cocked an ironical eye at me and said: 'Yes, yes, Madame Teissier du Cros, but before the war it smelled of manure!' I left the rest of the conversation to Helena till the moment came to produce my soap. Madame Fadat liked the look of it but was not exaggeratedly interested—no doubt she made her own soap. In the end she offered to buy it, which was not at all what I wanted. Even if I could have asked the black-market price, which *noblesse* obliged that I do not, what use was money to me in a land where it is of value only in conjunction with love? Obviously Madame Fadat felt no particular love either for me or for my family. But I was still hopeful. I insisted on giving her the soap as a present and I asked her to keep cheese for me whenever she could. To give her her due, she held out but few hopes; what cheese she had was ear-marked for old friends. She said that I could always look in when I went that way, just in case . . . and by then it was too late to take the soap back. It never bore fruit, and May must have felt justified in thinking me feckless.

Fortunately there remained our friends the Passets at Les Laupies, and there Helena and I went every week. We had nothing left to barter—I dared not take the remaining shirt—but we never came away empty-handed.

By this time François had come to join us for his month's holiday. He had obtained his complete release thanks to the complicity of an Austrian doctor whose job it was to examine prisoners on parole and decide who were unfit for military service and could therefore be released from their parole. This doctor most obligingly made out such a report on François's physical condition that his liberation followed as a matter of course.

François suggested that we push farther afield in our search for food. As Papa had given us a demijohn of wine, we thought we would try to barter wine for wheat in the Causse, the upland plains where wheat grows but no vines. We set out for Lanuéjols, on the far side of Mount Aigoual. We tried several farms, but though everyone wanted wine the rate of exchange they offered us was impossible. Then quite by chance we fell in with an elderly couple who were friendly because they knew the Coupiac branch of the family. They asked for nothing in exchange, but they sold us regularly both wheat and potatoes and eggs, and an occasional live rabbit. The ride home, a matter of some twenty miles or more, taxed my strength to the utmost, especially after François left and I had to go alone. My bicycle was so heavy, what with twenty pounds of wheat on the carrier, potatoes slung from the handle-bars, and eggs and sometimes a rabbit in a basket in front, that I could scarcely keep it upright while I mounted. When the road was uphill and I had to dismount and push my bicycle, I was sometimes reduced to tears, the more so that I had only my wooden-soled shoes with fragile uppers and my ankle kept turning. On one occasion my bicycle overbalanced and while I was desperately trying to save my eggs, the rabbit was as desperately trying to make good his escape. If his back legs had not been tied I would have lost him. It was all of a piece with the rest of our lives during the Occupation, and when I look back on it all I find the familiar feeling of exhaustion creeping over me once more, the weary, hopeless strain of the beast of burden. It seemed always to be our fate to have to carry weights beyond our strength, whether our luggage, since there were no taxis and few porters, or raw materials to provide food for our family. The luxury of luxuries seemed to us then to be able to go out and come back empty-handed.

But we had our comic relief and our lighter moments, in part thanks to a man called Jonget, whom I should have mentioned earlier, for he was part and parcel of our life in L'Espérou. But it is right that he should appear only at this point, for it was the odd friendship that sprang up between him and May Kalf that brought him to the kitchen door with gifts of salads and gladiolas, and thence to the kitchen table for a cup of 'coffee'. Jonget kept one of the Espérou inns, though when I say he kept it, what I really mean is that his wife did. Jonget himself was wounded in the head during the First War. He drew a pension and was exempted from work, an exemption which he took very seriously. His wife worked for two. She ran the inn and she did all the cooking, although Jonget had the reputation of being a really great chef. There was a legend that he once cooked a meal both for the King of England and for the Czar of all the Russias. I gather that his talents as cook were discovered when he was first mobilized, and that it was in the capacity of cook that he served his country. He rose to the top of the hierarchy, and when King George V (and on another occasion the Czar) visited the front, Jonget it was that cooked the meal he was offered. However that may be, Jonget felt himself in some way responsible for the English royal family and was as loyal to them as any Englishman.

What first drew him to May Kalf was curiosity, as he soon told Helena and me. Apparently discussion was rife in the village as to May's sex; was she a man or was she a woman? I shall leave to the reader's imagination the ins and outs of such a discussion between French peasants who dearly love a laugh. The problem solved itself the day May, who had been wearing slacks about the village, appeared in a skirt. The next day Jonget was round at the kitchen door with a bouquet of flowers from his garden, and a friendship was struck up which continued up to the time of Jonget's death, long after the end of the war. For though they never met again they corresponded, and when May went back, as eventually she did, to her husband in the Netherlands, she used to send him every Christmas a parcel of bulbs. Flowers were Jonget's passion and the only work he ever did was in his garden, though actually the impression given was rather that he had a thumb so green as to require him only to flit about the garden like an incongruous butterfly, touching a flower here, a shrub there, for everything to blossom.

He brought no flowers for Helena and me, but we often joined him in his inn for a drink, and every year in late September, when the summer visitors were gone and we had the inn dining-room to ourselves, there would be a solemn ceremony. After making certain he was unobserved, even by his wife, Jonget would gravely open a cupboard and bring out a bottle—always the same bottle—of English gin. For the royal family was not Jonget's only link with England. Before the war the tin mines of Villemagne were exploited by an English company, and the English engineers often came to L'Espérou and soon formed the habit of keeping in Jonget's inn a bottle of gin to mix with the French drinks he provided. The mines closed down some time before the war, and the engineers went home, but a bottle of gin remained. Like most Frenchmen, Jonget cared little for gin; it was not till the first summer of the war that he remembered the bottle's existence and started what was to become a solemn ritual. Liqueur glasses were produced and filled, and in silence we would drink to victory.

That summer too an evening came late in September when we gathered in Jonget's inn for the usual ceremony. But when at last he rose and went to the cupboard, his step was slow and his face clouded. He stood for a moment before us, the bottle clasped to his bosom, and he said, 'I can't give you a drink this year. I can only let you smell the bottle, or there won't be any left when victory comes.' And so it was that each in turn we put our nose to the bottle which he handed to us without ever letting go his hold of it, and through it we drew a deep breath that ended in a sigh. Then Jonget corked the bottle firmly and put it back, and for a moment we all sat in silence, gazing into the future and wondering.

We had one happy evening that summer. It was when we learned that the Allies had landed in Sicily. I had been out food-hunting and it was only on my return that I heard the joyful tidings. After dinner I went over to the Nicks' house to celebrate with Helena, and Madeleine who had now arrived. As the evening advanced, one friend after another joined us round the fire, several bringing a bottle each of white wine which they had managed to wrest from one or other of the hotel keepers. Our spirits rose as we drank toast after toast. Soon we began to give hilarious accounts of the various symptoms from which we were all beginning to suffer as a result of underfeeding. We had all of us escaped the more serious symptoms, the drying and cracking of the skin, the shrinking together of the skeleton with stiffness and great pain in the joints, which the doctors took at first for a mysteriously epidemic form of acute arthritis. But each had some minor trouble, and often we had the same. As for me, it was especially my memory that was affected. It was not only that my mind went a blank every time I had to introduce people. Far more inconvenient was the fact that the moment I left a room it would be as though a sponge had washed my brain free of all memory of what I had been doing. This very minor trouble had disastrous results, which were to repeat themselves the following winter. As I had too much to do and am impatient by nature, I would try to do several things at once. While the tap was running in the bathroom to allow me to wash Nicolas's clothes, I would go through to the kitchen to give instructions to Lucie, or do some other quick job that needed attending to. I would forget about the tap the moment I was out of the bathroom and on several occasions our downstairs neighbour had been flooded out. He was a man with a weak heart and a shop full of valuable books, so it was a serious matter. Yet I could never train myself not to leave a tap running, so certain I was that this time I would not forget. On one occasion I was so tired that I lay down just for a moment, to rest my back. I fell asleep and was woken by a furious ringing of the door bell. This time the flooding was so serious that the water had poured through from the first floor to the cellar where my neighbour kept his rare editions. Fortunately we were insured. But for years afterwards I would wake suddenly in the night in a cold sweat, thinking I had left a tap running, and for a long time I never heard the doorbell ring violently without a terrible leap of the heart.

I told them all this that evening as we sat round the fire. A young woman from Marseilles, a friend of the Scobs, capped my story with an account of a night in the hotel where she was staying. The hotel had been built with his own hands by the father-in-law of the present owner, with the help of the village carpenter. The partitions and ceilings are so thin that it is impossible not to hear what is going on in one's neighbour's room. One of the symptoms produced by an almost exclusively fruit and vegetable diet is a certain degree of incontinence. She told us how during the night, each time she grew drowsy she would be roused by her next-door neighbour, then by the one overhead, by which time she herself would have caught the infection and was forced to get up. But scarcely was she back in bed but the neighbour on the other side would follow suit, and then the one below, and so on, *aria da capo*, all night through.

And so at last, at the very end of September, we set out on our homeward journey with May Kalf. She persuaded me to travel with her in a first-class sleeper. My own identity card was a false one, made for me in the early days by the secretary of the Valleraugue *Mairie*. Before the war I had managed without an identity card, and I could procure none of the papers I would require to have one made through the regular channels. Both my marriage and birth certificates could be obtained only by application to Edinburgh sources, since by some error or negligence my marriage was never registered in France. As May would certainly be arrested if it was discovered that she, a foreigner, had left Paris without permission, I felt extremely nervous as we approached Moulins where the German control still took place. But May was right. We lay in the dark when the train stopped, scarcely daring to breathe. At last the door was cautiously opened and a shaft of light from an electric torch swept the compartment. We heard a voice whisper the magic word, '*Schlafwagen!*' and respectfully and silently the door was once more closed.

Nessun maggior dolore . . . No doubt; but which of us can resist the temptation to press the sensitive nerve on whose hinge the door springs open on lost happiness. At a time when what was frightening was the ease with which we settled into our present misery and came to think it normal life, it was vital not to remember our lost world—memory is indeed unbearable—but to recapture the very feel of it. And no doubt each of us had his own magic, his witch's cauldron from which he conjured up not visions of the future, for to all intents and purposes we had none, but the past itself. Mine was an incongruous cauldron enough. How often during the Occupation have I swung back the door of the *Métro* and paused to breathe in with rapture the smell, the inimitable smell of the Paris underground! And for as long as the spell lasted, for one exquisite fleeting moment, gone were hunger, cold and despair, gone cruelty and injustice; I was eighteen again and discovering a new country in a world still new where, as I said earlier, there was danger only from the other sex. Of course, it never lasted; it could not last, and it left me shattered. But I owe to the Paris *Métro* a deep debt of gratitude and I was incensed when after the war an English journalist dared disrespectfully analyse that very smell. I forget what ingredients he distinguished, but I remember that one of them was stale garlic. Stale garlic, indeed! The Paris *Métro* smells as surely of my youth as did the lilac-bushes on the Helden Platz in Vienna *im wunderschönen Monat Mai*.

Day by day in that last year after our return to Paris the tension rose. Notch by notch the screw was turned. We lived with one idea ever present: when were 'they' coming?—and 'they' for everyone now meant the Allies. The rumours which we handed on to one another were always dates, the date at which 'on the best evidence' we had been told the landing would take place. We lived too with in our hearts the terrible fear that Armand once expressed to us that winter, 'If they don't come soon, there will be no one left worth saving!' For facts were coming to light, and we began to know just what the numbers were on the lists of people shot each week. Our nervous tension was highest when we heard in some drawing-room where we forgathered with our friends that the prison of Frêsnes had been emptied. This meant that its inmates had been shot or deported, and that a rounding-up was imminent of new suspects to fill their place. I did not know then that François had taken advantage of his liberation from parole to join a Resistance movement, later called the OCM (*Organisation Civile et Militaire*). He wisely kept me in ignorance. I could never have borne the thought of the too precise danger that he ran; I had not the courage of Geneviève Armand, who faced everything with open eyes, both for her husband and for herself, and took the precaution only of sending all her children except the youngest, Nicolas's contemporary, into separate safety—illusory safety as it turned out, for when Armand was at last arrested, the Germans showed him that they had taken the trouble to find out the address of each, just in case . . . But though there seemed no reason, as far as I knew, why François should be arrested, I knew that he considered the thing possible, and for several days, until the news came that the prison was full again, I would rise every morning at six. We knew that the Gestapo called in the early morning, before 8 a.m., and I had a foolish hope that if I could hold them talking for a moment in the hall, then François might slip round to the nursery, since all our rooms communicated, and there escape through its window which gave, not on the Rue du Cloître Notre Dame, but on the little Rue Massillon. After eight o'clock I ceased to worry till next morning.

Armand and Geneviève once nearly did attempt to escape out of that very window. I shall tell the story here for I learned it only after all that happens in this book was over. At the end, Armand was in such danger that he avoided sleeping in his own flat. The habit of coming in the early morning to make their arrests was in a sense the Achilles' heel of the Gestapo, for its victims could sometimes escape arrest merely by sleeping out, and yet be safe at home or in their office the rest of the day. At the time I am referring to, the spring of 1944, Armand knew that the net was closing round him; one after another the people he worked with in the Resistance were being arrested, and he knew that he had no right to expect them not to speak under torture. He therefore seldom slept at home, but went from one friend to another for the night. One night he and his wife were sleeping in our flat, in the room whose window gave on the Rue Massillon. I had gone south some time before with the children, and only François was at home, and Madeleine Vinot-Préfontaine, a student who came to us *au pair* when Lucie, to our relief, left us to get married again. Some time in the very small hours of the morning the door-bell rang. Armand and Geneviève sprang from their bed and made ready to escape out of the window. François slept on, and it was Madeleine who woke when the bell rang furiously a second time. She opened the door, while Armand and Geneviève paused a moment and strained their ears to hear what was going on. There on the doorstep, hopping with fury, was our downstairs neighbour. Once more he had been flooded out, this time by Madeleine. She had left a tap dripping and the basin plug closed, and at last the water had overflowed and seeped through to where our neighbour and his wife lay peacefully sleeping in the room below. Such a razor-blade sometimes separated comedy from tragedy.

The food situation, too, was worse than ever. Our meat ration had dwindled to almost nothing, and we were driven to buying a small roast of beef every week on the black market. Wine and salt were also severely rationed, which was sheer sadism on the part of the German authorities. I remember how, the day our ration of wine was distributed and we could drink a glass of *gros rouge* with our food, it seemed to flow into our very veins, restoring our lost zest for life. Our salt ration was so small that it ran out early in the month it was supposed to last. It consisted of two probably half-pound bags, one of grey kitchen salt, the other of unrefined table salt. Both left a black deposit in the pan our food was cooked in. I have, I said so earlier, a great liking for salt, and often at that time my thoughts turned with new understanding to King Lear's Cordelia. When our ration was finished I would scour the shops, buying up all I could find of the celery salt that is sold as a condiment in small glass pepper-pots. A whole pot was needed to produce the slightest effect, so it was no real solution of our problem. In the meantime my sister Alice, as she later told me, had trained her small son Andrew, contemporary of my André, to taste the various bath-salts which in the Netherlands were still to be found in the chemists' shops, while she bought something at the counter to divert attention. When he came on a brand that tasted of salt he signalled to her so that she could buy some for her cooking.

We could not even fall back on smoking to divert our attention from hunger. François's ration kept us going for only a couple of days in the month, for he too now felt the need to smoke. I smoked not only my own fag-ends; I smoked any that I found in our ashtrays. But there came a day when, though several of François's friends had spent the evening with us and all had smoked, when I hastened to the ashtrays after they left I found them empty. Every vestige of tobacco had been surreptitiously swept into some discreet receptacle and taken home.

At this point we were in fact doing as many people did; we were growing our own tobacco. We grew it at Longpont. As in France tobacco is a state monopoly, this was strictly illegal; but so much of what we did was illegal that we scarcely gave this a thought. The real snag was that to be smoked tobacco must be treated, a long and complicated business. François would have had the patience to do the necessary if I had left him time. But the moment the tobacco leaves were dry, I would cut them into little strips with my nail-scissors and roll them into prickly cigarettes. They told me the hospitals were full of people who had done the same thing, but I was past caring.

The screw was turned in other ways than these. Sometimes in the night we were woken by the sound of an explosion. 'What's that?' I would ask, my heart in my mouth. 'It's nothing,' François would reply, 'Someone in the

Resistance must have blown something up.' He would sink back into sleep, but not I. I lay remembering another night, long, long ago in Metz in the early days of our marriage. I had been woken by what sounded like a pistol-shot, though no doubt it was only a burst tyre; and I lay in bed in a cold sweat while for the first time it dawned on me that just over the border lived what was now my hereditary enemy. I lay imagining what war would mean in a part of France the Germans claimed for their own, and with all my heart I wished I were back in my island.

Then there was the bombardment of the Paris suburb of Clignancourt, and though I was not afraid even when I heard wave after wave of aeroplanes passing over our heads, so sure I was that the RAF would throw no bombs on Notre Dame, the noise of the explosions was so terrific that I could not keep my teeth from chattering. I knew then that I was better fitted for life in enemy-occupied territory than for what the English people were facing every day.

In our topsy-turvy world bombardments seemed not to concern us and were rather things to be rejoiced at. I remember going for one of our weekend visits to Longpont at about this time, just after an RAF bombardment of the marshalling yard of Juvisy, through which we had to pass. Precarious rails had been put up to allow the trains to run very slowly through the damaged station. While our train crept along them, every single person in it was at the window, giving vent to their pleasure at the extent of the damage.

All through the last year of the Occupation air-raid warnings were frequent. When the sirens sounded we were supposed to make for the nearest shelter, and if we met a policeman we were forced to do so. It happened to me only once. I was taking Nicolas for his daily walk when the warning sounded, and I made for home as unobtrusively as was possible with a perambulator. To reach home I had to cross a bridge, and policemen were always posted on all the bridges. I was firmly led to a shelter and while I sat waiting for the all-clear to sound I happened to look up. The roof over our heads was made of opaque glass! The whole thing was a farce; everyone knew that Paris ran no real danger from the Allies, and it became a sort of game to dodge the police whose job was to direct us to the shelters. I remember an evening when François and I were again going to dine with Janine and Bob. Before we reached the underground the warning sounded. We decided to go on foot, hugging the walls in back streets so as to avoid the police, for we were determined not to be thwarted of our evening's entertainment. It was a long walk, and we had to take precautions at crossings and avoid large thoroughfares. We reached our destination safely and spent a very pleasant evening. An old pianist friend of Janine's was there, and he played Schumann to us after dinner. He so enjoyed himself, and we so enjoyed his playing, that we forgot the time and found ourselves in serious danger of missing the last underground and being out after curfew time. We rushed from the house and got the last train from the nearest *Métro* station. But when we came to change at Montmartre, we found we were too late. The *Métro* was closing. It is a long way from Montmartre to Notre Dame, and midnight, the curfew hour, was drawing near, but the pianist was afraid of facing the police alone, so we decided nonetheless to take him home with us. François and I each held him by an elbow and almost carried him as we hastened on, fortunately downhill all the way. When at last we emerged on the Place de l'Hôtel de Ville, a few minutes' walk from home, loud and solemn the twelve strokes of midnight sounded through the silent city, and we saw standing ahead of us, impossible to avoid, a policeman. He stopped us when we came up and asked what we were doing on the streets at that hour. François explained that we had missed the last *Métro*, but that we were only a few minutes from home, and he gave our address. The policeman asked for his identity card. By some oversight François had forgotten to have the address on his card changed when he left Oncle Robert's, so that it did not tally with the one he had given the policeman, nor was it only a few minutes' distance off. We thought we were in for a night at the police station, but, 'Get home as fast as you can!' said the man, and once more we all three broke into our ambling run.

My memories of our years in Paris are clouded. Even in

retrospect that air is unbreathable and the effort of sustained recollection almost impossible. But groping through the mist I stumble on this or that image.

Two Indo-Chinese, probably students, standing silently gazing at a bowl of rice displayed in a grocer's shop on the Boulevard St Germain, as a sign that the small ration of rice allowed to babies could be claimed.

A small spindle-legged boy who passed me in the Rue Lagrange, pushing his little brother in a go-cart. I looked at the baby—when you have children of your own you always look at other children, and this one was about the age of Nicolas. He lay half reclining, as though his spine were too weak to support him, and he gazed before him with such an expression of uncomprehending suffering on his face that I asked his elder brother if he was ill. The little boy looked surprised and said that no, the baby was not ill. I realized that it was only underfed.

The interior of Notre Dame one cold January day. I had not been able to resist going to a Bach concert the Germans were giving in the cathedral. I got little pleasure from it, chiefly because the icy wind blew through the billowing canvas that replaced the stained glass windows, in safe hiding; but also because I soon saw there were almost nothing but Germans present and I knew I should never have come. I should have contented myself with hearing the music through our windows, as I had done before when they gave the Christmas Oratorio. It was too late; I sat on till the end, my teeth chattering with cold. Then I joined the stream of people making for the doors. In front of me moved an immensely tall German officer, very thin, with something, seen from behind, of the thorough-bred horse about him. Then suddenly he turned and fixed me with such pale, cold, inhuman eyes that I stopped dead and moved on again only when a safe number of people were between him and me. Long afterwards, when Armand told us about the man that Himmler sent to visit him in prison, who said no word but coldly examined him 'with the eyes of a wolf', I remembered that officer and I knew just what Armand meant.

Very different was the young German soldier I once saw in the underground. He heaved off on to the floor the enormous rucksack he carried on his back, and stood easing his shoulders as though they ached. He cannot have been much more than sixteen. I found my heart melting towards him, he looked so like any other unhappy child. It seemed to me that he gazed with envy at the half-starved but un-uniformed French.

Then there rises up the drawing-room of an acquaintance who was of a well-known Jewish family and had been one of the social lights of the Paris banking world before the war. It was her at home day, or what was left of it; the routine of life goes on when everything else is lost. I had been there before, and I had to force myself to go again. I knew that I would come away with all my defences shattered. The room was full when I arrived; no doubt even more for the Jews than for ourselves the intensity of the feeling that bound us together was what made life possible. I sat among them, but apart; I had not suffered enough to be one of them. Tragedy had long since overtaken every person in the room. One woman's husband had thrown himself out of a window. Another's brother had drowned himself in the Seine, but not before he had carefully laid out his food-cards for some other member of the family, and changed into his oldest clothes. Another's nephew had been so badly beaten-up at Drancy, the concentration camp near Paris, that his ear had been torn off. He had managed to escape, and was lying in hiding, everyone knew where. A fourth's husband had been deported; she sold silk stockings on the black market to earn a living for herself and her little girl. All of them lived in a state of constant terror. For each one of them it was simply a case of, When? But what they spoke of was the price of butter on the black market (I think it was the equivalent of two pounds sterling the pound), and I was torn between bitterness at the thought that my own children were losing their health for lack of the price of butter, admiration for the light tone of conversation they managed to keep up, and tearing pity for what I knew of them, and knew only because our hostess told me it all in an undertone, sensing my bitterness.

The mist clears on another scene which is a part of the same tragedy but at the other end of the scale. I was standing in an interminable queue in front of a stall where there were cabbages for sale. The weather was cold and damp, and the long queue of weary people moved very slowly forward. As the mother of three children, I had a priority card which meant that I queued to the right instead of to the left of the cabbages, and that we moved forward a very little faster than the others. Suddenly a little old woman with the yellow star on her thin black coat came humbly up and stood hesitating on the edge of the pavement. Jews were not allowed to stand in queues. What they were supposed to do I never discovered. But the moment the people in the queue saw her they signed to her to join us. Secretly and rapidly, as in the game of hunt-the-slipper, she was passed up till she stood at the head of the queue. I am glad to say that not one voice was raised in protest, that the policeman standing near turned his head away, and that she got her cabbage before any of us.

A last and foolish image, but typical of the times we lived in: Armand was dining with us and brought with him a flat wicker box. I opened the lid and found lying at one end of the basket a large beef-steak and at the other a damask rose.

And through it all, how lovely Paris was! Traffic had dwindled to a few motor-cars, driven as the Nazis deemed the *Herrenvolk* should drive (on one occasion I only just snatched Nicolas's perambulator back from where a second later a motor driven at breathtaking speed by a German sailor would unhesitatingly have caught it with its front wheel), a very occasional lorry, and bicycles grown so precious they were stolen if you left them standing for a moment. To confuse memories of things lived with that of things read, the *fiacres* of bygone times, emboldened by a seeming return to a more leisurely age, crept out from their long hiding and conveyed about the city those who could pay their fabulous fares. The air breathed by the Paris trees was no longer petrol-poisoned, and gratefully they flourished. It was the Paris of Proust and Colette, the Paris of my Valleraugue plates. No; not quite. The gay leisurely men and women, the bustles and leg-of-mutton sleeves, the tailcoats and top-hats, the smocked workmen, all were gone.

The people in the streets were shabby and barelegged, for it was only in drawing-rooms that elegance subsisted; and their faces were yellow from underfeeding. But though we were all ugly and dowdy, beauty was round us everywhere. And we never went about with blind or indifferent eyes. We were so certain the city would be destroyed before the end that, projecting ourselves into a time when all would be ruins, we gazed and gazed with the nostalgic eyes of memory, imprinting each image on our minds and saying to ourselves, not 'How lovely Paris is!' but 'How lovely Paris was!'

It was at the end of May that we left Paris for the south in 1944. The German authorities issued an order that everyone in France must hand his identity card in to the police, and make regular application for a new one. They hoped by this means to round up Jews and resisters leading more and more hunted lives under false identities. It was a measure that plunged me in a serious dilemma. My own identity-card, as I said before, was irregular. When the secretary of the Valleraugue *Mairie* made it out for me, not only did he do so without my having produced the necessary papers; he also wrote my town of birth as 'Aberdun', to give it a French look, and passed over in silence my country of origin. If I handed it in to our local police station it would lead to inquiries. I decided to go boldly to Police Headquarters and explain my problem. They would know what to advise. The official who received me told me that my best course would be to leave Paris immediately and go to some place, if such existed, where I was known to the authorities. He explained that all applications for new cards were submitted to a German commission. The chances of their accepting mine were slight. 'You won't know their decision till they send us to arrest you,' he said. 'You had better clear out.' Obviously this meant that I must go to Valleraugue. But how was I going to get past the German check that still took place at what used to be the line of demarcation? I went home and explained the situation to François, who agreed all the more readily to my taking the children south at once, since as more and more trains were being blown up by the Resistance, the time was obviously at hand when it would be impossible to leave Paris at all. He in the meantime had obtained his new identity card and he decided to go part of the way with us to see us past the check point. He was confident that the presence of the children would make things easy.

And so towards the end of May we set out, François, André, Nicolas and I. Henri we had to leave behind for what in the circumstances must seem the most frivolous of reasons. He was to take part in his school play, and we felt that danger was no proper excuse for upsetting so important an event at the last moment. He would follow as soon as the performance had taken place.

That I took so calmly the prospect of facing the German control without identity papers shows how events had toughened me. By all the laws of my nature I should have been panic-stricken. It is true that I have great faith in my husband, but I admit that when the German official entered our compartment and demanded our identity cards, I quailed. François waited till all the others had shown their cards. He then calmly held his out, while I sat with Nicolas on my knee, trying to look detached. The official carefully examined François's card and then turned to me. François again held his card out, and assumed as stupid an expression as is possible for so intelligent a man. He said, 'This is my wife, and these are my children'. The official's face stiffened. He said that I must show my own card. François looked at him with candid eyes and repeated a little louder that I was his wife. The man showed signs of losing his temper, so François led him firmly out into the corridor and there explained in German that I was obliged for urgent family reasons to go south, that I had handed my old identity card in to the police in Paris, and that my new card had not reached me in time for the journey. The German was at last prevailed upon to let us through. Just as he turned away, Nicolas, who was the only one of my children to whom in his babyhood, from an obscure and rather silly need to defy the enemy, I always spoke English, held his arms out to me and in a voice liquid with sentimentality said, 'A kiss!' Fortunately it passed unnoticed. Nothing could now prevent our reaching Valleraugue. I never took seriously the very real danger of our being blown up, for the foolish reason that if we were it would be by friends, not enemies.

When we reached the south, it was to Mandiargues that

we went first. There a shock was in store for me. Papa gave me a blood-curdling account of the crimes that were being committed by the 'bandits', as the Vichy press called the *maquisards*. He told me stories of how they broke into isolated farmhouses and carried off what they could lay hands on, sometimes with the use of violence. I discounted much of what Papa told me; I knew by then that every resistance movement draws to it not only what is best in a country, but also some element of what is worst and that the Vichy partisans closed their eyes to the former and saw only the latter. But the precise accounts Papa gave of crimes committed in our very region, in one of which a small boy had been murdered as well as his parents, were disquieting. 'Has our poor country not suffered enough?' asked Papa. What could I answer? I did not wish to discuss the matter with him. If it came to a discussion, we would both argue not from facts but from pent-up passion, and it could lead only to a quarrel. But I wanted to know the truth, and whether or not it would be madness to settle with two young children in a house as isolated as La Coustète. I decided to go to Le Vigan and consult the Scobs. They would know what was really happening.

It was on June 5th that, making the excuse of my having to see the Valleraugue police about my identity card, I left Mandiargues for Le Vigan. I found Helena alone with the children. She made me very welcome, and when I asked her what she knew about the *Maquis*, with great airs of mystery she led me down a back corridor to a room that usually stood empty. She knocked at the door and it was opened by a man I had known slightly for several years, Pasteur Olivès, the clergyman of Ardaillès, a village in the Valleraugue neighbourhood. Olivès was one of the first to organize a *Maquis* in our region. His group was stationed at Ardaillès and had been joined, as I said before, by the few survivors of the Aire de Côte massacre. That very winter the news had reached us in Paris that there had been an SS raid on Ardaillès as well and that Olivès and his young men had been warned only just in time. But nine men whom the SS found in the village, none of them *maquisards* if I remember rightly, were arrested and taken to Nîmes and hanged. They were hanged from the railway viaduct and left hanging, so that no high vehicle could pass beneath without setting their bodies swinging. Olivès lived a hunted life. He was the last person I expected to meet in a house less than two hundred yards from the German blockhouse.

As soon as our greeting was over, Olivès questioned me closely about my family; were we all safe at Valleraugue? I explained the situation, and mentioned that Henri was to join us in a few days, specifying which day. Olivès sat silent for a moment, and his face looked white and strained. It was much later that he told me why. He knew that the Forces Françaises de l'Intérieur (FFI) had instructions to blow the Paris train up that day. He urged me to bring Henri south sooner. I told him that was impossible. You had to book your seat weeks in advance. We had got ours through Armand, but we hated asking for favours except in dire necessity. As far as we knew, there was no such necessity in Henri's case. Olivès could not tell us that such a necessity existed. What saved Henri was that he travelled not by the valley of the Rhône, but the mountain route. Even so, his escape was a narrow one. If I remember rightly, his train was the last to get through. Neither Oncle Ernest nor any of his family was able to leave Paris that summer.

Olivès then told us that he had been warned there would probably be a house to house search in Le Vigan that same day. I felt the icy grip of fear on my heart. I remembered my lack of an identity card, and my accent that betrayed me every time I opened my mouth. But at first I said nothing. I was ashamed in front of Olivès to make a mountain of what by his standards must seem the veriest molehill. He went on to say that a watch would probably be kept on all the exits from Le Vigan.

At last he rose to go. Timidly I then mentioned my lack of an identity card and asked what I should do. He said that if I liked I could leave Le Vigan with him. Some of his men were waiting in the neighbourhood with a vehicle. They had hand-grenades and would throw them if the Germans tried to stop them. I hesitated. I was not yet in tune with the atmosphere in which I found myself plunged. In Paris danger was everywhere, but it was underground; shorn lambs could keep the thought of it to some extent at bay. Here it was at your door. Deep inside me I was sorry to miss such an opportunity of having something stirring to tell my future grandchildren; I felt that I was letting them down. But I knew I must run my risks in my own way. I said I would chance the control and bicycle quietly out of the town.

Before Olivès left, almost in spite of himself he told us something that had the effect on us of a blood transfusion. He said that the message that the *Maquis* was waiting for had come through. This meant that the Allied landing in France was imminent. There was no need to swear us to silence.

Before I left, Helena gave me a rapid account of what had happened since I had left the region the summer before. Most exciting was her story of how Georges le Belge, the man behind the cash-desk in the butcher's shop, having fled from Le Vigan with the Gestapo on his tracks, was with the *Maquis* somewhere in the mountains. The rumours we had heard about him had apparently been true.

I left Le Vigan on my bicycle without any difficulty, and made my way to Valleraugue. I was received almost with open arms at the *Gendarmerie*. I was told to cast care to the winds; they would make me an identity card if I wanted one, but they added that I would need none so long as I stayed in Valleraugue. 'In the meantime,' they told me, 'if anyone makes trouble for you, send him to us. We'll answer for you!'

When I left the *Gendarmerie* I ran into Pasteur Couderc, our local clergyman. He too offered to make me a false card: he said that he was used to the job. All this determined me to settle with the children as originally planned at La Coustète. I made the house ready and bicycled next morning to Pont-d'Hérault, where I took the train. At the second stop, Ganges, a man got into our carriage. He was bursting with excitement. He told us that the Allies had attacked the coast of Normandy and were even then landing in France. Everyone began talking to everyone else in an uncontrollable explosion of joy. We reached St Hippolyte before I was aware that we had left Ganges, before even it dawned upon me that I had not really believed the announcement made by Olivès. I had been grateful to him for giving me something to keep me going; but this, this overpowering joy, was something I had not really expected ever to happen, at any time.

Papa and Maman saw things differently. They were convinced that the landing could never be successful and would mean only new and more dreadful suffering for France. But I was proof against pessimism. We left, the children and I, for Valleraugue. I was no longer in any fear of the *Maquis*. On the contrary: I believed that only in its shadow would we be safe.

The most immediate effect of the landing in Normandy was a tightening of the screw as regards food. The Valleraugue region produces little at the best of times. The arable fields are on narrow terraces that must be worked by hand and, though most of the villagers own a piece of land, they produce only for their own needs. Those of us who came from the outside, and had neither a pig nor a goat nor, most of us, a vegetable garden, were almost completely dependent on the outside world. Now that the railway system was dislocated we were in a serious plight. We could no longer count even on our rations, and it was too early for the fruit and vegetables grown in the valley. I would have to go far afield to find food for my family.

Fortunately Maman had engaged a maid for me for the summer, Antoinette, a cheerful soul with whom I could leave the children with a quiet mind. It was when I was food-hunting that I made my next contact with the *Maquis*. I had gone up to L'Espérou by bus, taking my bicycle with me. From there I rode to Les Laupies to visit the Passets. I came back with the usual load of cheese and milk and butter, too late to catch the bus home. I bicycled on, but before I had gone far one of my tyres punctured. I had neither the implements nor the knowledge necessary to mend it. There was no alternative but to walk. I pushed on for another mile, feeling very discouraged. At a turn of the road I caught up with a peasant tramping beside his ox-cart at the slow pace of another age. We walked together for a while and

he told me that he was, of all unlikely things, Portuguese.
I gathered that he had settled in France before the war. He
seemed to live in a world utterly detached from the tragic
web in which we were all caught. We soon fell silent. At
last I asked him whether he would be willing to take my
bicycle on his empty cart and leave it for me at Valleraugue
to allow me to continue by the short-cuts. He agreed and
we parted.

But I was not at the end of my troubles. My wooden-soled
shoes were quite unfit for the rough steep paths that cut
across the hairpin bends of the road. Before I had gone far,
I shed the sole of one of them. I struggled on till I came to
the road again, and there I sat down on a wall in despair.
Suddenly I heard the unusual sound of a motor coming
down towards me. When it rounded the bend I saw that
it was full of *maquisards*. Before even I had time to signal
to them to stop, it had drawn up beside me and the driver
asked if I wanted a lift. The young men squeezed together
to make room for me, and one of them put his tommy-gun
under the seat and took my basket on his knee. We started
off and as we drove I examined my companions out of the
corner of my eye, remembering what I had been told about
the 'bandits'. They looked pathetically young, probably
not more than seventeen or eighteen, and they were in
high spirits. They told me they had only recently joined
the *Maquis*. In the meantime we were whizzing down the
road at a breathtaking speed, swerving at the hairpin bends
in an unnerving manner. I became acutely aware what a
dangerous road it is, with its twists and turns and its seven
'devil's elbows,' and a sheer drop all the way at one side
or the other. By way of making conversation, one of them
explained to me that the boy at the wheel was learning to
drive and that the rest of them had come out to give him a
lesson. I began to regret the slow pace of the ox-cart. But we
were nearing the end of the descent, and my companions said
they would turn back at the foot of the hill because they must
not go too near a village. Thoughtlessly, I said that it was just
as well because one of my near neighbours was a member of
Pétain's Legion. They gave a shout of joy, seized their guns
and suggested making him a visit. I assured them that they

had much better leave him alone, and we parted on the best of terms.

I was lonelier than ever in Valleraugue, for the Lévi-Strausses had left. They had been preparing to go ever since, one cold winter day when the mistral was blowing, Papa had bicycled all the way from Mandiargues to warn them that they had better go into hiding. Rumours had reached him that there was to be a rounding up of Jews in the region. At the time they had hesitated, and so far nothing had happened to them. But they had at last made up their minds and had procured false identity cards. Before they went, they left as many of their possessions as they could in my keeping, including some bottled fruit which they said I might eat if things grew desperate. I missed them badly, and so did everyone else. The neighbour, Madame Daudet, who supplied us both with vegetables, said to me with tears in her eyes, 'They need never have gone. None of us would have given them away!' And it was true. If the people of Valleraugue were proof against anti-Semitism, it was in part because its absurdity was so well illustrated by that gentle, civilized couple.

In the meantime Helena and I discovered that a small lorry went every week from Le Vigan to Lanuéjols by way of L'Espérou to fetch coal from a neighbouring mine. When I say 'coal' I am using a euphemism for what in fact was coal-dust. The mine had been closed down some time before the war and had been re-opened to provide jobs for young men who would otherwise have to go and work in Germany. Luckily no one in authority ever came to see just what the mine produced. The driver of the lorry that fetched the coal, a friendly cheerful creature with a wife and nine children in Le Vigan, agreed to let Helena and me travel to and fro with him. I had to find my own way up to L'Espérou and join the lorry there. We had always to make the return journey sitting on the coal-dust, on which the driver laid sacks as protection for our clothes. On one occasion Jonget, too, was of the party, and at the last moment, on the homeward journey, the driver decided to join us on the coal-dust and let his boy drive. We each hollowed out a place in which to recline, and off we went in high good humour and feeling the best of company. The road climbs slowly between deep forests of pine and larch, and then suddenly emerges on to a high plateau with a magnificent view across the valley to the Causses beyond. It was at this point that I became aware of a strange sensation. It seemed to me that our friend the driver was making a tentative effort at pinching my hip. Soon it was clear that it was no effect of the imagination. My anger, though promptly roused, was as soon swept away on a flood of inward laughter. I had a sudden vision of my grandfather, Sir Alexander Ogston, surgeon-in-ordinary to the Royal Family in Scotland (but long dead), who used to maintain that one's duty is always as plain before one as a pikestaff. I saw him looking down from heaven on his grand-daughter, and I wondered where by his standards the pikestaff now pointed. My dilemma was no ordinary one. If I shook my poor friend off with harsh words, could I in decency require him to give me a lift the following week? Was I to sacrifice my finer feelings in order to provide food for my family, or to let them starve, comforted by the thought of my own high-mindedness? I decided to pretend not to notice, and at the first lurch of the lorry I rolled out of his reach. We remained on excellent terms, and I was back on the coal-dust a week later. The driver was back at his driving-wheel.

Since I came south I had had news of the Passemards. They had moved into Nîmes, where Passemard had been appointed Director of the Museum of Natural History. He had also joined, and had become the head of the Nîmes branch of, the *Milice*, a sort of minor Gestapo brought into being by the Vichy government. By all accounts he was seconded in his activities by Madame Passemard, but this may not have been true, since he alone was shot at the Liberation. I think it is because of the part played by Passemard that Papa never could believe what we told him at the time of the methods used by the *Milice*. When finally he came to admit that torture was used, I am certain he thought that the Passemards knew nothing of it; which is manifestly impossible. Yet it must have cost them a bitter sacrifice to do what they did or had done. They were not heartless people, and nothing would surprise me less than to learn that it was Passemard who told Papa to warn his Jewish friends that they were in danger. He was perfectly capable of going out of his way to save a Jew while mercilessly pursuing the *maquisards* whom he associated in his mind with communism, for him the evil of evils. If he had been a gangster like the Nazi leaders, or a coward or sadist like the men who served them, if he had even been stupid, Passemard would not be such a disquieting figure. But he was none of these. He was simply a man who believed that you can turn the clock back if only you are energetic and ruthless enough, and that to preserve our values it is necessary to turn the clock back.

Many Frenchmen see their country as a sacred person charged with an almost supernatural mission. Those who mentally are contemporary with the times they live in know that if such a mission does exist, then it is one that can never be carried out by brute force. But men of Passemard's stamp believe that force is necessary; they see France, by reason of her very greatness, as exposed to exceptional dangers and the victim of unscrupulous neighbours who use her as a battlefield. An even greater danger in their eyes is that of disunity within the country itself. They saw the Resistance as a movement of people swayed by foreign counsel, and destructive of the fragile unity restored by Pétain's government. They persuaded themselves—and their spirit is still alive today—that this inner enemy must be dealt with as in the good old days they would have dealt with witches and heretics. They were—they are—blind to the fact that France's real greatness is in the hands of the very people they condemn, and that the destruction of a certain passionate liberalism would make nonsense of their whole conception of France as a country with a mission.

I am going to skip to the middle of July, 1944. In the meantime I had received the last letter that was to reach me from François. In it he told me that Armand was in hospital and that his friends were all very anxious. I guessed that this meant he had at last been arrested. It was a haunting thought.

In our immediate neighbourhood the great event was that L'Espérou had been openly occupied by the *Maquis*. On one of our visits there Helena and I found Olivès and his men in the act of settling into three of the houses that are occupied only in the summer. Olivès had been living with a price on his head, or so I was told, since the Ardaillès affair, and until the *Maquis* came into the open he had no permanent shelter. Madame Teulon, who keeps a grocery in Valleraugue, once hid him in her house for three consecutive months, and thereafter always left her door unlocked, both by night and by day, so that he could take refuge there. I knew nothing of this at the time. I knew Madame Teulon only slightly, and nothing of her activities, which included honouring the food-cards supplied clandestinely to her for the *maquisards* by Charles Adgé, the secretary of the *Mairie*. She did so at considerable risk to herself, for their numbers far exceeded that of the customers she could reasonably claim to have in so depopulated a village. As I say, I knew nothing of all this, and once when I met Olivès on one of his rare open visits to Valleraugue, I offered him, in rather quavering tones, La Coustète as a shelter. Great was my relief when he said that he had one already.

On July 12th Olivès was joined at L'Espérou by other groups of the Aigoual-Cevennes *Maquis*. On the 13th I went down to Valleraugue to do my shopping, and there I was told by the excited villagers that an order had come down from the *Maquis* chiefs; we were to celebrate July 14th for the first time since the armistice, in spite of the interdiction on all such celebrations. A detachment of *maquisards* was coming down to light the ritual bonfire. I rushed home, determined somehow or other to concoct a flag. I tore a strip from one of my precious sheets, another off a blue counterpane (it was the wrong blue, but that was a small matter), I unpicked a red linen-bag and cut it to fit the other strips.

The next problem was a flagstaff. I had no proper tools or in my enthusiasm I might have cut down a sapling. I had to content myself with a broom-handle. I was a little uncertain about the order of the colours, but as the French for red, white, and blue is *bleu, blanc, rouge*, I presumed that the blue strip should go next the broom-handle. Then I remembered that somewhere among Henri's toys there was a little Union Jack my mother once bought for him at Woolworth's. I brought it out and stitched it on to a corner of my French flag. The broom-handle was too short, but I screwed it into the prop that once had held a garden parasol, and I hammered it into the ground. I then crossed over to the far side of the river to see how it looked from a distance. It was a triumphant sight.

In the early afternoon we went down to the village, all five of us, and spent the rest of the day there. A retired captain of the Marseilles police, a local man by birth, who had been an active member of the Resistance from the beginning, had managed to produce fireworks which were to be let off as soon as it grew dark. He was known in the *Maquis* as 'Triton', and that day he came out into the open and led the celebrations. The great moment of the day was when the detachment of *maquisards* arrived on foot from L'Espérou, armed to the teeth. They wore the dark green uniforms that had recently been looted from government stocks, badly cut and badly fitting, a little reminiscent of Robin Hood with their big hoods as protection from the rain. The young men's thin, set, badly-shaven faces were marked by the strain of constant danger, lack of sleep and underfeeding; but they all had the same look of having an inner purpose to sustain them. The whole village was at their feet, and everyone who could brought something out to offer them. I had nothing, so I generously dived down into Oncle Ernest's cellar and brought them up as many bottles of wine as I could carry. My sense of property was wearing so thin that it seemed the right and proper thing to do—and by what were then our standards, so it was.

As soon as darkness fell Triton let off his fireworks. He must have been storing them since the beginning of the war, no doubt for the victory celebrations. Many of them refused to go off, but a muted bang followed by a spark was all we required to set up a roar of enthusiasm. Then came the bonfire. All afternoon we had hung over the wall above the river-bed, gazing in admiration at the tremendous pile of wood the villagers had prepared. The Hérault in the summer dwindles to a narrow stream, leaving a broad expanse of stony ground on either side. It is there the villagers always make the July 14th bonfire, but I think it had never before been so big. When the solemn moment arrived, as many of us as could surged down into the river-bed in the wake of the *maquisards*. They set a light to the dry vine-shoots beneath the logs and with a roar the flames rushed upward. It was a terrific sight, but we had soon to beat a hasty retreat, for the heat was unendurable. We were all shattered by the emotion of the moment. The thought of the Germans at Le Vigan, only twelve miles away, made us feel delightfully heroic, and the knowledge that in all likelihood this would be our last summer under the heel of Nazi Germany went to our heads.

As gradually the heat subsided and it was possible to draw near the fire again, the *maquisards* in their excitement began firing volleys into the river-bed with their tommy-guns. The bullets ricocheted off the stones and with one loud cry we took to our heels again. It was at this point that I saw an odd scene. A villager I did not know by sight, a man of about thirty, was running with us, but I suddenly realized that he was not running for the same reason. He was in full pursuit of a village girl, and she was running not from the bullets but from him. He caught up with her, and for a moment they stood facing one another, a few yards apart. The fire flamed up and by its flickering light I saw the man's face as he manoeuvred to come within reach of the girl. There was nothing in it that could shock you; what it expressed was too pagan, too gay, too utterly free of the knowledge of any law. The girl looked back at him with the defiant, hypnotized eyes of a woodland nymph. It was a most unexpected sight in such a sober village. The crowd swept me on and I lost sight of them; but I thought of them long afterwards when Monsieur Jaujard, then *Directeur Général des Arts et Lettres*, told me what he saw from the window of his flat in the Louvre during the liberation of Paris. There was fighting going on all round when he looked out of the window, but there in the garden of the Louvre he saw four people; all of them were tranquilly doing what in normal times is forbidden. One was 'watering' a flower-bed; two were making love; the fourth was picking the roses.

The next thing I saw was our gentle, kindly little postman being led to the doctor's house to have his arm dressed. He had been wounded by one of the bullets. The evening's festivities were at an end. The *maquisards* were getting ready for their long climb up to L'Espérou. I took my sleepy children by the hand, Antoinette hoisted Nicolas on to her back, and we turned for home.

Exactly a week later, day for day, the Germans came to Valleraugue. It was a hot sultry day and the sky was grey with moisture wafted up from the Mediterranean by the south wind. It is the hardest weather of all to bear, for it saps your strength and clouds your spirits. In the early afternoon I went and lay down in the living-room, feeling depressed and weary. It was too hot to sleep and at last I got up and opened the shutters. I heard the sound of a motor and saw on the far side of the Hérault Olivès's car, easily recognizable by the French flag streaming in front. It was going up the road at a breakneck speed and soon disappeared round a bend. Scarcely was it out of sight but a large grey lorry followed at a slower speed, and to my horror I saw that it was full, even to the running-boards, of the sinister grey figures I knew so well. At the same time the sound of shooting broke out from the direction of the village, prolonged, one-sided shooting which made me fear a massacre in the village. The lorry disappeared round the bend after Olivès, and I stood on at the window feeling like death and straining my ears to hear what would happen. Then I saw it coming back and I told myself that Olivès at least must be safe, for there had been no sound of shooting from that direction. He had the advantage of speed on a dangerous road whose every turn he knew. Obviously the Germans had been afraid to go farther, with the risk that the *maquisards* might be lying in ambush behind every rock. I went downstairs to consult with Antoinette. She suggested we go higher up into the mountains behind the house. She was quite frank that she found me dangerous company. She put it very charmingly. She said, 'If anything were to happen to Madame because of her accent, I would be embarrassed to break the news to Monsieur'. I suggested we go up to the Mas du Conte, a hamlet perched on the top of the little hill that gives La Coustète its name. While we were still talking, Pasteur Couderc appeared. He came to fetch his little boy who was spending the day with my children. He gave me an account of what had happened so far. Olivès had come down in the morning to act as judge in a rather painful affair. The son and daughter-in-law of one of our few real collaborators were suspected of stealing the provisions intended for the prisoner-of-war parcels that went through the hands of the daughter-in-law in her position as president of our local Red Cross. I think, from what I was afterwards told by Olivès himself, that there was little doubt of their guilt, though the affair was never completely cleared up as far as I know. Certainly they left the region at the Liberation. In the meantime, as no official inquiry had been made, Olivès decided to take the matter into his own hands and get to the bottom of the affair. He summoned the couple to appear before him at the *Mairie* of Valleraugue, and it was in the middle of this unofficial trial that the Germans had driven into Valleraugue. Olivès was warned just in time to leap into his car and make for the mountains with a German lorry on his heels. The shooting I heard had made one victim, one of the men we could least spare, Triton. When the warning came he too escaped, but not with Olivès. He decided to remain in the neighbourhood, and keep watch so as to be able to inform the *Maquis* of what went on. He climbed up by a path at the back of Valleraugue till he reached the bare hill called the Rocher de Gache. He who had always warned the *maquisards* to keep clear of this hill because it affords no cover, took to it, confident that by lying flat and moving only an inch at a time he would escape notice. He was wrong, and he had been right in the advice he gave the *maquisards*. The Germans saw him move and fired their machine-gun till they got him.

I followed Pasteur Couderc down to the road when he and his little boy left. He added that it looked as though the Germans were going to stay the night, and that there were about a hundred of them. He too thought we would be wise to go up to Le Mas du Conte. I stood by the roadside for a moment after he left me, thinking of Triton and remembering how gay he had been on July 14th when he struggled with his damp fireworks. It began to rain, a soft hopeless drizzle. I turned to go home, and it was then that I saw coming towards me some twenty *maquisards*, with their guns on their shoulders and revolvers and hand-grenades at their belts. Their thin faces were grimly set. I ran to meet them and told them that the Germans were a hundred strong at Valleraugue. I said, 'For God's sake go back, you'll only get yourselves killed. They've got Triton!' They stopped dead in their tracks. There was a moment of silence and then one of them snarled, '*Ah! Les salauds!*' and they swung off down the road towards Valleraugue, I ran beside them, trying to make them turn back, but it was no use. I stopped at last and stood by the roadside stupidly weeping, as much because they looked so young as because I was convinced they would all be killed.

At last I turned back to La Coustète, straining my ears all the time for the sound of shooting from the village. I found Antoinette and the children all ready to go, with a shopping bag full of necessaries for the night. We locked the three doors and set out up the path at the back of the house, Henri carrying Nicolas on his back. The path goes only a part of the way and the rest of the climb is steep and difficult. The rain had stopped but the air was still heavy and damp. When we reached the top we found that the only inhabitants were an old couple. Except for theirs, all the houses stood empty and some were falling to ruins. They made us welcome and told us that they had the key to one of the houses and that we could occupy it for as long as necessary. The owner, a Nîmes postman, would, they were sure, be willing to let us use his house, for he was a Plymouth Brother and a good Christian. We went in, feeling nonetheless like thieves, and explored the house. It was very simply furnished, but there were plenty of beds. Antoinette said she would give the younger children something to eat and settle them for the night, and Henri and I went out to find water as there was none in the house. We found the village fountain in the middle of the little hamlet, a stone water-tank with clear mountain water spouting into it. We filled our can and Henri carried it back to Antoinette. There was still no sound from the village. I went and stood on the terrace of one of the houses, straining my eyes in the direction of Valleraugue, but a hill hid it from sight. It was then, on looking down, that I noticed I had forgotten to close the shutters of La Coustète and take the deck-chairs in. When Henri joined me again I told him I was going down to close the house properly. If the Germans came (by now I had a fixed idea that they would hear there was an *anglaise* in the valley) they would guess we could not be far off. Henri insisted that I let him go instead. He said that as a child he ran less risk and that my accent was liable to betray us all, but he had not been gone ten minutes before I was asking myself how I could be such a coward as to allow a small boy to run such risks. I set off down the hill after him and when I reached the house I found him busy among the deck-chairs. He started when he heard my step and seeing who it was cried, '*Maman! Tu me prends toute ma gloire!*' I think he had really hoped it was the Germans. Those were terrible times for a boy of his age. I know now that he was haunted by a story we had heard of a lad not much older than himself whom the Germans had caught and questioned on their way to Ardaillès, and who had refused to give information about the *Maquis*. He needed proof that he was made of the same mettle.

We left the house looking as though it had stood empty for a long time, and we climbed again to our eagle's nest. We were exploring the little hamlet when a peasant passed through on his way higher up and gave us the latest news. The Germans had left before the *maquisards* arrived, but it seemed probable that they would return the following day. We had better stay where we were. Still, it was with a more quiet mind that I wandered about the place with Henri. Tomorrow was tomorrow.

The first thing we found was a little graveyard. It contained five or six graves, and to my astonishment they all bore Polish names on their stones. It was not so much the fact of the names being Polish that surprised me—there are Poles all over France. What was unexpected was to find them buried in a private graveyard, for though there are a number of these in the region they are all Protestant and date from the times of the Camisards when no Protestant could be buried in consecrated ground. Our next find was the old village bread-oven, built of stone and standing in the shade of a fig-tree. At last we went behind the biggest of the houses where there was a broad grassy terrace overlooking the valley. Right in the middle of this terrace we found a square wooden lavatory-seat. It was not even one of the *petits cabinets de province* immortalized by the inimitable Frères Jacques, the Paris *chansonniers*; it was nothing but a seat without even the pretence of a shelter round it, although it stood in full view of the road that winds to L'Espèrou. It stood facing one of the loveliest views I know, for the ground below the grassy terrace with its incongruous burden falls step by step, from terrace to terrace, to the Hérault, and from it you have a circular view of the mountains opposite, from the Lusette to the hill that masks the Rocher de Gache where Triton was killed. Evening had begun to flood the valley, and gradually as we gazed its shadow rose, filling each hollow as it passed and flattening the hills to a deep even blue. What peasant-poet, I asked myself, had so loved to watch the changing hills that he had lost the old old instinct that drives man into hiding to preserve his dignity?

The Germans did not come back, and they buried Triton the following afternoon. Again a detachment of *maquisards* came down, and he was given a military funeral. After the service we all gathered in the Catholic cemetery. It was black with people come from all over the countryside. Although Triton had been a Catholic, it was Olivès who made the speech over his grave. He spoke with passionate conviction of the cause in which Triton had died, and with biting contempt of those who were not prepared, in such a cause, to do as much as Triton had done. My heart was in my mouth during all the early part of the ceremony; if the Germans had returned we would all have been trapped in the narrow Vallée des Salles where the cemetery lies. But from the beginning of Olivès's speech we forgot everything, and even when an aeroplane zoomed overhead and we—or at any rate I—thought that our last hour had come, we were so moved that we scarcely cared. The next day all the young men in the valley who had not already done so went up into the mountains to join the *Maquis*, and at L'Espérou the Maison Noire and all the other empty houses were occupied.

The day after the funeral I went over to Le Vigan to see the Scobs. I went with a double purpose; I wanted to tell them about yesterday's stirring events, and I wanted to persuade them to join me at La Coustète. I was certain they were in serious danger now that the *Maquis* was grown so bold, for their house stood almost next-door to the German blockhouse. There was nothing illogical about my fears. I found that Olivès had actually warned them that an attack on the German forces in Le Vigan was imminent. Even so they were hesitant. They hated leaving their house, and they were naturally anxious about Scob's mother, for whom there would obviously be no room at La Coustète. But it occurred to me that I could probably borrow a room for her at Oncle Ernest's. The bottles of wine I had looted for the *maquisards* from his wine-cellar were proving to be the thin edge of a wedge which was to go in a long way before we were out of our troubles.

The moment I was back in Valleraugue I went and discussed the matter with Georgette, who had taken Lucinde's place in the old house. She is the grand-niece of one of Lucinde's oldest friends, Élise, and as she was left an orphan, she was brought up by Élise and Lucinde conjointly. Something of old Lucinde's spirit lives on in her, and a great deal of her humour.

Georgette agreed that we need have no scruples about borrowing a room. We were deciding which room when the door-bell rang. At the door we found two *maquisards*, hung about with arms, who told us that the *Maquis* intended soon to occupy Valleraugue. They asked us whether the house was occupied; they had been told it was empty and they had instructions to requisition it for the *Maquis* command post. I said I thought there could be no possible objection, but that they must leave the whole of the first floor free for the widow of a Russian general. Even from Oncle Ernest's point of view I felt that I was doing the right thing. They were bound to occupy the house if they found it empty. It was better to make them as welcome as from my own point of view they in fact were, and to keep them out of the rooms that Oncle Ernest most cared about, which included his library. The *maquisards* agreed to what I asked, and I inquired when we were to expect them, but they would not or could not say.

I went back to La Coustète with a singing heart. The occupation of Valleraugue by the *Maquis* would amount virtually to our liberation. I then solved our own problem of fitting seven extra people into a house that with difficulty contained five by turning the great living-room into a dormitory for the children and the maids. I borrowed the beds I lacked from Oncle Ernest's service bedrooms. Given an inch I was taking an ell.

The Scobs arrived almost at once. But Scob's mother decided to stay where she was. She had been through the revolution in Russia, had fled with her family to their estate in Finland and been through both revolution and counter-revolution there, before escaping to France. I think she had no strong feeling one way or another about the Germans. She found it difficult to take them seriously after the Russians and, as she spoke fluent German, she thought she had nothing to fear from them. It seemed to her less of a hardship to remain where she was, even with the prospect of a battle next door, than to make an inconvenient change to a strange house in a strange village.

It was an immense comfort for me having the Scobs at La Coustète. Every evening when the children were in bed we would sit round the wireless, listening to the BBC news bulletin and *Les français parlent aux français*, and Scob would mark in with my lipstick on a map of France pinned on the wall the growing expanse of country that was falling into Allied hands. He had also to star the map with red dots to show which towns were one by one being liberated from within by the Resistance, most of them alarmingly far from any hope of military aid in the event of a return offensive by the enemy. Terrible accounts were coming in of the atrocities being committed in the Vercors by the Mongolian troops which the Germans loosed on the population with a free hand to carry out reprisals.

Meanwhile the food situation was growing desperate. The *Maquis* did its best to organize supplies, but the task was an impossible one. More and more people were pouring every week into our valley from Nîmes, Marseilles and Montpellier, where food was even harder to find than in the hinterland. There was meat perhaps only twice, when the *Maquis* made free distributions, and only very occasionally bread. The loaves were made with anything that came to hand, including bean-flour. They were damp, grey, unappetizing and indigestible, but we were not hard to please. We lived on vegetables and a little fruit supplied by our neighbours, the Daudets. And we did contrive to make a cake for André's birthday, August Ist. Helena had brought some sugar from Le Vigan, and we had an egg which made us feel there was nothing we could not achieve. We used potato instead of flour and the result bore little resemblance to a real cake. It was all there was for the birthday tea, but we set the table under the vine-trellis in ceremonious style, and André felt that the right thing was being done by him. We divided the cake carefully, so that everyone should have a slice, and the birthday child two, since that is the rule of the house. When the last crumb had disappeared, Scob wiped his mouth and remarked, 'Well! If the war lasts till 1970 I expect we'll find that good!'

Food was not our only problem. The children's shoes were worn out and they had few clothes that still fitted. Wooden shoes were not convenient on the uneven ground of La Coustète, but the Daudets' son, Robert, taught my children that by relaxing your feet completely you feel no pain when walking barefoot. When the weather grew hot I had ended by letting them go stark naked so long as they remained in our little property. The Scob children soon formed the same habit, and like mine wore clothes only to go down to the village. Michel, André and Edith went there twice a week. A Jewish composer, Mademoiselle Hass, a refugee from Paris, was living at Le Valdeyron, the property of Monsieur Marcellin Pellet, and she had organized a *solfège* class for the innumerable children in Valleraugue. We seized this opportunity of giving our children some normal employment and improving their education. They grumbled at first, for they loved their free life, but they resigned themselves to these lessons the less unwillingly that there was a tree on the way (though this we discovered only when its owner complained) from which they could steal plums. What they found difficult, if we were not at hand to remind them, was to remember to put clothes on for the occasion. Long afterwards André told me that once, when they were halfway to Valleraugue, suddenly Edith (now a rising actress on the Paris stage) looked down at herself and cried in dismay, 'But we're naked!' Like Adam and Eve before them, they felt ashamed and went home to dress.

The Pellets of Le Valdeyron are old friends of my husband's family, but it was only that summer I came to know them well. Old Monsieur Pellet, who had been French ambassador at The Hague before the war, spent the whole of the Occupation in his country house, with his daughter Janine, and a number of her friends. Except Monsieur Pellet, all occupants of the house were women between the ages of thirty-five and fifty. I found them entertaining company, and one of them, Vève Catelin, the sister of Jacques Catelin the film actor, had begun to take an interest in Henri. She set him to learn Lafontaine's *Fables* by heart, and gave him lessons in diction. Henri had no need to join the *solfège* class, but he went regularly to Le Valdeyron for these lessons.

Other neighbours were our cousins, the Chazels, and the Bargetons, who were back at La Coste. Edith Bargeton's husband, Daniel, had managed to get through from Paris.

I think it was during the first week of August that we made our last attempt at a social occasion. We invited Edith, Daniel and his sister Jaqueline to dinner. Huguette, Helena's little maid from the north of France, got egg-fruit and tomatoes from the Daudets and contrived to make them into a *gratin*, which was to be our *plat de résistance*. To make things look festive, we took advantage of the relative coolness of the evening to light a fire, and the table was set in front of it. We had named an early hour for dinner, knowing that the Bargetons would have to bicycle the five miles home. When at eight o'clock there was no sign of them we decided they must have been prevented from coming, probably because the *Maquis* was out on the warpath. We decided to begin without them.

It was the old story all over again. Scarcely had we eaten two mouthfuls of *gratin* but the evening air was rent by a loud cry from Huguette, 'Madame! There's someone on the bridge! There are two! No! There are three!' It was the Bargetons. Aghast we looked at one another. Not a word was spoken; there was no need. With the same swift gesture we simultaneously swept the contents of our plates back into the dish, and Huguette, who had come running upstairs for instructions, bore it and our plates off to the kitchen. When ten minutes later she laid the *gratin* solemnly before our guests, we carefully avoided each other's eyes. Its content had been neatly flattened out and Huguette had even managed to brown the top again very nicely in the oven. It looked as though butter would not melt in its mouth.

I think it was on August 9th that Helena announced her intention of paying a visit to Le Vigan. She had just heard that a stone of plums she had ordered from a neighbour before leaving had been delivered at her house. She was determined not to waste them. As she had some black-market sugar stored in her cellar, she said that she was going home to make plum jam. I tried hard to dissuade her, and so did Scob. It seemed foolish to have waited so long, and then perhaps to be caught out by the *Maquis* attack for no better reason than that there was jam to be made. While we were arguing the matter Huguette appeared. She announced that, since we had two other maids, we could easily spare her and that she would make the jam. She was not at all afraid. Scob said that he too would go; there would be plenty of work waiting for him, and besides, he could pay his mother a visit.

They set out the same afternoon on their bicycles. They returned the following day with dishevelled hair and almost speechless with emotion. The attack on the German forces in

Le Vigan had taken place that very morning, while Huguette was busy with her jam. Scob as usual made comedy of their experience. He described how tiny Huguette clung to the kitchen table with one hand while stirring the jam with the other, in a vain but determined attempt to prevent the blast from the hand-grenades from lifting her across the narrow kitchen every time one of them exploded outside. He also gave an uproarious account of his own desperate and fruitless efforts to persuade the *maquisards* not to invade his terrace as a convenient place from which to shoot at the enemy. Huguette doggedly stuck to her guns till the jam was safe in its pots. They then stole out by a back door, dragging their bicycles up a stony path behind the house, till they reached a rough road over the hills to Valleraugue. Scob had got his mother safely away to a neighbour's house when the shooting started.

The same evening Olivès called. He gave us a brief account of what had actually taken place. The *Maquis* chiefs were warned the day before that a battalion of Armenians had been sent from Mende to reinforce the German forces. They decided not to call off the attack. But they had another stroke of bad luck. The signal for opening fire was given too soon, before everyone was in position. The battle raged for several hours, but in the end the *Maquis* had to withdraw. They had not succeeded in ousting the Germans from Le Vigan. But they had made seventeen prisoners and had captured thirty saddle-horses. On the debit side of the balance sheet was the death of one of the most popular chiefs, Marceau. He was killed during the attack on the Armenian barracks.

But Olivès's real purpose in coming to La Coustète was to tell the Scobs that by way of reprisals the Germans had burned to the ground three houses owned by people notorious for their pro-*Maquis* sympathies. The Scobs' house was one of them. Madame Scobeltzine was safe.

Under the first shock we could do nothing but laugh. We felt so detached at that time from normal life, so uncertain of any future to be faced, in the Scobs' case deprived of all they possessed, that our view of the absurdity of human life was almost Olympian. What seemed to us especially funny was that a number of the Scobs' friends had left their more valuable possessions in the house, because Le Vigan struck them as such a safe place. But it was the thought of the jam burning away quietly, and the pots exploding one after the other, that made us laugh most.

The Scobs went back to Le Vigan the next day to see what they could save, though their doing so made me very nervous, for a number of arrests had been made. But when they got there they were warned not to go near the house. A German sentry was mounting guard over the smoking remains to prevent any attempt at salvaging. They made certain before leaving that Madame Scobeltzine was still safe in a neighbour's house. Scob's account of his mother's adventures set us laughing all over again. When the *maquisards* withdrew, at about ten in the morning, she received the visit of a German officer, come with a search party to arrest Scob. She explained in perfect German that her son as an architect was often obliged to travel, and that he had been absent for some time. While his men searched the house, the officer conversed respectfully with her, thereby confirming her in her belief that she had nothing to fear from the Germans. At last, or so said Scob, he kissed her hand and took his leave. Seeing that it was close on midday, Madame Scobeltzine put on her hat, and taking nothing with her but her handbag, she went back to her neighbour for luncheon, and to tell her the latest developments. When she returned for her afternoon nap, she found the Scobs' house in flames, and a couple of sentries mounting guard.

But I too had a story to tell. While Helena and Scob were in Le Vigan news had reached me that the *Maquis* was at that very moment occupying Valleraugue. I hastened down and found Oncle Ernest's kitchen full of *maquisards* whom Georgette was showing round. She introduced me, and the *Maquis* cook said, 'Ahh! Now we're beginning to meet Englishwomen!' and diving into a duffle-bag he produced several little bags of tea which he gave me.

I was next introduced to the *Maquis* chiefs. I was a little anxious in case they asked where the Russian general's widow was, and I also wished to make certain that they had done as I asked and left the first floor unoccupied. I escaped as soon as in politeness I could, and went upstairs.

They had been as good as their word, but I was afraid that when they discovered there was no one to occupy the rooms, they would overflow into all of them. I decided then and there to occupy them myself.

Before I left I accordingly told the three chiefs that my Russian friend had decided not to come, but that I was living in the house myself. One of the chiefs then asked me if I would be willing to lend them my flag which they had seen as they went past La Coustète on their way down from L'Espérou. I was delighted that my home-made flag should adorn a *Maquis* command post.

From Oncle Ernest's I went to Les Angliviel, the property of our cousins, the Angliviel de la Beaumelle family. I had been told that it was occupied by another command post and I was anxious about the library, which is full of valuable books. The village was overflowing with *maquisards*, and as I passed through the square under Oncle Ernest's terrace-garden, I saw German prisoners peeling potatoes for the *Maquis* kitchens. It was a glorious summer day, and when I reached the avenue that leads to Les Angliviel I thought I had never seen the place look so lovely. In the orchards on either side of the path the grass was lush and green, and a number of rather fine horses were grazing under the apple-trees, adding unexpected beauty to the scene. I felt as though I were having the sort of uncanny experience they love to tell about in Scotland, when time slips and you find yourself seeing, not what is there but what once was.

At the house I asked to speak to the officer in command. His *Maquis* name was Colas, and he was a major in the Air Force and very much on his dignity with the mere civilian I was. He waved an airy hand and told me the house would be treated with all due respect. Before taking my leave, I inquired about the horses. He said they were some of those the *Maquis* had captured from the Armenian battalion in Le Vigan. I longed to ask for permission to borrow a horse to ride, but was afraid he would think me frivolous at such a time.

On my way out I met the Angliviels' farmer's wife. She whispered in my ear that she had managed to lock the library up before the *Maquis* arrived. As I knew it contained not only valuable books, but also some letters written by Voltaire to the Beaumelle ancestor of his time, I was considerably relieved.

I went back to La Coustète and found the Scobs were back from Le Vigan. It was then they told me what had happened. We sat laughing till late, in the dark, because a pylon had been destroyed in the fighting and we had no electricity. After Scob went to bed, Helena and I sat on. Suddenly a reaction set in, and we felt exhausted and as though emptied of everything that makes you feel alive. Nothing was left but the dogged will to survive, though to what end we could scarcely have said. I remember standing by the open door and looking out. I saw the August night sky trembling with stars, and between the stones of the terrace-walls one by one the glow-worms lit their pale emerald lamps. I heard the passionate chirping of a cricket, but I could feel nothing. I remember that I turned to where Helena sat in the dark behind me. I said, 'I can see that this is a night made for love, but I can't even remember what it feels like to be in love!'

The next day events took a new and precipitous turn. It must have been August 12th. I went down to Valleraugue to see what I could loot in the way of fruit from Oncle Ernest's big fruit and vegetable garden, Le Mas Mouret, which lies on the outskirts of the village, and I was on my way home with a basket of unripe pears. I had to push my bicycle because I had nothing with which to fix the basket on the carrier. As usual I had shoes with wooden soles, and they made walking difficult.

At a bend in the road a large motor-car caught up with me and passed so close that I had to make an abrupt movement to avoid it. My foot turned, and my bicycle lost its balance, spilling the pears all over the road. I heard the car draw up and inwardly I cursed the driver, but I was too busy chasing pears to pay much attention. Then suddenly I was aware that someone was helping me. I turned my head and saw, busy among the pears, a man in the uniform of a lieutenant in the French regular army. He made some joke, but I scarcely took it in. I had seen no such uniform since our defeat, and I was so excited I could scarcely breathe. I longed to ask him what he was doing there, and where he came from and how, but the habit formed during the Occupation of never asking questions paralysed me. We joked together while we filled the basket as though there was nothing extraordinary about the situation. When the last pear was recovered I straightened up and looked about me. The motor was only a few yards off, and in front of it two men were waiting with expectant faces. One was one of the *Maquis* chiefs from Oncle Ernest's house, the nicest of them; the other I would have recognized as English even if he had not been wearing uniform. His hair was reddish-gold, greying at the temples, his eyes were blue and they had a faintly come-hither look

which I found comforting because it belonged to the world
I had lost. He wore a small moustache and his face looked to
me so pink that I could scarcely believe my eyes. I thought
his complexion peculiar to himself, but when I got back to
Paris and saw the English and Americans, and even those
of the French who had been in England with de Gaulle, I
realized that it was simply the normal colour of the white
race. It was we in occupied territory who had grown sallow
through underfeeding.

The French lieutenant led me up to the two men and the
Maquis chief stepped forward and ceremoniously performed
the necessary introductions. He told me he had been hunting
for me when he upset my bicycle, and he apologized. He
explained that he hoped I would perhaps make room for
the two newcomers in my part of the house. All the other
rooms were full. I said that I could make room for one, or
two if they could share a room. We decided to go back and
see. The French officer put my bicycle and my pears in a
sheltered spot and we drove off.

Our passage through Valleraugue was triumphant. I sat
between the Englishman, Major Sharpe, and the *Maquis*
chief, and all the villagers we passed smiled broadly and
stood looking after us. Major Sharpe very naturally took it
all as homage to his uniform, and it certainly did make an
impression; but a farmer's wife afterwards told me that they
were really smiling with pleasure that 'Madame François'
should at last have found a compatriot.

I showed Oncle Ernest's best bedroom to my three
companions, and Major Sharpe firmly but courteously
appropriated it. At the breath of ceremony for which my
shyness was responsible, the parachute-trooper hardened
to danger and discomfort had been metamorphosed. The
come-hither look had been banished from his eye, and in
its place was an expression of respectful interest. In fact,
he looked so much the upper-class English gentleman (as
indeed he was) on a visit to a country house, that I was
embarrassed at having even suggested he might share his
room—and with a foreigner. It occurred to me that perhaps
the Chazels would make room for the French officer; their
house is almost as large as Oncle Ernest's. We drove there

to inquire and found the Chazels all in their garden. Once more solemn introductions took place. Pierre and Françoise declared themselves happy to give their compatriot a room, and so we left him, and Major Sharpe and the *Maquis* chief drove me back to my bicycle. As soon as they were out of sight I abandoned my pears by the roadside and sped home with my glorious news.

I saw Major Sharpe again the next morning. Georgette always brought me breakfast in the garden (*Maquis* bread, *Maquis* jam and *Maquis* coffee), and seeing me there he came and joined me. He mentioned that he would like to get in touch with some civilian who knew the region well and could discuss with him what bridges should be blown up to hinder the movements of the German troops. He wanted to avoid indiscriminate destruction. I suggested Scob as a suitable person, and we arranged that he should come and lunch with us the day after the next.

I must explain that from the moment the *Maquis* occupied our village we lived in an atmosphere of alarms and excursions. The task of the *Maquis*, and this was to be especially true after the Allied landing in the south of France, when all over France the enemy was on the move, was to harry the German columns and hinder their progress by destroying communications. Even if they succeeded only in delaying them ten minutes here and twenty there, the cumulative effect was disastrous to the Germans' plans. This work was done by handfuls of *maquisards* set in ambush at strategic points along the road each signalling to the next when a German column entered their section. But we civilians were kept in complete ignorance of what was going on, and every time the *Maquis* went into action we thought it meant that the Germans were on their way to attack Valleraugue and that they had gone to intercept them. Day and night there were feverish comings and goings in the old house and shrill ringing of the telephone. But what I found most frightening of all was when in the night I would hear a *maquisard* going from door to door of the village, and another doing the same thing in Oncle Ernest's house, knocking loudly at each and crying, '*Alerte! Alerte!*' To this day I cannot bear the sound of knocking.

On the day when I breakfasted with Major Sharpe it was obvious from the excited atmosphere that something was pending, but I still could not bring myself to ask questions, even of him. I went home as usual to La Coustète for the day. Late that afternoon Scob suddenly announced that he intended to return the next day to Le Vigan. I told them my impression and joined Helena in a passionate effort to dissuade him. But he explained that he had just been informed that he must make an immediate application for war damages at the *Mairie* of Le Vigan. If he delayed he would get no compensation for his losses, which included not only all their possessions, but also everything contained in Scob's office, which had been in the burned house. It also included their friends' valuables, and Madeleine's diamonds which she could ill afford to lose. There was the future to consider, whether or not we believed in it. He must go through the ashes of the house with a fine comb, and he must make his application for war damages. Seeing that he was adamant, Helena said that if he went, then she went too, hoping this would give him pause. But no; he remained unshaken.

I left them arguing and hurried down again to the command post, determined to force one of the chiefs to tell me whether or not there was fighting going on on the road between Valleraugue and Le Vigan. When I reached the house I was told they were all at dinner. I took my courage in both hands and walked boldly into the dining-room. There was still no electricity, and they were dining by candlelight. It was so dark that, blind as I am, I could not distinguish where the chief sat whom I knew best and was least afraid of approaching. I went up to the one nearest me. It turned out to be Major Colas whom I had met at Les Angliviel. Obviously this must be a council of war. I felt so shy that no doubt I was abrupt when I put my question: was there any reason why the Scobs should not go to Le Vigan the following day? There was a pause during which no one spoke. I saw Major Sharpe's eyes fixed on me, but I dared not meet them. At last Major Colas said in as casual tones as he could assume that it would be far better if they waited for a day or two. What hurry could there be?

I thanked him and beat a hasty retreat. I hurried back to La Coustète, confident that Scob would have to yield. But no; he was as determined as ever, and Helena would do whatever he did.

I think I never admired Helena as much as I did the following morning when at an unearthly hour I saw her ride off in the wake of a determined Scob. I knew that she felt the same physical symptoms of fear as I did, but unlike me she paid them no attention.

They came back in the course of the day, having had a narrow escape. There had been fighting at Pont-d'Hérault. It had started just after they passed through. In Le Vigan their search through the ashes of their house had been fruitless. All they found were the blackened and twisted remains of the Scobeltzine family silver, brought with them by Scob's parents when they escaped from Russia and afterwards Finland. Apart from that there was nothing. The work of destruction had been done with characteristic thoroughness.

That evening, when I went down to Valleraugue for the night, I found the whole house in a state of upheaval. The *Maquis* was 'clearing out to spare the civilian population,' or so I was told by the discouraged-looking wife of the chief, Rascalon, who had changed from civilian dress into her *Maquis* uniform and was preparing to leave with the troops. My heart sank at the sight of the hand-grenades that lay about on tables, and the tommy-guns that hung from pegs in the hall among Oncle Ernest's waterproofs. I went up to the library to see if Major Sharpe were there. The room was empty, but while I was standing wondering what I should do, he came in laughing. He said, 'Do you know the latest *Maquis* rumour?' I said I only knew they were clearing out. He told me the *Maquis* believed there was a division of SS on its way to wipe us all out. I said, politely inquiring, 'Do you think that funny?' He said, 'They can't possibly send a whole division. There are only two in the whole south of France! We aren't nearly important enough.'

I said nothing. I disliked its being suggested even indirectly that I was not important. But especially I felt that what he said was beside the point. The prospect of a single

SS in Valleraugue would be enough to send me haring up into the mountains. Numbers had nothing to do with it. Major Sharpe then added that he saw no reason why he himself should clear out, since he was not allowed to join in *Maquis* action. I heard my voice courteously reply that of course not, he was most welcome to stay! Even as I spoke visions of what would happen to Oncle Ernest's house and to me if the Germans found me in polite conversation with an English Major in full uniform in a house full of arms, flooded all rational thought from my mind. And though we sat on talking for some ten minutes more, on one point I was determined: I was not going to spend that night in the old house. I escaped from the library as soon as in politeness I could. I seized my toothbrush and made for La Coustète.

All along the road lorries full of *maquisards* were drawn up. The young men were obviously in the best of spirits, as they always were when they were going into action. They shouted friendly greetings as I passed, but there was no repartee left in me.

That was a dreadful night. The sound of shooting broke out in the distance some time after I reached home, and after we had gone to bed I lay hour after hour with beating heart, trying to distinguish whether or not it was drawing nearer. When doubt became unbearable I would leave my bed and open the door of the room where the Scobs slept. I think that Helena was as wakeful as I was myself, but Scob was always asleep. I would call his name till he woke, and then beseech him to listen and tell me whether the fighting sounded any closer. He would raise his head for a moment and obediently listen, say, 'I don't think so!' and at once fall asleep again.

When we met the next morning on the terrace for breakfast, Helena and I were wan for lack of sleep. Scob was in as good form as ever. The sound of shooting had ceased in the early morning, but as we sat drinking our foul coffee in the bright sunlight there came a new sound, such a ghost of a sound that at first I said nothing, believing I was imagining it. At last I looked inquiringly at Scob to see whether he too had heard it. He was gazing into the far distance with a listening look in his light blue eyes. He said,

'That's not shooting. It's the sound of bombs. They must be bombarding the coast!'

It was then that the idea of liberation became for us a reality. Later in the day the news of the Allies' landing in the south was confirmed.

CHAPTER TEN

It was on the evening of the day the Allies landed that Major
Sharpe invited me for the first time to come and listen to
the news with him in the library where he had installed his
portable wireless-set. It was a battery-set, and required no
electricity, but as we had still no light I suggested we made
a fire. We went down to the cellar for wood and while we
were there it occurred to me that we might celebrate the
Allied landing with one of Oncle Ernest's best bottles. We
opened the trap-door that leads down to the wine-cellar and
Major Sharpe remarked that it was very like the moment
when you prepare to jump from your aeroplane. I pointed
out that there was a ladder. He went down it and came back
with a bottle of St Emilion which we carried up to the
library. There we sat solemnly by fire-light with earphones
on our heads, listening to the news. We had to open wide
all doors and windows, for the heat was now considerable
even after dark, and with a fire it was almost unbearable.
We then drank our wine and he told me something of his life
in the army. He had been parachuted first into Yugoslavia,
then into Savoy, and finally at L'Espérou. He said that the
discomfort in Yugoslavia had been extreme, but that the
danger was less than at Valleraugue because the Germans
were never nearer than eighty miles' distance. He found it
a strange contrast being in a civilized house with library and
bathroom, the guest in some sort of a compatriot, but with
the Germans only twelve miles off or less. I asked him how
he came to speak such good French, and he told me that he
too had Swiss governesses in his childhood. He added that
he spoke much better German. He lived in, I think, Danzig
before the war and spoke German like a native.

He then began telling me something of what was going on
in our own district. He said that the *Maquis* intended to blow

up the bridge at Pont-d'Hérault the following day. His own role was solely that of adviser and he was supposed to take no part in *Maquis* activities. He was also strictly forbidden to abandon his uniform; but he admitted that he intended to go along with the *maquisards* and that he was being lent a *Maquis* uniform for the occasion. He had nothing but praise for our *maquisards*. He said that he had only once been obliged to interfere to prevent physical pressure being put on a prisoner to make him talk. Except in that one instance—and it had been easy to dissuade them—the prisoners were humanely treated. Long afterwards I learned that three German prisoners whose wounds were dressed in the hospital installed by the *Maquis* in Oncle Ernest's Espérou house, and where Daniel Bargeton was working as doctor, had struck up such a friendship with their *Maquis* comrades that they followed as orderlies a regiment that was formed after the Liberation, solely of Aigoual-Cevennes *maquisards*. They went right through de Lattre de Tassigny's campaign in Alsace with this regiment, and even when it would have been easy to escape into Germany, they never attempted to do so.

Major Sharpe then disconcerted me considerably by telling me things about myself that it was impossible he should know. It was only when he saw me thoroughly alarmed that he admitted having been given to censor a letter which I had written to my father, and which the *Maquis* had offered to send over to England for me. I believe there was an airfield camouflaged somewhere in the mountains, or at least so I was told. Certainly they said the letter would be sent by air.

The next day was the one on which Major Sharpe was invited to lunch at La Coustète. Helena and I had a feverish time finding food. I think that even the *Maquis* had no idea now difficult things were at that time for the civilian population. Henri, who as the eldest of our children was the one most in need of food, remembers this period as one of intolerable hunger. He soon formed the habit of going a-begging in his uncle's kitchen. The men in charge would cut him huge sandwiches of cold roast mutton at which we adults gazed with ill-concealed envy. We dared not follow his example, but on this occasion we felt justified in demanding what we needed. Olivès and his men were at Cancabra. We got meat from him and bread and cheese from the command post. We had no fruit, but I remembered Emma Lévi-Strauss's bottled fruit. I decided this was an occasion which could be counted as desperate, and we took one bottle of cherries. We were doing what the French all did when they entertained, resorting to desperate remedies to produce a tolerably normal meal. When the guests were English or Americans, it was probably foolish because it gave the impression that our restrictions were a myth.

We fed the children early, knowing that our guest had serious matters to discuss with Scob. At the last moment we reminded them to put clothes on.

The hour for which Major Sharpe was invited brought a *maquisard* with a letter saying that he was going to be late and asking us to begin without him. This we dared not do. We knew that if once we started eating we would stop only when everything was gone.

When at last he arrived, the children surged up on to the terrace to meet the parachuted Englishman. All, all were naked, except Henri, and he remained in the background. I gasped, 'Where are your clothes?' They looked down in astonishment and then, with a start of recollection, André said, 'Oh yes! I fell into the *béal* and got wet, so we all took our clothes off'. Even as he spoke my vision shifted; I found myself seeing them with Major Sharpe's eyes, and it struck me for the first time that all their bellies were enormous. It came as such a shock that I spoke my thought out loud, in English so that the children would not understand. 'Yes,' said our guest cheerfully, 'I was just thinking the same thing. They remind me of native children.' I was so furious I could find nothing to say. Of course they were like native children, and for the same reason of undernourishment.

When the last of the bottled cherries had been eaten, conversation turned to serious matters. Major Sharpe took off the scarf he wore round his neck and spread it on the table. It had a detailed map of our region printed on it. I think I never wanted to steal anything as much as I did that scarf. He and Scob then fell to discussing what other bridges it might be necessary to blow up, and Helena and I sat and listened, and meditated on the odd fact that had transpired during lunch: we were all four of us the fifth child of our families.

It was at about this time that Helena and I met an old acquaintance. We were down in Valleraugue together and suddenly we both felt dreadfully hungry. We decided to cadge a meal off the *Maquis*. So far we had been very discreet and strong-minded about never asking for anything for ourselves, however hungry we felt. But hunger suddenly made us cynical. Even so, we dared not ask outright, but decided we would pretend we had our own food and that all we wanted was a place on the stove to cook it. After all, it was Oncle Ernest's own kitchen, to which I had a better right than they. Just as we hoped, rather than have us messing about among them they offered to feed us. Georgette, who was privy to the plot, said she would serve us in the garden. Soon, blissfully sated, we lay relaxed in Oncle Ernest's great basket-chairs, gazing in ecstasy at the pattern wrought overhead by the shocking-pink flower-clusters of a Lagerstroemia against the blue sky. Our moment of abandon was cut short by an invitation to drink coffee with the *Maquis* chiefs.

When we entered the dining-room we were surprised to see not three but four figures rise to greet us, and that the fourth, glorious in uniform, with the white cord of the FFE (*Forces Françaises de l'Extérieur*) on his shoulder, was Georges le Belge. He beamed at us, delighted to be seen in his true colours by Helena and me, who knew him only as the man-behind-the-cash-desk in the butcher's shop. As we drank our coffee, conversation turned to the reprisals the Germans had carried out in, I think, Tulle. The local *Maquis* had liberated the town and then been forced to abandon it. The inhabitants were made to pay for what Helena and I could only look upon as the imprudence of the *Maquis*. Lieutenant Georges saw things very differently. He seemed to look upon the number of civilians shot as a crown of glory won by another *Maquis* and greatly to be envied. We tried to explain our point of view, but he turned on us the same opaque look I had already seen in the eyes of the British officers when we argued about Mers el-Kébir. He said nothing, but obviously he too thought us incapable of understanding the military point of view. The other chiefs, none of them professional soldiers, were more reticent.

Ever since the battle at Le Vigan, the individual members of the Armenian battalion had been deserting in groups of two and three in the hope of joining the *Maquis*. They even brought with them some essential part of the German mortar, which made them confident they would be well received. Unfortunately *Maquis* feeling was high against them, because their battalion was responsible for the death of the chief, Marceau. I heard them discussing the matter one morning when I passed through the hall on my way to La Coustète. It was clear from what I heard that they intended to shoot them all. Major Sharpe came down the staircase just at that moment and greeted me. I told him what I had heard and asked him to interfere. He answered that, quite honestly, he had no objection to the lot of them being shot. I left the house feeling very taken aback, and by chance I ran into Scob as I was going through the village. He said that he would see what he could do.

We went back to the command post and found the discussion still going on in the hall. Scob asked them with airy nonchalance whether they needed an interpreter—the Armenians spoke Russian but no French. They immediately sent for the wretched men—there were about fifteen of them—and Scob began questioning them in Russian. He stood among the German and *Maquis* uniforms looking very unmilitary in his corduroys and clogs, but he dominated them. Not only was he head and shoulders taller than any of them; he had the patrician art of putting people at their ease without ever losing his ascendancy. He incidentally knew far better than I what nerve to touch to carry his interlocutors along with him.

At last he turned back to the *maquisards* and gave them a succinct account of what he had been told. The Armenians had first been mobilized by the Russians and made to fight the Germans. They had then been made prisoner by the Germans and sent to a concentration camp.

Those who after two years were still alive were finally put into German uniform and sent to reinforce the troops of occupation in France. '*Voilà!*' said Scob, and turning to me he suggested that we go home.

I followed him out, but I was almost as disappointed in him as I had been in Major Sharpe. I had expected an impassioned and Shakespearean plea for mercy. But Scob knew what he was doing. The Armenians were not massacred. They were put into a third uniform, that of the Aigoual-Cevennes *Maquis*.

In the middle of all these emotions, we had some comic relief the day the *Maquis* attacked a German column which had looted nine tons of Rocquefort cheese from the Rocquefort cellars. They captured the cheese, and brought it back to Valleraugue where they insisted on housing it in the Chazels' vast cellars. The Chazels came round and asked for permission to spend the day in Oncle Ernest's house. They were afraid the Germans might come for their cheese. They would only have to follow their noses to discover where it was. In the days that followed the *Maquis* made generous distributions of cheese to the population. We had no bread to eat with it, but we used great slices of it in place of meat. Fortunately it was fresh cheese that had not yet been put to mature in the Rocquefort cellars; even so we were soon sick of the very sight of it.

In the meantime I heard a depressing account from one of the *maquisards* of what had happened to my English friend's Bulgarian husband. He was notoriously pro-German, and his black-market activities were also well-known.

Black marketing and hoarding were counted no crime so long as we were under German rule, except by the Vichy partisans; but once the *Maquis* had liberated us both were severely punished. There had been a descent on the house at Le Puech-Sigal. All the provisions had been seized and the Bulgarian beaten. The *maquisard* assured me that he had come to no great harm, but I was haunted by the thought of what it must have been like for his wife and son. I never saw either of them again, but immediately after the Liberation I had a letter from her in which she told me that she was taking her son home to England and that they would not return.

On August 24th Henri and I went to Le Valdeyron. We found it a very different place from what it had been earlier in the summer. On August 14th, in time for the great battle at Pont-d'Hérault, the entire police force of Montpellier and all the *gendarmes* of the Hérault department had joined the *Maquis* at Valleraugue. One hundred and seventy of them took up their quarters at Le Valdeyron. Between the house, the 'pavillon', the farms and the outhouses, there was room enough. Women were in a minority at Le Valdeyron, and I found myself wishing that Raymond Lévi-Strauss could see the scene. Once at a tea-party we were both at, he remarked to me as we sat surrounded by women, all with cropped hair and wearing slacks, that what was lacking to complete the picture was a priest in his robe. I felt he would have appreciated this very different restoring of the balance, for by contrast with the stalwart Montpellier police, even slacks and short hair looked feminine.

On this occasion I had promised to play to Janine and her friends. I was afterwards given a glass of wine, and while I was drinking it someone turned the wireless on. The voice that came through told us that Paris was liberated, liberated from within by the Resistance. As soon as my benumbed mind grasped what I heard, I retired to a quiet spot in the garden and allowed four years' pent-up tears of self-pity to flow.

The last episode of that strange summer was a tragic one. Three spies were tried and shot. I heard about it from Major Sharpe one evening, immediately after the trial had taken place. He told me they were to be shot the next day. He added that there was evidence enough to justify shooting them in time of war, but not in peacetime. But this was still war. He kept from me what I later learned from Georgette, that the trial had taken place in Oncle Ernest's dining-room, while I sat in the room immediately overhead, unwillingly translating Pasteur Couderc's report on the French Methodist Missions which he had lost no time in drawing up for their American headquarters.

The room is haunted now for me, especially at dusk. How can they have believed that their lives were really at stake when they looked out through the tall french windows and saw the stage set for the garden scene in *Eugene Onegin*; or that night was stealing their breath as it stole the colour from the flowers?

Dawn snuffed them out like candles, against a wall starred the night before with glow-worms. The sound woke me, but by then I was so numb to all emotion except fear that I turned over and went to sleep again.

When at the end of the third week in August the wave of resistance swept down on to the plain and left us stranded in the mountains, our first feeling was one of desolation. After being in the thick of the action we were cut off from everything, and glory—for though vicarious, yet it had been glory—was departed out of our lives for ever. The bridge blown up at Pont-d'Hérault was our only direct link with the outer world. How many more bridges between us and Paris were in the same state? There seemed small chance of our getting home for a very long time; yet I was desperate for news of François.

The Scobs at this point decided to go up and occupy their house at L'Espérou; they had no other home. It was a bleak day for me when they left. Olivès, who was still at Cancabra, offered to take me to Mandiargues to see how Papa and Maman had fared. He was going on one of his rounds to distribute tobacco to the *maquisards* still in the region, and St Hippolyte was on his way. We had to go by a long detour through the mountains. He dropped me off at Mandiargues, and I found Papa and Maman shaken but in good health. There had been a battle very near their house. They had closed all the thick wooden shutters when the shooting started; they had buried the family silver in the garden at the back of the house, and themselves taken refuge in the inner courtyard round which the house is built. They had been forced to beat a hasty retreat into the house when stray bullets began to ricochet from the walls. The next day the peasants made prisoner a number of Germans found hiding in the vineyards. The poor men gave themselves up thankfully enough to civilians; their terror was of falling into *Maquis* hands. They had been told by their officers that they would be mercilessly tortured. The peasants' fierce hatred of their hereditary enemy fell flat at the sight of the wretched, hungry men, and soon they were being fed by the women of Mandiargues with loud cries of, 'Pecherètte!'

I spent half the night lying on a stone bench outside the house, waiting for Olivès and his motor. He turned up in the small hours of the morning and took me home.

I had made up my mind to leave Valleraugue; but it was not till the *Maquis* had been gone three weeks that I found a lorry which was going in the direction of St Hippolyte by the same detour I had taken with Olivès. At five minutes' notice I had to make up my mind to bundle Antoinette and the two younger children into it, with a minimum of luggage. Henri and I intended to find our way by bicycle.

The leave-taking was sad. Everyone was going through the same reaction as myself. I said goodbye to Madame Teulon in whose house Olivès used to hide. She and her family had played a heroic part in the shadow of the Resistance. There would be no recognition of what she had done because so many people all over France had done more. She must sink back into a humdrum existence which would yet not be normal life; our material difficulties were to continue hard for a long time to come. I said goodbye to Pasteur Couderc, to the Daudets and the Launes, and of course to Olivès. His wife and children were expected to arrive at any moment. He had sent them elsewhere for safety's sake, and unfortunately had chosen the Vercors. They were all going to spend a month or so at La Coustète to recuperate in peace and quiet after the emotions of the last two years. I looked in on the hotel-keeper. He and his wife had been staunchly pro-British throughout, and at the end his wife had lost her life in the Allied bombardment of Nîmes.

Henri and I then mounted our bicycles and set out on the first part of our journey. The shadow of all that had happened during the last four years was heavy on me, and I felt more depressed than I would ever have dared let myself feel during the Occupation. At Pont-d'Hérault we dragged our bicycles up on to the railway viaduct and crossed between the rails. Once we were over we carried them down again, and it was only when we were at last spinning along the Nîmes road, with no major obstacle between us and Mandiargues, that the cloud lifted and at long last realization of our freedom swept over me. I could have shouted out loud for joy. I knew that this was no return but a rebirth.

We had some difficulty in reaching Mandiargues, however. There were burned-out vehicles and fallen plane-trees across the road in several places, put there to delay the German convoys. And before even we reached Ganges one of my tyres punctured. At Ganges no one could repair it for me and I had to do the rest of the journey a hundred yards at a time, pumping at every stop and then rushing on feverishly so as to cover as much ground as possible before the tyre went flat again. And when at last we reached Papa's old house, we found that Antoinette and the children had not arrived. For three anxious days we waited. They turned up at last in a vehicle whose driver Antoinette had persuaded to take them, with reckless promises of largesse at the other end. The original lorry had apparently changed its mind and decided to go elsewhere, leaving them all stranded in a village in the mountains.

Now that the children were safe with their grandparents I began to study ways and means of getting back to Paris. No trains were running, except on short distances; the whole railway system was dislocated because so many bridges and tunnels had been blown up. There was a rumour that the Allied troops were generous with petrol, and I had some idea of borrowing Papa's little Simca and finding some other person who wanted to get back to Paris and could drive, a thing I have never learned to do. But it had stood too long unused and was to all intents and purposes dead. Then one day when I was in St Hippolyte a shopkeeper told me that he had just been on a journey to Lyons, travelling from Avignon with American troops. He said the GIs were very friendly about giving lifts to civilians and that they fed their passengers on the way. I went straight home and told Papa and Maman that I was determined to try my luck. They shared my anxiety about François and agreed to my going.

The next evening, carrying a couple of light suitcases, I boarded the train at the station of St Hippolyte-du-Fort. It took us to where Major Sharpe had had a tunnel blown up by the RAF There we all walked for about a hundred yards, and another train took us the rest of the way to Nîmes. In a café where I went for a drink I saw some British officers. I took my courage in both hands and went and asked them what my chances were of hitch-hiking north with American troops. They gave me excellent advice. They said I must find my way to Avignon. There I must walk out of the town by the Paris road. When a convoy passed me I must let the jeeps and all the lorries but the last go by. The officers would be in the jeeps at the head of the convoy and would be bound to refuse to take me because it is irregular for army vehicles to carry civilians. The last lorry on the other hand could stop without holding the whole convoy up.

From the café I went to the hairdresser to have my hair done: much was going to depend, I felt, on my appearance. I also bought a bottle of scent. I chose it solely for its name and without even smelling it. It was 'Vivre' of Molyneux. I set out in the bus that was running between Nîmes and the Rhône, with my confidence solidly renewed. I crossed the Rhône after nightfall in a crowded ferry-boat. I could just distinguish what was left of the bridge. It was in as ruined a condition as the famous old Pont d'Avignon nearby, and where its shadow fell the stars that shone so steadily in the sky overhead danced in the surging black waters. An icy mistral was blowing, and I was frozen by the time we reached the far bank.

It was as I dragged my weary way up to the town, a suitcase in either hand, that American kindness overtook me for the first time. A jeep passed me by and then stopped. The colonel sitting beside the driver asked whether I wanted a lift. When we reached Avignon he took me with him to the best hotel, but there was not a room to be had and we were told there was none in the whole of the town. The American was ill and could hardly stand; he told me it came of eating tinned food for months together in North Africa. The hotel-porter telephoned all over the place and at last found him a room, but the colonel refused to leave until they found one for me too. He dropped me at the address we had been given. I suspect that in normal times the place had been a house—or at least a flat—of ill-fame. It was a sinister-looking apartment, kept by a sinister-looking woman, and I discovered afterwards that she had stolen several things from a suitcase while I was out the next morning having 'coffee'.

As early as possible I took my two suitcases and walked out of the town by what I was told was the Paris road. I felt foolish asking the way to Paris, and very like the carrier-pigeon in the story which came home on foot because it was such an enjoyable day. Before long I saw a convoy standing by the wayside. Near it were a number of enormous American Negroes. I asked one of them if they were going north. He said they were and agreed to take me along, but he said I must walk on and that the last lorry would pick me up; their officers were white and would prevent my coming if they knew. So I walked on, but I walked on the wrong side of the road. I have never even after all these years grown accustomed to right-hand traffic. Before I had gone far the convoy roared past me. I saw my friend standing up on the last lorry, gazing from under a shading hand at the right hand pavement. He never saw me and I saw him too late to stop them. I felt very foolish and a little discouraged. My suitcases were beginning to drag on my arms, but I changed to the other side of the road and walked doggedly on. The next convoy that passed me found me waiting on the edge of the road. I made timid signals to the last lorry and it stopped. I said, 'Are you going to Lyons?' There was a shout of, 'This one speaks English!' and I was almost lifted into the seat between the driver and his mate.

All the men on the lorry were hilarious with excitement. They told me they really had the impression in France that they were liberating a country, whereas in Italy they felt they were simply replacing one occupying force by another. They had hated Italy and they said the Italians were dirty and dishonest and had far too many children. This last statement left me aghast. I was so saturated with Vichy propaganda in favour of large families that it seemed to me sheer blasphemy. Seeing my shocked face, one of them said I must forgive them if they were a little above themselves; they were excited at seeing white women for the first time since they left America. I said, 'But I thought you were in

Italy?' He answered cheerfully, 'That's right. North Africa, Sicily, Italy!'

We stopped at midday to eat by the roadside, and it was as I had been told; they shared everything they had with me. I had been living on grapes and *ersatz* coffee for the last two days and I thought their food wonderful, but they told me they were sick of it and that they longed for fresh food. I suggested they barter their coffee and biscuits at the farms we passed, but they said they were not allowed to. I offered to do the bartering for them, and they at once agreed. At several farmhouses I exchanged coffee for milk and cheese and eggs. We then went careering after the convoy to catch up before anyone noticed we had fallen behind.

We travelled slowly, stopping often to eat, and I soon got to know the officers. The first time I met them they were standing by the roadside. One of them held an open bottle in his hand and was smelling its contents. When I came up to where they stood, he asked whether I knew what it was that was in the bottle and he gave it to me to smell. I told him that it was *marc*, a sort of rough, strong brandy the peasants drink. He said, 'Can *you* drink it?' I said I could, and at his request I drank a very little out of the neck of the bottle. One after the other the officers came up and shook hands with me, saying, 'Pleased to have met you!'

We reached Valence only at nightfall, and we stopped on the outskirts of the town, at a *Gare Routière*. The commanding officer drove me into town to find me an hotel, but there was not a room to be had, so many houses had been destroyed. We went back to the camp and he said he would lend me a lorry to sleep in. While they were getting the camp ready for the night, I went over and knocked at the door of the French road-house and asked if they would allow me to wash. The people who kept it, a man and his wife and grown-up daughter, were very friendly. They all cleared out of the kitchen and left me with a basin and plenty of hot water. When I was ready they offered to make tea. An English officer had made them a present of several packets. We sat round the stove talking, and I let my gratitude towards the Americans overflow in a torrent of enthusiasm. They were rather reticent. At last the man set down his cup of tea and said, 'We prefer the English!' I felt the veriest snake in America's generous bosom, but a broad smile spread over my face as I listened in ecstasy while they told me that only the English really understood what things had been like in France, only the English had tact and consideration in their dealings with the French.

When I got back to my lorry I found that everyone had gone into Valence to see whether there was any fun to be had. A single sentry remained in charge of the camp. He gave me several packets of cigarettes which the officer had left for me. I was sitting behind the driving-wheel, blissfully smoking one cigarette after another, when I heard a small voice say, 'Madame!' I glanced down and saw a little girl looking up at me. She told me that she was frightened to go home alone. She lived outside the town and there were still Germans hiding in the woods. Did I think an American would go with her? I got down off my lorry and we went and laid our problem before the sentry. He at once exclaimed that he would take her home himself.

It was only when they had been gone for some time that it occurred to me how foolishly I had acted. The camp was unguarded. What would the officers say if they came back before the sentry? An hour passed and there was no sign of him. I began to be really afraid; perhaps the little girl had been sent as a decoy and the man was lying dead somewhere. In a fever of anguish I heard the jeeps draw up outside. When I told the officers my story they were as alarmed as myself, and obviously they held me in deep suspicion. They poured into a couple of jeeps and bade me get in with them. They were no longer the exuberant creatures with whom I had been travelling; they had become real tough guys, armed to the teeth and out to kill. With tommy-guns pointing in every direction we roared out of the camp by the road I indicated. Soon we were in the open country with woods on either side, and I began to feel very frightened. If we ran into an ambush I was going to make an excellent target with my red coat. Then suddenly, by the light of the torches they were brandishing on every side, we saw the sentry coming towards us, looking very pleased with himself. His face fell when he saw us. Our jeep jerked to a stop and the commanding officer asked him sternly what he thought he was doing. He explained that when he reached the little girl's home her parents had insisted on his coming in for something to eat and drink. I murmured something about my own responsibility. The officer contented himself with some colourful abuse.

Back in the camp he supplied me with a sleeping-sack, blankets, more cigarettes and several packets of chocolate. He told me they were bringing me supper and asked if he might have his with me. We were brought bacon and eggs and great cups of steaming coffee, and I sat beside him in front of the lorry, feeling it must all be a dream. I was brought back to earth by the officer's suddenly putting his arm round me and starting to make discreet love. It was as great a shock as when the lorry-driver pinched my hip on the way home from Lanuéjols. This time, too, I felt it would be mean to choke him indignantly off. He had been so kind! All I found to say was, 'It's no use. I'm so exhausted with it all that it's as though I were dead!' He continued kind. He at once removed his arm and we finished our coffee and sat talking peacefully, with the detached intimacy that is possible only between strangers who know they will never meet again.

I slept not a wink that night. This was due not only to the coffee, or even to the tea, which had been as strong as in any farmhouse in Scotland. I was so happy that it would have been sheer waste to lose consciousness. It seemed to me in that blissful oasis of time, which lasted for a whole night, that you had only to mop up the Nazis to discover what a glorious place full of glorious people the world is. I told myself that I must hang on till at least a hundred to make up for lost time. At last, and at what a cost, I had put salt on the tail of happiness!

It was not till the first grey glimmer of dawn that I admitted to myself what it really was that had touched off this sudden explosion of joy. If the officer had felt drawn to make love to me, then surely that must mean I was thawed back to life again?

From Valence to Lyons, along the bank of the Rhône, the road was strewn on either side with the wrecks of German lorries and armoured cars and even private motor-cars. I found it a glorious sight, and so did my Americans. Soon we could no longer express our joy, so many there were. By this time I was in as high spirits as my companions. Indeed, I look back on that journey as one of the happiest experiences of my life. It was like a dream to sit back without a care after having, for four long years, fought tooth and nail for the barest necessities, never knowing whether we were being amiable to people because we liked them or because we wanted something out of them. It was surprising even to me with what ease I shed the unwilling cloak of independence so hardly acquired and sank back once more into my natural role of clinging vine. I, who had set out so boldly on the roads of France to find my way by my own wits to Paris, trembled at the prospect of having only too soon to leave the protection of what, after the sinister Germans, seemed to be creatures from another and better world.

At Lyons we had to part company, and it was there that my real problems would begin. I was to face them less destitute than when I set out, for the whole convoy contributed to stuffing my suitcases with food of every sort, including a huge tin of boned turkey. They gave me soap and cigarettes; they even asked me, oh so tactfully, if I were certain I had enough money for so uncertain a journey. I had not, but I assured them I had more than enough. I felt lost indeed when the convoy took to the road, heading east this time. I stood by the wayside, waving back in response to their farewell signals till a bend in the road hid them and I was alone once more.

Lyons seemed to me huge, inhospitable and impersonal.

Several of the bridges over the Rhône were destroyed, and I had some difficulty in finding a room in an hotel. Above all, there seemed little hope of getting farther; most of the American convoys turned east at this point, or so my companions had told me. Before nightfall I found a room in a rather dingy hotel. There I ate some of my provisions and settled down with a cigarette to write Maman an account of my adventures so far.

The next day I set out once more with my two suitcases, asking as at Avignon which was the Paris road. I stood for a long time at a crossroads, but no American convoy passed and nothing that did pass showed any inclination to stop. After I had been waiting for some time I noticed that I had a rival. A young girl with a single suitcase was waiting a little farther down the road. After we had both waited in vain for some time, casting each other suspicious glances, I went up to her and asked whether she too was trying to get to Paris. She said she was, and I suggested we join forces. I could see that at first she was not very willing. No doubt she felt that two young women with three suitcases between them would have less chance of getting a lift than one young woman with a single suitcase. But my experience with the American officer had made me a little chary. I doubted whether I could count upon everyone's being so considerate. I felt we would be safer together, though I could see that our chances of a lift would be halved. I said nothing of my thoughts to the girl, but tried to break down her obvious suspicion by being friendly.

She soon agreed to our sharing the adventure, but as there was still nothing to share except my American provisions, and it was beginning to look as if we were bogged down in Lyons, I suggested we go into a café and eat some of my food. We were so ravenous that we decided to tackle the turkey, of which we made short work in spite of its size. We were soon in hilarious spirits and growing confidential. I told her something of my background, and she told me that she was a hairdresser's assistant in a Paris suburb, that she had fallen in love with an American soldier while in Burgundy during the Liberation. She wanted to get back to Paris as much in the hope of seeing him again as of joining her parents.

Like me, she had a foolish feeling that all Americans must be heading for Paris, and that as he had her address, sooner or later he was bound to turn up. She explained that they had actually got engaged, but that he had afterwards disappeared and had never written, a thing that often happened at the time. I remembered my travel-companions' joy at seeing 'white women' again for the first time after two years. My new friend was blonde.

Whatever was then the American opinion of Italian women, she at least must count as a 'white woman'.

In the café we fell in with some other people who were also trying to travel north, though their goal was only Beaune. We decided to share a taxi if we could find one provided with petrol, and one of the men offered to prospect the neighbouring garages. He came back with a large Citröen whose chauffeur had black-market petrol and was willing to take us as far as Beaune.

At Beaune my companion and I went to the nearest hotel, which turned out to be the best. It had only just been evacuated by a German general staff and was standing empty except of hotel personnel. We shared a room and slept like logs. The next morning we woke to find it was raining, which was depressing, for we had only summer clothes. There was nothing for it but to take up our stand by the roadside in the rain. Fortunately a single American lorry soon came along. The driver told us he was going to Dijon and bade us get in at the back. We bundled in among the cases of provisions and sat congratulating ourselves and wondering what would happen at Dijon.

What did happen was that we found a town seething with people like ourselves, desperate to find transport to Paris. We made no attempt to search for a room, for we had no thought of spending the night at Dijon. We established temporary headquarters in the open-air part of a café while we decided what we should do. The old plan of action was outmoded. If we left Dijon and took to the Paris road, anything that passed us would already have picked up its quota of passengers in the town, for competition was obviously keen. We sat listening to the talk of the people round us. Not one had been able to find a room; they had tried to hitch-hike with no success, since none of the convoys was going north; they had tried to hire transport, but there was no petrol. We began to feel desperate. There was no reason why we should fare better than other people.

At last I pointed out to my companion that I had one advantage over other people. I spoke fluent English. I told her I was going to see whether there really were no convoys going north. I left her in the café, with encouragement to sift the passing traffic for an opportunity with unfaltering, inexorable eyes. Our café was at a crossroads—it was for that reason we chose it—and at the point of intersection stood an American MP, directing the convoys according to instructions. I went bravely up to him and said, 'Look, I'm desperate to get to Paris. I know most of your convoys are going east, but if anything is heading north, will you stop it and let my friend and me get in?' He looked me up and down. 'Young lady,' he said at last, 'I'm here to make you get down off the trucks, not to put you on to them!' Seeing my face fall, and having made his point, he went on to say that he would do his best, adding encouragingly, 'The boys'll take *you* all right!' But what he seemed unable to grasp was that I had no wish to travel with 'the boys' if it meant going into the fighting zone, and he would not tell me whether any of them were heading north. I waited beside him hopefully for a while and we got into conversation. I told him that we were afraid of being stranded in Dijon where there was not a room to be had. He made me a generous offer. He said that if by four in the afternoon, when he went off duty, I was still stuck in Dijon, then I was to meet him at the same place and he would let my friend and me have his hotel room. He would find a place for the night in one of the barracks. I thanked him with all my heart, asked him to signal to my friend in the café if he found a convoy going the right way, and I went on to where I saw an American Negro mounting guard in front of what looked like barracks. I asked him whether he knew of anything that was going in the direction of Paris, and whether he could tell me what the MP either could or would not disclose, whether generally speaking any of the convoys were going north. He told me that he knew of nothing, and that it was unlikely any Americans were going to Paris. He also, after a few moments' conversation, told me that, if I were still in Dijon at six in the evening, I could meet him outside the barracks and he would smuggle my friend and me in for the night, rather than leave us to spend the night in the street. Him too I thanked, but I decided that if the worst came to the worst I would keep my date with the MP . . .

I went back to the café to tell my friend that at least we would have a choice of rooms for the night. While I was crossing the street towards her I saw that she was standing by her table signalling to me desperately. I ran the rest of the way and breathlessly she explained that in a small motor-car standing by the kerb was an FFI officer who was willing to take us to Auxerre. The officer told us that we would easily find a lorry at Auxerre, since the region sends vegetables to the Halles, the big Paris central market. We piled our suitcases into the back seat and both got in beside him in front. At last the end was in sight. We looked with pitying eyes at the people still sitting in the cafés we passed on our way out of Dijon, and our pity was tinged with triumph, for we resented their having made us feel so discouraged. The officer was excellent company, though he did not conceal from us that there was some danger in the wooded country we were about to cross. The little girl who told me there were still Germans hiding in the forests had been right. But somehow I could no longer believe in danger or disaster; I was confident we would get home.

We drove into Auxerre at dusk and found a town where half the houses seemed to have suffered damage. Our officer hunted down the only hotel that was still intact, and left us there with good wishes for a successful conclusion to our adventures. We found a room without difficulty; most of the people who got as far as Auxerre had found transport all the way to Paris and stopped only to dine. The dining-room was so crowded that we had to wait a long time in the sitting-room. Soon we were in conversation with a French officer of the regular army who was also waiting. He was in as high spirits as ourselves, and we decided to have dinner all three together. At last a waiter called us in, and while we were examining the menu our companion announced that

the wine was his affair and asked if we had any preferences.
I told him that I had none, so long as we drank Burgundy;
I had been charmed as we passed through the region to
Beaune to see the names of famous wines on the signposts.
There was nothing small-minded about this Frenchman. He
made the waiter a sign and proceeded to order a bottle of
each of the three wines whose names I had seen on my way
through Burgundy, and of which I remember only Nuits
St Georges. Our spirits rose still higher. Fortunately I had
then a very good head for wine. Besides, this was the only
form of danger, if danger there was, that I had learned to
cope with. We had a hilarious dinner; the officer had the
Parisian gift for talk, the quick repartee, the wide range of
topics, the instant grasp of allusion. By the time coffee came
(and it was real coffee), all our heads were a little light. When
I heard our companion order *marc de Bourgogne*, a vastly
superior and matured version of what I had drunk from
the Americans' bottle, I did have a moment of hesitation.
But it was irresistible. At last, swaying slightly on our legs
we left the dining-room and at the foot of the staircase we
bade our friend of an evening farewell. He kissed both our
hands and wished us good luck.

I had scarcely closed the door of our room but my
companion said to me with a gasp, 'How lucky you all
are! Among my friends it would be impossible to talk so
freely and drink so much without their taking it for granted
that you were ready for anything!' We lay in bed talking
till late, about ourselves, about people generally and about
customs in the different strata of life, but at last we fell into
the deep sleep of the happy.

The next day we took our luggage and went and threw
ourselves on the mercy of a *Maquis* post which was directing
the traffic on the road outside Auxerre, and no doubt
keeping an eye on who went in and out of the town.
They told us to wait beside them; they would put us in
the first convenient vehicle. Soon there were a number of
us waiting, and before long we were told to climb into a
closed lorry belonging to the Ministry of Prisoners of War.
It was a sort of Black Maria and when we were all inside
the door was hermetically closed from without. The rest

of the journey was dull and very exhausting. We did at last persuade the driver to open the door and let in some light and air, but there were no seats and we soon grew stiff from sitting on the floor, or weary from standing. The pace was slow and it took us hours, I forget how many, to reach the outskirts of Paris. We made no contact with our fellow-travellers. We had already recovered a sense of the distance that in normal times separates strangers, but which had ceased to exist when we were all caught up in the same tragic dilemma.

At the Porte d'Italie underground station they set us down, and our fellow-travellers rushed to a café to telephone to their friends. My companion and I went down into the underground and boarded a train, but at the first change we had to separate, for we lived in different parts of Paris. We made each other promises to keep in touch, and so we did for at least a year. But gradually we slipped stupidly apart. Back in everyday life each was soon caught in the system of constraints that for all of us goes by the name of liberty, that is different for each, and that leaves us so little free.

Left alone in the *Métro*, I breathed in a deep breath of the beloved smell and then looked about me. It was obvious from the very atmosphere that the enemy was gone. People's faces no longer looked grim and self-contained, and everyone was inclined to be voluble. Instead of gloomy Germans were boisterous, pink-faced Americans. When I reached my station the first thing I did was to telephone to François from the public telephone box. There was no answer from our flat. I tried Germaine, and soon there was joyful shrieking at either end of the line. She gave me the news I so longed to hear; François was safe and well. But he was not in Paris. He was commanding a detachment of FFI in Meaux. Everyone else was safe, and Armand had been liberated. There were a million things to tell and to hear, and I must come and lunch with her and Pierre the following day.

When I emerged from the underground into the Place de l'Hôtel de Ville, dusk was falling, but through the shadowy twilight I could see, at each of the innumerable windows of the town hall, three unostentatious French flags arranged fanwise, only the white of their tricolour folds still clearly visible against the soft grey of the stone. Night fell as I crossed the square, but even in the dark I could have told, or so it seemed to me, that 'they' were gone. The very air I breathed, that once had been saturated with suffering, felt light and buoyant. Perhaps—I hoped—the sap of *französische Frivolität* was stirring after its long sleep and making ready to rise again. From the direction of the Seine came the voice of a newspaper boy, crying his evening edition. Gradually as I drew near the river the words came clear, *'Liberté! Liberté du Soir!'*

Afterword

It is nearly fifty years since the final events recorded in *Divided Loyalties*. This afterword tells what happened later to the Teissier du Cros family and to others who played a part in the story.

JANET TEISSIER DU CROS. In the autumn of 1944 she and François were joined in Paris by the three boys, and she found work as a translator for the Allied Forces. She managed a brief visit to her father in Edinburgh where the display of haggis and black puddings in Wilson's shop in George Street gave her 'an almost holy feeling'. In the summer of 1945 they were all in Savoie, with the boys living on a farm and eating enormously. The family continued to live in Paris, where the boys went to school and Marie was born in 1946. Later summers were spent at La Coustète and l'Espérou, where they entertained many of the children of their English and Scottish friends. Janet often came over to see her father and sister Molly Dickins in Cambridge, her sister Flora at Woodstock, and her godmother Leila Rendell. She often stayed with me in London; so did Henri, and André joined my family one summer in Braemar.

In Paris Janet played chamber music with friends, worked at translations for the *Revue France-Asie*, and in the fifties became a regular contributor to BBC radio's Woman's Hour, with talks on everyday life in Paris. *Divided Loyalties* was published in 1962, and she used some of the money it brought her to improve La Coustète and buy the family's first car. In 1958 they had moved from the Rue Cloître Notre-Dame to the Rue Vaneau; when François retired in 1972, after his parents had died, they settled into the family house at Mandiargues. La Coustète was sold in the 1980s; the Maison Noire at L'Espérou now belongs to François' brother Rémi and his sister Claude.

About the time of Vatican II (1962–5) Janet became a Catholic—one of her reasons being the value the Church of Rome bestows on art and music. The plainness and severity of the services in the *temple* must have contrasted with the ritual and ceremony of the Scottish Episcopal Church in which she had been brought up.

From the end of the 1960s Janet suffered from arthritis, and from osteoporosis—a lack of calcium—which prevented her having operations on her hips. She gradually lost her freedom of movement and became dependent on crutches; but she never lost the ability—or the need—to play the piano. She continued to write, and completed the typescript of a memoir of her childhood and youth in Aberdeen and Edinburgh which she called *Cross Currents*. She had much pleasure from her grandchildren; but there was great sorrow in 1987 when Marie's daughter Laetitia died of leukemia, aged 11.

In 1980 she and François had celebrated their golden wedding; she had been looking forward to their diamond wedding in December 1990, but her last family celebration was to be her grandson Philippe's marriage in May of that year—when she was carried out to the orchard at Mandiargues for the wedding banquet. She died in the clinic at Ganges on 14 October 1990; and after the funeral at La Gardiole, when the only music was Bach, she was buried at Mandiargues. Her grave is at the end of the vineyard, beside those of François' parents, his brother Roger and her granddaughter Laetitia. She was 85.

MONSIEUR AND MADAME HENRI TEISSIER DU CROS, François's parents, continued to live at Mandiargues till he died in 1968 and she in 1971.

FRANÇOIS TEISSIER DU CROS continued his career with the Ponts et Chaussées, repairing the war damage to bridges and planning the layout of the future Paris-Lille autoroute. In 1947 he switched to research. He took a doctor's degree in Mathematics with the University of Paris, then in 1952 went with a scholarship from the British Council to Bristol University to work in physics, as research student under Professor Neville Mott. He came back to Paris to work in one of the physics laboratories at the Ecole Polytechnique, of which he became Director. After his retirement he was elected a member of the New York Academy of Sciences. He now lives at Mandiargues but keeps in touch with his old laboratory in Paris.

HENRI TEISSIER DU CROS. After graduating from his Paris lycée, he spent 1950–51 at Edinburgh University, then attended the Ecole de Science Politique before being called up to serve with the Army in Algeria. After a course at the Ecole Nationale d'Administration he joined the Civil Service, in the Conseil d'Etat, and since 1981 has been a Conseiller d'Etat. He is also a municipal councillor at St Hippolyte-du-Fort, and President of the Institute for the Deaf there. His biography of Louis Armand was published in 1987. He has two sons.

ANDRÉ TEISSIER DU CROS. After engineering school in Paris he worked as a consultant engineer. In 1982 he moved to the United States and set up an engineering consultancy, Gean Overseas that takes him frequently to Europe, India and Japan. He is now an American citizen, living in Atlanta, Georgia. He has two daughters.

NICOLAS TEISSIER DU CROS studied architecture in Paris at the Ecole des Beaux Arts and has since practised in Paris, first in partnership and then as a freelance. He has two daughters.

MARIE TEISSIER DU CROS trained as a landscape gardener at l'Ecole Paysagistes de Versailles. In 1969 she married the architect Antoine Dalbard; they live at Ganges. Their only child, Laetitia, died in 1987.

GERMAINE DIETERLEN. After the war she resumed her work as an anthropologist in French West Africa with Marcel Griaule of the Musée de l'Homme. She has published several books which have won her an international reputation. She is an honorary member of the Council of the International African Institute in London.

RAYMOND LAZARD. Arriving in America late in 1940, he soon crossed back to London to join the Free French, was sent on a mission to Central Africa, then in 1944 joined the US Air Force as liaison officer with the Ponts et Chaussées where—with a three-year break as a freelance engineer in the United States—he worked till his retirement. He lives in the Dordogne where he has organised a group of former Résistants to fight against racialism in the whole of France.

THE SCOBELTZINE (or SCOB) family. Scob resumed his architectural practice in Paris and then at St. Cloud; they still went to L'Espérou in summer. Helena worked for the Cimade, a non-governmental association concerned with the rights and welfare of refugees and immigrants; then became head of the Department of Political Refugees in Paris until her death in 1974. Her father, Pasteur Nick, had during the war sheltered Jews, Communists and Résistants while continuing his ministry among the workers of Lille. He died in 1954.

RAYMOND LÉVI-STRAUSS died soon after the war, but his wife continued to come every summer to Cancabra, their house at Valleraugue. Their son Claude, whose collection of Marxist books Janet had concealed in Oncle Ernest's library, is internationally renowned for his anthropological writings.

LOUIS ARMAND. From 1944 Armand was the moving spirit in the reconstruction and modernisation of the French railways, becoming Director-General of the SNCF in 1946. A whole-hearted European, he was involved with Euratom, the scheme for regulating civilian nuclear energy activities in Europe. Among his many achievements were election to the Académie Française, and the reform of the Ecole Polytechnique where he and François Teissier du Cros had been fellow-students. He died in 1971.

PASTEUR LAURENT OLIVÉS continued his ministry in the region;

and in 1984 took part in a conference at Valleraugue on 'Les Cevennes, Terre de Refuge, 1940–1944'. A book of this title, containing the papers given at the conference and much additional material, was published by the Club Cevenol in 1987. It records the key part that Protestant ministers organised by Pasteur Boegner (the head of the Church whom Janet had met in Edinburgh and heard preaching at Le Vigan in 1941) played in rescuing and hiding families of Jews and anti-Nazi Germans.

DONALD CASKIE. The minister of the Scots Kirk in Paris who called on Janet at Mandiargues in 1941 continued his visits to St Hippolyte-du-Fort and other prisons in Vichy France, and included in his pastoral duties the organisation of an escape route into Spain. In 1943 he was arrested, and imprisoned first in Italy and then at Frêsnes near Paris, accused of spying, and sentenced to death. Thanks to the efforts of a German prison chaplain the death sentence was finally lifted, and when the Allies liberated Paris in August 1944 he was able to go back to the Scots Kirk in the Rue Bayard and hold a thanksgiving service. He continued as minister there till 1968; in 1967 he published his wartime memoirs, *The Tartan Pimpernel*. He died in 1983.

Janet Adam Smith
25 January 1992